Wave of the Gulf

Pen sketch of the author, done by his cousin, Henry Ziegler

Wave of the Gulf

By Jesse A. Ziegler

Ziegler's Scrapbook of the Texas Gulf Coast Country

— □ —

The Naylor Company
San Antonio, Texas

1938

*This book is dedicated to my daughter,
Jessie, who has given me much
assistance and inspiration
in my work.*

FOREWORD

Just as "great oaks from little acorns grow," so this book has become a reality. Having always been interested in the development of Texas, particularly the Gulf Coast section, I frequently contributed letters to the newspapers expressing my thoughts on timely subjects. Often I received personal letters agreeing with my views or taking issue.

When the Centennial celebration was proposed a decade ago, just as I had reached my three-score-years-and-ten, I became interested in this great movement. And why not? My family for four generations had become deep-rooted in American soil and I had watched and been a part of the commercial development in one section of Texas. I began to write letters encouraging the Centennial movement. As the movement gained momentum, my letters were more frequent and I began writing historical articles. It became a hobby with me to write of the people, places and events which would be memorialized during the Centennial year. I heard from friends everywhere and it gave me particular pleasure when I heard from descendants of subjects about whom I wrote.

My friends urged me to write regularly and suggested different subjects. These I wrote and each new subject suggested another until the dozen have grown into hundreds and the end is not in sight. The Centennial movement created interest in the events of yesteryears and the people who trod the same roads and traveled the same streams as we of today. Needless to say, their going was somewhat different from ours.

In 1936, I published a short collection of historical articles under the title, "When Texas Was Young," which was used by the Houston Chamber of Commerce and a number of firms for Centennial souvenirs, as well as going into Texas homes, schools and libraries.

This book is a fulfillment of a promise to those who have asked me to compile the articles in book form. I have made no attempt at fine writing and have no thought of any literary effect. My sole desire was to chronicle accounts of pioneers and incidents of the Gulf Coast section of Texas. Some of the articles herein may contain duplications. Others may arouse question as to their accuracy. I mention this because there are some stories and traditions that have been repeated so often as to become accepted as fact and to be believed by many as true.

I gratefully acknowledge the assistance and cooperation of Lloyd W. Gregory, Max H. Jacobs, George W. Cottingham,

W. N. Blanton, W. L. Clayton, L. W. Kemp, Miss Julia Ideson, Mrs. H. F. MacGregor, Miss Martha Schnitzer, S. G. Reed, Francis G. Hickman, George B. Dealey, Silas B. Ragsdale, Allen Bartlett, A. W. Grant and Alfred Jones.

Thanks are expressed for cuts and photographs furnished by Southern Pacific Railroad, Houston Chamber of Commerce, Port Commission, Galveston Chamber of Commerce, Ziegler Brokerage Company, Acco Press, and Verkin Studio.

It has given me great pleasure to do this writing and each published article has brought some pleasant memories, as well as letters from friends over the United States. If it brings entertainment and pleasure to those into whose hands this book may fall, then I shall be gratified. I can only feel and say

> *"My heart is ever dreaming of the joys*
> *That long have fled*
> *With the live ones, that time's slipping*
> *Numbered with the dead."*

JESSE A. ZIEGLER

THE AUTHOR

Jesse A. Ziegler was born in Galveston, March 5, 1857, the son of Jacob and Minnie Boettcher Ziegler. The elder Ziegler of Bavaria, Germany, came to Texas from Ohio by way of New Orleans and assisted Thad and Jerome Hooper in building the first cotton compress in Houston in 1851. He was prominently identified with the cotton industry in Galveston and his five sons, Jesse A., Harry L., William, Charles and Jacob, followed in his footsteps.

Jesse A. Ziegler acquired his education at Crawford's Private Academy in Galveston. He spent the first twenty-six years of his life in his native city, coming to Houston about 1883. While in Galveston, he was a member of the Washington Light Guards.

His connection with the cotton industry dates from 1871, making him the oldest cotton man in Texas. He owned the Varney Plantation between Houston and Sugarland during the famous Jaybird-Woodpecker political era. He is a former director of the Houston Cotton Exchange and still maintains his office in the old Cotton Exchange Building, now called Merchants Exchange Building. He is the only living member of the original membership of the Houston Cotton Exchange and of the Galveston Cotton Exchange staff of 1874.

Mr. Ziegler is prominently identified with the Sons of the Republic of Texas, Sons of the Confederacy, Secretary of the National Frontiersmen's Association, and Vice-President of the Harris County Historical Society. He is an honorary member of the Houston Constructive Writers and Speakers Club and a member of the Episcopal Church.

Mr. Ziegler was for many years an active worker in the development of the Houston Ship Channel, as well as other civic enterprises. Now that the progress of Houston is definitely established, he has turned his interests toward historical writings and research and has proved himself to be a competent chronicler of Texas history, particularly that of the Texas Gulf Coast country.

CONTENTS

xi

ILLUSTRATIONS

PART ONE

HOUSTON

SETTLEMENT

Arrival of Austin and Taylor With the First Settlers

As my stories deal largely with the Pioneers, it is proper to say a few words of the plantations and their owners who produced a civilization and a society in which we dwell to-day. In November, 1821, Stephen F. Austin sailed for New Orleans to lead the first immigrants to Texas. He reached the Brazos River on the thirty-first day of December, 1821, proceeded up that stream, and on January 7, 1822, settled in what is now Washington County. From that time on, especially between the years 1823 to 1830, there was a great influx of settlers.

In 1819, Anson Taylor settled near the Coushatti Indian Village on Trinity River, and in 1820 Colonel Knight and Walter C. White from Colonel Long's camp at Bolivar burned off a cane brake and raised a crop of corn at a point on Buffalo Bayou.

The era of the Texas colonists extends, as I have said, from 1820 to 1830. The Battle of Velasco was fought in 1832. San Jacinto, in 1836, was the decisive battle that gave us independence from Mexico. Stephen F. Austin died in 1836, and was buried at Peach Point (though his remains were removed later to the State Cemetery at Austin).

The first settlers of Brazoria County were Josiah H. Bell, Breit Bailey, James H. Pelly, Prim, the Bradleys, Amos and Daniel Rawls, Damon, and a little later, David Tilley, James and J. T. Beard, Thomas Widley, T. J. Pilgrim, the Tews, the Shipmans, John T. Pitts, John Brown Austin, Warren D. C. Hall, the Alsbuys, Mrs. (General) Long, Major Cavitt, and John Austin. All of these were planters and settled at Brazoria in 1828.

At about this time came James T. Perry, brother-in-law to Stephen F. Austin, and settled at Peach Point. Then came the large merchants, and the bankers, R. and D. G. Mills, John Adriance, and Patrick McGreel.

Jared L. Groce brought the first cotton seed with him and one hundred slaves from Virginia in 1825; he also built the first gin and produced a hundred bales of cotton, one-third of the cotton production. Such was the rapid increase in the production of cotton that in 1834 it was estimated that the crop of cotton brought six hundred thousand dollars.

To give you an idea of the magnitude of the business

1

then at Brazoria and at Columbia (which produced ninety per cent of the total), R. and D. G. Mills, John Adriance and Patrick McGreel often took in five thousand dollars cash in one day, besides the credit sales and business which was credited.

Each of these men carried a stock of five hundred thousand dollars and Morgan L. Smith of the Waldeck Plantation carried an equal amount. It was estimated that there were over a hundred plantations of a thousand to six thousand acres, a few of which were on Buffalo Bayou and on the San Jacinto and Trinity Rivers.

HOUSTON, THE MELTING POT

Beginning of Houston and Influx of Foreigners

Pioneer Houston, "that little village on the banks of Buffalo Bayou," was a melting pot of the nations.

A majority of the early settlers, those accompanying Stephen F. Austin and other grantees of his type, were of the average American native stock. But when the latter colonization era came into full swing there was a great influx of all nationalities to Houston, at that time, the gateway to fertile coastal and inland regions of Texas.

When the Republic of Texas was but six years old, in 1842, the first noteworthy period of colonization began. It continued through 1846. As Houston's possibilities were seen and recognized, the trek from abroad was initiated by the Adelsverein, a German colonization company comprising twenty-one princes of the Rhein. During the life of the company they furnished conveyance to between fifty and sixty thousand German colonists to Houston and Texas, and as a result, the first census of the United States in 1850 showed that of the total inhabitants of Houston, forty per cent of them were German speaking people.

The percentage of these Germans might not have been so high in Houston as elsewhere in Texas, but there was a contributing factor, as thousands of German families arriving in Houston and destined for interior colonization points, learned from friends upon arrival here that epidemics of yellow fever, cholera and small pox were raging inland. As a matter of personal safety they decided to remain in

2

Houston. The quite natural result was that many took up permanent residence here. Among them were Prussians, Austrians, Swiss, Hungarians and Bohemians. Mostly they were of the peasant class but included merchants and mechanics, and a sprinkling of doctors, lawyers, engineers and school teachers—and I doubt not, one or two most excellent "brewmeisters."

Later on, when Col. Tom Pierce completed the Galveston, Harrisburg & San Antonio Railway to San Antonio, he cooperated with the Land Commissioner of Texas in bringing thousands of Englishmen, Welshmen and Scotchmen to the state, extending them land-grants that would delight the heart of the small farmer-rancher today.

I recall, even now, witnessing the landing of these pilgrims at the wharves in Galveston. It was a picturesque sight. They would disembark, loaded down with fine old silverware, beautiful, life-size oil paintings elegantly framed, tapestries, fine linens and other similar items that perhaps had been in their families for generations.

Imagine it! These were to be taken to log cabins, adobe houses with mud floors. Forsooth, it was a case of the "Harp that once through Tara's halls." There was something about these periodic landings of the immigrants that impressed my childish mind as "gorgeous," doubtless because of their foreign, usually highly-colored raiment and the unusual type of household goods that they were taking, innocently enough, to a wilderness infested by savages, or at least so, I thought.

Many of these English immigrants had earned previous experience in Australia. Accordingly, once settled, they stocked their farm-ranches with fine strains of sheep and cattle. Others went in for the raising of fruit and grain, and of course, cotton. Many among them who were not inured to the hardships of colonization, in due time became discouraged, packed up their belongings and returned home.

Many, however, remained in Houston.

Being only a child myself, my interest quite naturally was drawn to the English children and from them I learned to play the English game of cricket. Among the Scotchmen, their playing of the bag-pipes fascinated me, but it was one of the arts, I am sure, for which I was never intended. My one attempt to master it came to an abrupt end with the bag and the pipes wilting in hopeless confusion in my childish arms. But I remember particularly, a very fine looking

Captain Douglas who weighed three hundred and forty pounds, who not only played these pipes magnificently, but also danced the "Highland Fling" as nimbly as a sixteen year old girl.

Among the other nationalities, an outstanding character of those days was Henry Castro, a Frenchman from Alsace, who secured colonization grants equal to those of Stephen F. Austin, and was instrumental in bringing over a large number of French and Germans from the Alsace-Lorraine district. These subsequently settled at Castroville, creating a beautiful little township where many of their descendants yet reside in control of the lands of their forebears. A number of the Frenchmen, however, returned to Houston, and joining with the French cotton buyers from New Orleans, founded a French colony in Houston.

Proceeding still further with the varied nationalities composing the Houston of that day, when Count Telferner built the "Macaroni" railroad (so nicknamed because of the many Italian laborers employed in the building of it) he brought over hundreds of Italian mechanics, artisans and laborers. After the road was completed and their labors finished a great majority of these nationals gravitated to Houston. They mingled here with the Italians who had preceded them, gradually entering the truck farming industry on nearby lands, or engaged in other pursuits with which they were familiar. Thus Houston had also its Italian colony.

The results of these early national migrations to Houston are to be observed today in the various foreign societies and clubs long established in Houston by the Mexicans, Italians, French, Germans and others. Collectively and individually, they always have played an important role in the civic and commercial status of the city.

Transportation in the early days to, and even into, Texas, was accomplished largely by water routes. Many schooners and brigs came in from Maine, bringing lumber, brick and building material from which the first real homes of Houston were constructed. Many of the "down Easterners" who manned these ships remained to take up their residence here. Among them, I recall Captain Latham, Captain Hawthorn and others,

After the War Between the States came the Yankee cotton-buyers in large numbers. Eventually they become permanent residents of Houston, joining with those of the Yankee element who had preceded them.

4

HOUSTON

Strange was the fact that in those days scarcely a Mexican was to be seen in young Houston. Perhaps it was too close to San Jacinto and memory sometimes lingers, yet, San Antonio continued chiefly Mexican at that time.

The building of various railroads, the H. & T. C., the T. & N. O., the Katy and the I. & G. N., contributed to the cosmopolitan population of the new city. Work on the roads attracted laborers from all parts of the world. These were eventually distributed all along the respective railroad lines. Houston fell heir to many of them as permanent residents because it was customary on pay-day to come to Houston either to cash checks or make purchases. Those whose funds gave out, as the funds of many did, were compelled to seek employment locally.

Norwegians, Swedes and Portuguese came into Houston from their original contact with the wharves and docks of Galveston and along the Buffalo Bayou. It became so that almost any language could be heard on Houston's streets.

Then, with the post-Civil War period, came the Negro problem. Promised gloriously by the "carpetbag" regime, forty acres and a mule, that there would be no work, that Uncle Sam would take care of them the rest of their days in idleness, the Negroes came in quite large numbers. Alas! It was a bubble which soon burst; the actual conditions confronting them upon emancipation did not develop the "hog heaven" some of the credulous had imagined. As a matter of fact, a great many of the older and loyal Negroes refused to accept freedom and continued with their former masters. Others, after affording brief trial to the new order of things, returned empty handed and empty stomached to their former homes. Be it said, in fairness to the Southern "master," that always the worthy ones were taken back into the family fold, paid regular day wages for their hire and treated considerately. Many lived out their lives in the service of the family in which they were born.

Still, others of the Negro Race, however, were able to grasp the new situation with sufficient intelligence to proceed upon their own; there were likewise instances where they proved thrifty, law-abiding citizens and thus laid the foundation for the present benefits accruing to the Negro as a constructive citizen of the South.

Amusements of the several nationalities differed as greatly as their origin. It was natural that they resided in groups of their own and leaned to social gatherings of like character.

Many of them still wore a foreign type of dress and the various folk dances of their respective countries provided colorful scenes.

To jump a few years, another interesting phase of Houston, in regard to dress, came with the fall of the Confederacy. After surrender hundreds of officers of the "Army in Grey" wended their way to Houston in search of a land of new opportunities. Virginians, Kentuckians, Tennesseeans and Carolinians in abundance were numbered among the newcomers. There were more colonels, majors, captains and doctors to the square foot of sidewalk than could, perhaps, have been boasted of by any city of similar size in the nation; many were talented lawyers.

Practically all of them, however, naturally were in sore straits financially. They came and lived, attired in their grey uniforms and a change or two of linen; the lawyers brought their thumb-worn copies of Blackstone. I heard, on occasion, two noted jurists relate, how, when they landed in Houston, they possessed only three dollars and seventy-five cents between them; that they rented an office on credit, and hung out their "shingle." They, subsequently, became men of great legal prominence.

Every Sunday morning one would see these former officers, now returned to civilian life and attired in their only wardrobe, the grey uniform, wending churchward. Here, some of them taught Sunday School classes, others occasionally preached lay-sermons, still others went merely to attend services and greet friends.

With the former officers' coming, though, there also came to Houston much of its social elegance and fine old customs for which the city became noted. One charming item that I yet remember distinctly was the annual "tournament" reclaimed from "days of old, when knights were bold," —when the young men, clad in purple and velvet, plumed hats, tights and doublets, would mount their steeds and, spear in hand, charge at top speed down the line of overhanging posts and capture the swinging rings. Their "fair ladies" would attend, equally bedecked, sitting their mounts on the side-saddle of those days, their huge picture hats displaying ostrich plumes . . . and skirts trailing almost to the ground. To my youthful gaze, it seemed to me a picture from fairyland.

At the close of the tournament amid a royal court setting, the "knight" who won the championship would offer the queenly crown of the tournament to his lady fair. Then, at the close of the day of sports, the occasion generally would end with a brilliant ball at the Hutchins House. At these affairs the ladies usually wore dainty colonial costumes, their male escorts being clad accordingly. Favorite dances were the minuet and the Virginia reel, calculated to reflect all the grace and charms of the dancer.

Yet another colorful custom of the day was that occurring on the fine spring and fall days when the "dress parade" occupied the social elite of Houston. About four o'clock of the afternoon there began gathering from the residential sections of the city, beautiful high stepping horses, attached to every conceivable type of vehicle—the French Barouche, the German Landau, the Russian Hack, the low-swinging, American Phaeton, and so on, down to the Irish dog cart. All would turn into Main Street and merge into the flowing stream of vehicles, the occupants of which represented the flower of Houston's society. To the appreciative onlooker, there was something in the passing review which quickened the senses, what with the gold and silver trimmed harness flashing back the bright sunlight, the immaculately attired men and the stylishly dressed women.

Here and there a more stately vehicle would hold an elderly, grey-whiskered gentleman of the old-school, his "missus" beside him, the two of them bowing gracefully to passing friends; the younger element flashing by, as youth is wont, in conveyance more ornate, or perhaps on horseback, displaying a favorite mount. Now and then would pass by a rubber-tired "sulky" drawn by a magnificent pacer or trotter, the occupants destined out Main Street towards Bray's Bayou, or mayhap in the opposite direction toward Harrisburg Road, then a beautiful lane cut through tall pine forests that lent an aroma with a wonderfully exhilerating effect. Occasionally, some of the more pretentious conveyances carried drivers and footmen in livery; but a majority of the inhabitants were far too democratic to adopt this style.

So far as I know, such affairs are no longer to be seen in America. One beholds them, perhaps only in Havana or Mexico City. We took life in the Houston of those days much more slowly and seemingly much more peacefully. I sometimes wonder, perhaps, far happier!

There was something about the Old South of that period that bespoke a cultural tone of rich elegance, a quaint, elusive, intangible charm that, with all our wealth of commerce today and the social grandeur that it provides, we seem, thus far, unable to bring back.

FIVE TRAILS

First Commercial Routes to Houston

When the Allen brothers, founders of Houston, issued their first map of the city, the plat showed only a small affair. Most of the business was conducted near the banks of the Bayou, where the steamers and other small craft landed their passengers and cargoes. Properly speaking, the city began with Commerce Street, which skirted the Bayou. It extended south to Prairie Avenue, so named because it was vitually the end of the city and where the prairie began, beyond that the rabbit, bird and duck hunting commenced. Contrast that with the corner of Prairie and Main streets today, busily alive with its hastening throng of shoppers and other minions of commerce.

The north side of Buffalo Bayou came to life with business houses and residences as the city began to grow and expand.

Running out of Houston, there were five distinct roads or "covered wagon" trails, now called "state highways," which, in point of beauty and utility, are rather wonderful when compared to the muck-and-mud trails of those days. Leading among them were the San Felipe Road, to the northwest; the Washington Road, which ran nearly parallel to San Felipe; the Richmond Road, more to the west; the Montgomery Road, to the north and the Liberty Road, to the east. Each of them were little more than mere Indian trails, but with the coming of population and commerce, were straightened out and made into wagon roads.

San Felipe Road began at Dallas Avenue, as it was subsequently named, and skirted Buffalo Bayou, being the first road of note to lead to San Felipe de Austin, second capitol of Texas, and the home of Stephen F. Austin, where much of the original commerce of the state was carried on.

Washington Road led out what today is Washington Avenue, turning north at Eureka to Hempstead, Brenham and Austin.

Montgomery Road followed a winding path to "New Kentucky," located near the edge of Montgomery County. This

8

was one of the oldest of settlements, dating back some one hundred and ten years ago. During the Centennial year, the Chamber of Commerce and the Historical Society of Texas, for the information of generations to come, placed a marker with appropriate legend at the former location of New Kentucky. In the early days of its existence, Harris County had but four hamlets and voting places of importance—Harrisburg, Lynchburg, Stafford and New Kentucky. Nothing remains now of the once thriving settlement except a fine, flowing well built about 1826. New Kentucky's inhabitants were gradually lured away to Montgomery and Houston.

Liberty Road likewise led to one of the very early settlements, an infant village which grew into what is now the town of Liberty. At Liberty the Liberty Road merged with the historic Spanish Trail, which was the road to Nacogdoches and to the United States through Louisiana. There was at the time no noteworthy trail running north from Houston to Dallas and through Indian Territory to the United States, although a portion of the travelers occasionally turned aside at Nacogdoches and followed the trail to Marshall, and thence to Jefferson on the Red River and Caddo Lake.

Richmond Road, fifth of the five trails, turned aside from South Main Street, at a point considerably from its present course, and carried the traffic to Fort Bend County, the Brazos and Colorado "bottoms" and to San Antonio and the older settlements of Texas. The two rivers had no bridges, but were crossed either by ferry or at established fords.

Neither was there any bridge across the bayou at Houston when the city was first established. Cotton and other commodities, as well as passengers, were ferried across the stream at the foot of Main Street. All of the roads had a cross-trail enabling wagons and teams to turn aside and cross Buffalo Bayou far to the north and west of the city. This cross-trail brought them into Washington Road, where they might ford the bayou, or tie up for the night at either of the two famous camping spots, "Vinegar Hill," located where the Southern Pacific Depot now stands or the "Old Indian Camping Ground," at the intersection of Houston Avenue and White Oak Bayou.

Eventually, there was built the long bridge over the Bayou at Preston Avenue and while it was a very crude and rickety affair of hewn logs, it afforded entrance to the city for the long caravans of ox and mule team wagons. Subsequently, in the "Forties" a more commodious and substantial bridge became absolutely necessary to accommodate the growing traffic and the Preston Avenue bridge was supplemented with one of wood and concrete at the foot of Milam Street. This latter was replaced in time with the little iron bridge that served the city for so many years.

The interior counties of Waller, Montgomery, Grimes, Washington, Austin and Fayette were beginning to settle rapidly with the incoming colonists, and the commodities and products from their plantations and small farms poured into Houston for a market. Houston also was their source of supply.

All these factors, aside, however, from the tireless energy and business acumen of the pioneer merchants who came to Houston in the days of its infancy, accelerated the growth of the city. Friendly regard for the merchants as well as patronage of the inhabitants of the early interior colonies adjacent to Houston helped. The city drew its sustenance then, as now, from its great interior trade territory, just then coming into bloom.

The tillers of the soil came in great caravans of covered wagons, replicas of the "prairie schooner," drawn by long teams of huge, unwieldy oxen, or multi-spans of mules.

I have stood upon an eminence and watched these caravans come winding into the city like a long snake, composed frequently of as many as a hundred or more wagons. They came in groups or caravans not only for the social companionship to be had, but equally so because of the necessity of presenting a strong front to their common enemies— the raiding Indians, Mexican bandits and renegade Americans who in those days were wont to prey heavily upon any suspecting traveler who came their way.

Usually the trips were made semi-annually by the groups from as far up as Travis County, and from the other counties named, when their crops were laid by in the fall and hunting was plentiful, and again in the early spring. The wagons were loaded according to the product of the given community. Some contained cotton, wool, hides, beeswax and tallow. Others bore cured meats of several kinds, thick hogsheads of plantation molasses, ripened sugar-cane, melons, grain or other produce of the farm and dairy.

The old Kentucky long-bore rifle was a fixture across the

10

knees of the driver; the men who tramped alongside the oxen carried their pistols and bowie-knives.

If these excursions were business trips, they were none the less social picnics, as frequently the feminine element of the family came along. Camp was made en route every night. Supper was served "al fresco," and the assembly gathered around the customary roaring campfire to indulge in social chit-chat, sing-songs accompanied by the guitar, the banjo or fiddle—and among the younger element, perhaps a bit of courting on the sly!

Hunting was a pastime along the way, and always by the time the caravan arrived in Houston, the wagons were decorated on the outside with a festoon of wild turkeys, squirrels and rabbits, venison, and occasionally a black bear. And always there trailed behind or alongside the wagon the inevitable long eared "hound," or the Central Texas specimen of "coon-dog."

Entering Houston, camp generally was pitched, as related, at one of the two camping grounds. When weather and roads, and camping room among those already there, permitted, Vinegar Hill drew much favor as being nearer the city proper, and as adjacent, also to the free cotton-yard camping grounds. After supper each night social gatherings prevailed, climaxed frequently by the old-fashioned barn-dance in which both elders and youngsters participated.

When morning came the visiting farmers took their products to market, finding ready disposal at profitable prices. Gradually, the wagons began to gather around the city hall square, and I have seen, in later years, the streets of that entire section filled with these wagons, displaying their offerings much as do the incomers at the Farmers' Market in Houston today.

After sales were effected, then came the family and farm purchasing with the proceeds; and the Houston merchants vied with one another for the ready cash of the visitors. Quite naturally, they bought supplies sufficient to last them for the next six months until their caravan came again. There were heavy purchases of groceries and dry goods of the staple kind, and of hardware heavy and light, farm implements, furniture and bedding, and seeds for the new crop; and boots and shoes and headgear ranging from the ten-gallon Stetson hat to the muffler cap; saddles, harness and like accoutrement.

All told, these caravan trips as a rule required about three weeks to complete, weather, of course, and conditions of roads

11

considered. One week coming, a week in which to sell, purchase and visit among friends, and a further week in which to make the return trip home.

Houston, while comparatively small, represented "the city" to these visitors and afforded considerable entertainment not available to them in the interior. There were no "movies," of course, but there was the "magic lantern" show, fascinating in its day to young and old alike. (I wonder how many children of today know what a magic lantern is!) Occasionally there was the traveling minstrel show, or some stock company, or a noted actor or actress at the small Opera House— all of which provided high amusement for the visitor from the interior. And, to those who had the time and could afford it, there was the fascination of a trip to Galveston on a real steamboat!

Trade from the Brazos Bottom by these early people was carried on by eight and ten-yoke ox-teams, or similar mule-teams. They brought cotton, sugar and molasses, entering on South Main and wending their way to Market Square. Some of the cotton was billed to Galveston and was trans-shipped by boat at the foot of Main Street, or carried in later years out Congress Avenue to the Galveston, Houston & Henderson Railroad; and woe to the wagon or cart that was caught at the turn of the corner when these ox-teams made the turn. The oxen never stopped, just exerted an increased strain against their yokes and went ahead, with the result that little was left of the vehicle except crushed wheels and axles. Few now living remember the degree of stubborn contrariness of some of the old lead-oxen.

On the camp nights mentioned, Vinegar Hill and Indian Camp Ground (known also as Beauchamp Springs) presented a genuine pioneer sight of frontier days. Camp fires were lighted. The visitors were in picturesque garb, and the evening wind wafted "The Arkansas Traveler," "Turkey in the Straw," "Dixie" and "Yankee Doodle" in the breeze.

Some years afterward, when the Iron Horse of the railroad began to rear its head, it was the signal for the gradual decline of the prairie schooner and the covered wagon. The day of the oxen was drawing to a close and the mid-day of even the mule team and horse team was at hand.

The covered wagon and its great caravan, however, had its day and served that day right nobly and well. The early merchant of Houston depended on them; he sent out his runners on horseback to meet and greet them and apprise

12

them of the fact that he was "doing business at the same old
stand," and to solicit their patronage.

Houston owed its early progress and growth to this form
of transportation. Its trade territory extended as far west
as Albuquerque, and as far north as the Indian Territory
and the Red River.

SAMUEL L. ALLEN AND THE EARLY INDIANS

In the tiny Indian village of Conaserga, New York—heart
of a wild unsettled country that, only until a short period
of years since, was still occupied chiefly by the descendants
of the early Indian tribes—Samuel Allen, last of Houston's
famed six Allen brothers, was born April 12, 1808.

The father of the Allens had purchased what was then
termed an "Indian Improvement," being a portion of the
lands originally set aside for use of the Indians, all of which
was not subsequently required by them. As the elder Allen
related, the family's only neighbors comprised several nearby
Indian families, upon their first settlement of the soil, some
of them not at all inclined to be friendly.

As a result of this occasional unfriendly attitude, there
occurred one incident that brought neighborly relations with
the Indians almost to an unhappy climax.

When young Samuel was somewhat beyond three years of
age, he went one day to the pasture with a neighboring boy
to assist in locating their horses. While his older companion
was driving up the horses, Samuel was instructed to wait for
him at a place of safety known as "The Gap."

Unfortunately, while waiting, the lad was tempted by a
nearby apple tree and concluded to climb it, eating freely of
its ripe, red fruit. An old squaw belonging to one of the
tribes, catching him in the act, shook him out of the tree,
and with a club beat him over the head until he became
unconscious. Thinking him dead, she threw him into a
clump of bushes, covered him with dry leaves and left him
to lie there all day. She returned late in the evening and sur-
prisingly found him alive; at his condition she became
frightened and ran to some of the white settlers reporting
she had found a white child who apparently had been kicked
almost to death by a horse. Leading them to the spot, young

13

Allen was recognized and taken to his parents who already were conducting a search for him. Recovering, he told the true story of the attack. Excitement ran so high it was feared violent measures of retaliation would be imposed. However, the manly husband of the squaw, upon learning what had occurred, went directly to the boy's parents, offering to surrender the woman for such punishment as they deemed proper. This served to quiet matters and the affair was dropped.

As a boy, Samuel Allen evidenced the marks of genius. Before he was twenty he had mastered the trade of tool making and had established a reputation for superior products. When he reached his majority he went to Baldwinsville, New York, and entered the mercantile business there. He continued to follow this line for a matter of some fifty years, first in New York and later in Texas.

When his brothers A. C. and J. K. Allen came to Texas, Samuel followed them in 1834, in company with Charlotte M. Allen, who had spent some time in New York visiting "the folks back home." Samuel and Charlotte came first to Natchitoches, in Louisiana, and from there rode on horseback to Nacogdoches, being protected en route from Mexican bandits by the friendly Indians.

Samuel Allen remained in Nacogdoches until 1838, when he came to Houston, then a village scarcely two years old. In Houston he entered the mercantile business, locating his store on the banks of the Buffalo Bayou where the firm of W. D. Cleveland & Sons now stands.

His residence, a two story mansion, he built on the bend of the bayou, just east of where the Peden Company building now is located. The home was so situated that he could hear the bells and whistles of the arriving steamboats coming around the bend, and proceed to the boat landing in time to welcome old friends and new arrivals.

In 1846 Allen associated himself with T. M. Bagby, extending their sales as far up as what was then Indian Territory. This business continued until the Civil War. Later he engaged alone for a short while in the teaming business, following the German colonists to New Braunfels. At New Braunfels he again established his merchandising and continued until 1887, when he returned to Houston. Engaging anew in Houston, he built the Allen warehouse, a rambling, immense structure for those days that covered the entire block where the M. & M. Building now stands.

14

Reference to this warehouse brings back to me a flood of memories of more than a half century ago. I became Allen's neighbor when I bought the Houston Press sheds and grounds just east of him. I recall in particular when the two of us were seated one summer's day in the shade of his wall, there came riding up the road Chief Minto of the Alabama tribe of Indians, followed by a large file of his braves. They rode single-file up the trail toward us, each of them loaded with wild game, skins, furs, hides and various Indian wares of barter and trade. They saluted and passed on, proceeding to the hide houses and other points to dispose of their loads.

I arose and started to return to my office but Mr. Allen exclaimed:

"Stay awhile, Ziegler, and see the real fun; they'll all be back presently, scampering for home like the wind."

True enough, somewhat more than an hour later I was startled to hear a commotion of galloping horses, shooting and wild Indian screams. Here came the Indian braves on horse, riding like mad.

Behind them came the city marshal and several of his deputies, shooting into the air and uttering unearthly screams that blended with the frantic yells of the Indians. All passed in a cloud of dust but before long the deputies and city marshal returned, laughing and joking.

It was customary, as I found out later, for the Indians to make their sales, then proceed to the barrel-houses uptown. At these bars they spent their all and soon became gloriously drunk. The City Fathers of Houston had long since learned that it was cheaper to frighten them out of town than to arrest them and throw them into jail; that would compel the city to keep and feed them for a week.

Nothing, in fact, was more pleasing to the Indian than to be kept and fed, with no work to perform—and in those days there was, as a matter of course, little work to be done.

I stood there many times after the incident, more or less amazed, watching the onrush of the redmen across the little iron bridge at the foot of Milam Street, then the only means of passage to the North Side; their legs dangled over the sides of their small Indian ponies, as they proceeded to the city limits and far out the Liberty Road, en route home.

As a matter of fact, the Alabama Indians were always of a friendly nature. De Soto, the Spanish explorer, had so found them in his early contacts with the tribe. Indeed, he cultivated them particularly in order to wrench from them their tribal secret concerning the Phantom City of Gold—a mythical source of gold supply, the whereabouts of which, of course they would (or could) never divulge.

In Alabama they had settled at the junction of the Coosa and Tallalpoosa rivers, held by the French, but finding themselves molested by the French colonists and mistreated they returned to Texas and settled at Peachtree, some seven miles from the present town of Livingston, about 1815.

Their name signifies "Here We Rest." Always friendly to the Texas colonists they took an active part against the invading Mexicans whenever the latter came their way, and provided General Houston with valuable information concerning Santa Anna's movements prior to the Battle of San Jacinto.

Later on, General Houston spent a night with them in their home environment, learned of their conditions, did what he could at the time to remedy the situation and was made their first "White Father" when he induced the State Legislature to grant them, in 1845, two sections of land in the Big Thicket of East Texas. Here, they were able to fish, kill wild game and rest to their heart's delight.

I can recall, in those balmy days of barter and trade, now a half century past, how, on occasions, I would buy from the incoming Alabama Indians a string of black bass, or a brace of canvas back ducks for fifteen cents; a quarter of venison for a half dollar. Today, the ammunition required for the kill would cost twice as much.

John House, uncle of the present James H. B. House and T. W. House, had a standing price, or reward, as the Indians termed it, for a twenty pound bronze wild turkey. Daylight frequently found the Indian hunters waiting at the little red bank of Mr. House's, with their lot of turkeys spread on the sidewalk, waiting for him to make his selection. That was fifty-three years ago.

Samuel Allen, slender in stature and a mild, gentle mannered man who never used profane language, strong liquor or tobacco in any form, held his own in a rugged age, commanding the friendly admiration and respect of the more rugged element, as well as the culturally inclined.

There were other tribes of Indians with whom Samuel Allen was on equally friendly terms; notably the Tonkawas and even the ferocious Coronkowas, the famed giant-cannibal Indians of the Texas coastal region. Both of these tribes were friendly to Sam Houston. Like the Alabamas, the

16

Tonkawas were friendly to the whites. The Coronkowas, or Karankawas (the name is spelled different ways) as a rule dealt the whites a great deal of misery, particularly the early colonists and explorers.

Jean LaFitte had to contend with them when he settled upon Galveston Island. When one day six of his men disappeared, he found to his amazement the Karankawas had captured and eaten them!

In retaliation, he loaded his cannon and attacked the tribe.

A fierce battle lasting two days ensued around his fort at Three Trees—swashbuckling buccaneers against cannibal Indians. When the smoke of battle cleared away, LaFitte with the loss of seven men, had killed 60 of the Indians and had driven the remainder from the Island. They never returned.

Noah Smithwick, in his "Evolution of a State," bears out this story of cannibalism of the Karankawas. He relates interestingly an occasion when the Tonkawas, normally a peaceful tribe, had borne with patience as long as they could, the cruel onslaughts of the Karankawas. Finally, turning upon them, a bloody encounter resulted in the defeat of the latter and the capture—alive—of one of the cannibal Karankawas.

The peaceable Tonkawas borrowed a large kettle of iron from one of the colonists who had no notion of its intended use, cut the Karankawa to pieces, and boiled him along with potatoes, corn and onions. They proceeded to gobble up the stew thus made, smacking their lips with great gusto. The owner of the pot, with a small party of other whites, came upon them in the midst of their feast and were horrified to learn of the use to which the utensil had been put. The Tonkawas, however, were not cannibals at heart or by practice—the instance was merely one of sweet revenge.

Old Chief Minto of the Alabamas was instinctively a gentleman at heart, and a cavalier compared with the majority of the members of these early Indian tribes. Minto was greatly liked by all of the early settlers. His besetting sin, however, was his great fondness for strong drink. He became lugubriously drunk on occasions and it always became a trying problem to dispose of him peacefully.

John Kennedy, father-in-law of the late William Foley, operated a store on the corner of Travis Street and Congress Avenue. This store drew both the admiration and trade of

Old Chief Minto, for, as he put it, "his whiskey is the strongest!"

Cornelius Ennis was another merchant who gained the confidence and respect of the Indians, and enjoyed a large part of their trade. He once presented Chief Minto with a rickety old buggy. But when Minto hitched his pony to it, the animal kicked the vehicle to pieces. This gave the venerable chief an excuse for remaining in the city two days longer while the buggy was being repaired—during which Minto celebrated as usual by imbibing deeply.

Indians—they furnished many an anecdote and incident for the early Houstonians. There are many yet living who recall that in the early "Seventies" we had in Houston the only State Fair then in existence.

When these fairs were on, Governor Coke and the Indian commissioner would bring down as part of the exhibit a tribe of the fierce Comanches; others who had participated in the battle with Custer at the Little Big Horn were sent down from the Indian reservation as a further drawing card for the fair. Their tepees, sleds and other paraphanalia filled the "Indian Village" at the Fair, and frequently they remained on as much as a month later to attract visitors to their camp.

I recall also that when Sa-Tan-Ta and Big Tree, the Comanche chiefs who had fought the Rangers for a long period, were captured near Austin, and were being transported to the Huntsville penitentiary, they were encamped between trains on Vinegar Hill.

Both they and old Chief Geronimo of the Apaches, who was likewise encamped there between trains en route to prison in Florida, drew hundreds of curiously inclined visitors, among them myself.

Geronimo was the most brutal and ferocious specimen of manhood I ever saw. His features literally reflected the satanic cruelty of his internicine nature.

He had finally been captured by General Miles near El Paso, after depredations which had cost the government over a million dollars in property, and countless loss of lives. Yet, when the close confinement of the Florida prison caused Geronimo to develop lung trouble he was pardoned and allowed to return home, to pass in peace among his fellow tribesmen.

Since those days the Happy Hunting Grounds of the Big Thicket, which gave the Alabamas sustenance, have changed. I once spent two days in the Big Thicket on a wild turkey hunt. I saw on that occasion a stag swimming over the lake with a pack of hounds swimming in pursuit. Behind them on the shore stood the hunters sounding the call on their cow-horns. The picturesque sight has remained vividly with me these many years.

With such inroads made by the hunters of that period upon the Big Thicket, it was not many years before practically all of the wild game was killed out. The Indians then turned to the cultivation of their little patches cleared in the thick undergrowth; yet, in due course, the virgin soil itself became exhausted, and the Alabamas lived in actual want, upon charity.

Since the coming of Clem Fain of Livingston to help them, the Alabamas have advanced. Today their old tepees are gone. In their place stand neat cottages, a school, and a church presided over by Rev. and Mrs. Chambers. Their dress is modern American, except when on exhibition tours or official missions—not the colorful garb in which I knew them more than fifty years ago, when they looked and were treated as vagabonds.

Lo! the poor Indian is no more! But the name of their early friend and benefactor, Samuel Allen, will be known to countless generations, as one of the founders of the greatest metropolis in the South.

INDIAN DAYS

Early Trade With the Indians in Houston

One hundred years ago, I am told, the first Indian trading post stood where the east end of the Preston Avenue bridge now rests, north of the Farmer's Market, and it was here that a vast amount of "swapping" went on between the Comanche Indian braves and their white visitors.

My first recollection of this Indian trading post site goes back some sixty years ago. It was then what impressed me as a high and imposing hill (long since been leveled off). Upon the summit stood a large, rambling cottage, the home of that early pioneer, Horace Dickson Taylor, "originally the first frame house built in Houston." Mr. Taylor was one of the earliest traders and cotton warehousemen of the city and did

19

considerable trading with the Indian tribes who came this way from time to time.

Houston was one of the chief stopping points for friendly Indians, as they journeyed en route to Sour Lake Springs, where they camped each spring and summer. They attributed high curative powers to the mineral waters to be found there.

My first personal recollection of these Indians goes back to 1871, to a band that impressed me at the time as "warlike Comanches." The occasion was the holding of the first Texas State Fair at the Macatee Warehouse and Cotton Yard. These Indians were a fierce looking lot and battle-scarred. Governor Coke of Texas and the Indian commissioner had granted them a leave of absence from the Indian Territory and loaned them to the fair association. As I remember them, they were quite a large band, highly decorated with their war paint and bedecked in feathered head-dress. They came with their sleds, crude affairs on poles, tepees, dogs, squaws, papooses and household effects. The sleds, serving as their form of wagon, were piled high with buffalo robes and other plunder of various sorts.

They pitched camp on what was then known as "Vinegar Hill," west of the Macatee wagon yard, and south of the Southern Pacific deport.

The Indian braves nearly always rode their horses bareback, performing at times feats of horsemanship that excited the envy of even the cowboys from the ranges. The Indian squaws divided their time between the campfires, cooking, washing, looking after the younger children that ran to and fro dressed only in their birthday clothes, or in selling beaded moccasins, leggings and other articles of Indian make to camp visitors.

The Indian braves were more or less ingenious in extracting money from the visitors. I recall, in particular, one game of skill that always appeared lucrative. Slender stakes would be driven into the ground and notched at the top. Into these notches the visitor would be induced to place a silver dime or quarter. Thereupon, the Indian would step back, say twenty paces, and let fly an arrow from his bow, the object being to knock the coin from the top of the stake at the first shot without splitting or knocking over the stake. If successful the coin became the property of the archer; if not, the Indian paid a forfeit. It impressed me at the time as a somewhat one-sided affair. I spent some time watching but

failed to see a single Indian miss his mark on first short. As
a matter of fact, while not generally known outside of the
followers of archery, there is quite a technique in the handling of these powerful bows used by the Indians. The average man, unfamiliar with their use, would scarce be able to
string one of the bows, much less draw back an arrow to
firing position in the bow.

It was customary for Uncle Sam to provide his Indian
wards on trips of the above nature with rations of chipped
beef or dried buffalo meat, corn meal, flour, coffee and sugar.
As a race, the Indian was exceedingly fond of sweets. Some
of the northwestern tribes ate dogs, regarding them as quite a
delicacy, and to be served only on state or special occasions
when prominent guests were present.

Indian bands visiting the fair were always accompanied
by a guard of Federal soldiers. These prohibited the visitors
from passing whiskey or other spirituous liquors to the Indians, although many of the youths and men visiting at the
fair would fill the tobacco pouches of the Indians. They
usually had capable interpreters with them, and for a silver
dime or quarter, the average Indian brave would relate a
story of having to do either with his personal career and activities, or else an old Indian legend. As an actual talker,
the average Indian could scarcely rate as loquacious, their
verbal utterings were brief, assisted by signs, grunts and expression of countenance.

No race of men has ever been more at home on the horse
than the Indians. I have watched tirelessly their games of
skill in special exhibitions of this nature. One of their favorite
acts was that of picking up very small objects from the ground
while racing bareback at breakneck speed. Rarely did they
miss.

Too, if one wanted a wild mustang pony broken to ride,
an Indian brave, for a small sum, would mount and ride
him until utterly pacified. After some two or three workouts
of this kind, the average mustang proved sufficiently docile
for any normal horseman. They charged, usually, about five
dollars for the course.

About 1874, when the Fairgrounds association bought the
fourteen hundred acres in south end, what was really the
first Texas State fair was opened. A large delegation of Indians attended this fair. One of the tribes had fought against
General Custer. Immense fellows, they appeared to me most
ferocious and scarcely half civilized. Their tents were pitched

21

at McGowan and Travis where the R. C. Duff home later was built. They remained in camp there for several months, giving exhibitions of skill and workmanship, and proving one of the biggest drawing cards of the fair.

It will be remembered that one of the last big Indian battles in Texas was fought at Packsaddle mountain, near Kingsland, situated at the junction of the Colorado and Llano rivers. This battle occurred in 1874. In 1900, however, I visited in Kingsland spending some time at "Camp Pajama."

Judging from the amount of arrow heads and spear heads recovered at so late a date, the battle must have been a stout affair. Camp Pajama is a most delightful spot and was named by the late M. L. Robbins, general passenger agent of the Southern Pacific.

It was about the year 1889 or 1890, that the great Apache chief, Geronimo, was on exhibit for nearly a whole day at the Grand Central depot in Houston. He had been captured near Fort Sill. This ferocious old chief had cost the government over a million dollars and the lives of many soldiers and civilians before he was finally captured. He was en route to Florida for confinement, with two hundred other braves, in a federal prison. Remaining in prison in Florida for an extended period, he contracted tuberculosis from the close confinement. Because of this he was released to go among his tribesmen.

It is a matter of record that in the late "Eighties" the Indian tribes often came down as far as Burnett and Llano, and even into Marble Falls and near Austin on their occasional raids. When Austin was first made the capital of Texas, the legislature would regard adjournment of the legislature as prudent, in order to avoid an especially dangerous raid on part of the Indians.

I recall sitting in the office of P. J. Willis and Brother, when R. S. Willis was handed a telegram from Captain M. M. Roberts, one of his star salesman, who covered West Texas for the firm. The telegram read, "Attacked by the Indians. Escaped in my ambulance with two Milburn wagons."

This attack occurred near Mason, Texas, in 1882. Captain Roberts later became adjutant general of Texas. In 1874, when Governor Hubbard was the state's chief executive, he brought to the Waco state fair an entire Indian village, the largest gathering of red men I have ever seen. At that time the Katy railroad had been completed only to Indian Territory, and I used it in making a trip to St. Louis. Fort

Worth then was little more than a frontier army camp and the first two-story brick house had just been completed in Dallas. Denison was full of Indian "bucks" while Fort Scott, Kansas, was little more than two or three stores and a few scattering houses of the "shotgun" type. In many of the towns along the route, I noted numbers of Indians in their native garb. Comanches still infested the western part of Texas.

When Captain R. E. Belding of Gonzales, veteran salesman of the San Antonio district, would come to town, all his friends would gather around him to hear of his latest hairbreadth escapes from the Indians, Mexican bandits and bushwhackers, all equally as bad as the Indians.

Another veteran star salesman now, who had more actual Indian encounters than any other, is Captain B. F. Blanton, now in his eighty-fourth year and still going strong. He is the father of the general manager of the chamber of commerce of Houston, W. N. Blanton; a real pioneer of the famous Chisholm Trail. He is the son of Ransom Gwynn Blanton, a Virginian who helped the Allen brothers launch Houston on its path to metropolitan greatness. He was born in one of the wildest sections of Texas, near Fayetteville in Colorado County.

Outstanding among the adventures which Blanton encountered in his long career as trail driver, cowman, buffalo hunter, merchant, cotton gin operator and traveling salesman, is the one when Ham White held up a stage coach on the road from Austin to San Antonio at the fork in the road. He was sitting next to a newspaper man who had just recently purchased a gun which he displayed with much pride, telling the world that he would not submit to a holdup, not while he was in possession of that shiny, new pistol. In the midst of the bragging the coach was stopped and ahead was a masked man with a wicked looking six-gun trained on the occupants of the stage.

"Pile out!" he commanded, and out they piled, including the newspaper man, who Ham first disarmed, pocketing his treasured gun. Then he cleaned everybody out and rode away. During the rest of the day this newspaper man had nothing more to say.

You have all heard of the capture of Cynthia Ann Parker, and every school boy knows the history of her rescue by Captain Sul Ross, and the sad end. In 1880, I visited Fredericksburg and became acquainted with the Fisher family, who had a ranch a short distance away on the Pedernales. One moonlight night the Comanches swooped down on these folks, captured their only son, who was about fifteen years old. Later the neighbors located him in Indian Territory, going to what is now Oklahoma with eight or ten wagons, and brought him back. His parents fell on his shoulder weeping with joy; they gave him a fine Kentucky horse, a shotgun and some clothes to make him feel at home; after about three months he disappeared one night.

Later they found he had returned to his Indian squaw and his two papooses as he had learned to love this wild life best. On his visit to his people he informed them that he had accompanied the Comanches often on raids. One night, seated on the home gate, he tried to steal away from the Indians but he was too closely watched, but they did not attempt any bodily harm.

Like the passing of the day, the Indian is fading from the face of the earth. No longer does he roam the plains of a free and untamed country. His trek has ended, and now at the end of the trail, he vanishes with the setting sun. Destroyed by the progress of a race gone mad, he awaits the day when his race will have vanished from the earth, consoled perhaps, by the thought that we too will someday stand at the end of the same trail.

FROSTOWN AND TALLOW TOWN

Forebears of Houston—German Settlement

Older than Houston is the little German settlement which was built up before the coming of the Allens. Unquestionably, Frank R. Lubbock was one of the most outstanding men during the days of the Revolution and Civil War. We find his name everywhere but his history will go down for all time in this state as the Confederate governor of Texas.

Historians have quoted him for more than four decades, particularly on his amusing account of the coming of the "Laura" and his three days' trip from Harrisburg to Houston, but his crowning narrative was his attempt to "find Houston," the famous city which the Allens had so extensively advertised. Lubbock said they sailed up White Oak Bayou to where the Merchants and Manufacturers building now stands, and on discovering their error, "backed downstream and found a few clapboard shacks on the bayou." But had they looked around a little more closely, they would have discovered the little settlement, "Germantown." Historians claim that Mrs. Mary Wilkens, her two daughters and her son-in-law were the first settlers of Houston, in 1822, fifteen years prior to Lubbock's visit. It is more than probable that settlers were scattered all over this section of the state, when the battle of San Jacinto was won.

Mrs. Wilkens had had constructed a dwelling, the first house in Harris County, at a point about one and a half miles south of Buffalo Bayou, where it makes a bend at Frostown, on the northeastern limits of the city, beginning at the I. and G. N. railway track, and running east on Magnolia Street, bounded by Buffalo Bayou. Altogether it comprised eight blocks. At first it was called "Germantown," as it was built up almost entirely by Germans, who are considered practical and thrifty people. They settled this little hill as it was the best drained land in this immediate section. The German population was from the beginning the largest of all. There were also Austrians, Swiss, Prussians and Hungarians, all speaking the German language. When the first census was taken in this state, the German speaking people comprised forty-five per cent of the inhabitants. This little addition is shown on Borden's map.

In 1836 a surveyor by the name of Henry Smith Rider landed on the peninsula now called Morgan's Point. Two days later John Iams James landed on the same spot and joined Rider. This was in May, 1822 and these men are presumed to have been a surveying party sent in advance of Mrs. Wilkens, all hailing from New York State, according to notes left by Green and Wise.

This was the only thickly settled section in 1826, with about twenty inhabitants. In 1836, it had grown to half a hundred men, women and children. Augustus C. Allen and John K. Allen had lived at Nacogdoches until 1835 when they came and settled in the Frostown settlement, where they were living at the time of the battle of San Jacinto. They were real master real estate agents. They were land speculators but saw the vision of a great city at the head of navigation. Accordingly, they bought a portion of the John Austin survey (the present site of Houston) from a Mrs. Parrot and began the work of platting it and advertising it to the outside world. The good job they did is remembered with pride by all who have seen the city grow from its humble beginning. The city began its real development in the "Seventies."

But just below it on the bayou was another important place known as "Tallow Town," which sprang up during the War Between the States. This was Houston's dinner pail. It was estimated that one hundred were employed there in killing cattle and cutting up the meat, but they killed the cattle mostly for the hides and tallow which brought big prices. This was long before John D. Rockefeller's kerosene came into use. Probably five or six thousand head of cattle were slaughtered to feed the forces of General Magruder stationed from Harrisburg to the seven forts at Galveston. I have often been told by the early residents of Galveston that beef was given to all who came and asked for it and the balance was burned. This is quite a contrast to the prices now.

As far as appearance is concerned when the writer first saw Frostown sixty-five years ago, it was a beautiful settlement. Many of the prominent people of this day descended from its citizens. I can remember the homes of the families of F. W. Heitmann, H. F. Fisher, John F. Usener, Ignatz Veith, Vetter Schmidt and others later very prominent, all bordering on "Quality Hill." Our veteran ex-mayor, John T. Browne, lived there once and Thomas Kehoe, one of Houston's best known cotton men, claimed it as his home. Mr. F. A. Heitmann gave a graphic description a few years ago to the press. He was reared there. Schrimps Field, about forty acres just north and east of the old gas works, was on a splendid hill.

Here it was that the early colonists had their folk festivities, brought from the fatherland, some of the newcomers even wearing their native dress. It was a picturesque sight to see the younger element and often the older ones joining in a

26

game of "Blind Man's Bluff," "Ring Around the Rosey," "Drop the Handkerchief," games almost unknown to the present young generation. The homes all had beautiful flower gardens and well kept vegetable plots which helped to sustain them. There were small goats which roamed the hills by the dozens. These goats were milked regularly. The Swiss and Germans knew the value of goat's milk and all kinds of foods were made out of the milk. There was a drink, "kumiss," which even up to two decades ago could be found at all northern soda fountains. The writer has often thought that Gail Borden, who surveyed the place, as well as the city of Houston, obtained his idea of condensed milk from the thick goat's milk, which was fed largely to invalids and children. However, the idea came to him, and he gave to the world a product never to be forgotten. He was one of the earliest to contribute toward the child health program and saved the lives of thousands of babies.

One reason why Frostown was settled so quickly was the fact that the German colonists came and, finding friends or relatives here whom they had known in the old country, they remained instead of traveling on into the interior. Germany had started a colonization program and when the immigrants came, they knew they would not be alone. When the papers and letters came from home, groups would band together and read to each other. Few can remember the linen blue envelopes plastered all over with sealing wax and marked "via Queenstown, Liverpool, Southampton, London, Bremen, Hamburg, Havre," giving the name of the clipper ship as a routing. Often the letters would come dated on a certain day of the month, but actually written in installments, ten to fifteen days apart, as time was no object. It often took about four months for the clipper ships to cross the big pond. There were no telegrams in those days and few newspapers. The feminine elements of the settlement gathered in late afternoon at the German "Kaffe Klatch," for coffee and cakes, while the men gathered at the taverns, and in this way the news was spread.

The Turnverein was founded eighty-three years ago and the newspapers and magazines were placed on file from all of the larger cities in Europe. Even the New York papers were to be had in the files. Houston was a cosmopolitan city in the early days and the English, Finnish, Italian and other nationalities had their societies and meeting places. Seventy years ago the Caledonians (Scotch) danced to the horn pipe and gave out to their neighbors the news from home.

The old Borden map recently discovered and secured by Miss Julia Ideson shows a block laid out for an arsenal. Near here there was the arsenal "swimming hole" and the "Russian swimming hole," where all the boys from the Longcope Square later disported themselves regularly in the well-known swimming-ponds wearing nothing more than heavenly smiles. Now they are bankers, merchants and the like. At Longcope's Square was played the old town ball game, with a flat bat and a rubber ball. If a good strike was made, it would roll either to Quality Hill or Frostown. The game was similar to baseball but lots more fun for us.

I have often fished on the bayou near Quality Hill and Frostown and caught trout, perch and gaspergou. On one occasion I saw a porpoise swim around the bend at Frostown. The water is so contaminated now that even an alligator gar cannot live in it. Few remember when we would swim across the bayou from bank to bank, swallowing a bit of old Buffalo Bayou water on a dare, in the days of "Auld Lang Syne"—when it was Frostown and Tallow Town—and Houston, as a big city, was just a dream.

CIVIC RECOLLECTIONS

Mud Bog Days Recalled

Comparisons, as the hoary proverb remarked, are sometimes odious.

That should be true if one compares what one has at present with what he possessed in the past. It does, however, create some degree of smug satisfaction to contemplate one's present possessions and find them of a richness not even approached by that which he formerly owned.

It is safe, therefore, to compare the Houston of today, with its broad avenues, well paved streets and rapid traffic arteries, with the early village of some eleven thousand souls as I first knew it.

Time was when Houston was famed for its mud. Not that the mud had any medicinal or healing qualities which might have made the city attractive as a health resort, as Sour Lake and its mud baths of a generation or so ago, but solely because, during the rainy season, the mud existed in such tremendous quantities, was of such great depth and clung so tenaciously. Far from healing, it was in every respect most irritating.

Houston was popularly known, from town to town, as "Mudville" and Galvestonians and others poked merciless fun with a derisive reference to Houstonians as "mudcats." For Galveston, already had become "citified" with its paved and well drained streets. It had only sand, and still has it.

My first graphic description of Houston was received by me in 1864, when my mother returned to our home in Galveston after having spent a week here with relatives and friends. Her visit had taken place during the rainy season. At the dinner table that evening, my father inquired how she had enjoyed the week's stay, and somewhat of her impression of the Bayou City.

"As a place of residence I would not live in Houston if they were to give me the city," she exclaimed. "The place is a sea of mud that is knee-deep and clings like cold tar. The men carry six-shooters by day—and a lantern by night!"

Eight or ten years later I made my first trip to Houston. On the origin and history of the city, its founding by the Allens, I was fairly well posted. Accordingly, I looked forward with a keen sense of appreciation to an opportunity to inspect the city at first hand.

En route on the G. H. & H. train from Galveston, as we neared what I thought might be Houston, the conductor called "Allen's Station." I pricked up my ears, but was surprised to find out that the stop was really the station for the famed Allen's Ranch, an Allen, incidentally, not related to the Allens who had founded Houston. Another Sam Allen, the cattle-king of this region in those days, operated this great ranch house whose acres flanked both Simms and Buffalo bayous. On Buffalo Bayou he had his private boat landing, a noted stop-over. His cattle were numbered by the thousands, and his landed estate seems to me to have occupied the greater portion of soil between Houston and Galveston. Allen's home was a two story, Colonial structure with broad verandas, and the scene at one time or another of much gaiety and entertainment.

In the later "Seventies," the firm of Allen, Pool and Company, operating the ranch, failed for a half million dollars. Nick Weeks, of the Galveston Island City Bank, was made receiver. The cattle upon the ranch increased so prolifically that, together with the enhancement in land values at that time, within four and a half years the receivership was terminated and a handsome profit was returned to the estate—a result regarded as most remarkable at the time. An echo of this estate was noted early in 1937, when Mrs. Rosa Allen, in her suit before the Supreme Court of Texas, recovered judgment against the Port of Houston and title to certain portions of the old Allen ranch property valued at about two hundred and sixteen thousand dollars.

The train continued on and as we neared Harrisburg, a young lady sitting opposite me turned suddenly to the window and exclaimed, "Look, what beautiful Christmas trees!" Peering outward, I gazed enraptured at my first sight of a pine forest and joined in her enthusiasm, especially when I spied a small number of wild deer come bounding out of the woods, take a surprised look at our moving train and then gallop madly back into the shelter of the forest.

After a ride of some three and a half hours from Galveston, as compared with the less than an hour ride today, we arrived at the depot in Houston, a very small wooden affair known as "Allen's Station," located at the foot of Congress, about where the old I. & G. N. depot formerly stood.

I was told it was only a short walk up to the city. For the purpose of sightseeing I decided to "hoof it."

Congress Avenue I found a teeming thoroughfare, chiefly active with business houses, a majority of them filled with patrons. A sidewalk had been built along both sides of the street. Its composition, however, was crude, consisting of clamshells and black asphalt, a composition of little stability which did not last long. I remember, in fact, that under the subsequent rays of the hot summer sun, the asphalt melted and ran so that the pedestrians' shoes became "be-gobbed" with large chunks of the mixture!

Congress Avenue, itself, only a mud road at the time, reflected a busy traffic of various types of wagons and carts drawn by ox or mule-teams, some of them of eight yokes. There were drays that impressed me as quaint—scarcely three feet high, and about fourteen feet long, so arranged as to enable one man to load three bales of cotton and five barrels of flour. The interesting purpose of this extreme width was that the wheels might fit the ruts made by the feet of the oxen! This type of dray with their wide wheels, so far as I know, can now be seen only in the museum of Henry Ford's Magic City.

En route to the center of the city, I paused at Congress and San Jacinto to contemplate the magnificence of the rose-garden cultivated by Mrs. G. H. Bringhurst in her immense front yard. It, like the wondrous, old-fashioned garden maintained by the Roberts family at what is now Byrd's corner on Main Street, was one of several similar showplaces of the city. I never had seen flowers grow in such luxurious beauty. Compared with these gardens, Galveston had only a paucity of flowers.

I continued on and came presently to Main Street; even then it was a "Main Street" to delight the imaginative pen of Sinclair Lewis. The passing throng included types of people new to my youthful eyes, and I think I must have stood fascinated. Everywhere around me were the immense ten-gallon hats peculiar to the cattlemen and plantation owners of that day; and here and there the sleek, booted professional gambler; the native Mexican in his picturesque garb, or the elderly citizen of distinction wearing the small blanket or great scarf thrown around his shoulders, as we see today in certain pictures of Sam Houston taken during that period. Sam Houston's shoulder blanket was, in fact, as well known in Washington when he was United States Congressman and Senator, as it was in Houston.

There, too, was the typical farmer of the day whom one could identify half a block away by his "galluses," and their wives, with rotund, happy countenances peeping out of the deep, old-fashioned sun-bonnets, or the yard wide bandannas.

I registered at the Barnes House, famed inn that stood where the Rice Hotel now stands.

Sprawled in the street on both sides of the hotel were heavy yoked ox teams, making traffic almost out of the question for anything more than a man on foot or horseback. Around the sidewalk on each side of the hotel was the wooden and iron hitching rail, to which the cow ponies and other horses belonging to the patrons were hitched. The sidewalks themselves turned out to be a structure of wooden plants and supports very much like a lengthy platform. High, it had to be, to avoid the splash of soupy mud from Houston's main thoroughfare.

I contemplated the street in amazement. Reared in Galveston, I never had seen such a vast amount of mud; it was not only deep and morass looking, but stretched in both directions as far as I could see.

Over at what is now J. C. Penney's corner, at Texas and Main, some jokingly inclined wag had driven down a four-by-four post with a sign on it declaiming "No bathing, please!" An hour later I passed it again. The original sign had been taken away; a stovepipe hat had been placed on the post, and a new sign announced to mildly surprised pedestrians, "Don't kick me—I'm down here on horseback, trying to get out!"

Around the corner, on Fannin Street, I noted an "H-M-T" (hug-me-tight) buggy in the middle of the street, stuck fast and tight in the deep mud. The driver was nowhere in sight. Apparently he had cut the horses free from the buggy, allowing to flounder out of the bog as best they could. Around the bog were scattered a number of card-board cracker boxes, empty sardine and salmon cans, and the accompanying pepper-sauce bottle, indicating that the driver had remained with the buggy and had consumed his "commissary" probably purchased for other purposes, hoping that someone would come along and assist him out. It had been, I was told, one of those proverbially "unusual" rainy seasons, and I observed many other carts and buggies stuck fast in the mud in various parts of the city, deserted by their owners until the mud should dry sufficiently to allow excavation of the vehicle without danger of the excavator himself sinking into the morass!

I noticed also in parts of the town where no sidewalks existed, that the pedestrians would make their way by frequently hanging to the picket and rail fences, gaining foothold on firmer but smaller piece of ground just beneath the fence, or sometimes on the bottom rail or footboard. Occasionally I would see their feet slip, and down they would go into the sticky mire over their shoetops or halfway up to the knees. It is little wonder that one carried a lantern by night.

However, in all fairness to the early days of Houston when it was a village, there also was an altogether different side to the story. If the streets and sidewalks deep with adhesive mud were discouraging to the inhabitant or visitor, the wonderful old shade trees and luxurious, old-fashioned flower gardens that lined the streets were an equally offsetting delight. In Galveston we had no trees. In Houston they grew naturally, or the Allen brothers had planted them

The new magnificent San Jacinto Memorial Shaft at San Jacinto battle ground.

while laying out the city. The effect was beautiful. Aside, possibly, from New Orleans, I do not recall any American city that boasted of a greater number or more pretentious trees than Houston. It is a great misfortune that they were sacrificed to civic progress.

As I continued my inspection of the future metropolis I turned and found my way to Market Square. It impressed me as the busiest portion of the town. The sidewalks were dotted with vendors of every kind of produce, fruits and vegetables, flowers, breads, pastries, and what-not. It was the custom for the rich and poor alike to go to market on Saturdays particularly.

Each carried his great basket. Dignified, stately and wealthy old gentlemen elbowed with the laborer and hired-man, not only for the purpose of driving hard bargains with the vendors, but also for the sake of visiting socially during the shopping hour with their fellow citizens who likewise attended "market day." I remember distinctly, in later days when I resided in Houston, seeing among others in the crowd B. A. Shepherd, founder of the First National Bank, Dr. Erich Schmidt, Charles Miller and other Houstonians equally prominent in their day. On these Saturday marketing days the crowd was so great that one could scarcely hand pick his way through the aisles.

This was in the day when all of the dinky, small, six-windowed horse cars made the turn at Market Square; and which, incidentally, reminds me that in the middle of the street car track was a narrow board walk on which the mules drawing the street car would walk. In rainy weather pedestrians always used these walks. They provided excellent footing until the mules came along. Then, there was no alternative but to step off into the deep mud! The only way there to successfully use the walk was to time the cars; otherwise it was a case of "love's labor lost."

As I continued my ramblings I found no "corner groceries" of the type known later on, or anything in the nature of the food emporiums such as we have today. There was but one restaurant in Houston. Frank Colby, later to become one of Houston's institutions as a caterer to sated appetites, had just come to town. He established his first place of business at Franklin and Travis. Here was the only place in the city where one could obtain an order of ham and eggs or anything in the nature of prepared dishes, except at the hotels

or the town boarding house; or, of course, at the railroad
station eating house some distance from the heart of the city.

There was, however, something about Houston even at
that time that made the newcomer feel at home here. Notwithstanding the mud and the "unusual" weather, I liked the
place immensely, and could visualize that it had the possibilities— the location and possible resources—from which to build
an eventual metropolis that would far surpass even the
optimistic claims already made by the Allens.

Ten years later, in 1883, I made Houston my home.

It was the same year that the Inmans of Atlanta, great
cotton merchants of their day, arrived.

Texas had produced that year the greatest cotton crop
of all time. Jepperson, the statistician, estimated the yield at
from 9-16 to 5-8 of a bale to the acre, a yield which may
never be equalled again, as the virgin soil that produced it
has suffered much deterioration since then. That year every
empty town lot from Houston Avenue to the I. & G. N.
bridge was filled with bales of cotton.

To take care of the overload, two additional compresses
were built. Houston had become of such importance as a
cotton center that the Cotton Exchange built its first permanent home, still a worthy structure, at Travis and Franklin.
In cotton transactions the town took its place alongside of
Galveston and New Orleans. Houston thus received its first
great impetus toward its present metropolitan status.

About the same time, the inhabitants began to pull Houston out of the mud. Lower Main Street was paved with
white granite slabs, which after a heavy rain glistened like
the marble streets of ancient Rome. Congress Avenue was
paved with "Nicholson" blocks, made of cypress and bois
d'arc tightly welded together. They were not altogether successful. Heavy rains caused the blocks to expand, buckle
and wash away by the hundreds. Franklin and other streets
were filled in and were given a coat of gravel.

A commercial club was organized. This club brought
about the sale of the two mule-car lines and replacement in
due course with electric trams. Subsequently deep water
transportation was agitated and brought about. Houston
began to throw off its swaddling clothes and began to have
real and genuine "growing pains."

QUALITY HILL

Houston's First Fashionable Residential District

It seems strange now, when the ultra-fashionable of Houston are domiciled in their palatial homes in River Oaks, Riverside Terrace, Braeswood and Montrose, to contemplate that the first "blue blooded" residential district of the city occupied a portion now so far removed from anything of the sort. It is a striking example of what time and progress do to a rapidly growing community.

Houston's first residential district of the "socially elite" was called "Quality Hill."

Quality Hill was not a large area, as civic properties go; in fact, Houston's "four hundred" of that day was a comparatively small, closely allied social circle, environed on the north by Buffalo Bayou, on the east by Crawford Street and on the south and west respectively by Congress and Austin streets.

Nature itself had aided the "four hundred's" seclusion, for, just before reaching Quality Hill, running north and south through the town, had constructed at Caroline Street, for drainage purposes during the heavy rainy season, a vast gully, ranging from twenty to forty feet in depth, known as Fred Smith's Creek, which emptied into Buffalo Bayou. In later years, the citizens supplemented this with "Calhoun Ditch," running east and west across the city.

Recently I had an opportunity to inspect what remains today of the once famed Quality Hill. It was a beautiful morning and as I was making my way across the intersection of Main Street and Frankin Avenue and stepped up to the opposite curb, a fine large sedan of the latest model drew up beside me. Its occupant, one of my old school boy friends, hailed me.

I glanced appreciatively at his sleek-looking conveyance, surmising that he desired only that I give heed to his swanky new purchase, but he exclaimed enthusiastically:

"Get in here—this is just the morning for an exhilerating drive."

Nothing loath, I accepted with equal pleasantry and he inquired, "Now, where shall we go?"

"Let us drive down to old Quality Hill and see what

35

is left of the glory that was Houston's in its early days,"
I replied.

Continuing on Franklin, we came presently to Crawford
and turned aside to Commerce. It was here that once stood
the beautiful southern home of William J. Hutchins, pioneer
merchant of Houston, who built the old Hutchins House,
an inn famed in its day where the Southern Pacific general
office building now stands. The Hutchins House was the scene
of many brilliant balls and social affairs of that period.

Perhaps one of the most elaborate functions ever to
take place in that famous old structure was the wedding of
Hutchins' daughter, Ella, to Lord Stewart of England, a
son of General E. B. Nichols of Houston, who, having been
educated in England, was adopted by the preceding Lord
Stewart. The wedding at the time was regarded as one
of the outstanding international marriages.

Unhappily, however, upon the death of the senior Lord
Stewart, it was found that under the English law of succession, the estates and title could not be entailed to an alien.
This resulted in the return of the new "Lord Stewart" to
Houston as plain Frank Nichols. Among much old plate
and jewels, I recall that Mr. Nichols brought with him
the famous "Black Diamond," once owned and worn by
Mary, Queen of Scots, herself one of the earlier Stuarts.
I saw the wondrous gem on several occasions, exhibited at
church fairs and similar fetes, but of its final disposition I
know not.*

The wife of "Lord Stewart" subsequently became Mrs.
Seabrook Sydnor, and was so known and endeared over a
long period of years to a majority of old Houstonians.

A little farther up Quality Hill stood the imposing homes
of the Gentrys, the Waldos, Tinsleys, Cochrans, Hamblins
and Cages, and other social and commercial leaders of the
day. Just around the corner stood the colonial residence of
Colonel Cornelius Ennis. Yet another type of ante-bellum
architecture was the old Longcope home, constructed of beautiful white brick, ornamented with green shutters after the
fashion of the times. It boasted also of fancy-worked, black
iron railings and balconies, after the old Spanish or French

* Shortly after this was written, I was informed by Charles J. Phillips,
prominent Houston attorney, that the Black Diamond still rests in Houston, the property of Mrs. Alfred D. Smith. In a subsequent chapter of
this book its entire Houston history will be told.

styles. In its palmy days the residence stood out like a thing of beauty. Alas for the working of time! It presents now a dilapidated appearance, going slowly to ruin, and is now occupied as a Mexican rooming-house of the cheaper type.

We turned and drove (with a sigh for the passing of those olden days) out towards Rusk Avenue and that section which, perhaps twenty years later, became the next "silk stocking" residential section of the city. There was noted, in passing, the former homeside of Judge Peter Gray, one of the most learned jurists and gallant gentlemen of that period.

Then came the old home of William R. Baker, also on Rusk. A great brick structure of Southern Colonial design, it was the scene of much splendor in its day. It was here, during the Civil War, that General Bankhead Magruder of the Confederate army made his headquarters in Houston.

He had arrived here fresh with the laurels of having won the first battle of the Confederacy at Big Bethel Church, which for more than a century was the national camp-meeting grounds of the Baptist Church of Virginia. As a merited promotion, General Magruder had been given the command of the Southern armies of Texas and Louisiana. His brilliant recapture of Galveston from the Yankee forces on New Year's Day of 1863 is a tale often told. His aide-de-camp, Captain N. P. Turner married Mr. Baker's daughter, the wedding taking place at the old Baker home, being another of the brilliant social affairs of the period. Captain Turner was the consummate "Beau Brummell" and was known all about the city as "The Lord Chesterfield of Houston."

In driving down Rusk and McKinney avenues, I recalled distinctly that in the city's earlier years these thoroughfares had been lined on either side with magnificent oaks, the towering branches of which spread across the street until they almost intermingled and it was a stirring sight to drive under the bower thus created. With the coming of the telephone and light wires, these were cut away, giving way to a progressive municipality. Yet I could not but entertain a twinge of regret at the thought of their passing. They were much akin to that wondrous specimen of oak remaining at the corner of the Scanlan Estate on Main Street. I never pass and contemplate the latter but that I am reminded of Joyce Kilmer's melodious creation, "Trees." As the Persians are wont to say, "May its shadow never grow less!"

Presently my companion and I turned to Post Office Square where once stood four pretentious homes, belonging to the Waldos, Boyles and other prominent Houstonians, all of which, in time, gave way to construction of the present Post Office.

Across the street, on the corner of Caroline and Rusk Avenues, stood the attractive home of Colonel Charles Dillingham, one time receiver of both the I. and G. N., and the H. and T. C. railroads, in turn, and later chairman of the South Texas Commercial National Bank. Farther down, at the corner of San Jacinto and Rusk avenues, stood the charming white and yellow home of William D. Cleveland, Sr. Alas! The homesite of Colonel Dillingham is now occupied by a parking lot and a hot dog stand; while that of Mr. Cleveland boasts only of a parking lot. Yet, these properties, I believe, remain in the hands of the respective families and it occurs to me that it was scarcely these particular soils the party who coined the phrase had in mind when he exclaimed, "dirt cheap." It would, in fact, be interesting to compare the prices originally paid for these respective locations by Dillingham and Cleveland, with the quotations upon them today.

I happen to know that Charles J. Grainger, maternal grandfather of Mrs. Natalie Taylor Carlisle, paid eight hundred dollars for his homesite at Fannin and Texas avenues, now occupied by the Shell Building, and that he purchased from Sam Houston for seven hundred and fifty dollars, the plot of ground now occupied by Foley Brothers . . . trifling sums in the light of today's values.

We turned now into McKinney Avenue and noted a corner occupied by another parking and sales lot, where formerly had stood the home and grounds of the late Captain J. C. Hutcheson, father of Federal Circuit Judge J. C. Hutcheson, Jr., and Palmer Hutcheson, the attorney.

A short way east on McKinney remains the enlarged cottage residence of the Pillot family. It is particularly distinctive by reason of the two great, black iron dogs that guard the front entrance. These iron dogs, said to have been cast in France, have a most interesting history. One of my friends, now approaching fifty, tells me that some eighty-five years ago his mother, when a child, played and frollicked around these same dogs, and that the homesite was then considered a farm on the outskirts of Houston.

The Pillot residence probably stood near the outskirts of the very limits of the city as not far from it there once stood a little shack store known to travelers upon that road as the

"First and Last Chance," maintained by a George Elser. The proprietor proclamied to the public that, for quenching one's thirst, it was the first chance coming in and the last chance going out. Eventually, R. E. Paine, Sr. built his home across the street and in due time the "little shack" gave way to the growing pains of Houston.

McKinney Avenue was "way out" during the period we have in mind, and we soon lost sight of landmarks familiar to our four-score years. We turned back and reentered Main Street once more to get our bearings.

The early home of Charles House stood at Main and McKinney; the same residence was subsequently occupied by Dr. W. R. Eckhardt and his family.

Now, all of the magnificent homes of yesteryear's Main Street are gone. Years ago the E. P. Hill properties occupied a block a short distance out Main Street. When Hill was the owner it was centered with a large residence, and it was the purpose of the owner to deed it to the city for park purposes. Today it is occupied by outmoded apartment houses and business buildings. Had it become a park it would have constituted a much needed and beautiful area, but the actual transfer was never effected. The plot had been planted years previously with oak trees from acorns taken from the Great Oak standing at the first capitol of Texas, in Columbia. Capt. A. M. Darling had filled his pockets with the acorns on one of his missions to the capital, and had planted them upon his return to Houston. Only one of these immense oaks, I believe, today remains upon the block.

Farther out Main there yet remains the original home of J. I. Campbell, one of the lumber magnates of his day. This residence was subsequently purchased and used as a home by Mrs. Augusta Jones, aunt of Jesse Holman Jones, the capitalist and chairman of the Reconstruction Finance Corporation. Many of the younger years of Jesse Jones were spent there. Business structures are closing in upon it, and the once impressive mansion appears to be falling into decay.

In the fourteen hundred block on Main Street, the splendid home of Captain James A. Baker stood. That block is now filled with business buildings.

On Main Street, too, there formerly stood many other expensive homes during the period of two generations ago. I recall among them those of the Nelms, the W. T. Carters, Henry S. Fox, the Taubs, Kaiser and others. The site of the

Fox home is now occupied by a prosaic appearing drugstore and other commercial buildings. The Major Dickson home and the James E. Masterson home have given way to a block of business houses.

With the vision of past glories of these mansions of the "Nineties" imprinted clearly on our minds we turned into Milam Street to Hadley Avenue. Here yet stands the once pretentious mansion of Gail Johnson, the son-in-law of Gail Borden, who founded the Houston Post. Gail had the house built for his bride. Unhapply, she passed away before its completion and through other hands it passed to J. O. Ross, whose family for many years occupied it as their home. The Johnson residence, too, was the scene of many debutante and other sparkling social events. Casual inspection reveals it is currently being used as a boarding house.

As we turned into lower Louisiana Street we contemplated the site of the former home of T. W. House, occupying the block between McKinney and Lamar. It was, in its day, an imposing structure, with the entire block covered with stately palms, neatly maintained. Until its recent demolition to make way for a used-car lot, the property served during the recent depression as headquarters for housing Federal Transients.

Not far from the "House of House" was the lovely residence of James Bute, its grounds and fountains comprising one of the show places of Houston. It, too, has given way to the inevitable parking lot.

Another home equally attractive in its appointment of grounds was the James T. D. Wilson place, which covered an entire block. It was the site of profuse flowers and shady nooks. The Rice Hotel Laundry now occupies the spot.

Near here was the B. A. Shepherd block, bounded by Lamar, Dallas, Travis and Milam. Its floral gardens rivalled those nearby. Subsequently the site was occupied by Mr. Shepherd's son-in-law, O. L. Cochran and his family, and after Cochran, came W. H. Palmer and family.

Memories, as some writer has suggested, make life beautiful; sometimes forgetfulness alone makes it possible. This is a truth. The enjoyable drive around parts of Old Houston brought me to a realization that where we had our boyhood playgrounds, our baseball park and circus grounds—on old Bremond Square where the Lamar and Lamar Annex Hotels now stand—is now the home of cold stone and steel converted ino modern sky-scrapers. Progress stops at nothing . . . "the play must go on."

WHEN THE PLANTATION BARONS CAME TO TOWN

The plantation "baron" of the early days, making his periodic pilgrimage to Houston or Galveston, traveled in state much akin to that of the overlords of ancient feudal days. In the palmy days of the immense river plantations, his lands were worth at least one hundred dollars an acre in gold, and that was at a time when gold commanded a high premium over currency, sometimes as much as one dollar and forty cents. The plantation baron was, in truth, monarch of all he surveyed.

Well do I remember as a child, when one of these plantation owners arrived in Houston over the venerable Columbia Tap Railroad, an institution that had its terminal at San Jacinto Street and McKinney Avenue, then at the edge of town, but now a busy mart not a dozen blocks from the center of the city, occupied chiefly by automotive and parts supply houses.

The Columbia Tap was often referred to as "Joe Bonney's Road," Bonney being general manager, superintendent, baggage master, freight agent, ticket agent and even chief engineer. He checked in the freight and delivered it, collected fares and drove the engine. The plantation barons really owned the road. They built it, paid for it and operated it until eventually it was sold and became a part of the International and Great Northern.

It might be said, the barons also owned Joe Bonney, took great pride in his management of affairs and more or less made him. Bonney was a great character of those days; a man of much personal charm and universally known and liked. The town of Bonney, some forty miles out of Houston, was named for this genial pioneer of railroad days.

The road itself was facetiously called the "tri-weekly," for many times the train would start out on Monday and find its way back to the starting point by Saturday, for boiler blow-outs were frequent and parts of the engine often were found along the right-of-way. Bonney generally gathered them up, patched them back into place, and, in such fashion, would limp back to Houston. One could get off the train, they said, pick blackberries along the tracks, run and catch up with the coaches anywhere between Houston and Columbia.

When the barons came to town, M. Westheimer or genial

41

Joe Baldwin would have a "grape-vine" telegraph announce
their arrival, creating much-to-do and turning-out as a consequence. Their best spick and span hotel bus awaited
them at the station, drawn by four fine horses and driven by
a Rocky Mountain Express driver, whose claim to fame was,
among other things, that he could "turn the coach around on
a silver dollar and have fifty cents left in change."

The sovereign of the river plantation alighted usually
dressed in a long-tailed coat, a silk waist-coat, puffed shirt,
and pantaloons of the period. Too, he wore the customary
large sombrero which resembled the present-day ten gallon
hats now often presented to notables who visit Texas. Our
river baron added to this raiment a Mexican blanket or
cape over the shoulder, giving a prodigiously picturesque
touch to the whole attire.

His "missus" attended him, she dressed in the fashion of
the day; large hoop-skirts, a huge poke-bonnet, with perhaps
a rich Cashmir shawl or a lace mantilla to adorn her sloping
shoulders.

The young daughter who came with them dressed similarly
to her mother, and quite frequently brought along her
favorite pet, sometimes a poll-parrot or canary bird, encaged.
Usually the mother and daughter brought along their personal maid and with the three of them and their hoop-
skirts, little or no room was left in the hack for the master of
the house. As a result, he perched himself democratically
alongside the driver on the front, outside seat.

With great flourish and a clatter, the coach and four
moved off down the street in a dash of break-neck speed,
headed for the Hutchins House, or the Barnes House, then
situated on the present site of the Rice Hotel, but which,
in those days, was noted for being the original capitol of
Texas.

A platoon of porters and clerks in double column met
the occupants of the coach upon arrival at the hotel, extended the usual acclaim of cordial greeting, and transported
the luggage. The "barons" never pretended to know anything about the weather, but came with overcoat, linen duster,
overshoes and umbrella.

Once ensconced at the hotel the baron proceeded to hold
court. The cotton factors, the bankers and wholesale merchants of the town vied with each other in honoring the
planter and his family. They, as a rule, found him in a
mood receptive to pleasure. Only after a big flood, or an

early attack of the army or leaf worm, when his crop was short, did the planter baron worry about "figures." His lands often yielded two bales of cotton to the acre, against which he paid out the then usual charge of two and one half per cent for selling, and two and one half per cent more for advances made him, or for the purchase of farm implements and supplies, a surcharge that enriched the cotton factors and wholesale merchants of that day.

Frequently, after two or three days spent in feasting and a reception at the hotel for the wife and daughter, the next stage of the journey occurred. The four-in-hand coach was called out and again, the coach clattered down the street at crack of whip, to the old Allen Station at the head of Congress Avenue, where the family could entrain for Galveston. Or, disdaining the transportation of the railroad for something more unique, the party would proceed to the Buffalo Bayou Steamboat Landing and embark for Galveston by passenger steamer.

The selection of a passenger steamer in those days was an event in itself.

The planter often waited on a certain boat, or made an engagement for himself and family two weeks in advance, in order to make the trip with his favorite captain, or perhaps with a particular steward who had before tickled his palate with the choicest of wines and deliciously cooked game brought in from the Big Thicket.

The captain having reserved his best stateroom for the party, and the bandmaster, who also having been apprised of the coming, awaited the party with his band on the dock, upon their arrival struck up the familiar "Dixie," or "My Old Kentucky Home," or "Carry Me Back to Old Virginny," —where many of the planters had been born.

Then would the gang-plank be lifted, and the boat pass down the bayou to what was known as Constitution Bend. On its arrival at Harrisburg it tied up a few minutes to permit friends and well-wishers of the passengers who had accompanied them this far, to disembark and return to Houston. At Harrisburg the steamboat took on additional cargo and the real trip to Galveston began. The engineer, joining in the enthusiastic reception to the party, would fire up heavily, load on extra steam, and give a long blast of the whistle.

When eventide came, with the San Jacinto Battle Ground passed and the broad open stretch of the Bay lying before the vessel, the big table of delicacies was cleared; dancing began, chiefly among the younger set, and there would be quadrilles, lancers and the Virginia Reel.

All of this, however, was too tame for the baron. He with his friends and companions generally mounted the "Texas," as the pilot house barber shop was called. This compartment was soon cleared out and the table arranged for the gentlemanly game of draw poker, a pastime engaged in by almost every man of the time. I have quite often seen the tables piled with gold and silver; greenbacks were tabooed for a long time after Lee's surrender (they were called "shinplasters"). Many times big games were played and stakes ran high.

In one instance to my knowledge a Brazos steamboat owner and planter won a large and elaborately fitted steamboat at a single sitting. The winner was the much-famed Capt. Bill Jenkins, who for years carried ten silver dollars about with him, continually shuffling them like poker chips as he talked, until, in the course of time, they were worn as thin as cardboard.

These draw poker games often continued long after lights out was sounded. Then came a brief rest of two or three hours, breakfast, and Galveston would be at hand.

Galveston usually repeated the Houston reception. "Old Man" Gregory had painted his big hotel bus white; set off by the four Kentucky thoroughbreds which drew it, the one-coach cavalcade resembled Mardi Gras in the ride from the dock to the hotel. The coach took on the party, and would dash down Tremont Street to the Waters House, built and owned by Old Colonel Waters, himself a large planter at Arcola. This plantation was later owned and operated by T. W. House, and finally was disposed of to the Scanlan sisters of Houston. Colonel Waters at the time mentioned operated one of the most pretentious hotels in Texas.

Another day of feasting and entertainment and the planter-baron and his party again dashed through the streets behind the four-in-hand, to embark on one of the Morgan steamers to New Orleans, there either to visit indefinitely, or to continue on to London, Paris, or New York. Sometimes, when the planter felt he needed rest, he detoured for the season to Saratoga, or Wakesha in Wisconsin, or to Green Brier or White Sulphur Springs in Virginia.

Nothing was too good for the cotton planter in The Year of the Big Yield.

POETIC NAMES OF STREETS IN HOUSTON

Taken From the Borden Maps

One of the most interesting discoveries relating to early Houston was in a collection of four very rare maps of the city of Houston, now safely ensconed in the office of Miss Martha Schnitzer in the public library.*

The collection consists of four original maps dated 1836, 1837, 1839, and the fourth and largest bearing no date, but apparently some years later in origin.

The first map is a rather tiny affair, perhaps fifteen by twenty inches, and contained in an apparently very old gilt frame. In it, the southern limits of the little village of Houston are indicated by Prairie Avenue; a name well applied at the time, as beyond it lay prairie.

As relating to this first map, which is identified by the legend: "Plan of the City of Houston, 1836—surveyed by G. and T. H. Borden," it is proper to mention that the Allen brothers bought the land on which they plotted the village from a Mrs. F. F. L. Parton, whose first husband was John Austin, and from whom she had inherited the land grant. At the time she lived in what is now the Fifth Ward, and the Allen brothers boarded with her. They purchased from her the lower half of two leagues situated on both sides of the bayou, but the greater portion of it on the south side; and it was on the south side, immediately adjacent to the bayou that Houston first began.

In the margin of this map there is still legible notation, written by hand in ink, that it is the original map surveyed by Borden and is countersigned and attested by John K. Allen for "A. C. and J. K. Allen," and dated in June, 1836. It is witnessed by J. P. Holman and T. P. Gazely. The entire village at the date of this map was only three blocks in part, beginning with Commerce Avenue on the bayou and extending to Prairie. It shows about sixty blocks then plotted. Another hand written notation is: "The above was previous to the sale of any of the lots shown, and those who have purchased and shall hereafter purchase, will continue to do so according to the plan of the town as it is herein prescribed, and they will call upon the witnesses later to testify to the same,

*The Borden maps were discovered by Julia Ideson of Houston.

as the plan of the City of Houston." This, too, is signed by G. and T. H. Borden.

It is interesting to note that some of our present streets then bore different names; La Branch and Austin streets, were then dubbed Milton and Homer. Upon the north side of what is now Texas Avenue, then a prairie, there was set aside between San Jacinto and Fannin, what is shown as a "school reserve." This area was given to the Christ Church and continues to be occupied by the church. Farther west, between Milam and Travis, where the Chronicle building now stands, was marked "church reserve," which later became the original site of the Methodist Church, subsequently known as "Shearn" Methodist.

This same map shows also the present court house square, which now contains Harris County's fourth court house on that site. Directly west two blocks, bounded by Travis, Preston, Milam and Congress, is block thirty-four, known then as "Congress Square." This was subsequently renamed Market Square and is the present site of the present city hall. It is my understanding that the original deed to the city of Houston is so conditioned that this block of ground reverts to the Allen heirs, should the site not be used for a city hall, or equivalent civic purposes.

The second map of the collection is larger than the above, being approximately twenty-nine inches long and twenty-one inches wide. It also is signed in the original by A. C. Allen "for A. C. Allen and J. K. Allen," and in the right hand lower portion contains an insert map of the coastal and nearby interior regions of Texas. Bordens were the surveyors. The lettering is quite dim; however, the date is clearly indicated as 1837.

On this map, where Bagby Street now runs, the name inserted there is "Calhoun Street," and no Bagby then existed. As the city expanded, Calhoun Street was moved to its present location; Major Bagby, at one time, owned a large tract of land in that portion of the town, and made his residence about where the library now stands.

No market square is indicated on this map, indicating that block thirty-four had not yet been deeded to the city for that purpose. The city had, however, moved its southern limits farther out, and Rusk Avenue is shown as its boundary. On Rusk Avenue, between Fannin and San Jacinto is found a new "school reserve." This is the site of the Texas Company building now. Also on Rusk, between Travis and Milam, was an additional "church reserve."

At the bottom of this map is a most interesting insert extolling the advantages of Houston's location, and a prophetic vision of what might be expected of the city's future. Whether the authors knew it or not, their statement of 1837, probably made for sales purposes only, is astoundingly accurate of what, eventually, has come to pass. It is headed: "The City of Houston," and relates: "Situated at the head of navigation, on the west side bank of the Buffalo Bayou, is now, for the first time, brought to the public notice, because until now the proprietors were not ready to offer it to the public with the advantages of capital and improvements. The City of Houston is located at a point on the river which must ever command the trade of the largest and richest portion of Texas. By reference to the map, it will be seen that the trade of the San Jacinto, Spring Creek, New Kentucky and the Brazos must necessarily flow to this place, and will, at this time, warrant the employment of one million dollars of capital; and when the rich lands of this country shall be settled, a trade will flow to it, making it beyond a doubt the great interior commercial emporium of Texas."

There follows a further account of what the city must, by reason of its strategic location and potential resources, come to be; and for purposes of comparison with development of the city to its present status, the comments contained are most interesting.

The third map of the collection is yet larger, being about thirty-five inches long and twenty-two inches wide. It is also the best preserved map of the three. All the blocks south of Lamar, east to Live Oak and west to Brazos are platted. The legend indicates that it "is sketched and partly surveyed by A. Girard, late chief engineer of the Texas army," and is dated in January, 1839. In it are now shown both the court house square and the market square. A large plot on the north side of the bayou is shown unplotted, but marked as belonging to A. C. Allen, and a similar tract is shown as belonging to A. C. Baker.

Perusing this map, it is interesting to note that in that year there ran parallel to Washington to the south a street called Monroe, and the north, Adams (later changed to Railroad Street), then Girard, and Susan, and I cannot but wonder who this particular Susan was, and why the distinction of having a street named for her in those early days. Both the

47

fair Susan and her proud little street have long since passed into memories.

Chartres Street on this map is designated as "Charter"; and later on it was spelled "Chartre" on a subsequent map of the city. South of Lamar, the streets are not shown, but the blocks are platted as far out as Clay Avenue of the present day. Beyond Clay is a great tract of land bordering the entire city, and designated as belonging to Baker and Holman. North of the city, bordering White Oak Bayou, are two additional large tracts, listed as belonging to a Dr. Evans and A. C. Allen, respectively. This apparently included the present Taub property between Dart Street and White Oak, on White Oak Drive.

The fourth and largest map of all is thirty-six inches by twenty-four inches, but bears no date, although inspection would lead one to believe that it must have originated about 1840 to 1842. The entire South Side is platted into blocks, and a portion of the North Side is similarly treated. At Magnolia and Jackson streets there is an entire block designated as "armory block," this designation was also shown on the third map. The Capital block is shown at Texas and Main streets, location of the Rice Hotel, but only half the block is shown as devoted to that purpose. Christ Church is plainly shown on its present site, and "academy block" is indicated at the present site of the Sam Houston High School. The first school on this site was known as the "academy," but this poetic name did not last long; it was soon changed.

The name of the surveyor is not shown on this map. My belief is that it was one of the Borden maps as they were the leading surveyors of that time, and took an active interest in the commercial life of both Houston and Galveston.

Gail Borden became one of the first collectors of customs at the port of Galveston. It was there, that he produced his now world-renowned "Gail Borden brand condensed milk."

On this fourth map, north of Commerce and between Hamilton and St. Charles, the names of trees were favored in designating the streets. Running parallel, the names of Magnolia, Maple, Hickory, Holly, Fir, Elm and Bay. A number of these still apply. Oddly enough, after St. Emanuel, running north and south, were three streets known as West Broadway, Broadway and East Broadway, respectively, then St. Charles and Live Oak. Broadway now exists only in Harrisburg. On this map Chartres Street appears as Chartre, La Branch is "La Branche" and "Carolina" has been changed

Houston Port and Ship Channel Today

The Port of Houston as it appeared in 1876. ∿∿∿

to Caroline. Lamar Square is unknown today. Prairie and Hamilton, with the intersecting streets passing through, bisected a square in which there was a fountain.

The maps were located and obtained from Edward S. Wilson of Daniel Boone Tavern, Columbia, Missouri. Mr. Wilson stated that the maps came to him from his maternal grandfather, Walter Norton Brown, who with his family, lived in Houston as late as 1908, and owned a set of abstract books, hence the maps. Mr. Wilson relates that his grandfather paid three hundred dollars for one of the maps, and believes it to be the original map dated 1836. These maps were purchased by Miss Annette Finnigan, long active in the civic betterment of Houston. She has made many rare contributions to the Art Museum and the public library.

It is pleasing to learn that, aside from their historical value, our city engineering department has found them useful in establishing original property lines along the bayou.

When the contractor was preparing to clean up the site of the new United States parcel post building, at the location of the old H. & T. C. depot, a chest of maps was found. Among them are many prints of the layout of Houston of other years. One of these blueprints was mailed to me by L. B. McDonald, vice president and general manager, and was particularly interesting. There are designated the old passenger and freight depot of the H. & T. C. railroad. Also on the print is shown the two blocks where old Alexander H. McGowan operated his iron foundry. Another historic spot on the map is the Allen warehouse site, now the Merchants and Manufacturers building. It is here also where A. A. Szabo, Hungarian exile from Austria, erected his first gin.

It was just east of this location that the writer's father, Jacob Ziegler, assisted Thad and Jerome Hooper in building the first cotton compress in Houston in 1851.

Other historic points on the print are the location of the first T. & N. O. depot, built north of Liberty Street, on the hill; the spot where the old G. H. & S. A. freight depot stood at the intersection of Wood and Liberty; the block where the A. C. Allen home stood, east of the present Peden building; the old freight depot of the G. H. & S. A. C. W. Sedgwick then was agent for the road, with five clerks and two train dispatchers. Today the Southern Pacific lines are at this site, employing some four thousand clerks.

Truly, the acorn has grown into an oak!

HOUSTON'S MAIN STREET SIXTY YEARS AGO

My first introduction to Main Street was in 1872, when Houston had a population of about eight thousand, and when Peter Louiselle was an intimately known caterer of the "Barnes House," which was the original capitol building of Texas. He was as broad as he was tall, wore large shirts with puffed sleeves and immense cuffs, large shirt collar that extended nearly half way down his chest to meet a gold chain a yard long. He loved to entertain "the boys." He invited me up from Galveston, with four or five others, for a dinner and gave us a feast fit for a king.

The Barnes House stood well into the block, where now the Rice Hotel is located. In front was a kind of court yard, where twenty cowboys had hitched their ponies to the universal rail. Several yoke of oxen lay on the street. Where the Binz building now stands was a little red frame store. Here was the end of town; everything beyond it was a beautiful garden. Main Street was paved with large white granite blocks, from Commerce to Texas Avenue, that glistened like the "white marble streets of Rome" after a heavy rain. This was the first and only hard surface street for years. Main and Commerce marked the site of the store of William M. Rice, the little red brick under the viaduct, which is still standing, possibly seventy years old. The William D. Cleveland store was opposite, and the intersections were so jammed and blockaded that it was difficult to cross the street. At one time eighty per cent of the commerce of Texas passed this corner. Ox-teams, mule teams and the long ten-foot tailed drays (which can only be found today in Henry Ford's Magic City) passed here trying to reach the boat landings.

Where the Converse building stands was a little two-story brick building occupied by F. W. Heitmann, and across the street was the wholesale produce firm of Baldwin and Cargill. The upper stories of these buildings were offices of Ranger and Company, where the big cotton history was made in 1863. They bought cotton and shipped it to Mexico. One lot of six hundred and eighty bales they bought for six cents. When it arrived in Liverpool, they sold it for one dollar and fifty cents and one dollar and ninety cents per pound, making them millions.

Adjoining this office was Captain Henry Sherfius' implement store (the blockade runner of the Civil War times). Op-

posite stood the auction house of Major Bob Burns and Theodore Lubbock. On auction days, a big Negro with a red flag
and a twenty pound bell would parade around the streets ring-
ing it loud enough to awaken the dead of the San Jacinto
Battle. Where the Traveler's Hotel now stands was the old
Bacon and Bagging store of Bob Cohen. Adjoining this was

Main Street and Texas Avenue in 1872

Franz Illig's furniture store. On the sidewalk of this store, one
often saw many rocking chairs filled with friends engaged in
conversation and often enjoying mint juleps. The corner was
the City Bank. On the opposite corner was the little red brick
building of the First National. Adjoining was the two-story
bank of T. W. House and his wholesale grocery store opened
from the side street on Franklin. Often six or eight yokes of
oxen would remain for half a day to take out bacon, bagging
and ties, and groceries from this store.

Small stores lined both sides of the hardware store in the
middle of the block with dry goods and others adjoining it.
It was a common sight to see men sitting in front of these
stores with checker boards on their laps and other men standing around silently watching. Across the street was the dead-

51

line. No lady would venture on that side of the street or half way up the other street for many years for fear of encountering a drunkard or witnessing some pistol play. Where J. C. Penney's store is now, there stood for years a little fruit and candy shop. Often teams were bogged in the mud opposite this store in the street. I saw a sign on a post which read "no bottom." Next day, a wag had placed on the pole a battered stovepipe hat and another sign, "Don't kick me. I am down here on horseback and trying to get out."

On the Woolworth corner stood the Masonic Temple. The older Masons will bear me out in saying it was the finest decorated interior of any building in Texas at that time. They sent to New Orleans for artists who frescoed the walls. The plastering showed handsome moulds that cost thousands of dollars.

The only store south of the Masonic Temple was that of Latham's furniture store, now the Kress store. Beautiful gardens continued to Calhoun Ditch and "Calhoun River" at times carried the storm waters off into Bray's Bayou. Another big ditch was built at Elgin which was the head of Slaughter Pen Bayou and a sweet gum swamp. Gustave Fosgard often stated that he swam a horse across and had seen three feet of water and more in it many a time.

Where the Second Presbyterian Church stands was a large pond, where I killed wild ducks. Our old merchant, Charles P. Shearn, built a cottage there. It was the last house out to the country, and where Fort Bend County started. No one would be arrested for killing prairie chickens as there was "no law in Fort Bend County." Just south on Calhoun was George Elser's store, "first and last chance" to get water or beer as nothing else was nearer than Richmond.

The beauties of South Main Street centered on the Hill block, where giant oak trees, planted from acorns from Columbia were located. Where St. Paul's Church stands was a strip of dense timber and farther south was the George Hermann wood and sawmill site, now the Hermann Park. Another large strip of woods was at Bray's Bayou, making three distinct and dense woods on Main. Compare this with the fine store to the old time when wild animals roamed unmolested there, and the magnificent skyscrapers where only a few years ago were corn fields.

Opposite Rice Institute were bottomless quagmires for forty years. Thousands of loads of trash were dumped there. Many old residents of Houston came from Virginia and

Kentucky. They introduced tournaments at the old fair grounds in the "Seventies." Ladies on side saddles, with long plush skirts, flowing plumes on wide hats and buff gauntlets would accompany their knights wearing colors, when they performed with their lances and rings on the frames.

It would be difficult to describe the style and beautiful sights of the old parades which occurred about four o'clock in the afternoons. Many doublet teams appeared on Main Street. These fine horses and carriages often cost more than the eight-cylinder cars of today. The harnesses, mounted with silver and gold, were beautiful and often cost as much as one thousand dollars. The carriages came from every part of Europe, footman and drivers in livery, and made a most interesting parade.

Contrasted with the Main Street today, our old Main Street of sixty years ago was only a rough beginning of what the "Master hand" of progress has done in making Houston the South's foremost city.

FIRST WAREHOUSES AND CAMPING GROUNDS IN HOUSTON

Oxcarts and Covered Wagons Start Houston's Growth

Houston derived her first impetus and growth toward her present metropolitan status from the patronage of immense wagon-trains from outlying counties and the interior of the state. The motive power employed was either long yokes of oxen or four to eight-mule teams. The wagons were loaded top-high with baled cotton, hides and wool, bacon, lard, hogsheads of molasses, barrels of sugar, grain, butter, cheese and eggs.

The merchants and brokers of early Houston had to provide suitable facilities for sheltering these incoming wagon-trains and storage for their cargoes. Hence originated the old camping grounds and warehouses of pioneer Houston.

The first cotton warehouse and camping ground of which we appear to have record, was the large two-story warehouse of Tom Whitmarsh, erected about 1850 just east of where the W. D. Cleveland store now stands. Since that a portion of the old foundation and walls of this building could yet be seen. It was so erected that long wooden chutes were used to slide the cotton and the other baled and bagged

53

commodities from the great sliding doors of the first stories down to the waiting steamboats and barges on the bayou. From there, the cargo was freighted to Galveston and other nearby ports for either consumption or transshipment. Deliveries were made in those days, even as now, on the basis of "ship-side proposition."

Later came the renowned Macatee warehouse, built in 1858, covering the entire block where the Macatee Hotel now stands and surrounded by high brick walls. It received the greatest portion of trade coming in from the Brazos and Colorado section on Washington and San Felipe roads, and being just across from "Vinegar Hill," where the Southern Pacific depot now stands, was one of the most popular stopping places in the county. With the senior Macatee at that time were associated as partners, Major Ike Stafford and Captain E. B. Schneider. This partnership was dissolved when the War Between the States started, Captain Schneider withdrawing to become captain of the Turner Rifles. Captain Stafford, then twenty-two years old, was one of the youngest officers in the Confederate army. He was later promoted to major.

Mr. Macatee continued his warehouse, camping ground and commission business until the Macatee Hotel was built, which has served as a hostelry for over three-quarters of a century.

I have seen as many as two hundred wagons unload at the Macatee place in a single day. The charge for storage, sampling and weighing cotton was fifty cents per bale—in addition the farmers had the privilege of camping for the remainder of their stay.

The first Texas State Fair was held upon the old Macatee warehouse grounds.

The old Louis Pless warehouse, that of a distinguished German merchant of the period, was a two-story structure standing on the southwest corner of what is now the location of the Merchants and Manufacturers building, and over a term of years he conducted an extensive business there. The remainder of that land was taken up by Samuel L. Allen, who erected a tremendous galvanized iron warehouse and engaged in the business of storage, forwarding and commission. His operations, including the trucking of supplies by wagon-train, extended as far north and east as the Red River and Albuquerque, New Mexico. Allen, like the other camping ground owners, made no charges to the farmers for the use as they saw fit. Their stay usually depended upon the weather and conditions of the roads. During the great blizzards of 1895 and 1899, there were hundreds of farmers marooned in the camping yards for nearly two weeks.

H. D. Taylor was another prominent commission merchant and forwarding agent of that period. His last warehouse was erected where the Sidney Meyers produce store now stands, at Commerce and Travis; but it was destroyed by fire and in later years he became a wholesale grocer. This was sold to the Schuhmacher Grocery Company, the Taylor family engaging in the lumber business yet continued by the firm.

A warehouse of equal importance was added in 1889 by J. Ziegler and Company, the writer being the junior partner. It included a three-stand reconditioning gin-plant and as reflecting how crudely business was then carried on, our firm was allowed to flag all trains, except those with United States mails, to allow the great barges loaded with cotton to pass under the railroad trestle without danger of taking fire from flying sparks of the locomotives. The engines were nicknamed "pine knot burners" from their use of wood or any substitute fuel that might be handy.

Somewhat later, Henke and Pillot erected a warehouse and free camping ground on the former site of the old Wiggins and Simpson foundry, taking in nearly two blocks.

Where the Martha Hermann Square now lies was an entire block fenced in for a wagon yard to take care of a portion of the business coming in from the Brazos on the San Felipe Road.

These wagon trips usually required about three weeks to come and go and complete their transactions. On John Robinson circus day, I have seen as many as three hundred wagons arrive in the course of the morning. As late as 1877-78, one could see ox-teams lying all day in front of the Barnes House (where the Rice Hotel now stands) waiting orders from their owners, who had stopped at the Barnes House. A similar scene was the corner of Main and Franklin, where the First National Bank now stands.

Closely adjacent was the T. W. House plantation commissary and wholesale grocery; and here the ox-wagons remained half a day waiting on a load of bacon, flour, beans, bagging, ties and other staple commodities for the interior farms. Oxen, once they started the turn, held an utter disregard for anything in their way. Many times the light posts or carts were caught in the turn and demolished.

These wagon-trains, however, were, as indicated, one of the chief sources of revenue for the then growing Houston. Through them Houton's trade territory extended west to New Mexico, and north to Indian Territory. The government forts, extending from Brownsville to Fort Sill, Oklahoma, were supplied regularly from Houston by these wagon-trains.

The camping yards of these wagon-train travelers was always an interesting scene at night. The campfires were built, the guitars, banjos, harmonicas, fiddles and accordians were brought out and while the roasting venison and wild turkey proceeded, one was regaled with airs and melodies of the day. Later the dancing of the Virginia reel and even the minuet was deftly performed.

With the coming of the automobile, the camping ground of yesterday is the parking lot of today; and the end is not yet.

VINEGAR HILL

One of the First Camping Grounds in Houston

Echoes of Washington Avenue, impatient traffic, crumbling mortar and steel, the ruins of Houston's historical hostelry, grinding brakes of the locomotives and long black coaches, reberating down the corridor of time, the scene changes to a grassy slope, that for scores of years, strangely resembled a Roman market square, a refuge for roving gypsies, wandering redmen, traders and outlaws, that was known as "Vinegar Hill."

By day, the hill with its tents and squalid huts was alive with half-clad children, playing crude games while their parents bartered for horses, furs, beads, food and "moonshine."

By night, gray fogs crept up the bayou and swallowed the hill, leaving the sallow rays of candlelight, the pale, flickering flares of camp fires and the faint strains of a "fiddle" to mark the scene.

During the first state fair in 1870, Vinegar Hill was alloted as a camping ground for a side show of a band of

Comanche Indians, many of whom had fought against General Custer.

Long after the fair had closed its gates, the hill echoed the yells of the bloodthirsty Indians, who remained to vend their wares of trick entertainment.

After the capture of Geronimo, the great Apache warrior who for years depredated and fought in Texas and New Mexico, he was brought through Houston and one of his last requests was that he be taken over the Vinegar Hill site, where he had spent many of his earlier days.

Riding single file over the narrow Liberty Road, Chief Minto of the Alabama tribe of Indians, now stationed at Livingston, brought his redmen to the village of Houston, to dispose of wild turkeys, deer and other produce.

From Produce Row to the saloons, the Indians partook deeply of the cup that cheers and often they were driven out of town by the police.

Traversing the rough winding trails from surrounding counties, caravans of sixty to eighty wagons twice each day often camped on Vinegar Hill.

These trips to Houston were a combination business and holiday affairs. After their produce of wool, hides, beeswax and other materials were disposed of, the traders secured supplies for another six months and then there were days of merrymaking. The traders were banded toegther for protection against the outlaw "bushwackers," renegades who roamed this section of the country following the Civil War. Many of the drivers were highly educated men, some having been graduated from Oxford College, England, who later became the merchant princes of Texas.

When the Northern army of occupation came South after the Civil War, part of the camp was stationed on Vinegar Hill.

Another legend reports the first game of baseball played in Texas was staged on Vinegar Hill. Natives, so the story goes, never forgave the Northerners for bringing baseball, which they called a "steal" of the old game of "town ball." A good batter, using the Vinegar Hill special, which was a large flat board, could knock a home run that sailed from the spot where the Macatee Hotel stands past the Tennison Hotel location.

The favorite Sunday afternoon sport of many Houstonians was to climb the hill and witness the battle between that team and the Fifth Ward "nine." These games usually resulted in a fist fight that covered the entire hill. The participants, calling a halt, topped the afternoon's entertainment off with a visit to the old Schneider's swimming hole.

Along the edge of Vinegar Hill, there was an alley called "no man's land" of Squatters Row, and over this settlement lorded the "queen" of the hill. This queen, a double-fisted black Negress, more than six feet tall and weighing almost two hundred pounds, was the terror of the countryside. Perhaps it was her disposition, but most likely it was the effects of too much moonshine that prompted the black queen to whip her subjects. When she started roaring down the alley, men, women and children fled in her path. The town bell would toll at most any hour of the day or night and it required the city marshal, his entire force and many volunteers to quell the riot. When the black queen charged, it brought out the "Black Maria," to transport her to the "calaboose" where she spent half her time.

Vinegar Hill, with its light and shadows, its covered wagons, Kentucky rifles and assortment of people held all the disorder and fascination of a curio shop.

Two years ago this spot was covered with the new Southern Pacific station and another veil was drawn around the picturesque neighborhood. The few remaining of the old guard perhaps will take a last lingering look at the spot, that added many a colorful chapter to the early days of Texas history.

HISTORIC OLD NOBLE HOME IN SAM HOUSTON PARK

A Rendezvous of "Ghosts of the Past"

Unquestionably, the oldest house of historical import standing today in Houston is the old Noble house, a great white, colonial designed edifice that graces the southwest portion of the park, fronting in the general direction of the Dallas Avenue entrance. Bare, white mansion of a period long past, many ghost-like tales have emerged from it.

Its construction was started soon after the Battle of San Jacinto by a noted character of those times, one Kallem. Before its completion, it was sold by Kallem to E. W. Noble, who completed it as a home for his bride, a Connecticut "school-marm." The two had met during the course of one of her visits here and become enamored. Taking no chance of losing her, Noble persuaded her to marry him and remain here.

A brief glimpse into the life of Kallem, original planner of the house, is not without interest. He was reputedly a sportsman and maintained a somewhat notorious gambling house on Main Street. In consequence, he made many enemies and they in turn caused him considerable personal embarrassment on occasions. He also maintained in connection with his gambling establishment, a small race track, operated perhaps, with as much regard for the eternal fitness of things, as was his gambling house. The net result was that patrons of both places, going broke, would console their outraged feelings in an attempt to "take it out of Kallem's hide."

It is related that, anticipating these onslaughts, Kallem's Negro slave kept always in readiness a sturdy mount on which his master could easily escape, and that mounting, he would dash off to his trusty stronghold, the incompleted house above mentioned. In the event his enemies forestalled his retreat in that direction, he would veer off to Fort Bend County. Strangely enough, he had built the house without a stairway and for a purpose; arriving there ahead of his pursuers, he scaled quickly to the second story by means of a ladder. Drawing the ladder up after him, he left no means of ingress by his attackers and, protected, was enabled to "bang away" at them at his pleasure. Doubtless, too, the lack of stairway was intended as a protection against surprise attacks at night.

Back to the history of the Noble house, its present location was formerly a farm of some fifteen to twenty acres. It had, in fact, at one time been a "tan yard," as was disclosed by the discovery of a number of vat cans on the place. Originally, the farm was more level than the terrain of the park would now indicate. There was merely a gentle slope from the western boundary of the farm to Buffalo Bayou and, of course, there was no Buffalo Drive between the two. The deep gully now traversing that portion adjacent to the Confederate monument and the marked lower level of the ground toward the northern boundary of the park was caused from excavating great quantities of mud from which to make mud-brick in the very early days of the city.

As a result of these excavations, a great pool was formed and made what, in the early days, was called "Old Cypress Swimming Hole," because of the large cypress trees then surrounding it. Next to Schneider's Swimming Hole on White Oak Bayou, it was the most favored spot of its kind near the city. Here it was that those who constituted in later years the "Old Guard" of Houston, dignified bankers, stately lawyers, astute merchants, gathered as boys, disported themselves in the waters of the pool and battled with "chaw bacon" (knotting of clothes) with no more raiment than was worn by Adam. Bathing suits were either unknown or unwanted. Many is the boy who, drying and preparing to dress upon its banks was mercilessly bespattered with fresh, slimy mud flung with charming aim by companions not yet ready to "get out."

The former school-marm mistress of the Noble house induced her Aunt Salome Metcalf to come to Houston and live with her. She first married a Mr. Kelly, who became prominent in the affairs of both Houston and the Republic of Texas and left three daughters who were likewise prominent in the social affairs of the city: Mrs. O. C. Drew, Mrs. A. A. Wettermark, whose husband was a partner of B. A. Shepherd, and Mrs. Charles Marsden. The parents separated, however, and Mrs. Kelly subsequently married the distinguished Hungarian patriot, A. A. Szabo, a grand old man of his day, who operated the first powder mill for the Confederacy and later the first and earliest cotton gin in Houston. He, also, was City Treasurer for nearly twenty years until death removed him. For much of this story I am indebted to his daughter, Mrs. Eloise Szabo Witte, for years the principal of one of our Houston schools.

Originally, the Noble home was sheltered by a cordon of fifteen giant live oak trees, giving the mansion a beautiful environment. Through the successive storms of 1875, 1886, 1900 and 1915, fourteen of these original trees were demolished, only one of them remaining to stand as sentinel over a glorious past. It is possible that this remaining live oak is the oldest tree on the city. I recall none at the present whose age surpasses it. My belief is that the great Scanlan live oak at the corner of Main and Pierce streets, magnificently beautiful that it is, does not antedate the life of the Noble oak in Sam Houston Park. The latter, according to a statement made to me by one learned tree-ologist indicates a life approximating three hundred years.

What constituted originally, the eastern section of the little farm was purchased by the Masons of Houston, shortly after the lodge was organized and converted into one of

Houston's first cemeteries. Even today, there will be found here, ornate tombstones dating back to deaths occurring in 1836, and among the graves yet existing, those of some of Houston's most prominent pioneer civic builders. My recollection is that the burials there were discontinued about the turn of the century. Meanwhile little care has been given to the grounds and many of the tombs have been vandalized.

Sam Houston Brashear, one of the true pioneers of Houston, for years coveted the Noble house and its surrounding grounds and when he became Mayor of the City in 1898, induced the council to purchase the place. If I recall correctly, the sum paid approximately thirty thousand dollars; a price that many protested at the time as being entirely too high. Contemplate, however, what the city would have to pay for it today. At that, there were about five acres not included in the deal. The parents of our present Charles and George Byers had previously contracted for the lesser portion and retained it. This was their homesite at the entrance of the park, the house being environed by one of the prettiest old-fashioned flower gardens it has been my pleasure to see.

Mayor Brashear, with the Park Commission co-operating, converted the grounds into Houston's first park. The Noble house was remodeled and made a museum wherein was housed Houston's first collection of historical relics. There are many yet living in Houston who will recall having climbed the outside stairway to view these relics. The first floor was reserved for offices and other relics and curiosities.

At the rear of the house, was established Houston's first zoo. Many old-timers will remember the cages of animals occuping that portion of the grounds.

Farther over, toward the eastern portion of the grounds were the various items of play-equipment for children: swings, merry-go-rounds, parallel and horizontal bars, swinging-rings and what-not, and close by a cement wading pool of shallow depth for the tiny children. Some of these yet remain to delight the present younger generation who attend the park.

In the deep gulch toward the mid-western portion of the grounds, an intriguing nook among the bowers was created and the club-women of Houston contributed an attractive bronze drinking fountain cast in the form of one of Palmer Cox's "Brownies." It cost, I believe, approximately four hundred dollars. It remained there for more than twenty years to delight and refresh the passer-by, then it was stolen one night by miscreants and sold to a junkman for old bronze. I am told that the junkdealer paid two dollars and eighty-five cents for the statue. It was promptly recovered by the police and returned to its place.

North of the Noble house and about midway of the grounds a large sheltered band stand was built. Here, on Sunday evenings, the old Herb and Lewis Band of Houston and other bands, regaled the throngs with tuneful melodies of the period. Upon a tall tower, nearby, an electric searchlight stood sentinel over the surrounding grounds, playing its white stream of light upon distant seats, nooks and crannies of the park, to the embarrassment of springtime lovers.

In due course, old cannons from ancient ships and fields of honor were added to the grounds, accompanied by huge, round cannon balls. Later, the ship's bell from the famous "Harriet Lane" (Federal gunboat captured when General Magruder retook Galveston from the Yankees), was placed in its small belfry. Today it occupies a conspicuous spot for inspection of visitors.

Thus was the rambling old thicket farm converted into a spot of beauty and pleasure for Houston's citizenry. On Sunday afternoons it was a favorite driving place of Houston's horse and buggy days. Visiting the park on those occasions, I have stood and witnessed in admiration the passing of shiny, new carriages of all types, American and European. One might note the English hack, the French barouche, the German landous, the low-aproned phaetons and carriages, or even the Irish dog-cart, the majority of them drawn by sleek-looking, high-prancing thoroughbred horses.

Meanwhile, the Robert E. Lee Chapter of the U. D. C., co-operating with the D. T. R., and other women's organizations, had been active in a movement to erect in the park a suitable monument to the Confederacy. Their efforts finally bore fruit to the point that the distinguished sculptor, Professor Louis Amaties, was commissioned to fulfill their plans for a memorial to the heroines of the Confederacy. On January nineteenth 1908, thousands of Houstonians gathered to witness the unveiling of the beautiful bronze monument, "Spirit of the Confederacy," the crowning effort of a long and faithful service of a self-sacrificing womanhood of the South. Today it may be seen towering from its lofty mound upon a huge base of red granite from the Burnet County quarries, a memorial also to the Sons of Texas who served and suffered in the "Lost Cause." It is fitting, in connection, that we of the South should keep bright within our memory the dauntless courage of those soldiers of the South, so well reflected in the lines:

"They led the charge on many a field,
Were first in many a fray;
And turned the tide of battle
On many a glorious day!"

On the occasion of the unveiling, the Louisville Courier Journal and other leading southern papers sent their art-critics and correspondents to attend and offer comment. They vied with one another in encomiums and praise of the completed work of Professor Amaties. It was referred to as "graceful in outline, vigorous in conception, most delicate in execution and perhaps the crowning achievement of its sculptor, possessing as it does the strong southern appeal." Another leading comment described it as "The figure of a nude angel, a young warrior, vigorous in outline, brawny of muscle, his arms folding upon the hilt of a sword, with which the palm-branch of peace is entwined; a fair face with concentrated brow, and the introspective eye gazing perhaps restfully far into the distance."

The unveiling was a brilliant affair, yet marred by one of the saddest accidents ever occurring in Houston. Henry W. Cortes, alderman at the time, and co-worker of Mayor Brashear in improving and beautifying the grounds, drove toward the entrance of the park in his carriage drawn by his favorite pair of high-spirited, thorough-bred Kentucky horses. Just before the gates were reached, the horses became sorely frightened and although Mr. Cortes was one of the most thorough horsemen I have ever known, the team became beyond human control. In their ensuing mad dash, he was thrown from the carriage, landing head first upon the hard gravel pavement and was picked up lifeless from a crushed skull.

The ancient Noble house, Sam Houston Park and all that it contains may be seen today from the towers of the Gulf and Esperson buildings, scarce ten minutes walking distance. Unhappily, however, it is in a neglected state, fast becoming one of the "forgotten" parks. Yet, it is one of the most favored spots in the city where one may, at lunch time or in the cool afternoon, pause and find that restful period of mental peace that, at times, even the best and sturdiest of us require.

THE OLD WILLIAM MARSH RICE HOME

Probably Oldest House in Houston Continuously Occupied as Residence

It is my belief that there is no home of the ante bellum period in Houston, continuously occupied as a first class residence, that is older than the old William Marsh Rice house, long the home of the D. B. Cherrys, now located at 608 Fargo Avenue.

That location is not, of course, the original site of the home. Had it been placed there when first built, the home would have been so far removed from the then village of Houston proper, passersby would have regarded it as "far out into the country." As a matter of fact, its present location on Fargo Avenue appears to be the third site on which it has rested.

In point both as to its method of construction, following the building practice of that early pioneer period, and beauty of interior finish, it impresses me as a wonderfully interesting structure. Built of the most select material and staunchly constructed, it has withstood valiantly not only the ravages of time but the hardships of transportation involved in the occupancy of the three sites mentioned. Its history, too, is equally interesting.

Originally, construction of the house was started by General E. B. Nichols, about 1850, to be used as his home. He was at that time associated with Colonel Tom Pierce, later prominently known as the builder of the Southern Pacific Railroad, but then engaged in operating a fleet of twenty-two vessels plying between Maine and Boston and Galveston. For use in constructing the home, General Nichols brought by sea from the forests of Maine the greater portion of fine heart-timber and white pine, as well as the brick employed, and reshipped these by water from Galveston. From Pearl River, Mississippi and from Florida, he secured the long leaf yellow pine. From other distant points came the hardwoods and other expensive woods used in the interior finish.

General Nichols, however, did not finish the home. In the course of its construction, Colonel Pierce transferred him to Galveston, appointing him as resident agent there of his lines. General Nichols thereupon sold the house to William Marsh Rice, with whom he was then associated as partner.

I am told that at that time the house stood facing the County Court House, being located on San Jacinto Avenue. The partnership, however, between Mr. Rice, General Nichols and E. J. Hart continued until the Civil War period, when the two latter withdrew, General Nichols becoming active in the Confederate service and Mr. Hart moving to New Orleans, where he subsequently became one of the South's leading wholesale druggists.

Mr. Rice completed the house, adding even to the luxury of the interior originally contemplated. It was moved to the southeast corner of San Jacinto and Franklin streets. It is my understanding that the original cost of the house was eight thousand dollars, a considerable figure for those day, when both material and labor were comparatively cheap. I have known the old home for a matter of sixty years and for a long time, after the occupancy of Mr. Rice, it was known as the "Evershade Mansion," being occupied by Captain Charles Evershade (father of the later Paul Evershade of the South Texas Commercial Bank) one of the original Morgan Line Captains. He had been sent out from New Orleans in the early "Seventies" to take charge here of the Morgan interests and was superintendent of the Texas Transportation Company, a small road running from what was then called Bonner's Point in the Fifth Ward, to Clinton. He was also connected with the Houston Direct Navigation Company.

When I first saw the Rice home, it was painted snow white, with the proverbial green blinds typical of the southern home of that day. On friendly terms with Captain Evershade and his family, I frequently visited the home and became quite familiar with the details of its interior. It was of Grecian type, leaning throughout to what is known as the Georgian design. The present hip-roof was originally quite flat. The Corinthian columns, fluted, stood as a work of art in themselves, even the caps being highly hand carved. The doors, likewise, were highly carved and decorated, with deep windows running perhaps twelve feet from the ceiling, while the smaller doors opened upon the broad gallery. Inside, the ceilings are high and both they and the panelled walls decorated. Maine white pine was the material used; hand carving being prominent throughout. Mr. August Bering, the veteran builder of Houston, related to Mr. Cherry that he was apprenticed at the age of fifteen years to the master woodcarver who supervised the work on the Rice home and was employed there in the sharpening of tools and on some of the minor work of carving. As reflected by the ingenious work upon the panels, wainscoting and other parts of the interior, assuredly the master-carver was possessed of superior artistry. The stairs and ballustrades were highly treated and the rooms ornamented with plaster of paris mouldings popular during that period.

Some years later on, about 1886, occurred the failure of the old City Bank of Houston and the Houston Savings Bank and affiliated institutions. Residents of the city were hard hit and real estate values slumped to perhaps an all-time low. Who owned the Rice home at that time I do not recall. It was, however, thrown on the market at a sacrifice and both the house and its grounds, the latter somewhat extensive, were purchased for the sum of twenty-five hundred dollars by John D. Finnegan, pioneer hide and leather merchant of Houston. Mr. Finnegan later offered the place for sale against sealed bids. The offer being noised about, Mrs. Cherry, our noted local artist, inspected the place. The colonial effect and other details of the home found response in her sense of the artistic. She longed for the old house and induced Mr. Cherry to bid for it. He made a bid with the proviso that should his bid not be the highest, he was to have the privilege of making a further bid, a type of bidding that while unusual, was apparently used occasionally in those days.

Oddly enough, Mr. Cherry's bid appears to have been the only bid made. It was accepted on the basis that the house be moved from the premises. Having purchased a plot of ground on what is now Fargo Avenue, but then far out on the bald prairie, Mr. Cherry cast about for means to move the house to that location. Difficulties confronted him. No house mover could be found who would undertake the job, and it was feared that he would be under the necessity of tearing the house down and reconstructing it. Finally, however, he was fortunate in locating a Mr. Wallace, formerly a master housemover of Wichita, Kansas. The latter procured huge rollers and other needed equipment formerly used in Galveston and undertook the contract that had been declined by other contractors in Houston. To his credit, be it said that he did a painstaking and excellent job. The only route practical required nearly three miles transportation on rollers and consumed some forty-six days to complete, many traffic intersections being blocked before the journey was over. I was the proud owner at the time of a fine Kentucky thoroughbred that I delighted in driving and often chided Mr. Cherry for the many detours I found it necessary to make at one part of the city or another, while the house was journeying. I recall that in part, the house proceeded south to McGowan, then west toward the Kirby place and outward toward the bald prairie, over gulleys, ditches and morasses. When it would arrive at street car tracks, permission had to be obtained to cross and only at night could it be moved. Where a telephone wire or electric light barred the way, permission again was obtained to proceed. Finally the old mansion reached its destination at what is now 608 Fargo Avenue. The structure was intact in the year of 1894.

It is noteworthy that even the chimneys, constructed with the Portland cement of those days, brought from England, withstood the trip without injury. After re-location the house reflected its sturdiness of structure by passing unscathed through the Galveston storms of 1900 and 1915. Its floors, of the puncheon type, are two or more inches thick. The sills, from solid heart pine, are tongued and morticed by wooden pegs, reinforced with hand-made, old fashioned, iron nails. The uprights and sleepers are of the long leaf yellow pine, of the type that resin and pitch has hardened and seasoned until it has the appearance and hardness of bois d'arc. Kept in the proper state of repair, a hundred years from now may find the old house still intact, as I am told that the rot never penetrates long leaf yellow pine, treated, or of the type, as above.

The Rice home was one of the last great homes of early Houston to be moved. Such moves are no longer made. It would be impossible today to get a permit to move a house of that size one twentieth of the distance within the busy area of Houston. That is why we see so many of the old homes wrecked on the spot. Nor, perhaps, would it be possible to build today a house of the same material and handiwork. I doubt that workmen could be found, competent in the building methods of those days and certainly the great pine forests from whence the immense, broad slabs were taken for panelling and other purposes, no longer supply these items.

At the invitation of Mrs. Cherry, it was my pleasure to again visit and inspect the interior of the home, after a lapse of fifty years. They are to be congratulated in preserving this distinctive old edifice for future generations, not only

67

because of its example of early southern architecture and the splendid methods of those days by which it was built, but also because of its association as the early home of William Marsh Rice, eminent benefactor of the Houston of today and to whom the following youth of our land must always be grateful for his endowment of the Rice Institute.

To those who hold appreciation of this early day architecture and the methods employed, such as I have held, I am sure the Cherry's would accord the same privilege of inspection they were kind enough to extend me. They are proud of the old mansion, as well they might be. Surrounded as now it is, by thousands of homes, I cannot but contemplate, in retrospect, when that plot of ground was the home of the jack-rabbit, the field-lark and the wild-turkeys.

THE GABLES, ANTE BELLUM MANSION

While strolling down the recent acquired business section of McKinney Street, looking around me I discovered familiar landmarks of yesteryear. Suddenly I looked up and before me was the old renowned "Gables." This structure has often reminded me of Nathaniel Hawthorne's "Scarlet Letter," where he describes the house of seven gables so beautifully. But the scene shifts from romantic old New England to good old Houston's McKinney and Austin streets.

It was here during the ante bellum days, some of the enterprising citizens, for humanity's sake, as well as an investment, erected a low built hospital, now named infirmary or sanitarium. It was operated, during the War Between the States, as a home for the heroic sons or the surviving of the Battle of San Jacinto from Fort Bend, Matagorda and Brazoria counties, who received treatments for chills, fever and malaria to make them fit as members of that famous fighting Regiment, "Terry's Rangers" of Hood's Texas Brigade, as it must be remembered, ninety per cent were Houstonians and friends from the adjoining counties who recruited here. When fit for service, they marched to the battle torn fields of Virginia, and the siege of Vicksburg and Mississippi Valley. Many of them still rest on the banks of the mighty river, where the beautiful National Cemetery stands today, one of the most beautiful spots of the land. But many returned maimed and wounded to be cared for by their relatives and friends in the hospital at McKinney and Austin streets, in Houston.

It was the home of the survivors who fought under General Lee and the Stars and Bars, while convalescing. After peace was declared General Granger arrived with part of the army who fought for the Stars and Stripes in the summer of 1865, but during the terrific epidemic of yellow fever in 1865-67, it was turned into a Federal Hospital, and hundreds of them never left the hospital alive, having succumbed to the dreadful disease. Congress later, however, made several appropriations to have all soldiers who died here from the North, exhumed and taken to their home burial places and Greenwood Cemetery in Brooklyn, N. Y., where thousands lie today.

The day soon came when the city expanded and the land became valuable and the vicinity became a residential district, and it was sought for a southern mansion. The hospital was torn down, but some of the timbers went into the new building that took its place, as it was long leaf pine from Calacieu River, and through the various evolutions of building, it became the "Gables" of today.

It was in the spring of 1889, when Samuel K. McIlhenny, one of Houston's pioneer wholesale dry goods men, (and later became the partner of the writer as Ziegler and McIlhenny, cotton merchants), constructed a mansion and established it as one of the historical homes of the Old South, before the rush of commercialism, and put aside the old custom of southern hospitality.

There was always true and gay hospitality in this home, as Mrs. McIlhenny was always fond of young people and surrounded herself with them. She was a great civic leader and the family name was known throughout the land, and friends from all over the adjoining counties dropped in on her. Many social gatherings and civil affairs and receptions were held in the spacious large halls.

The large open fireplaces often glowed with coals from the oak and cottonwood logs, which was reflected on the swinging chandeliers. The large room contained much antique and old fashioned furniture. The walls were covered with paintings from a master brush and the interior furnishings, decorations, and hanging draperies were perfect.

The walks around the home were lined with hollyhocks, and gladioli, which the Germans named so beautifully and appropriately, "heavens' ladders"; all kinds of bright bedding plants, sweet allusiums, petunias entwined with woodbine, all of which is now only to be seen in the wholesale seedman's catalogues, as nearly everybody is content today, with "lawns."

There came an evening when glad cries of swarming children coming from everywhere, made merry, as the occasion was the eve of Rosalie's wedding day, which was a beautiful and glorious affair when she became the bride of Charles H. Lucey. Many are still living that remember when she smilingly parted with her bridal bouquet, throwing it to her girl friends. It was a happy marriage and one of the greatest events of the year. But a little later it became one of the most tragic occurances that this section has ever known, and which will linger in history for time immemorial.

Mr. McIlhenny admired "Gables" and purchased one of the handsomest cottages in the city, the "Old Dr. Fielding" home, with its high mansard roof held down by English tiles. Many can remember it as it stood near the old San Antonio and Aransas Pass depot.

He dismanteled it, reloaded it on flat cars and carried it to the flats at Seabrook, where he rebuilt it, facing the Bay, as a summer home.

It was on a Saturday when Mr. and Mrs. McIlhenny, their daughters, Rosalie and Anita, together with young David Rice, a cousin and son of our esteemed citizen, David Rice, watched the waves and wind as they came higher and higher and soon turned into a hurricane. The friends of McIlhenny implored him to bring his family to the station and to the city but he felt so secure in his well built home that he refused even after they had sent a switch engine for them. The last seen of them, when nightfall came on, was they were all clinging to the mansard roof when it parted from the house, and they were thrown into the raging flood. Mr. McIlhenny, the only survivor, was found wondering around on the prairie, twenty miles west at Genoa, his reason gone but by careful nursing he recovered and lived twelve to fifteen years longer.

Fortunately, Mr. Lucey, and Mr. McIlhenny's only son, Sam, could not reach them and remained in Houston, to be saved from such a disaster. It was called the great Galveston storm, September eighth, 1900.

Mr. McIlhenny never returned to the old home, and he, shortly afterwards, sold it to Colonel Newton and his wife, as they had just sold the old Sour Lake Hotel and its one thousand acres. Colonel Newton then moved the old home, from the corner to the middle of the block, making it larger and added the gables, making it a private hotel and one of the most fashionable boarding houses in the South. It was called the "Gables" and afterwards the "Drummer's Home." The dining room cuisine was of the best in the state and drummers came hundreds of miles to be there over the weekends. The spacious lobby and dining room was known all over the state.

Mr. Benson lived there and had sold the old Sour Lake to Colonel Newton for the Travellers Protective Association, who had acquired it from Sam Ashe.

It later became the home of the Young Women's Christian Association and the Girls of the "Blue Triangle" held their monthly gay receptions and the most influencial and prominent ladies of the city looked over them and mothered them there.

The "Gables" is still a well known boarding house, but when the time comes it will answer the "call of the house wrecker" and the glories and the history of the old home will be gone, where the Z. Z. "The Thaliens" often danced the cotillion to the strains of "Home Sweet Home" well into the small hours of the next day.

But, as often is in the old and large families, they die out as in this case, but the name of the family will live for ages to come.

McIlhenny Street in the south end bears the family name, also in the south end is Rosalie and Anita avenues which were named for the daughters, who will also be remembered by their friends for years to come as beautiful and lovely "daughters of the Southland."

FIRST STREET CAR SYSTEM IN HOUSTON

It affords a feeling of luxurious thrill to the older inhabitants of Houston when they compare the rapid, smooth traveling, comfortable busses running on schedule over well paved streets of today, with the crude transportation facilities that we endured only a few decades back.

One hears many sighs, from time to time, for a return of the "good old days" but who of us—as spoiled a people as we are—would seriously care to swap the comforts of today for the discomforts that we tolerated good naturedly a generation ago?

The first "street car system" of Houston provided those dinky little cars with four to six windows, the motive power of which was a diminutive mule scarcely larger than the donkey of today. Patterned, too, after its big brother, the railroad train, the "locomotive" had a bell. It was a deep-toned bell suspended from the neck of the mule and tolled, it seemed to me, somewhat dolefully to apprise prospective passengers that the street car was coming!

A single wide plank was laid between rails in the center of the track, on which the mule could gallop, however he seldom stirred himself to a gait of that speed and the weary drivers expended little effort to improve their usually tardy pace. The rear hides of these mules had become so toughened from constant urging on of the whip, that consequently, a longer whip was developed that would flick the forepart and shoulders of the mule, and many drivers had produced from long practice a technique so accurate that they could, with one deft stroke, flick a large fly from the ear of the mule without particular pain to the ear.

There were times when these stubborn mules would come to a dead standstill and utterly refuse to move, despite all urging of the whip. On such occasions, the driver would step out and light a newspaper under the haunches of the mule. It was a certain remedy required to produce locomotion.

Hoofing it down the plank walk, the bell would tinkle out its "sort of runic rhyme" with the beat of the hoofs of the mule upon the board. This sound was always welcome to the ears of the waiting passengers.

There were no conductors as a matter of course. Boarding passengers would proceed up the aisle and deposit in the coffee mill shaped box just to the rear of the "motormen's" elbow, their small, yellow pasteboard tickets, marked "Good for One Fare—Five Cents." This was long before the buffalo head nickel, but the yellow slips passed everywhere locally the same as gold, up to a given quantity. As a matter of fact they came in handy, as there were no small denominations of coins at hand, and the "picayune," then minted in New Orleans as a silver half dime, and from which the New Orleans Times-Picayune derived its name, had only arrived in Houston in small quantities.

A limit of two dollars worth of these street car tickets would be received as part payment on merchandise purchased at any of Houston's stores. They had, however, their disadvantages also, for if one was caught in a heavy rain, or perspired too freely, the pasteboard squares would become moisture soaked and fall to pieces, thus making them difficult to identify sufficiently for redemption. (It was this fact, probably, that later brought on the punched out metal car tokens.) The street car company profited by this and there is little doubt that ten to fifteen per cent was beyond redemption.

I recall also that when they were first issued, they were looked upon somewhat dubiously as to passing face value. For example, it required two of them to purchase a glass of beer, or five in payment of a good cigar.

The fare box was similar to a huge coffee mill, with an orifice at the bottom, leading to the box below. The box was always locked with a large Yale padlock to which there was only one key. This was retained by the collecting "auditor" who opened the box at the end of the run, downtown, where the central office was located. Here the driver would alight, remove the tickets and tie them into bundles with string. The operation usually required a delay of about twenty minutes. Meanwhile the passengers accumulated and waited. If the number of tickets did not correspond with the "passenger list" the shortage was taken out of the drivers' pay checks.

This last mentioned phase reminds me also that the so-called "racket" is by no means a modern practice. The proverbial small boy soon learned the value of these tickets. They would go into "cahoots," board the car, and while the others engaged the driver in conversation the chief culprit would drop in the box a huge grasshopper held captive by a stout thread. The grasshopper never failed to grab onto one or more tickets, and the whole was lifted out by the thread and the operation repeated as time would permit. The proceeds were split among the "gang." Another was to affix a piece of gum to a long, slender stick and pick up the tickets through such contact.

Another phase that made life interesting to the "Motormen" of these early day mule-cars was the element of danger constantly present to the driver. Not that the danger arose then as it does today from excessive speed, but solely from the heels of the fractious mules. While the animals were small, they possessed a terrific kicking power. Harness was frequently torn to shreds and the dash-boards of the street car smashed to pieces with kicks far more vicious than those of the kangaroo. One prominent driver, now pensioned after a service of more than forty years with the original and succeeding companies, who leaned over the dash-board to ply the whip upon an enraged mule, received, unexpectedly, a kick that disfigured his countenance for life, only a portion of his nose remaining.

Quite often during rainy weather the rails would spread and the car would jump the track and on such occasions the male passengers would get out, flounder in the mud until the car was lifted back on the track. It was either that or wait in the car until word was passed to the barn and the "wrecker" arrived, or likely as not come to find that the wrecker itself had stuck in the mud en route. Ordinarily, the cars were so light and small that both driver and passengers felt safe against long delays.

Houston's first street car track was laid on Preston Avenue from Market to Allen's Station, then the East End depot. There, it turned and circled back on Congress Avenue. Another track began at Preston passing out Travis to Francis, a point then far out into the country. It made its subsequent terminus on Main Street, about where the Slaughter Pen Bayou then crossed—a famous stream long since filled in and obliterated.

The old mule-car operated on little if any schedule. At the far end of the line, the driver would sit and "snooze" wearily waiting for a load. This required about twenty minutes. Downtown, the same operation was repeated at Main and Preston, where the Citizens Bank now stands. There was also the Washington and San Felipe street lines, in all, about five and one half miles of track.

The company originally incorporated in 1856, the prime movers being T. W. House, E. W. Cave, John T. Brady and his brother William Brady. In 1872, when the Fair Grounds Association purchased some forty-five acres in South End and moved the Texas State Fair from the Macatee wagon-yard near the present Southern Pacific depot, the street car company laid its track to the entrance of the ground at McGowan and Travis. The rolling stock on this line, however, was exceedingly crude; open flat cars purchased from the railroad, with benches built lengthwise and no upper covering to protect one from the elements. They carried about forty passengers.

Boarding one of these cars one evening about seven o'clock

after the usual annoying wait, I found my seat; the driver cracked the whip over the two large mules necessary to pull this type of car and we started for town. No sooner had we gone two block than the rails spread and the car skipped the track. The men on board flailed in the knee-deep mud and placed the car on the track beyond the spread. Two blocks farther, the rails again sagged and we repeated the performance. After several experiences of the kind, I finally arrived at La Branch and Crawford in town about eleven o'clock that night. It had required four hours to travel the distance from McGowan and Travis. Today the "Zephyr" travels from Houston to Dallas in the same time; what a comparison of transportation facilities!

Two separate mule-car companies then operated in Houston; these were purchased by H. F. MacGregor and his associates, who later sold them to O. M. Carter and a Mr. Allen, who had only recently come from Omaha. Seeking profitable investments, Messrs. Carter and Allen bought one hundred and forty-five acres from the Brashear estate northwest of Houston, at a price of forty-five dollars per acre, and established the addition of Houston Heights. They also purchased the street car company and extended its lines, now electrically operated, out the Heights Boulevard and to the piney woods. H. F. MacGregor lived to see his original street car system grow from five and one-half miles to two hundred miles.

The old street lamps, artificial gas affairs that had to be lit by hand as dusk each evening and at best afforded comparatively little light, were now replaced by the electric carbon street lights.

And yet, withal, it seems to me even now, in retrospect, that those "good old days" had in kind no less merit and value than is possessed by the present day.

OLD HOUSTON ACADEMY

Their Gallant Boy Captain, William Manor Stafford

It would have gladdened most any heart to have stopped and witnessed, at any of the schools, some of the seventy-thousand or more students who enrolled, the past opening of the season, in the different schools of the city; their happy faces made a picture. The high school cadets of the different parts of the city were brushing up their guns, shining up their buttons and equipment. The elementary students had laid away their fishing poles to get down to a season of hard work.

How different it was in the olden days, when there was only "the little school house on the hill," where only "readin'," "'ritin'," and "'rithmetic" were taught from the little blue spelling book, McGuffy's Sixth Reader and the Universal Geography; these being about all the books that any boy possessed.

In 1844, H. F. Gillett advertised in the "Morning Star" that he had opened the Houston Academy on Main and Preston avenues and published that his tuition was two dollars a month for teaching arithmetic, grammar and geography, and for advanced scholars in English, Latin, and Greek, the tuition was to be four dollars a month.

It was in 1853 the Houston Academy was opened by A. W. Boyd and H. Morse, and in 1857, on September first, the corner stone of the Houston Academy was laid on the academy block set aside by the Allens, where the present Sam Houston High School now stands. It was not a public school and the tuition was four dollars a month.

I remember ten years later when my father paid six dollars in gold (one dollar-twenty-five cents to one dollar-forty cents premium) for my schooling at Crawford's Academy. My brother's tuition was also the same amount. This little Academy had possibly one hundred cadets, fashioned after the cadets of Sam Houston High, Reagan High and others today. Some of them only had wooden guns at first. When the state of Texas seceded from the Union to join the Confederacy, the school was soon abandoned as nearly every boy asked his parents or compelled their guardians to allow them to enlist in the Confederate ranks. As history tells us, only on rare occasions was this denied and they all volunteered in defense of their state.

The boys began to drill, securing real guns and after the awkward squad was perfected for fighting they elected as Lieutenant, William Manor Stafford. Only in his teens, eighteen years of age, he was a son of one of the oldest families and a relative of Obediance Smith, on whose survey the present city of Houston stands. I believe the only lineal descendant today of the Smith and Staffords is our esteemed attorney, Richard M. Franklin. The Lieutenant was also a descendant of Colonel Ben Fort Smith, the San Jacinto veteran and the great Indian fighter, who built the first hotel in Houston where the First National Bank stands today, in which was held the famous First Annual Ball that Mrs. Dulie Harris and Mrs. Adele Looscan so vividly described in their stories.

Lieutenant Stafford came from a fighting stock and in a short time carried his company to Galveston. This company was merged into Major Van McMahan's regiment. They occupied the old Hendley building with two cannons directing their fire against the Federal gunboats, at the Battle of Galveston. He was made Captain for his gallant service and McMahan's regiment were loudly heralded for their activities in capturing the enemy. After the battle of Galveston he sought more active service when he fought in Arkansas and Indian Territory to the close of the war.

He was not the only fighter in the family, however, for his brother, Major Ike Stafford, only twenty-three years old, the junior partner of W. L. Macatee, resigned when the war was declared and also formed an Artillery Company. He carried his company to the Rio Grande to protect the border of the state from the Federals and also the Mexican bandits.

As stated previously, Captain Stafford won his laurels in the battle-torn hills east of the Mississippi and in Arkansas. After the war he returned to Houston and engaged in business for a short time, but moved to Galveston later where he engaged in business with Jacob Vedder. He married his partner's daughter, Kate, to cement the partnership more closely. I remember their happy wedding day as a neighbor boy.

He continued with his father-in-law and then joined the firm of Shepherd & Stafford. When the big cotton firm of Inman & Company came to Houston he became their Galveston agent and acted as such for many years, but was often seen on the streets of Houston where he was hailed as "Houston's Boy Soldier."

He became my Captain in the Washington Guards. I say "my Captain"; I was only one of the big four which the Houston Light Guards remember as we often drilled against their famous Company, beating them twice, but went down in defeat forever after, like all opponents of this crack company, who became the champions of the United States.

It was in 1878, during the great Negro riot and draymen strike, one thousand Negroes, armed, met and demonstrated at the Market Hall, that Mickey, the policeman, killed one of the rioters. The feeling ran high and the great Confederate veteran, General T. M. Waul, was placed in charge of the five or six military companies on the Island. Martial law was declared and for three days we were ordered to our armories and the police department was doubled. Each and every soldier was awarded thirty rounds of ammunition and when the battle was eminent, Captain Stafford, calling our company to order, standing in front of them said, "Boys, each and every one of you has been awarded thirty rounds of ammunition. I warn you, do not fire a single shot, but when the order is give 'fire' shoot to kill." Fortunately, after three days of rioting the police billies caused many broken heads and subdued the mob and peace reigned once more.

A Father Kirwin story, given to me by his niece, Mrs. Katherine Vedder Pauls of Galveston, shows the magnificent character of the boy soldier, written by her, "Near the Cathedral Door."

"The late afternoon sun shown softly golden on the old Colonel as he stood by the cathedral door. A military bearing, rightfully his, for he had been the youngest captain in his regiment in 'sixty-one,' kept his shoulders erect, while his head, silvered by eighty years, was bare and bowed, as, hat in hand, he stood in quiet meditation.

"Many times the Priest, watching from within, had seen him thus. Had seen him even in passing, lift his hat with reverent gesture while his eyes seemed dimmed by tender memories.

"The Priest was curious to know the meaning of this act of reverence and meditation, and so, approaching the Colonel, he questioned him gently. And with courtesy and dignity the Colonel told a little story of many years ago.

"Bishop Odin, of the Catholic diocese, had a dream of a beautiful cathedral for St. Mary's parish. And with true zeal and sincere endeavor, set about achieving the success of his dream. It was not hard for his parishioners to follow their inspired leader. And every one who could give time, labor and such materials as he or she was possessed of, to help towards its building and completion.

"Among these was the mother of the old Colonel. She was a member of St. Mary's parish and an ardent worker in her church. (This faith was forced on all the people at that time.)

"She with her husband and family had come to Galveston

in 1845, and they had brought with them many slaves. It was too late in the season for work on the plantations and for a while they idled the days away to their hearts' content. Then the father of the Colonel heard of a wonderful soil around Lynchburg, Texas, admirable for the manufacturing of bricks. So, taking all of his slaves there, he started a brick industry at Lynchburg and sold them through a firm of well known business men of Galveston.

"Transportation at this time made bricks as precious as gold and jewels and almost as costly and difficult to procure. And as her gift and contribution, the Colonel's mother gave more than four thousand bricks, which went into the construction of the treasured walls of Galveston's first cathedral.

" 'And,' smiling, the Colonel added, 'although I have not followed my mother's faith, I feel a personal interest in the church that meant so much to her. I feel I have a sentimental claim on it through her, and so, it is always my pleasure in passing, to lift my hat in respect to her church, and in tender reverence to my mother's memory.'

"And bowing once more, with hat lifted high above his silvered head, he passed on his way."

He was a wonderful man and soldier.

But to go back to the Academy, it soon lost its name and in December, 1877, by vote of the people, the city took charge of the school and the present school system was born. But the memory of this old Academy still lingers with these who attended, many years ago.

HOUSTON'S EARLY FIRE-FIGHTERS

*City's Fire Department Older than City Itself
Antedating Incorporation*

It sounds paradoxical to suggest that the "fire department" of a city is older than the city itself. Yet, if we include in the history of our present elaborate Fire Department, the early origin and unbroken line of development to its present status, the statement is true.

Before the incorporation of the city, the Allen Brothers organized a company of fire-fighters known as the "bucket brigade" to protect the tiny village they had founded, from the frequent brush fires that threatened the town. In case of fire breaking out in the brush and undergrowth around the bayou or on the adjacent prairie, a bucket line was formed and wives joined their husbands in passing down the line to the fire buckets of water taken from the nearest source of supply. Sometimes the source was a nearby well or cistern. More frequently, perhaps, the water came direct from the bayou or a tributary creek.

Walking south in the six hundred block on Fannin Street, just beyond the Sterling Building entrance, one observes laid in the sidewalk, close to the wall, a marble slab bearing the legend: "Protection No. 1, Established 1838." It means little now to the average pedestrian. But ninety-five to ninety-eight years ago, it meant much to the pioneers of the little village of Houston. In those days Houston was a small community of log huts, clap-board or slab constructed homes and numerous tents scattered here and there. It became necessary that a more effective organization be formed to cope with the fire hazard.

Thus it was that the Allens organized a fire company and received a charter for the first organization of its kind granted within the new republic, "Protection No. 1." A search of the records indicates that the first equipment of 'fire engine' of this company was a large barrel mounted on wheels. It was rushed, boggy streets permitting, to the scene of conflagration and the contents used as a fire-extinguisher. This was supplemented, of course, by the bucket-brigade and line passing a continuous supply of water. Each member of the company made it a rule to keep one or two fire-buckets at their home and place of business and a small ladder to scale the walls.

As an auxiliary to the above, in 1847, a force-pump was mounted on a chassis or wagon and a long suction pipe added to a home-made engine on wheels, the end of the intake hose being lowered into the nearest water. The 'engine' operated somewhat akin to the late railroad hand-cars, there being a handle-bar on each side of the beam; and man-power, furnished by the members of the company taking turns about, the water being sucked in at intake and forced through the outlet hose upon the fire.

Attached to this machine were two long ropes. When the fire alarm was sounded, the members rushed to the engine-house, caught up the ropes and assisted by citizens en route, pulled the engine through the streets to the location of the fire. I have been told many years back by some of the then old-timers that they have seen as many as two hundred men aid in pulling the engine. Notorious for its deep, black mud, as Houston was in those days, perhaps on occasion it required that many 'pullers' to get the equipment there.

The alarm was usually sounded by the great bell atop the Market House. Later, when the railroads came, the switch-engines augmented the alarm with their whistles. Today, in the small towns of the interior, the populace will be awakened in the night by pistol shots intended as fire-alarm.

In those early days, when the fire alarm sounded in Houston, everyone rushed to the fire-house, then situated on Congress Avenue near the Market Square. It was a breach of citizenship not to respond to the alarm, and as late as 1853, women often worked at the pump alongside their husbands. I have often seen the little fire-machine carried to the fire, and boy-like, I would attempt to man the handle-brakes of the pump, only to be lifted off my feet into the air, and deposited again as the opposite brake-handle was raised.

In 1852, T. W. House, Sr., W. D. Cleveland, Sr., and Wm. Marsh Rice purchased an engine in Boston. This arrived in 1853 and Liberty No. 2 Engine Company was organized. The engine was a beauty and cost some two thousand dollars. This engine, with the force-pump of the previous company and the bucket-brigade, made up the entire fire department of Houston until 1858, when Hook and Ladder Company No. 1 was organized, and a home-made truck was constructed for the wall-climbers. T. W. House, while Mayor of the city in 1862, organized Hook and Ladder Company No. 2.

In 1876, J. H. B. House was elected Chief of the Fire Department. During that year the famous 'carpet-bagger' Market House was burned down, a total loss. It had cost the taxpayers of Houston four hundred thousand dollars under the carpet-bag regime. It was rebuilt, duplicated by Tom Lucas, contractor of that period, at a cost of approximately seventy-five thousand dollars. In constructing the new market-house, however, Mr. Lucas made use of the old foundation, thereby reducing considerably the expense of the new house.

One of the next great fires of Houston was the burning of St. Joseph's Infirmary on Caroline and Franklin, in 1894, with the loss of several lives, including three or four of the good Sisters. They gave their own lives in an effort to save the patients.

This fateful disaster occurred during the government of Mayor John T. Browne, who, as a result thereof, made a thorough reorganization of the fire department and both modernized and increased its equipment.

In these early days of the department, it was considered an out-standing distinction, socially and otherwise, to be honored with the office of Fire Chief. Among these early chiefs were Jos. F. Meyer in 1888, W. H. Coyle in 1882, Judge J. K. P. Gillespie in 1886. I recall one instance, in fact, when a prominent citizen of Houston declined to run for Governor of Texas, in order to enjoy the privilege of being Fire Chief of Houston.

I recall, too, a period during which the fire department of the city consisted of Hook and Ladder Companies Nos. 1 and 2, Protection No. 1, Stonewall No. 3, Capitol No. 5, and Eagle No. 7, with an additional volunteer company organized by the Turner Rifles from among their own membership. The cost of the equipment at that time amounted to around nine thousand dollars, as compared to a valuation today of approximately two million one hundred and twenty-six thousand dollars. But that isn't all. The nine thousand dollar figure mentioned first, had reference to an all-volunteer fire department. Today, annual salary cost of the Houston Fire Department is six hundred and sixty-five thousand dollars, with an additional annual salary cost of twenty-five thousand dollars for the Fire Prevention Bureau recently organized. If we waive the thought that comparisons are sometime odious, it is interesting to note, in passing, that while, since that time, the population of the city has increased about thirty-one times, the value of the city's fire-fighting equipment and properties (salaries excluded) has increased two hundred and thirty-six times. An excellent showing of proportionate fire-protection as the city grows.

The Volunteer Fire Department of Houston was accustomed to hold its annual celebration on San Jacinto Day. These were truly gala occasions. The highly decorated parades were gorgeous affairs of floral adornment, each piece of equipment being literally covered with flowers. I have seen the vehicles decorated with the real flowers, both cultivated and wild. There were also colorful silk conveyances of each company which bore proudly upon her throne, the beautiful young lady elected as 'queen' for the occasion. Even the manes and tails of the horses (they were, of course, horsedrawn vehicles during that period, the motive power equipment coming much later) were prettily entwined with ribbons and their hoofs gilded or silvered as might best harmonize with the decorative scheme as a whole. Allotted to each machine was two ropes twined with ribbons, to which the firemen of that company held on as escort to their queen.

One of the greatest of these annual parades was described by the Houston Post in their 1886 Post, San Jacinto edition. The parade was led by Herb's Light Guard Band, followed by the city council, the San Jacinto Veterans, distinguished visitors, the Light Guard and other Military Companies, and then the entire Fire Department. Bands were interspersed throughout, mingling national marches and southern airs. If the position of Fire Chief in those days was a highly honored one, no less so, proportionately, was rank and file membership in the Volunteer Fire Department. Each of the brave firemen had his circle of admirers among the onlooking throng and as his truck passed in review, their hero received the cheers and plaudits of his supporters. The particular parade above mentioned was stated to be more than a mile long.

Occasionally, during the annual parades, fire-alarms would come in. In such instances, the engines covering that district would leave the parade, galloping for the fire, and the remainder of the parade would close up and proceed.

Among some of the great fires occurring in Houston during those years was that of October, 1882, when the International Press burned, and along with it some fourteen thousand bales of cotton. Very little was salvaged and coming, even, at the time that Texas produced its first monster cotton crop, it worked a severe hardship upon buyers and shippers. Somewhat later, another great fire broke out on the east side of the block on Main, bounded by Congress and Preston. J. R. Morris and Sons had just completed a fine, four-story, ironfront building. This was destroyed with a large stock of merchandise. Other merchants in the block suffered almost total losses.

Houston's all-time record in great fires thus far, however, was broken in February of 1912, when a fire started about eleven o'clock at night, at Hardy and Opelousas in the Fifth Ward. Fanned by a gale estimated by some at sixty miles per hour, this fire spread rapidly beyond control. It crossed the bayou to the south side and spread east as far as the Houston Packing Company. A clean sweep was made of approximately forty blocks, and the loss, including a tremendous amount of cotton, was estimated at twelve million dollars. Galveston fire-fighting equipment was called in to assist the local fire-men, involving the making of a new train-record between the two cities.

The fact that Houston has not had a major conflagration within the past twenty-five years is, I think, indicative of the present excellent status of our Fire Department and its equipment. Its effectiveness, too, is reflected in the comparatively low rate of insurance that Houston now enjoys.

When we contemplate the present great fire-fighting establishment of the city, however, we should look back with appreciation upon the tireless and unpaid efforts of Houston's famed Volunteer Department of other days. True, the latter organization was almost as much social in nature, as it was effective in fire fighting; even the funerals of its passing members were conducted fraternally in fireman style, similar to events of like kind conducted by the Masons, Odd Fellows, Knights of Pythias and others.

Happily, there yet remain in active service in our present Fire Department, two 'old timers' who served in the old volunteer companies: R. F. Ollre, of Central or No. 1, and affectionately known as 'Kid' Ollre; and Henry Donnelly of No. 2. Two others whom I recall as members of the old volunteers, but not now in active service, are W. B. Hill, kinsman of our present Sheriff Norfleet Hill and A. H. Roper.

In conversation a few days since with Chief R. F. Ollre and Tom Graham of Central Fire Station and later with Chief J. H. Davidson, they talked most interestingly of the early history of the Volunteer Companies. Among other items, it was recalled that Protection No. 1 was later removed to Texas and San Jacinto (from a previous location on Texas near Fannin) and became a hose reel unit; that Liberty No. 2, after purchasing its 'engine' returned it and the company disbanded; that Stonewall No. 3, hose reel, once on Preston, was later on Smith between Preston and Prairie, and Mechanics No. 6, another hose reel unit, was located on Washington beside the Houston Infirmary, across from where Weingarten's now stands. Mention was made, too, of North Star No. 7, in Fifth Ward and Alamo No. 8, Bell and San Jacinto, both hose reel units, but short lived. Curtain No. 9 in the nine hundred block on Hardy was named for Martin Curtin, former chief. Seibert No. 10, named for Billie Seibert, an old time volunteer fireman and ran the Turf Exchange at Prairie and Main, and a brother of F. C. Seibert, once Fire Chief of Houston. It was located on Chartres between Congress and Franklin, where it yet remains. Hook and Ladder No. 1 was on Prairie and San Jacinto, Fred Christian being the 'foreman.'

Conversion of the old Volunteer Fire Department of Houston was begun on January 1st, 1893, when the members went on part pay. In July of 1895, the members were placed on full pay.

In the earlier days of the old Volunteer companies, nearly every citizen of prominence served a substantial period on one or another of the companies. Or, if actual physical service was not included, they contributed largely to the support and maintenance of one of the companies.

In beautiful Glenwood Cemetery today stands a tall and impressive column, a monument to these heroic fire-fighters of another day, surmounted by a splendid statue of that 'noblest Roman of them all,' Colonel Bob Brewster.

ARRIVAL OF THE STEAMBOAT "LAURA"

One Hundredth Anniversary of the Coming of Houston's First Steamboat

What well might be termed the first official opening of the present Houston Ship Channel, occurred one hundred years ago with the arrival of the little steamboat "Laura."

Historians differ as to the exact date of the Laura's arrival. Carroll, in his early recollections of Houston, refers to the date as New Year's Day in 1837. Mrs. Adele B. Looscan has stated in her writings that the boat arrived here on January twenty-sixth, 1837. Lack now, one hundred years later, of a specific date, in no sense lessons the importance of the occasion, nor interest in the various historical accounts of the voyage.

The Laura had previously plied the waters of the Brazos between Columbus and Matagorda under command of Captain Grayson, a hardy seafaring type, renowned in that period for the excellency of his seamanship. Regular trips were made from Matagorda to West Galveston and occasionally to Brownsville and intermediate points. Its initial trip was up

Buffalo Bayou, the official opening of that stream to Houston via steamship travel.

The most noted passenger on board the Laura on that first trip was Frank R. Lubbock, later a distinguished Governor of the State of Texas and who affords, in his memoirs written years later, a highly amusing account of the voyage.

The Steamer "Laura" in Buffalo Bayou at foot of Main Street

The Allen brothers had advertised the newly laid out city of Houston extensively, painting a far more glamorous and prosperous future for the town than then appeared probable. The owners of the Laura, falling victims to the lure of the well planned advertising campaign, in turn circularized their trade territory, advising of their voyage to Houston, and succeeded in obtaining a heavy cargo and passenger list for the new "inland port."

Proceeding upstream from Clopper's Bar (now Morgan's Point), the Laura's first stop was at Harrisburg, Governor

Lubbock relates that it required three days for the little steamer to make the trip from Harrisburg to Houston. It was found necessary en route to make frequent stops for the purpose of cutting down overhanging trees, shrubs and vines, or blowing up log-jams, to enable the boat to proceed. Finally, they unwittingly passed Houston altogether and reached what they believed to be their destination, a point on White Oak Bayou above the junction with Buffalo. Here, they paused, being unable to proceed farther and some of the passengers made a cursory survey of the banks. Checking his bearings, it suddenly occurred to Captain Grayson that they had overshot their mark, whereupon, he was forced to back out to White Oaks, the stream being of insufficient width to permit the turning around of the Laura.

Presently the lookout discovered another clearing on the banks of Buffalo Bayou, with a few small shacks. Investigation proved this tiny hamlet to be the wharf-front of the "City of Houston" that the Allens had advertised in so colorful a fashion.

Truly, the Allens had spared no printer's ink in their effort to provide the infant Houston its place in the sun. Alas! that they could not have lived long enough to have seen their wildest dreams of a future Houston come true.

In one instance they paid a bonus of more than one thousand dollars to bring the seagoing steamer, "Constitution" then plying between Galveston, New Orleans and Carribean ports, up Buffalo Bayou to Houston, in order to prove the feasibility of making Houston a deep-water port. There was one incident of rather humorous nature in their later efforts in this direction that I shall never forget. It was in 1886. Samuel Allen, then my close neighbor, called me up one morning and exclaimed: "At last, Ziegler, we are a salt-water port!"

It appeared that Sampson Heidenheimer, an enterprising wholesale grocer and cotton exporter of Galveston had bought two sailing vessels in Bremen, Germany, took them to Liverpool and there transferred them to British registration and flag, as being safer and more economical in point of operation. For ballast, Heindenheimer had the boats loaded with salt at Liverpool and the voyage to America began. It was his desire to bring the boats direct to "Head of Navigation" at Houston. Finally, it was found necessary to complete the last lap of the trip by transferring the salt to barges and thence to the warehouses of the Direct Navigation Company, located where the new E. A. Peden Building now stands, adjacent to the San Jacinto bridge. That night, a terrific cloudburst ensued in White Oak Bayou at Houston, causing a sudden rising of the bayou, wherein its banks and the warehouses were overflowed. The water receded almost as rapidly as it had risen but all that remained of the great cargo of salt was some eight to ten thousand empty, water soaked sacks. The salt had dissolved and washed away with the flood. The following morning's issue of the Galveston News came out in streaming headlines: "Houston at last a salt-water port, God Almighty furnished the water and Heidenheimer furnished the salt." There followed a description of the flood, with much good-natured sarcasm thrown in. Galvestonians enjoyed the joke no more than did Samuel Allen himself.

In 1837 there also came to Houston, some months following the Laura, an auxiliary steam yacht owned by a Mr. and Mrs. Houston (pronounced "Howeston") of England. The husband was a wealthy naturalist of note, engaged in exploration and collecting new and unusual specimens of flora and fauna. Leaving Galveston, they steamed across the bay and up the bayou to Houston, encountering, of course, considerable difficulty in making the trip. That they were both interested and favorably impressed, however, is gleaned from an account of the trip written by Mrs. Houston in her later memoirs. She relates: "We entered Buffalo Bayou River and found it bordered by magnificent trees, overhanging vines, tall reeds and bull-rushes, in the midst of which appeared countless herons, cranes and other water-fowls. At various times we saw thousands of wild ducks and geese flying overhead or disporting themselves upon the waters of the river. As we proceeded upstream, the river became narrower and the banks higher. Frequently we encountered narrow bends and turns in the stream that so crowded passage of our boat that we were caught either ahead or astern. At length, the stream gradually widened, the banks became yet higher and were sheltered by great magnolia trees, most beautiful in their dress of full bloom and affording a perfume of such sweetness as to be highly intoxicating. Both gray and red squirrels could be seen scampering across the ground or leaping from branch to branch of the trees, from whence came in fine voice the songs of many mocking birds. Added color was lent to the scene by great numbers of blue-jays and cardinals, or red-birds."

Her book, "First Voyage to Texas" was published in London in 1844, and contains, among other interesting discourse, an interesting account of the Battle of San Jacinto.

The "Constitution," however, was really the first large ocean-going vessel to come up Buffalo Bayou. Its size made it, at the time, an unwieldy vessel to undertake the trip. Considerable difficulty was experienced in negotiating some of the bends in the bayou and I understand that it finally had to back down stream in order to make the return trip, being unable to turn around. This, however, would have been needless had their navigator understood and employed a "trick" subsequently used successfully on many occasions. It was discovered and first used by Captain John Atkinson, and later by the Captains of the Morgan Line steamboats. It was performed by steaming the prow of the boat directly into the bank of the bayou, or, if available, up the mouth of a small stream or inlet, then backing the boat across the bayou. This was accomplished, in course of time, by many vessels of larger tonnage than the "Constitution."

In passing, it occurs to me that Constitution Bend on Buffalo Bayou greatly advertised by John T. Brady when he laid out Magnolia Park, was named on commemoration of the Constitution's visit to Houston.

In April of 1837 and I believe on San Jacinto day, the schooner "Rolla" came up to Houston. In many of the old prints of that period may be seen sailing vessels coming up the bayou under full spread of sail.

Somewhat later on, the "Yellowstone" came up the bayou to Houston and the inland water route was an assured realization. This boat, like the "Laura," had been engaged in the Brazos River trade at Brazoria and Columbus. Brazoria, it must be remembered, had been the principal port through which Austin's colonists had passed. Sailing from New Orleans on the schooner "Hively," in 1821, they passed Galveston Island, where, history relates, not a single human being was noted; only the three trees "Tres Palacious" marking the location of Jean LaFitte's former rendezvous, were visible.

While during the interim many large ocean-going vessels had plied the waters of Buffalo Bayou to Houston, yet another singular incident is found in 1863. A large seafaring blockade runner, with a great cargo of munitions of war steamed up the bayou and unloaded a portion of her hazardous cargo at the foot of Caroline Street, where the

Schumacher grocery store now stands. Much unloading of cargo was accomplished at this point by the incoming boats because of a large sandbar that facilitated the work. The blockade runner came up to Houston on the crest of a big freshet. Her return to Galveston was delayed, however, because of threat of another Federal attack upon Galveston and it was feared that the ship would be captured. It finally went downstream on another freshet. Shortly afterward, a schooner loaded with torpedoes, bombs, guns, bayonets and sabres, transferred from the blockade runner, came to anchor just beyond the iron bridge at the foot of Milam near Henke's ice-house. Through some mishap, the ship and its cargo sank and was abandoned by the Confederate authorities. Up to some fifty years ago, at each heavy norther, the hull could be plainly seen. It constituted a serious menace because of the disposition of small boys and others to prowl over the hull or dig in the mud for portions of its cargo, much of it still highly explosive. From time to time various accidental explosions occurred from the salvage recovered, resulting in shattered panes and show windows in that vicinity, as well as the loss of a number of lives. It has now long since settled in the mud.

The "Cayuga," later renamed the "Branch T. Archer" in honor of one of San Jacinto's heroes, was another one of the early steamboats to negotiate the trip to Houston. It was brought to Houston by John R. Harris, under command of Captain Isaac Batterson. Originally, the boat had been intended for use on the Trinity River, but trade upon the bayou having developed far more profitably, the "Cayuga" was diverted.

It appears to me as passing strange that, comparatively speaking, so few fatalities occurred in the operation of these early day steamboats over their period of some seventy years. The boilers and engines in most of them were extremely crude affairs and the fuel consisted chiefly of pine-knots and cord-wood, with little regard for limits of steam pressure, or loads placed upon the poorly constructed engines. History records that in 1839 the "Henry A. Jones" blew up and burned in Galveston Bay with considerable loss of life. In 1840 the "Farmer's" engine or boiler exploded, killing its skipper, Captain Webb. The "Star State," placed in operation on the bayou in the "Forties," met with a number of accidents. On one occasion, it was swept with fire and the passengers were saved only with the greatest of difficulty. Mrs. Peter W.

Gray, one of the beloved pioneers of Houston, was forced to jump overboard and nearly drowned before being rescued.

The real, or "classy" steamboat life on Buffalo Bayou began when Captain John Atkinson went to Cincinnati and bought three palatial steamers then the equal of anything on the Mississippi. They were brought to Houston under the names of "Thomas M. Bagby," "Diana" and "Captain Charles Fowler." Later was added to bayou craft the steamship "Lizzie," which many now living will recall went to her doom after the Galveston storm in 1900.

While full recognition in later years is accorded in the Houston Post, Chronicle and the Press, the Chamber of Commerce and the Cotton Exchange, for their untiring efforts to promote the interests of Houston's present day ship channel, the real founders of the steamship trade upon the waters of Buffalo Bayou were T. W. House, T. M. Bagby, C. S. Longcope, Captain Fred Smith and Major E. W. Cave. From the very first, Cave was a staunch enthusiast for and believer in deep water for Houston. As a small boy, I sat often at his knee, listening to him expound the merits of Buffalo Bayou. It seemed to me that so glorious and optimistic a future did he paint that did those who came after the Major accomplish the things that he dreamed, they must needs give Aladdin's Lamp the most vigorous polishing yet received. It must be remembered that the Buffalo Bayou of Major Cave's day was a deeper, more beautiful and more picturesque stream than the head of the bayou today. Too, its current was stronger, as it was fed by many large springs and creeks that have since given way to progress and city-building. Noted among the several larger springs was Beauchamp Springs, once the source of water-supply for Houston. The banks, too, instead of wasting away as they did in later years, were held intact by the spreading, drinking roots of great cypress trees, thousands in number. Audubon the great naturalist in his account of his first visit to Texas, refers in terms highly appreciative, to the beauty of old Buffalo Bayou, its trees, banks carpeted with luxuriant grass and masses of wild flowers.

Somehow, even now, I cling rather tenderly to the stream's olden name, Buffalo Bayou, and find that with forethought and difficulty do I refer to it as Houston's ship channel, the sea-road to America's largest inland port. In point of rank, it has, with recent years, climbed steadily in value of exports and imports handled to a position in the foremost ranks of the five great ports of America.

Little old Captain Grayson on the steamboat "Laura" a hundred years ago, 1837, was given the privilege to carry the first torch in a procession of what has now developed into magnificent accomplishment of a pioneer's dream.

CHARLES MORGAN

Father of Houston's Ship Channel

The initial efforts, considered in connection with the progressive steps of development which have brought the Houston ship channel to its present far-flung effectiveness, read like romance.

The first record we have of this now important waterway, was when Leonard Groce, son of Jared Groce, of the historic Groce's Ferry of Texas' pre-revolutionary days, in 1826 delivered to John R. Harris, founder of Harrisburg, one hundred bales of cotton. This cotton was carried down Buffalo Bayou by schooner and exported to New Orleans, one hundred and ten years ago.

The first sea-going vessel, of which we have record, to come up the bayou to Houston, was the "Captain Kelsey," a small steamer that undertook the voyage from Galveston, and which was owned by a Mr. Houston and his wife, wealthy English citizens, who were on a pleasure trip to Texas. Small, locally owned crafts had, of course, negotiated the bayou prior to the time of the arrival of the "Captain Kelsey" in 1836.

In January, 1837, the steamer "Laura" from Velasco, was the first locally owned steamer to come to Houston from Harrisburg. This voyage required three days to accomplish.

Charles Morgan, founder of the Morgan Steamship Line, might appropriately be termed the "Father of the Ship Channel." Morgan was a pioneer and the state's best friend in its early industrial development, by reason of his untiring efforts to provide Texas with its first regular line of steamships. As early as 1835, while Texas was yet a part of Mexico, he sent one of his ships, the "Columbia," to Galveston. Subsequently, during 1840-42, he had as competitor Commodore Cornelius Vanderbilt, who operated a service to Galveston comprised of two or three steamers running on regular schedule. In due course, however, Morgan, in order to kill off competition and control the entire trade, bought Vanderbilt out, and the "transportation king," as Vanderbilt was then known, never regained a foothold in handling the products and commerce of the empire of Texas.

Morgan, continuing his activities, developed a tremendous volume of business, moving in and out of Texas, for the line he had established, and consequently became the leading patron, by far, of the wharves at Galveston.

Meanwhile, Buffalo Bayou, as such, had remained very largely in status quo until the year 1866, in which year the Houston Direct Navigation Company was founded and began its initial operation of deepening the bayou and dredging a canal across what is now known as Morgan's Point. The city of Houston appropriated some two hundred thousand dollars for this work.

Morgan, who had then for many years controlled the ocean-carrying trade between New Orleans and Texas ports, and who now maintained a large fleet for that purpose, became more or less disgruntled with the facilities and rates accorded him at Galveston. In an initial conference with the Galveston port officials, Morgan asked for broader facilities and cheaper wharf rates than were then effective. The city of Galveston at that time owned about one-fourth interest in the Galveston wharves.

After several conferences between Morgan and the Galveston wharf interests, the city of Galveston, exerting a dominating influence through their ownership of a portion of the wharf stock, turned a deaf ear to Morgan's entreaties. The latter became indignant and threatened to cross Galveston bay with his ships and make use of Houston as a terminal port, unless Galveston treated with him more reasonably. Galveston, in effect, hooted at the idea, and told Morgan to go ahead, do what he pleased, notwithstanding that at the time he was their largest and most lucrative customer.

With his ultimatum turned down, Morgan turned immediately to Galveston Bay and Houston's Buffalo Bayou. He first purchased the city of Houston's interest in the Houston Direct Navigation Company, and put to work a large engineering force to deepen the channel across the bay and dredge a cut through the present Morgan's Point. The great storm of 1875 destroyed a portion of the cut through

Morgan's Point, together with a small fleet of vessels and a number of workmen. Nothing daunted, however, Morgan's staff resumed work within thirty days and continued until the cut-off through Morgan's Point was completed.

Morgan then claimed the cut as his own, and placing a log-chain across the canal, demanded toll payment for all ships passing through. This tariff was regularly enforced and the toll collected until 1891, when relief therefrom was had as will be touched upon later on.

A railroad now came into existence, known as the Texas Transport Company, following a right-of-way beginning at what was then known as Bonner's Point, where the Southern Pacific freight sheds now stand on north San Jacinto, and running a distance of some ten miles to Clinton. For a number of years, therefore, the Morgan Line steamers gave Galveston the go-by, much to the latter's chagrin, and passing by the Galveston wharves, proceeded directly to Clinton.

This constituted a bitter blow, both financially and in point of prestige, to the port of Galveston and the Wharf company there, now realizing the error of its former way with Morgan, repented thereof and complied altogether with Morgan's demands. The latter thereon discontinued his steamer service to Houston.

Morgan had thoroughly demonstrated what could be done with Buffalo Bayou as an ocean-going ship channel, provided proper efforts were made. Immediately there arose a popular demand from the citizens of Houston and interior merchants who were dissatisfied with the Galveston Wharf Company's charges. Congress was accordingly petitioned and the two senators from Texas, together with the congressmen concerned, urged the development of this important waterway, in the bright future of which the supporting population firmly believed.

In the late "Seventies" a bill was introduced in Congress for the purchase of the Buffalo Bayou ship channel by the United States government, with the view of opening and developing it as one of the country's great water-ways. A corps of engineers, headed by Captain R. B. Talfor, assistant United States resident engineer, in Galveston, Houston's staunchest friend, and a strict advocate of the work, was sent by the government with instructions to inspect the work already done and to report on what appeared to be the possibilities of the stream as an effective waterway. They reported that twelve feet of water, as an average depth of the channel to the foot of Main Street in Houston, could be had.

Houstonians then got busy. One of the conditions of the proposed sale of the channel to the government, which sale had then been pending for some time, was that the government should, in the purchase of the channel, refund to Morgan the amount expended by him in the preliminary work and proceed to carry out the remaining terms of the undertaking as originally accepted by Morgan when he took over the channel and its development from the Buffalo Bayou Ship Channel Company.

Fortunately, our congressman from Houston, Honorable Charles Stewart, was made chairman of the deep water committee. It was an inspiration to listen to him advocate the measure to be taken, and the undertaking itself was to be completed to the foot of Main Street in Houston as soon as possible. The ship channel proper was to extend from Clinton to Red Fish Bar and from Red Fish Bar to Bolivar.

In due course the government did work here and there on the channel spending about one hundred and forty-seven thousand dollars. When these sums were exhausted, the channel from Clinton to Bolivar varied in depth from fourteen to thirty feet. However, it amounted to something; progress had been made and an inspection in 1880 showed that the channel through Morgan's Point and Red Fish had actually deepened. This was brought about through a "scouring" process of the flowing waters and tidal action.

Houston Direct Navigation Company had expended some two hundred thousand dollars before it had transferred the work to Morgan, and Morgan had spent probably seven hundred thousand dollars more in bringing the work forward to Clinton.

Houstonians and Harris County citizens continued to press Congress for further and more liberal development for the channel. I recall, fifty-three years ago, the festivity of the occasions when the congressmen and notables of the time were taken for a trip on the bayou and were told of the possibilities of the ship channel.

Notwithstanding the forensic ability displayed on these occasions, there was much delay and it was not until 1891 that the money was finally paid to Morgan and, with the booming of cannon, the log-chain across the channel at Morgan's Point was removed and a "free Houston waterway thrown open to the world." The work of the government, financial co-operation of Harris County citizens has been continuous since the chain was removed in 1891. With one exception, when no river and harbor bill was passed, each succeeding Congress has made some appropriation for the work, which helped deepen and straighten the bayou, even though they were small appropriations. Buffalo Bayou was always deep and not sluggish, and had the remainder of the channel been likewise the problem would long since have been solved.

The government was regularly petitioned, all kinds of information furnished, and "pounds" of statistics provided from the Houston Cotton Exchange, there being in the earlier period no Chamber of Commerce.

Congress finally passed a bill appropriating one million two hundred and fifty thousand dollars for development of the channel, provided that Houston would furnish an equal amount. Officially, Mayor Baldwin Rice of Houston consulted with the Harris County commissioners. The result was that the Houston Navigation District was formed and an election held for the navigation district to issue bonds to the extent of the above price. The proposition was carried overwhelmingly in 1911, thus assuring for Houston the fifth largest port; in point of value of commodities handled and as a cotton export, it is the leading port of the world.

As it now operates, the Houston ship channel extends from the city of Houston to the Gulf, using the Galveston jetty-entrance to Bolivar Road, then across Galveston Bay up to San Jacinto River and Buffalo Bayou to the public terminals at the turning basin, and during the present year, a great program has been brought to completion. Now, through a further allotment of three and one half million dollars from the Public Works Administration the program contemplates the deepening of the entire channel from the present depth of thirty-two feet, to a possible depth of thirty-six feet. The present width of the Galveston bay section is 400 feet and river section is to be widened from 150 to 250 feet at the bottom. A total of twenty million dollars has been spent to date.

The public terminals are owned by the city and Navigation District. Those comprise some fifteen wharves, with nineteen private wharves in addition; the Manchester terminals being located some two miles below the turning basin. Each public wharf, of concrete, is five hundred feet long and two hundred feet wide, and fifty-eight regular steamship lines are

Allen Station—First in Houston 1857

Early Days in Houston

established. The management of the turning basin facilities lies with the port commission.

In contemplating the present status and importance of the Houston ship channel, and the vast amount of untiring personal effort expended over that period of years necessary to bring the project to its ultimate success, I hold sincerely to the belief that we should accord honor where honor is due. Well within that scope most certainly would come: Major E. W. Cave, C. S. Longcope, C. C. Pillot, Honorable Thomas H. Ball, Mayor Baldwin Rice, R. S. Sterling, R. M. Farrar and Mayor Ben Campbell. The latter decided that Houston needed a harbor board to protect and further the interests of the city as a leading port. In 1915 the following were active in the work in furthering the channel: R. H. Spencer, A. S. Cleveland and Burke Baker. These men went to New York to endeavor to interest the Morgan Line in establishing a service between New York and Houston. They were unsuccessful in this but did induce the Southern Steamship Company to establish a Philadelphia-Houston service. Morgan Lines are now the largest users of the ship channel so far as handling of general merchandise is concerned, after revising the previous decision. In equal prominence as a faithful worker in the cause, stands Captain Charles Crotty, Assistant Port Director, formerly of the United States engineering department.

Since May, 1922, the administration of the port has been under a Port Commission of five members, serving without pay, two appointed by County Commissioner's Court, two by the City Council and the Chairman selected by both bodies in joint session.

This Commission, with the late E. A. Peden as its first Chairman, followed by Governor R. S. Sterling and for the last seven years by J. W. Evans, and its members of outstanding public spirited citizens, have built up a port second to none in the south and ranking as fifth port of the nation in 1936. The executive officers as Port Directors under this Commission have been B. C. Allin from 1919 to 1930 and J. Russell Wait since that time, with a staff of assistants to handle all details of this growing port.

All in all, we must necessarily concede that the citizens of Houston as a whole, from first to last, constituted themselves a "Committee of One" to "talk and work and boost" for Houston's deepwater project.

PIONEER DAYS OF THE HOUSTON TURNVEREIN

Because of the leading role enacted by the Houston Turnverein, over a period now of some eighty-four years, in the social, fraternal and athletic development of Houston, it is obviously interesting to view the organization somewhat in the light of retrospect. To those who find some pleasure in delving into the records of pioneer Houston, a peek into the origin, early history and erstwhile accomplishment of Houston's Turnverein is altogether entertaining.

In the great hall of the Turnverein's handsome new building now located on Almeda, the attention of the visitor is immediately attracted to a series of nineteen large portraits. These portray, for future generations, the original charter members who met one evening in January of 1854 at the home of Peter Gable, a distinguished pioneer German citizen of Houston, to form the Turnverein. Among them were college men, professional men, mechanics, skilled and technical engineers and men from all walks of life who had been lured from their native land by the bright prospects and opportunities to be had in the newly created Empire State. Many of them had come here in the infant days of Texas as a Republic, seeking refuge from Prussian tyranny, severe hardships of the Napoleonic Wars, or perhaps even religious freedom.

It is interesting to note that when the first United States census of Houston was taken in 1845, forty per cent of the entire city population was German speaking.

In 1839 the capital of the Republic had been removed from Houston, chiefly, I believe, to satisfy certain political reasons that were based upon private profit. This created a situation somewhat in the nature of a local panic. Scores of merchants moved to Galveston and the interior. Property values drifted to low ebb and the Allen brothers, promoters of Houston, received their first severe set back. About the same time there came a serious epidemic of yellow fever, small pox and cholera and the city presented an appearance similar to Goldsmith's "deserted village." Street pedestrians were few, and a sign upon the capitol building bore the fateful legend "For Rent." Scarce a day passed without demise of one or more of the town's prominent citizens and fear was imminent that the passing of Houston would soon become a matter of history. Fortunately, the month of December was at hand and with the coming of cold weather, the epidemics were stamped out.

Then, on December the eighth, the steamer "Correo" came up the bayou from Galveston and landed a party, consisting of some two hundred new German immigrants, with their modest household effects. Their arrival dispelled the atmosphere of gloom that lay over the city. The citizens turned out to greet the newcomers and the only newspaper, the "Morning Star" came out in box-car letters heralding the arrival of the "blue-eyed, florid-complexioned Germans." The effect of this substantial addition to the city's fast dwindling population was both psychological and practical; the business and social life also received the needed impetus.

It was from such type of men, came the founding of Houston's Turnverein.

At first, membership in the organization was limited to German-speaking citizens. Subsequently this was found impractical and the provision was amended to include a broader field.

The Turnverein's first hall occupied a frontage of one hundred feet on Prairie Avenue, where the Cotton Exchange now stands. There was, from time to time, much discussion of enlarging both the ground and the building but the finances of the society were frail and no definite action was taken. Finally, one evening in the summer of 1885, when a number of the younger element were engaged in ten-pins, in walked Dr. Edward Flewellen, pioneer resident of the city, who owned the remainder of the Prairie Avenue frontage and other portions of the block. Mounting a small bench, he called for quiet and exclaimed: "Boys, we've been talking back and forth for a good many years about the sale of my property to you. Other matters have now arisen that necessitate my coming to you with the statement that here and now is your last chance. I am giving you now, the last call as the auctioneer says, upon it. If you want the property you must take it now at the price we have heretofore agreed upon; otherwise it will be sold tonight to other parties."

I was among the listeners present. We did want the property and there was no alternative but to take it, regardless of the Verein's finances. Accordingly, a hurry up call was sent out to other members and there we underwrote the required down payment by giving our personal checks. In less than six months the Verein had repaid the entire amount advanced by the group present that night.

While the original Turnverein was a German organization, its membership naturally kept alive their traditions and folk-customs of the fatherland and took official notice of feast and other holidays peculiar to the German people. It also took a most active part in the leadership of any movement to the development and progress of the community, social, commercial or patriotic; its membership totaled 1,100.

Let us consider some of the early activities of this group.

They were among the very first to establish public schools where the children of all nationalities and faith came. These schools were presided by most excellent tutors brought here from other states and learned institutions abroad. If the parents of the children were unable to pay the stipulated tuition, the deficit was made up by the association members.

They were the first society to create and equip a local fire-fighting company, the personnel of which was taken exclusively from their membership.

When, during the Civil War, their adopted State of Texas seceded from the Union, they were again among the first to organize from their membership a military unit in behalf of the southern cause. Their company, the Turner Rifles, became known as one of the outstanding military units of war, leaving to those who came after, a most cherished record of valorous accomplishment. At the beginning of the war they were the first local unit to leave the city. Previously, they were assigned to Galveston, to protect that city from the outlying federal blockading fleet. From here they were transferred to the more active theatre of war in Mississippi. In the fighting around Vicksburg they invariably carried their objectives, even though on occasion they suffered severe casualties.

Another phase of the constructive civic work carried on by the members of the Turnverein, was their organization and development of a chapter of the Howard Association, forerunner of and later merged with the Red Cross Society founded by Clara Barton. The laudable service of this chapter was rendered under most trying local circumstances, particularly during the various epidemics of cholera, yellow fever and small pox. In many instances there were no doctors, nurses, or even established undertakers available; medical and hospital supplies were scant and the members of these Howard Chapters were and necessarily had to be, men of great resourcefulness.

HOUSTON

It was the early membership of the Turnverein who brought to Houston with regularity the city's first classical musical programs and concerts. Under the direction of Professor Gustav Duvernoy, these affairs attained a state of excellence creditable to a city greater than Houston. He will be remembered by many now living as principal for some twenty years of Houston's High School.

In later years, the Turnverein again took the lead in establishing summer night open air concerts. By this time the association had increased its membership to a total of some fourteen hundred, by taking in both passive and active members and had also acquired ownership of the entire block bound by Prairie, Caroline, Texas and Austin streets. These summer night concerts were rendered by band or orchestra, accompanied in many instances by creditable vocal and instrumental numbers. That they were exceedingly popular was attested always by the large attendance. Socially, the Turnverein had advanced to the status of being not only among the oldest organizations continuously active in the state but also the largest. Their annual balls were undoubtedly among the most brilliant social affairs in the state during the period mentioned.

Their hall had been greatly enlarged, affording commodious quarters and modern conveniences of the day. It served the larger gatherings and public functions of that time much as does the city auditorium of today. Many state conventions were held there; the first No-Tsu-oh ball, various noted political affairs, including the "Clark Convention" during the Hogg-Clark campaign and other assemblies of equal importance.

My first introduction to the Houston Turnverein was in 1875, when the Jahn Turnverein of Galveston came up to compete in their annual tryst with the members of the Houston organization. These competitive affairs covered a wide range, including events musical, military, athletic and skill at various games. To me, the piece de resistance that year was the act offered by Captain E. B. H. Schneider and his five sons of Galveston, who performed some of the most brilliant and hazardous feats I have ever witnessed on horizontal bars, flying trapeze, parallel bars and swinging rings. The father would lead out, followed by the respective sons in turn and the principal standing by to protect the younger sons from accident. I witnessed Captain Schneider, at his then age of seventy-one, perform the marvelous back-swing from

101

one aerial swing to another, with the ease, accuracy and agility of a young man of twenty, a feat regarded so hazardous by performers of today that, I am told, none of the performers in the greater circuses of this period ever undertake it.

Captain Schneider was not only a trained athlete and acrobat but also one of the most effective disciplinarians and drill-masters I have ever known. His courage was dauntless and carried him always into the thickest of the fight. I recall in the Battle of Galveston, when he was firing the cannon on the "Cotton-clad" Bayou City, one of his gunners removed his thumb from the vent, causing a premature explosion that resulted in severe injury to one of Captain Schneider's eyes. The effect of this injury was apparent for many years afterwards. He will also be remembered by those who knew him as Tax Assessor and Collector of Harris County for some fifteen years.

As Captain of the Turner Rifles, he would drill and march his company for hours at a time. I recall an instance when the company left the hall to drill on San Jacinto Street; they passed north to where the Schumacher Building now stands; Captain Schneider gave the command "Forward" just as the troops reached the bayou and without a moment's hesitation the entire company plunged into the waters and undertook to swim across. With the exception of one man they arrived at the opposite bank; this one man was unable to swim and drowned. If this had been known he would not have been required to undertake the feat. (The bayou of that day was not polluted with oil and unclean waste but was clear and fresh, being fed amply by numerous springs above the city.)

Another interesting character of the Turner Rifles was Louis Mueller, skilled in gunsmithing and the use of explosives. He was drafted from the local military unit by the Confederate Government and placed in charge of the manufacture of a very effective type of percussion cap created by his inventive genius.

Other early members of the Turnverein whose names are outstanding in the industrial development of Houston, were Henry Schulte and Peter Gable, both of whom engaged in the brewery business and whose products were known throughout the state. The astute and honored Jacob Binz, not to be outdone by these distinguished brewmiesters, addressed himself to the gathering of the wild mustang grapes, muscatels, etc., and being without barrels and kegs for his vinuous products, established a barrel and cooperage factory.

102

No story of the early days of the Turnverein would be complete without reference to the "annual celebrations" of the organization. Over a long time these were outstanding events. Many could not afford to close all day but each made an effort to be at the evening's program.

At break of day, the Turner flag was raised on top of the building, the band played the national anthem, and the old cannon was carried to the banks of the bayou where salutes were fired. At eighty-thirty o'clock the military commenced their program. The command "Fall in" was given; they were marched several times around the hall, put through their drills and then faced in single file toward the athletic equipment. Here each member of the company went through the particular act in which he excelled. I recall that my contribution had to do with the rapid scaling of a swinging ladder; an act that I performed in those days with cat-like ease, but that I would scarcely relish at my present age.

After so vigorous a program, we were delighted at noon to sit down at the annual stag-feast, a meal that left nothing to be desired. For a week the hunters would scour the woods and prairie for the choicest game to be had. It was not unusual to see upon the heavy laden board a wild black bear, sixteen point buck, wild turkeys, squirrels, o'possums and rabbits. Too, there were several roast pigs with apples in their mouths. The salads, pies and cakes were prepared ahead of time by the members' wives. Tax on imported wines was slight and the table presented a array of German wines, sparkling Burgundy, Moselle, Mumm's and Louis Roeders, sufficient to warm the cockles of the heart of a connoisseur.

Outside in the "garden" the members dined al fresco amidst rose and grape arbors and the wisteria vines that grew in abundance. Occasionally one would observe three and four generations of a given family at one of the tables. Wines flowed freely, folk-songs of the fatherland were sung, while the younger children performed the rustic dances of the old country.

The Balls that brought a close to the day's celebration were brilliant and colorful affairs. Beautiful women, in satin, silks and velvets. True enough, all did not possess these luxuries of dress, for as the wife of one member told me, many of the wives would meet for nights previous and create their tarleton dresses by candlelight and oil lamp and under the soft lights of candelabra in the hall, these dresses

103

shone with a brilliance that suffered little by comparison with the more expensive garbs.

The suppers at these annual dances were another outstanding feature; I have never seen more appetizing delicacies nor more delicious wines.

THE HOUSTON COTTON EXCHANGE

It was in the spring of 1883, that a small group of men, many of them already gray-bearded, was seated in rickety chairs drawn up around two small wooden tables in the small dingy old room located in a building at Main Street and Franklin Avenue, the site now occupied by the handsome and imposing structure of the Houston National Bank.

The group of men gathered there were reviewing the blackboards on which cotton quotations and the like were being chalked up as the wires came in.

Providence had been kind to the cotton fraternity the previous season by proffering to Texas the big bumper crop and the largest per acre ever known, or perhaps that ever will be made, as the virgin soil found by Stephen F. Austin is long since gone. According to Shepperdson's, the only statistician at that time, the estimated yield was placed at between nine-sixteenths and five-eights of a bale per acre, total acreage and crop considered, a monster crop. The total crop was seven million bales compared to five million four hundred thousand a year previous.

Every compress in the city was blocked; every warehouse, all empty lots on the North Side from Houston Avenue to the I. and G. N. bridge were filled with cotton.

The large firm of Inman and Company of Atlanta had established itself during the season and was the largest buyer in the state, purchasing heavily in the interior from merchants on daily limits, a method of purchasing cotton then only recently introduced.

H. W. Garrow and Company was also a heavy buyer and spinners from all over the East had their headquarters here as did the Greek house of Ralli Brothers and representatives of large European buyers, all of them attracted by the magnificent staple produced. A staple of one and one-eighth was common; and one-fourth plentiful, and there was some staple to be had of one and five-sixteenth to one and three-eights inch.

It had been an excellent year, everyone had made money. Spirits were running high among the little group gathered around the two tables. It was market closing time, and the conversation veered to other topics of interest.

Presently, in the course of the discussion, the suggestion was offered that Houston should have a regularly established Cotton Exchange and Board of Trade, and then and there the foundation of the present Houston Cotton Exchange was laid.

Subsequently to the calling of one or two preliminary meetings committees were appointed to work out the details and to select a site and plans for the proposed structure.

Milby and Porter had just completed a building where R. M. Gordon and Company are now located, at Travis Street and Franklin Avenue. Mr. R. M. Porter was a member of the committee in charge and the members authorized him to secure the site on the southwest corner of Travis and Franklin, part of the Joseph F. Meyer estate.

Eugene Heiner, a leading architect, planned the red-faced Philadelphia brick, with white coping and trimming that stands to this day a monument to the enterprise of those early day founders, and to the greatest of Houston fifty-three years ago.

It was, in fact, the city's first sky-scraper, the Binz Building at Texas and Main streets being constructed some four years later.

Recently, the original Cotton Exchange Building was cleaned with electric brushes and remodeled throughout as a modern up-to-date office building. With its excellence of construction and simplicity of architectural design, it will be modern fifty-three years hence.

The formal opening of the old Cotton Exchange was an elaborate and festive affair. At the house warming, the debutantes of that day were entertained with a magnificent Ball given on the floor of the Exchange. Music was hidden in the balcony, behind palms, the walls and columns being beautifully decorated with flowers and vines. Dancing continued until after midnight, when supper was served. It was an elaborate spread.

Eugene Bremond, son of the railroad king, Paul Bremond, opened an excellent cafe in the basement. The cuisine was wonderful, all wild fowl, turkey, venison and so forth, being brought in from the woods. Champagne corks popped freely, for these were the days and the land of plenty.

It would require a more facile pen and mind to describe effectively the bustle and activity of those days. Cotton was arriving from all over the state and from western Louisiana by rail, small sailing vessels and small steamboats of light draft brought in from the rivers. Hundreds of long-tailed drays, mule teams and even ox teams could be seen everywhere. Caravans often of a hundred to one hundred and twenty-five covered wagons came from Austin, Grimes, Montgomery and other outlaying counties.

W. L. Macatee, H. D. Taylor and Sons, Ziegler's Warehouse and the Allen warehouses remained open day and night, free of charge to the farmers and incoming wagons, thus affording them a convenient camping ground. At that time the covered wagon trade was one of Houston's chief sources of revenue. Teaming was carried on extensively even after the Southern Pacific and H. and T. C. railroads were built.

In bad weather it often required four to five days for the farmers to make the trip by team from the adjacent counties. Wagons came, however, from the Red River, north Texas and the western section of the state.

It was often asked what was Houston's trade territory.

"As far as Albuquerque, New Mexico, all along the string of Forts from Brownsville to the Panhandle and Indian territory," was the fitting answer.

Not only was cotton brought in, but also tallow and beeswax, these being the general substitutes used then for kerosene that came later on. There were large shipments of wool, hides, Spanish moss and similar commodities that came into Houston in exchange for bacon, bagging and ties, staple groceries, dry goods and other merchandise for the home and farm.

The Inmans built a large press in Houston that year, John W. Sander's father, a partner in the firm, coming from Atlanta to supervise it. Other compress companies were quickly formed and a building boom got under way. Houston had cast off its swaddling clothes and was recognized as the coming inland cotton market of the world.

The activity and prosperity continued over a long period of years, culminating with Houston's recognition as the paramount cotton market in the country. Larger crops have been produced and brought in a growing harvest of gold in return for our white staple, creating at the same time profitable employment for many thousands in the various allied lines and along the route to foreign markets.

For the nonce, King Cotton's crown is "badly bent." At the present all eyes are on Congress in the hope that it will eventually afford the South relief from the unhappy status of the cotton industry of the past few years, and that they will bring back to us the sound and profitable fundamentals of which our fathers and grandfathers made use of to wide advantage.

THE EVOLUTION OF HOUSTON

Interesting Sidelights on its Growth from Coastal Village to Cosmopolitan City

The tiny little map of the original plat of Houston, as made by Surveyor Borden for the Allen brothers, founders of Houston, was a crude and small affair, compared with present day maps of the city that show all the subsequent additions.

That primitive map indicated Prairie Avenue as the southern boundary line of the village. Beyond that was all that the name implied, a rolling prairie and Prairie Avenue was so named accordingly.

Very old-timers will recall particular locations on the vast expanse beyond Prairie Avenue that were designated by the names of "Oates Prairie," "McClure's Prairie" and the like. The great prairie, dotted here and there by low-lying swamps, extended to the Galveston County line. As a whole, it was unbroken by trees and scarce a house appeared on the landscape in the outlying territory.

Houston lay dormant for a great many years before any additions were made to the town. Perhaps the first additions of any consequence were the Sydnor and Foster additions on the North Side of Buffalo Bayou. Primarily, however, these two additions were, in fact, more the basis of a lottery scheme of that period, rather than any undertaking in the way of real estate venture on the part of those promoting them.

The first great impetus in the city's growth came with the monster cotton crop year of 1882-83; the same year in which the great Inman cotton interests of Atlanta were attracted to Houston because of its outstanding importance as a cotton center. The city at that time was practically "smothered" with cotton. Every vacant lot from, approximately, Houston Avenue to Hill Street was covered with baled cotton. Railroad yards stood congested with cotton traffic awaiting space in which to unload. New warehouses, compresses and oil mills were built and many new domestic and foreign cotton firms opened important agencies in the city. This created in turn an influx of new residents, with a corresponding increase in the demand for houses and housing facilities.

Thus it was that Houston experienced its first real growing pains. There was no "boom" at this time; just a steady, substantial spreading out of the residential and a portion of the business district.

Houston suffered its first real "boom" a trifle later and there are a number of our residents yet living who will recall vividly the wild days of that period. The cyclonic trading in real estate began first in Galveston, then adjoined to Houston for a similar orgy here.

In the years 1886-88, Galveston obtained one of the largest deep water appropriations that Congress had, up to that time, awarded six million eight hundred thousand dollars. A concerted drive was made by delegates from Galveston, Houston, Denver, Omaha, Kansas City, Wichita and other inland, midwestern cities for an outlet to the sea through Houston and Galveston. The late Presley K. Ewing of Houston, traveled these mid-western and northern cities and with a silver-tongued oratory unparalleled at the time, enlisted their active cooperation. The result was that Congress appropriated the above amount for deep-water improvements at Galveston. Galveston and Houston drew world-wide attention.

Almost immediately there swarmed to Galveston the countless number of land-grabbers and real estate promoters who had infested and brought about booms in the same cities above mentioned. Their bubbles there having burst, they now sought greener fields. Under their Aladdin-like touch, property and real estate values in Galveston soared over night to figures unbelievable. Millionaires were made on paper until, as one enterprising firm, Cash and Luckel, expressed it via circular, "Come to Galveston!" "Millionaires are so common upon the street that no longer does one pay them any attention." L. C. Luckel now lives in Houston. Values in Galveston doubled and trebled and the wild scramble went on. Alas! when the boom burst, many native Galvestonians received a severe drubbing financially. They took back many millions of dollars worth of homes and vacant lots on which only one-fourth or perhaps one-third or a half had been paid.

Houston's turn came next. Practically the same crowd of imported "magicians" applied the same tactics here in Houston and, if possible, with even greater effect than in Galveston. They caught Houston perhaps at its lowest ebb, consequently, the contrast between the two extremes appeared greater. Houston had just experienced the failure of the old City Bank and the Houston Savings Bank; a great many of the merchants and citizens had been caught in their failure; business was more or less at a standstill and property values at rock-bottom. I recall one prominent home in the down town section, having commodious grounds and the house alone costing eight thousand dollars to build, that sold for a pittance of two thousand and five hundred dollars; nor was its owner particularly pushed for money.

I recall nothing in the life and progress of Houston since that time, comparable to the boom that followed. Vacant down-town offices were filled to overflowing by rental and sales-agents and their patrons. Every vacant lot was placarded with signs bearing the legends, "For Sale," "For Lease" or "Sold." The newspapers were loaded with advertising of a promotional nature and the mails swamped with sales literature calculated to catch the eye and hold the mind. Transactions, sales and re-sales were so numerous that the County Clerk and his two assistants became hopelessly overwhelmed with recordation of instruments; meanwhile, values skyrocketed anywhere from one hundred to five hundred per cent. Ten-acre plots in the outlying environs of the city were purchased, sub-divided into lots and resold. I recall one instance of this kind where the original purchaser bought one of these plots for one thousand and seven hundred dollars. That plot rapidly passed through several hands and finally sold for a total of seventeen thousand dollars before the first purchaser had received his recorded deed from the County Clerk's office. There were many other transactions equally fantastic.

Hacks, buggies and other conveyances were at a premium, insufficient to show prospective purchasers over the city, so great was the influx of speculators. Men, women, old and young, bought and sold like mad. Then the bubble burst, liquidations were rampant and those holding pyramided equities saw their dreams of wealth collapse. As in Galveston, original owners took back hundreds of properties on which only partial payments had been made. Of course, in many instances where brick and mortar had gone upon downtown lots, the transactions were carried through and the new owners held the sack, for several years.

Time marched on and with it came Houston's first addition of prominence, Houston Heights, a separate municipality in itself. Founded by O. M. Carter, a newcomer from Omaha, Nebraska, he supplemented it by purchasing the several mule-car lines in the city, consolidating them, converting the whole into an electrifed system and extended the lines to the boundaries of the Heights.

The old Fair Grounds, comprising some one hundred and forty-five acres, beginning on McGowan Street, was sold, subdivided and eventually created further additions to the city: Fairview, Westmoreland and Hyde Park.

Meanwhile, the I. and G. N. road, desiring to expand, took the smiling Horace Booth into the confidence of their plans. They had purchased the Magnolia Park Railroad and now, through Mr. Booth, proceeded to buy up a great portion of the property in and around Quality Hill, Houston's original residential section of the socially elite. Edward Larendon had bought the old Smith Block; brick structures had been erected and preparations made for permanent business. When it was suddenly made public that the I. and G. N. planned to cross Main Street and connect with the Magnolia Brewery, located on the north side of Buffalo Bayou, an application was filed with the city council for franchise to construct a track in Commerce Street to cover this extension, but the city council refused to permit them to go any farther than the east side of Main Street.

The plan resulted, however, in the removal of many residents from the eastern portion of the city affected by the above and a new area of residential section comprising some forty blocks came to life east of Austin Street and out as far as St. Emanuel Street.

Once again the railroads proved an impetus to city-building. The Rock Island Frisco merged and cast longing eyes upon a portion of the new section. They brought to Houston one of their leading attorneys and land-men, Edward Lazuras from St. Louis. Locating at one of the local hotels, he quietly went about getting options and titles on a great section of the residence section of the city, involving Prairie,

Preston and Texas avenues, beginning on the west of Crawford and extending many blocks eastward. It took several years to complete these transactions and when the announcement was made of the completed purchase, Houston was amazed. Again it was believed that the railroads would push forward to Main Street. This, however, was not the intent and the Rock Island, stopping at Crawford, built their new depot. In justice to the Rock Island interests, it should be offered in passing that original property owners in that section fared splendidly in point of profit. I recall in connection a curiously interesting example: L. F. DeLesdernier, father of our present John DeLesdernier, Mrs. Thurman Adkins and Mrs. M. B. Carr, traded a small boat-load, comprising about two tons, of hay for the quarter block of Prairie and Jackson streets (about where one enters the gates of the station now), built their home and was paid by the railroad approximately thirty thousand dollars for the property.

This move on the part of the Rock Island again caused expansion in Houston's residential area. Homes began to dot the section beyond McGowan Street, spreading to the south and west. It was further stimulated by the advent of the Gulf, Colorado and Santa Fe, as this road tapped into Houston from its line at Alvin. Meanwhile the Missouri, Kansas and Texas built into Houston from Smithville via the Fifth Ward. The growth and expansion that followed these various factors caused Houston at times to resemble a city on wheels, so great was the movement of cherished homes from one section of the city to the other. Main and other principal streets were frequently blocked by homes en route to other parts of the city.

Houston experienced another period of stimulating growth immediately following the great Galveston storm in 1900, when some ten thousand inhabitants of that city and nearby coastal regions moved to Houston. Later, however, many Galvestonians returned there, helping to build that city to its now greatest population.

Long before this the downtown business section had begun to expand and subsequential office buildings made their appearance, even if cautiously so. I recall that when Jacob Binz built Houston's first sky-scraper at its present location, there were many pessimists who proclaimed loudly that Mr. Binz needed a "guardian" and would never find tenants to fill it. That such pessimists are always with us is reflected

111

upon again in the comments made S. F. Carter who built the present Second National Bank Building at Main and Rusk streets; they proclaimed just as vehemently that Mr. Carter needed a "guardian" and wouldn't fill the building within forty years. Only a few years later, it was necessary to increase its height by six stories in order to supply demand for office space. Recently Mr. Vandervoort told the writer that the building was one hundred per cent occupied and a long list in waiting.

Prior to the above came Houston's first exclusive residential addition of note, Courtland Place, guarded by an imposing entrance that opened a beautiful esplanade. Flanking either side of the tarvia street were spacious homesites, splendidly landscaped and shrubbed. Here the "old guard" of Houston enshrined themselves in the magnificent homes of that period and built a high brick wall across the far end of their beautiful lane, that it might not become a thoroughfare. Commercial vehicles were permitted only in the rear alleys. Thus it remained for some years until Mayor Baldwin Rice's umbrage and openly decreed that "No set of men in Houston are big enough to wall themselves in, to the exclusion of all natural traffic." The barrier was removed, opening traffic into the now Montrose section and an ordinance passed requiring that future additions to the city of Houston conform to civic arrangements. If, as its long-time Mayor, Baldwin Rice demanded much of the city, he also gave much. His palatial yacht of that period, the "Zeeland," maintained at his personal expense, served as host on many occasions to national and state dignitaries whose influences were needed and obtained, on behalf of Houston and its deepwater project.

By this time a program of city expansion was under way in all directions. On the east, Magnolia Park, Central Park, Eastwood and Forest Hill additions came into being, under the guidance of J. R. Cheek, F. W. Vaughan and other enterprising developers. J. W. Link and H. B. Jackson, moving to Houston from Orange, Texas, opened the beautiful Montrose section in the southwest portion of the city. On the north side, an equal number of smaller residential areas were developed; the splendid homes pushed farther south on Main and adjoining streets until progress was stopped by the "Hump" of the Southern Pacific Railroads running from Eureka to Blodgett Station. Their roadbed, some eight to ten feet higher at points than the surrounding land and with

The Southern Pacific Crossing Buffalo Bayou in An Early Day

but few culverts, hemmed in the city as with a wall. When heavy downpours of rain occurred, water accumulated in that section of the city to the depths ranging from four to six feet. Finally, sufficient pressure was brought to bear upon the railroad to cause abandonment of this line and lowering of the grade to street levels. The surrounding terrain thus drained, the new additions of Riverside, Washington Terrace, Southmore, Braeswood and others came into being.

Meanwhile, the Hogg Brothers interests and their associates, after spending hundreds of thousands of dollars upon its arrangements and beautification, placed River Oaks, Houston's finest residential area, upon the market. It arrived, apparently, just in time and has filled rapidly.

Jesse H. Jones, coming to Houston from Dallas, Texas, as a youngster about the close of the last century, had much to do with the constructive accomplishment of Houston. He engaged first under the direction of his uncle, our then lumber-king, M. T. Jones. Alert and enterprising that he was, it was not long before he engaged in his own behalf, leasing Bremond Square, early playground of Houston's older citizens; he covered the entire block, fronting Main Street between McKinney and Lamar avenues, with the Jesse H. Jones Lumber Company. Subsequently, under his guidance, this area, Southmore, and other equally prominent additions hav-block. Meanwhile, he undertook and in due course executed a building program for the downtown business district that included the Rice Hotel and annex, the Gulf Building and many similar edifices. Nor did he neglect the residential area, Southmore and other equally prominent additions having been financed through his various subsidiaries.

Tribute as above also should be accorded to the trustees of Rice Institute. Through timely loans and leases, the many millions of that institution have from the first been employed in the commercial and residential upbuilding of Houston. They have wrought right well, indeed, their part in bringing Houston to the forefront.

Nor would any history of Houston's evolution be complete without acknowledgment of the active part therein played by Houston's "father of Texas Lumber Industry," the now venerable John Henry Kirby. Coming to Houston in 1890 from the practice of law at Woodville, Texas, Mr. Kirby actively identified himself with the city's progress. In due course, he purchased the old Stevens Dairy farm, situated at the head of Main Street where Alabama now crosses and

113

where Main Street then came to an abrupt end. This he subdivided into city lots, provided graveled streets and drainage ditches and sold off under the name of Kirby's Main Street Addition. It was one of the first substantial additions to Houston and advanced Main Street to Bray's Bayou. Busy intersection that Main and Alabama now is, one would scarce think of it as once a pastoral scene.

Important, of course, in the development of Houston, has been the facilities provided by Houston's ship channel, concerning which the late Will Rogers remarked, "Houston had the nerve to dig a ditch and bring the sea to its door." It was definitely made possible by creation of a navigation district in which both city and county joined and matching the millions supplied by the United States Government with other millions raised at home. Its completion to present status has been the means of bringing to Houston countless great firms, including the largest cotton concerns in the world, Anderson, Clayton and Company, George H. McFadden and Brothers and others of equal note. As result, the largest cotton terminals in the world have been created at Houston.

It has been my privilege to witness the growth of Houston from a village of eleven thousand souls, mud-bog streets and mule-car lines to its present modern structure and metropolitan area. The outlying subdivisions are now encroaching upon the Galveston, Brazoria and Fort Bend County lines; the end is not yet. I look to find in Houston within the next five to seven years, a magnificent city of half a million people and were I to tarry among you for another quarter-century, doubtless I should then be numbered among Houston's "other million."

A VISIT TO AN EARLY DAY RIVER BOTTOM PLANTATION

I stood long, contemplating the charming picture before me, thousands of acres of rich, alluvial land, more productive than those of the headwaters of the Nile. Stephen F. Austin had found that the land surrounding the spot where I now stood, carried a deposit of from five to seven feet of alluvial soil that would require no fertilizer for centuries to come.

It was near where Sugarland is now located, the plantation I had come to visit being located on Oyster Creek and extending to the Brazos River, owned at that time by Samuel Gordon. It is now more than forty years ago that I made the trip.

Before me was cotton, corn, sugar-cane, as far as the eye could see in the given direction. In another section of the plantation baron's domain immense herds of cattle were feeding. How different the sight there from any of the rural scenes with which my eyes had been familiar before. How entirely different were the methods and systems employed there from those prevailing in the regions where I had lived.

At one moment I was struck with surprise at the vast amount of land under the care of a single proprietor and apparently, the comparatively few human hands required to perform the needed labor.

On one hand lay the cotton and corn fields and near the manor, the vegetable and home-garden, while farther on lay the seemingly boundless prairie, dotted here and there with its numerous "islands" of timber. Among these roamed a particularly choice herd of some six hundred head of mine host's cattle, well fed, active and vigorous.

Along the road toward the manor, my host suggested, "Ride through the furrow and let me see if I can see the top of my buggy." I turned aside in the light buggy and entered the furrow. The cane was fifteen feet high and I was lost to his view. The cotton grew to five or six feet high and even higher in places, yet was literally covered with bolls; corn waved its tassels eight and ten feet above the earth.

We turned back to the road and proceeded toward the manor, a magnificent structure of choice brick, and even the sugar-mill, ginhouse and the many cabins of the servants quarters were of brick.

115

The front of the manor was a thing of beauty in itself; broad lawns on which, here and there, rested pieces of statuary, brightly colored shrubs and the whole surrounded by long beds in which brilliantly colored flowers were massed.

The manor house was, of course, colonial in style, and alighting at the veranda, I discovered as we approached the door that the entrance was a duplicate of a colonial entrance planned by Thomas Jefferson when he was a young architect and which years before I had seen in Virginia.

At the door I was greeted by the charming hostess, the Lady of the plantation, who ushered us into a commodious living room, brought to a proper degree of warmth by a large fireplace on which glowed four or five great logs. The mantel surmounting it was of broad dimension and of beautifully carved marble. The room itself was furnished with solid mahogany furniture of massive proportion as befitted the size of the place. Over the door of the living room, I noted with interest the old Kentucky long-barrel rifle that rested upon the horns of two antlers. On other portions of the wall hung artistic paintings and likenesses, one in oil, of the family ancestry.

Presently, the noon meal, dinner, as it was then called (doubtless because it was entirely too bonteous a repast for a lunch) was announced by tolling of the great bells outside that gave forth paens of wonderful tone capable of being heard on a clear morning, I was told, for a distance of some five miles. It was related to me by the master of the house, in touching upon the history of these bells, that they had been cast in Philadelphia. The original owner of the plantation had attended the casting in person and dropped therein fifty Mexican silver dollars for the purpose of enhancing the tonal qualities of the completed bells.

Seated around the large mahogany dining table, the lord of the manor offered grace, such being customary at all plantation homes and at all meals. The dinner, splendidly prepared, by a "black mammy," was served by her in dishes of silver and delicate china. The thought came to me that the woods and the prairie, as well as, the home garden, had been called upon for all the delicacies of rare game and palatable products they would provide and, truly, that good natured black mammy must have been a past mistress in the art of cuisine, so great was the appeal to the appetite of the dishes she provided. My mind turned for the moment back to the "black coffee, bacon, corn bread and molasses" in which

I had indulged in so many occasions at the smaller, tenant farms and I could not but rejoice that I was dining on the larger estate. When the time came for it, our coffee was served on the veranda, accompanied by rich, double-cream and what an aromatic and stimulating delight it proved to be. Sitting there, quaffing my cup, there came to me an incongruity that had occurred only a short time previously; I was on a visit to a large ranch-farm. Coffee had been served and the servant inquired, "Will you have cream in your coffee?" I acquiesed and much to my amazement she brought forth a can of Borden's condensed milk. That was her idea of cream, notwithstanding, that the ranch contained four or five thousand head of cattle. Somehow, it seemed to me a total loss, when gallons of cream might have been had right at hand for the mere taking of it.

After the dinner and the serving of coffee, the host provided me with an excellent mount and the two of us rode over the vast estate, observing the cattle, the various crops and the work going on in the fields.

At sundown we returned to the house and partook of the evening meal. Subsequently, we occupied large easy chairs in the living room and discussed, before the open fire, the leading topics of the day, while some of the younger members of the family turned for diversion to a splendid library contained in the bookcases around the room. Looking over this later, I was pleased to note such volumes as Pope, Shelley, Shakespeare and other classics.

Shortly, there appeared before us a darky with his banjo, accompanied by a male quartet from among the field hands and a number of young pickaninnies. They rendered for us a number of old southern melodies and Negro spirituals and the youngsters performed, most commendably, as tap-dancers. A male quartet with plantation songs followed.

The hour growing late, we eventually retired. The bedrooms were large and airy. My own couch turned out to be a haven of repose and comfort. It was one of those magnificent specimens of old-timy beds, four-posters and canopy with drapery, a fine old feather mattress with overcovering of wool and silk. I slept wonderfully and was reluctant to answer call early the next morning, even for a most excellent breakfast. Even more reluctant was I, shortly afterwards, to bid my host a cordial farewell, to return home with the memory of one of the most enjoyable twenty-four hours my life had known.

PART TWO

TALES OF THE COAST COUNTRY

FAMED JEWEL OF MARY STUART, QUEEN OF SCOTS, LOCATED IN HOUSTON BY JESSE A. ZIEGLER

The much discussed and historically famous black diamond once owned and worn by Mary Stuart, Queen of the Scots, during her reign from 1553 to 1558; a reign terminating when she was beheaded by the virgin Queen Elizabeth of England, has come to light in Houston. It has rested in the safety deposit vaults of one of the Houston banks and for nearly two decades has been the property of one of Houston's most charming matrons.

December the twenty-seventh, 1936, I received from Charles J. Phillips, prominent attorney in Houston, who had read one of my articles in the paper about General Nichols' son, Frank Nichols, once Lord Stewart, a most interesting expression concerning the stone. Before quoting from Mr. Phillips' letter, however, it is proper to digress for a moment to relate somewhat of how the famous diamond came to America, paused for a long period of years in Galveston, and then found its way to Houston.

The story properly begins with a reference to the interesting career of General E. B. Nichols, a veteran of the Mexican War, and for many years a most distinguished citizen of Galveston and Houston. When the War Between the States broke out, he severed his connection with William Marsh Rice, for whom he materially assisted in laying the latter's great fortune that eventually made possible the present Rice Institute in Houston, and organized a Southern regiment. General Nichols served under General G. Bankhead Magruder, in the recapture of Galveston and after the war, among other ventures, he turned his energies toward railroad building, and in conjunction with William Marsh Rice, Colonel Tom Pierce and others, promoted the building of the Southern Pacific Railroad.

It was through these activities that General Nichols came to be a close friend of Lord Stewart of England, and later consigned to him his son Frank, that the latter might be educated in England. Lord Stewart, favorably impressed with Frank Nichols, placed him in Oxford University, and treated him in all respects as a son. In fact, having no issue of his own, Lord Stewart finally adopted Frank Nichols and made him his legal heir. Eventually, the senior Lord Stewart died, leaving his possessions and title to Frank Nichols.

121

On a subsequent return to Houston, the young Lord Stewart met and married Miss Ella Hutchins, beautiful and charming daughter of the distinguished Houston pioneer, William J. Hutchins, for many years proprietor of the famed Hutchins House, located where the Southern Pacific Building now stands. Their wedding was one of the most elaborate affairs ever held in Houston, and of international import at the time. The union resulted unhappily, however, and the young bride did not return to England with her husband. She later became the wife of Seabrook Sydnor of Houston, accomplished much in behalf of the city both in her club work and commercial (real estate) activities, and, with her brother, the late Spencer Hutchins, Ward McAllister of Houston in his day, enjoyed an immense social popularity.

Upon the return to England of the young Lord Stewart, the English parliament decreed that no alien, even through adoption, could inherit either the estate or the title of the late senior Lord Stewart. Shorn of the inheritance, Frank Nichols scorned the honorary title accorded him by his friends, requesting that he be known only as Frank Nichols, and returned to make his home in Galveston. He brought with him from the personal effects of the late Lord Stewart only such family plate, jewels, etc., has had been willed directly to him. Among these was the famous black diamond ring, once the possession of Mary, Queen of Scots, herself a Stuart. The ring had passed down consecutively through the family line to the late Lord Stewart, however, the spelling of the name had meanwhile, through succeeding generations, been changed.

Reverting now to the letter from Mr. Phillips: he relates, in part, how he knew Frank Nichols intimately from about 1906 to 1915, when, subsequent to the Galveston storm of that year, Mr. Phillips moved to Houston. The two of them had resided for an extended period at the same Galveston hotel. In their conversations, Frank Nichols had often dwelt upon the years spent in England, his education there, and considerable of the story concerning the famous black diamond and other jewels he had brought back to Galveston with him. Mr. Phillips states that Mr. Nichols was then a man of about sixty years, very polished in manner, affecting the broad "H" of the Oxfordites, and, as a rule, dressing immaculately, largely after the Oscar Wilde fashion of that day. He tells also of how Frank Nichols often wore the black diamond, related its history on various occasions, and now

122

and then placed it upon the finger of a friendly admirer. Mr. Phillips described the stone exactly as I had remembered it from my early days, although nearly sixty years must have elapsed since I last saw it. It was a peculiarly cut stone, coming to an apex on top, possibly after the fashion of diamond cutting of that period. My recollection of the story accompanying it is that its cutting was not altered after it left the possession of Mary, Queen of Scots, now nearly four centuries ago. In keeping with its rare and unusual color, black, it was set in a mounting of black that appeared to me to be a fine quality of onyx. Mr. Phillips' impression was that the stone weighed some two karats. I believe, however, that if removed from its mounting and weighed, it would be found to exceed that estimate. Most assuredly, it has the appearance of being very deep.

Mr. Phillips, like myself, did not know what finally had become of the stone. He believed that its present whereabouts might be ascertained by tracing through mutual Galveston friends. There follows, though, what impresses me as a strange coincidence, and brings to this story the desired climax.

There are many who firmly believe in mental telepathy. I do not know. It has been my pleasure to contemplate such things without having arrived at any definite conclusion. Personally, I have witnessed in the course of a long career, many profoundly interesting incidents of that nature. Be that as it may, it was by mere chance that, immediately after receipt of Mr. Phillips' letter, I had the delightful pleasure of meeting one of my former friends of old Galveston days, Mrs. Alfred D. Smith, now a resident of Houston, and wife of the late distinguished pioneer bar pilot of that name. Mrs. Smith exclaimed that she had greatly enjoyed reading my article on General Nichols and his family, and was particularly interested in my reference to the Mary Stuart black diamond. "I know," she continued, "that you will be happy to learn that I am the proud possessor of the ring, and that for these many years it has been locked away in the safety deposit vault of my bank. I shall arrange for you to have a look at it."

I accepted an invitation to call at her home later; and there, after the lapse of nearly sixty years, it was my pleasure to gaze again upon the famous black diamond that once adorned the charming hand of a gracious queen. Upon each side of the mounting was emblazoned a shield, the portent

123

for which I know not. Inside, in microscopic letters, appears the legend placed there in subsequent years: "To the memory of Sir W. W. Stewart, age seventy-five, August twenty-eighth, 1735."

It appears that Captain Smith, late husband of Mrs. Smith and a boyhood friend of mine, later became a close friend of Frank Nichols. He had, at the urgent request of Mr. Nichols in his declining years, purchased the ring along with a pair of cuff-links and a handful of other small jewelry at a moderate price, a sum far below the historic and actual value of the black diamond itself. The transaction was effected, however, in the nature of a friendly courtesy to Mr. Nichols. Captain Smith had no use for the jewels, but merely kept them and upon his demise that passed to their present ownership by Mrs. Smith.

Being interested, naturally, in what might be the future of the historic jewel, I inquired of Mrs. Smith, "Now that this treasured relic had again come to light of day, what do you propose to do with it?"

In her characteristic way, she replied, woman-like, "Oh, I don't know; just keep it, I suppose. You know, I never wear it; in fact, I seldom wear jewelry at all."

What a magnificent bauble that ring would be for the gallant Texan suitor of today to bestow upon his prospective queen! Yet, I doubt if the ring would be a fitting gift, as just as I had completed and was preparing to mail the foregoing story to the publishers, the postman brought me a most interesting letter from Mrs. Maude Nichols Benson of Galveston, a niece of the late Frank Nichols, former Lord Stewart. She stated in part (the words being my own) "The black diamond of which you write, was not only the property of Mary, Queen of Scots, but, authoritively, was the last and the only piece of jewelry worn by her to the scaffold when she was beheaded. A most unusual stone, it was set with apex up instead of down. Cousin Reba Gaines, daughter of the late J. S. Brown, understands that the ring is in possession of the widow of Uncle George B. Nichols, who was the main beneficiary of Uncle Stewart's will and did receive much of the jewelry. His widow, however, has long since remarried and we do not know her present name or address. It is through Cousin Reba Gaines that I have been able to obtain the foregoing data concerning the black diamond ring."

There is, of course, no doubt now remaining as to the present whereabouts of the Mary Stuart black diamond, and what an exciting morsel of history it is to know that the last piece of jewelry worn by Mary, Queen of Scots, upon that final eventful occasion, now rests tranquilly in our midst.

WINDSOR-SIMPSON WEDDING BRINGS RECOLLECTIONS OF HOUSTON SHIP CHANNEL

It impresses one as paradoxical to suggest that so romantic an event as the nuptials of Edward, Duke of Windsor, and Wallis Warfield Simpson, has its connecting link with so prosiac a subject as the commercial activities of the Houston ship channel. Yet, it seems to me that all romance, if it proves substantial, must have a practical foundation or background; and even Edward and his bride appear not to have overlooked the necessity of providing for their future financially.

Comtemplating that event, I am reminded of the fact that while we have heard much in the news headlines of the past year of Wallie Simpson, little mention has been made of her very estimable recent husband, Ernest A. Simpson. Fortunately, he is known quite favorably to a number of Houstonians prominent in shipping, cotton and brokerage circles. Without exception, they regard Ernest Simpson as affable, thoroughly constructive in his viewpoint, both as an executive and in his attitude toward life as a whole, and a man who is altogether attractive in point of personality. One hears him spoken of now among his Houston acquaintances as "the London shipping agent," a handsome-appearing man of brunette type, who visited among us several times.

As a matter of fact, the great shipping firm of Simpson, Spence and Young, of which Ernest A. Simpson is now one of the directing heads, is one of the largest ocean traffic concerns in the world, with offices at practically all principal ports. They are one of the pioneer shipping firms specializing in general cargo, and from their early days have taken a direct interest in the activities of the Houston ship channel.

It was my pleasure to meet and come to know the senior member of the firm, Ernest L. Simpson, and father of the present Ernest A. Simpson, when the former visited Houston many years ago in behalf of the firm's interests here. He was then a man of approximately fifty-five years, of quiet and conservative demeanor, but possessed of an air of courtesy and affability that immediately inclined his acquaintances toward him.

It was about 1894 that the firm of Simpson, Spence and Young decided to become active in Texas. They came to Galveston and organized the Texas Transport and Terminal Company. The late Jens Muller was employed at a salary said to be twenty thousand dollars per year to look after the firm's interests. If I remember correctly, their Texas concern was chartered with a capital of two hundred thousand dollars. A few years later, Frederick H. Sage of Galveston was made their local agent and carried on an extensive business, representing also at times the Creole Line and the Hamburg-American Line, the French Line and the Holland Line. The writer served as their local agent in Houston for some fifteen years, until the Company opened an office here.

The senior Simpson was a great believer in Texas, being supported therein by his associate, Frederick H. Sage. It was the latter who saw the great possibilities of Houston as a future inland port and strongly advocated the promotion of the channel, endeavoring meanwhile to influence Mr. Simpson to acquire property at Port Houston that later might be used for wharfage purposes. This Sage, incidentally, was a grand-nephew of the late Russell Sage, and visited here frequently before finally taking up his residence. His summer home was maintained on Clear Lake, near Seabrook.

In 1912, when our Turning Basin was completed, the elder Mr. Simpson, then visiting in New York, came south to visit the firm's offices at Galveston, and also to inspect the Houston ship channel. It was upon his arrival in Galveston, that Mr. Sage phoned me to show Mr. Simpson the Turning Basin, and endeavor to interest him in the future of the infant port. I secured the most pretentious car available in Houston at that time and with other friends carried him to the Turning Basin. There, I exposed to him what the late Will Rogers once characterized as "the ditch that Houston dug to bring the sea to its doors," expatiating as eloquently as I could the vast possibilities of the infant project in years to come. It is true that at the moment, it occurred to me that some of my predictions might be a trifle extravagant. If so, however, it did not for an instant dampen my ardor as an enthusiastic "seller of Houston," and I am sure that I spoke at great length upon the greatness to come of the locality immediately surrounding us. Alas, for Mr.

Simpson's conservative sense of vision; for all of my sales-talk, he did not grasp the same type of future of the project as that of which I spoke. He saw the turning basin only in the raw. There was absolutely nothing in sight but the bare banks of the channel; not a plank, a hut or bulkhead of any kind yet constructed; not five dollars worth of improvements. The only sign of life around us was an old Negro, his mule, blind in one eye, hitched to a small cart, hauling a load of sand. Mr. Simpson was not impressed. I was told later that he had been persuaded into an unsatisfactory real estate investment here before and the "flavor lasted" and he had not forgotten the experience.

Now, compare the desolate scene we looked upon that day as we stood on the banks of the Turning Basin, with its present day status of some two hundred million dollars worth of improvements bordering upon the ship channel, the result of only twenty-five years of intensive growth and cultivation.

As we turned from our inspection of the basin, Mr. Simpson inquired, "Ziegler, if this project is as big in its possibilities as you say, why is it that Houston is not doing something about it?" I was forced to explain that the dredging of the basin had just been completed and that the government had matched dollars with us in a recent bond issue of the Navigation District, and that if he would give us time to make our accomplishments effective, he would see the project I had predicted. I urged that his firm establish themselves here permanently and purchase now, while it was cheap and later use it for wharfage and warehouse purposes. His New Orleans representative, a member of the party talked against this idea and said it would be years before this "dream" would be realized.

Thus it was that the firm of Simpson, Spence and Young made no investment in channel frontage. I believe they would have returned two years later but with the World War coming on, shipping was temporarily at a standstill; however, Daniel Ripley and Company and the Leland Harrison Lines secured concessions and dock privileges at Port Houston, and later the Southern Steamship Lines of Philadelphia secured terminals and existing docks were enlarged and others built.

In 1914 a small brig came up the channel for a cargo of commercial fertilizer. The only dock available was that of the Armour Fertilizer Works on the channel as at that time the docks and sheds of the Turning Basin were filled to overflowing with cases of flying machine parts, war supplies and material of various kind. The brig loaded at that dock and sailed promptly. Nearing destination, it was torpedoed on the west end of the Irish coast. Later, another bark came up the channel, loaded at the same above dock with a cargo of cottonseed cake. It made the voyage safely until they ran afoul a German mine in the British Channel. These were the first solid cargos transported over the Houston Channel after its completion and the shipping firm of Simpson, Spence and Young, who chartered these ships, as well as many other available then in Charleston, Galveston and New Orleans, may be said to have been pioneers in the development of the Houston ship channel. Their headquarters then were in New York, later moved to London. The senior Mr. Simpson is still active in the firm; their Mr. Sage, now since passed away, was always an active supporter of the channel in its infancy. About 1920 he sent the Company's vice-president to me, again for the purposes of interesting the firm in the activities of the channel. Upon visiting the Turning Basin, with its vast improvements of eight years time since Mr. Simpson's visit he exclaimed: "I cannot understand why Mr. Simpson did not visualize what I am seeing today. What a pity your advice was not taken by our firm in 1912 or at least in 1914."

Overtures were made to the firm from time to time to enter Houston. It was necessary in those early days of the channel to go begging, so to speak, for patronage of the channel, whereas now the greater shipping firms are pleased to obtain entrance and facilities at the port. At present there are between ninety-five and one hundred separate shipping lines entering the port, with a patronage last year of over five thousand vessels.

In 1923 the firm of Simpson, Spence and Young decided to come to Houston. It was during one of the boom years, and their representative Mr. S. A. Dunlap found office space in the business district scarcely to be had. They finally obtained the old quarters of the Second National Bank, just vacated at Main and Preston streets. Facilities at the Port were another matter. There was no space to be had at the time, as Ripley and Company and the Leland Harrison Lines had to be accommodated. Eventually a shifting around was accomplished and space allocated to the Simpson, Spence and Young activities, who then brought in the French Line, the

Creole Line and others, as well as many chartered boats. They have continued actively in Houston ever since.

Houston has ample cause to be appreciative of the share of development of its channel by this Company and to hold a more than passing interest in the fact the Ernest A. Simpson succeeds to the present managing interest of his father in the firm.

REMINISCENCES OF A "TENDERFOOT'S" ARRIVAL IN HOUSTON

It is characteristic of the autumn of life that we "Old-Timers of Houston" fall now and then into a reminiscent mood. Who of us but find pleasantly interesting a retrospect of Houston as we knew it more than fifty years ago, when we contemplate the splendid Southern metropolis it now constitutes?

This morning, I sit writing in my office. Outside, it is one of those beautiful, exhilarating spring mornings; a morn of such bright warmth as to cheer the heart even of old Dick Dowling as he looks with disdain upon the loungers of the City Hall Square. Nowhere, I am sure, does Spring come quite so beautifully, so balmy or so inspirational as it does in Houston and its environs. Not to have lived in Houston in the Spring is a failure to have seen Spring at its utmost splendor.

Through my office window, I can gaze over the tops of adjacent buildings to the forks of White Oak. In that region, not far distant, but now environed by the busy marts of commerce, I can spot the erstwhile location of "Old Schneider Swimmin' Hole," one of the seventh heavens of Houston's boyhood of a period now long past. Here it was that they disported themselves throughout the spring and summer with no more raiment than a heavenly smile. Among the habitues of that pool were boys who later became presidents of Houston banks, great merchants, distinguished lawyers, and even international statesmen. I am told that when the eminent E. M. House, power behind the throne in Wilson's administration, and who was born at the corner of Capital and Smith streets, visited Houston shortly after Wilson's inauguration, he and his old boyhood companion, T. C. Dunn, Sr., then guiding official of the Union National Bank,

129

walked over together to revisit the site of the old swimming hole that they had frequented as youngsters. They spent most of the afternoon there. Part of the time, undoubtedly, was spent in reminiscing; but certainly also a portion of the time was devoted to business, as it was not long after that the Union National exhibited a healthy increase in volume of business, occasioned by their appointment as active United States Depository for government funds disbursed in this territory. Forsooth, swimmin' holes have their advantages in business as well as in point of sport!

Back to my office, however, a glance at the calendar reminds me that with the coming of Spring, I shall have been a resident of Houston nearly fifty-five years. As a sprig of a youngster, I had visited here several times some ten or fifteen years before that, and as a young "sand crab" from Galveston, in my boyish way had stood amazed at what I found and saw in the "frontier" town of Houston.

Looking back now upon my final arrival and extended stay here, the first thought that comes to me is that I am glad I came. I doubt very much whether I should have had as much fun, as much excitement, or have been as happy anywhere else, and I am certain that no other people could have been so hospitable and kind, so patient and so long-suffering under trying circumstances, as were the people of this section.

I came to Houston with the harvesting of the great cotton crop of the season of 1882-83. Probably another crop like it, in point of bale-to-acre ratio, will never be had. The virgin soil that produced it no longer exists.

Even then, I had great faith in the town aside from its importance as a growing commercial center. There was "that something" about it that fascinated me. I had come from Galveston, then one of the great cities of Texas; but I longed for the great open spaces and the huge trees. In Galveston we had none of them, and very few flowers. Be it said in justice to my native city of Galveston, however, that they have since materially improved their status in that respect.

I recall distinctly on my first trip by train from Galveston, a young lady on the adjoining seat, as we neared Harrisburg, jumped up and exclaimed, "Oh, look at the beautiful Christmas trees!" I looked through the window and beheld my first sight of a magnificent pine grove, and I agreed with her as to the effect given. Our rapture over the sight was short

130

lived. A merry "Ha! Ha!" arose from a number of other passengers immediately around us. They had been reared among the piney woods of East Texas and looked upon the young lady and myself as "city-slickers" who had never seen the great outdoors.

At the end of a four hour trip, we rolled into what was then known as "Allen's Station," the little depot situated at the east end of Congress Avenue, and alighted. (Note that modern transportation now makes the same trip in approximaely an hour.) There we were by one of Houston's "street cars," a small contraption with six windows, drawn by mules so small that they impressed me as "jack-rabbits." Being anxious to observe the city more leisurely, I scorned the cars and walked up Congress Avenue to the city.

The city council had recently passed a new ordinance requiring property owners to lay sidewalks or suffer confiscation of their property. These sidewalks were made chiefly of a combination of cheap asphaltum or pitch and white clam shell. The pitch, however, could not withstand the hot rays of the sun and often became quite sticky, even to the point of melting and running. To aggravate the condition of the walks, the street-urchins would pick out the clam shells and throw them at the sparrows, blackbirds and turkey-buzzards, the latter apparently the only scavengers the city boasted at the time. In mid-summer it was worth almost the value of a pair of shoes to attempt to traverse these walks.

The day of my arrival, however, there had been a tremendous rain, and I received my baptism in Houston' famous mud. The street was a sea of it, deep, sloppy and tenaciously sticky. I noted that in front of every store and house was a wide block of cement or wood in which was embedded a long, flat strip of iron with a sharpened edge. These were the oldtime mud-scrapers to be used before entering the places. Unused to such at Galveston, and such being the nature of Houston's mud, it required some residence here before I became proficient in the technique of cleaning my shoes upon these scrapers. One could better understand that had he, like myself, been reared, so to speak, upon a sand-pile, and then suddenly transported to a bog containing mud that "sticketh closer than a brother!" Houston's inhabitants, however, were altogether cheerful about the situation. They all avowed that the "splendid rain would make a great crop." In my ignorance, I think I must have wondered at the time

131

whether Houston's population was engaged in the raising of water-lilies

En route to the town proper, I recall a deep gulch, about where Caroline is now, that was called, I believe, Fannin's Creek. It began somewhere south of town and traversing Congress, Franklin and Commerce streets, emptied into the bayou. Near the bottom there was a small footbridge of narrow planks. One scrambled down to this as best he might, there being no descending handrail. I managed the descent fairly well. Crossing, however, and undertaking to ascend the steep embankment of the other side, I almost met my Waterloo. The base was hard clay highly glazed and slickened by the recent rain. One took two steps upward and slid back three, and in the slide backward was peculiarly lucky if he managed to land on his feet. There was a couple of times when I didn't! It was aggravating, too, because in those days we wore tight breeches. Such hazardous lanes of traffic were truly no place for a sand-crab from Galveston, accustomed to flat sandy surfaces.

Finally, as a result of several frantic efforts, I made the grade and was rewarded by coming upon the home of Mrs. Bringhurst, shortly farther on, and her beautiful rose garden. This was at Congress and San Jacinto avenues. It impressed me as one of the most beautiful sights I had ever seen. Roses in fact, flowers of any sort, were extremely rare in Galveston.

I registered that day at the famous old Hutchins House, located where the Southern Pacific building now stands. The trip and walk uptown had increased my appetite immensely. I wanted the good, old stand-by, "ham and eggs," and plenty of them. Strangely enough, there was only one place in town where these could be had on short order. That was at the restaurant of Frank Colby. He had recently opened a place across from the Hutchins House, where the Kentucky Bar now stands at Franklin and Travis streets. The staff consisted of Colby, the veteran waiter, Jack Arto, a cook and a dishwasher. His food and service were excellent, making him a legion of friends; and did I dine? It seemed to me that never were common-place ham and eggs so palatable, nor a cup of steaming coffee quite so delicate and rare. The only other eating places in Houston were the hotels, the depot lunch counter and the boarding houses. Compare that with what must be five thousand or ten thousand eating places of the short order variety that are scattered over Houston and its environs today.

Houston's citizens were hospitable from the start. I received the glad hand immediately from many of its inhabitants. "We are glad you are here. Stay here; you will like it and you will prosper." Their assurances were prophetic: I did stay, I did prosper, and I have always liked it.

It was only shortly afterward that I induced Charles Wolkarte and his brother to sell me a cotton condensing plant at the corner of Liberty and McKee streets, and there I engaged profitably.

Being from early youth an ambitious hunter, I was not long in becoming acquainted with old Captain Dunn, John D. Woolford, Bud Massie—afterward County Clerk of Harris County—Max Yeager, uncle of Leo Hahn of the Houston National Bank, and other local Nimrods. In due course they invited me to attend a hunt with them in the Big Thicket where they were going in search of wild turkey. I had never hunted wild turkey; perhaps even I had never seen a wild turkey in his native haunt. Setting forth, we arrived at Big Eddy in the late afternoon and pitched our camp. As a tent-maker, I was not entitled to the name of "Omar Khayyam" (who, incidentally, was not a tent-maker as his name implies, but an astronomer and mathematician of note, as well as a poet of distinction); therefore, while the rest of the party made camp, I wandered off into the woods. Just as dusk came on, I descried a flock of "wild turkeys" roosting on the dead limbs of what had once been a giant oak. Fixing the spot carefully in mind, I returned to camp, joined my friends at supper and related to Mr. Woolford what I had found. "Good!" he exclaimed. "We'll go after them at sunrise." Approaching the location next morning, he suggested, "Now show me where the turkeys are roosting." I pointed to the flock which were easily seen from that distance in the early morning light. Woolford looked at me in disgusted amazement and exclaimed, "Ziegler, don't you know that wild turkeys never roost on a dead limb. Those are not turkeys. They are turkey-buzzards!"

Convinced that I was no turkey hunter, I undertook during the day to retrieve my signal error by a solitary squirrel hunt. Wandering deep into the woods, I was gone for several hours; and I really did get the squirrels; but attempting to retrace my steps I became hopelessly lost. Realizing it, I wondered from mound to mound, climbing now and then a convenient tree, hoping to recognize in the distance a familiar landmark. Finally, late in the afternoon, giving up all hope of finding my way out of the thicket, I stopped at a small stream and firing both barrels of my gun, followed it by a great "halloa!" as loud as I could scream. To my amazement, Max Yeager's voice sounded within twenty feet of me, "Hey, Ziegler, for cripe's sake—how can I catch any bass with you raising all that hell!" I had wandered in a complete circle and returned directly to camp, but didn't recognize it when approached from the new angle. The tenderfoot had learned that he was no woodsman.

Another time, I left Houston for Duke's Station in Brazoria County, in search of plover and prairie chicken. Luck was with me and when dusk came on I had bagged an ample number of each. The only home in that section at the time was that of Bud Taylor, the sage of Pierce Junction. He received me kindly, as was the custom in those days, and I enjoyed an excellent supper and a good night's rest. The next morning, however, I was determined to go to Fort Bend County for further hunting. The day there was bountiful also and I remained late upon the prairie. As darkness descended I came upon a little white cottage. Riding up to the gate, I called the customary "Halloa." Much to my surprise, when my host came to the door, I discovered that he was a swarthy Mexican. More or less dubious, I had no alternative but to ask for lodging for the night. With an air of cordiality he made me welcome, unhitched my horse, gave him feed, put up my phaeton and set me down to a plain, but very wholesome meal. When bed time came, I placed my shotgun close at hand for safety, as I had often heard that the average Mexican was very treacherous, and had no desire to be stabbed in the back with a knife by my Mexican-herder host. Fatigued from the day's exertions, I slept most soundly. In the morning I was awakened by my host's call to a good breakfast, found my horse and phaeton awaiting me outside, and he politely declined my proffered pay for the accommodation, but did accept a portion from my sack of game. I have never feared Mexicans since then; in fact, in later years I came to have many staunch and loyal friends among the race.

With the present paucity of game in this vicinity, it seems difficult to believe that fifty years ago one could leave the Market Square at two o'clock in the afternoon and return home at dusk with a fine bag of plover, snipe, prairie chicken and the like.

On a further occasion, I had the pleasure of a successful

hunt with Captain D. P. Shepherd, a most interesting character of Houston's earlier days. Commercially, he was one of the most enterprising men I ever knew, reminding me somewhat of the "get-rich-quick-Wallingford" type of the present day. Among other items, he built the first flour mill in Houston, across from the Henke Ice House. Somewhat visionary, yet most of his "dreams" were of constructive nature. It was his purpose to throw dams across Buffalo Bayou, build up the water supply, tap the Brazos River and build locks to assist navigation. A company was formed for that purpose, and it was contemplated also that mill-races would be constructed and water-power utilized for grinding flour and meal and for operation of factories. In brief, he planned a Fall River or New Bedford for Houston. Alas, after he had constructed two dams on Buffalo Bayou (a portion of one of which can yet be seen from the bridge on Shepherd Drive), he found that the state would not permit him to tap the Brazos River, and the entire scheme fell through. Successive floods on the bayou washed away his dams, and there remains only the memory of a once great dream.

Just below that bridge on which Shepherd Drive crosses the bayou, there existed years ago a long bar of very fine, white sand that glistened beautifully in the rays of the afternoon sun. Coming from Galveston, I thought I knew all about sand, and coming upon this bar in the course of an afternoon's tramp through the woods, I stepped boldly out upon it. To my horror, I discovered that I had stepped into quicksand and was sinking rapidly. Happily, my youth on the Pirate Island had taught me a few tricks to be employed against quicksand. Using them all, I managed to flounder out of the mire. At that, I barely escaped with my life, and was certain at one time that I wouldn't.

I recall, too, another occasion on which I hunted squirrels in what is now Houston Heights. After bagging a few, my dog led me to a big, hollow tree, at which he barked furiously. Feeling certain of another squirrel, I leaned over to look closer into the hollow. Instead, I saw ensconced there a beautifully striped cat. At about the same moment, the "cat" started "spraying." Fortunately, both the dog and I jumped to safety in time. Even at that, however, the experience was heartily discouraging for further hunting in that neighborhood, and we returned to Houston. I found out I was no squirrel hunter.

135

In course of time, I bought a two hundred and fifty acre farm south of Stafford's Point, near Oyster Creek. It always impressed me as a beautiful little tract. In fact, I sometimes wonder if the quiet beauty and restful solitude of that little farm is not largely responsible for the splendid centennial that Texas was enabled to celebrate in 1936. The Mexican General Filisola with his three thousand soldiers en route to join Santa Anna, camped there over night, and impressed next morning with the beauty of the place, he tarried. Had he continued on and joined Santa Anna at Harrisburg or Lynchburg, the story of San Jacinto probably would have been far different. Houston and his small, ill-accoutred army might have found the odds far too great for conquests.

Notwithstanding that my regular week-end visits to the farm for purposes of supervision were altogether pleasant occasions, it was never a financial success. The cotton I raised and sold for seven cents a pound, cost me ten cents to produce, and I suspect that every head of cabbage grown thereon reflected a production cost of one dollar. Cotton there grew to enormous heights. I have seen it often at twelve to fourteen feet high. It was a standing joke in those parts that now and then a cotton picker, working from the top of the "tree" had fallen and broken his neck.

Economy was not always the watchword in the operation of these farms and ranches. Just out of Richmond there was a large ranch owned by Captain Dabney Walker. It contained many thousnds acres and was well stocked. Having an excellent breakfast there one morning, I was asked if I would have cream with my coffee. Imagine my amazement when, answering in the affirmative, I was served with condensed milk from a can, and yet there were some forty thousand head of cattle grazing upon the broad acres of that domain.

Another great ranch that old-timers of Houston will recall was the famous Allen Ranch, extending nearly all the way from Harrisburg to the coast. It had its own railroad station on the prairie, and its private boat landing on the bayou. Employing more than a hundred cowboys, it could have formed at least the nucleus of a military company in time of war. The history of that great ranch brings to mind recollections of one of the greatest legal battles in all history. It extended, I believe, over a period of twenty-six or seven years, during the course of which all the principals on both sides passed on. That, however, is another story and for the future.

136

The period of fifty-five years, is not, in itself, such a great span of life, yet, a residence of that period in Houston is quite long enough to have marked many changes in the growth of the little town of some eleven or twelve thousand that I found in Houston. Of those who were here when I came, not many are left. Some have moved away; but nearly all of the middle aged have since passed on. There is scarcely a doctor, lawyer, printer, dentist, blacksmith, baker, undertaker or shoemaker in Houston at present whose shingle hung out when first I came to Houston; and I can count upon my fingers those engaged in mercantile pursuits who still continue under the same firm name. Such are the changes I have seen occur in Houston during the interim . . . But, I am glad I came!

EARLY DAYS OF THE SOUTHERN PACIFIC

Colonel Thomas W. Pierce, Original Builder of the Road

H. M. Mayo, in a most interesting unpublished manuscript of the early history of the present Southern Pacific System, states in part: "As was practically the case in the development of many of the larger railroad systems of the country, the Southern Pacific in Texas and Louisiana represents the gathering and tying together of a number of separately organized rail properties. The Southern Pacific lines in the two states, forming that section of the transcontinental route, New Orleans to El Paso, had their inception years before Huntington and his colleagues in California began the organization of the Central Pacific. The corporate organization now operating between Houston and El Paso and known as the Galveston, Harrisburg and San Antonio Railway, began its existence as the Buffalo Bayou, Brazos and Colorado in 1850 at Harrisburg, and the actual work of construction was commenced the following year." This was preceded, however, as Mr. Mayo goes on to relate, by what might properly be termed the "first chapter" in the history of the present Southern Pacific, written ninety years ago, when the Republic of Texas granted, on January ninth, 1841, a charter to the Harrisburg Railroad and Trading Company. Some work of grading, etc., was completed, but two years later the charter was allowed to expire, the properties being taken over by the newly organized Buffalo Bayou, Brazos and Colorado Railway Company. Among the incorporators of the new company were found such prominent names as General Sidney Sherman, John G. Todd, William Marsh Rice, B. S. Sheppard and W. J. Hutchins. General Sherman, being possibly the most distinctive force behind the then ambitious project, there was named for him the first locomotive, a diminutive affair weighing only ten tons, but representing the latest in improved steam motive power. By 1855 this road had reached the Brazos River, opposite the little village of Richmond, thirty miles from Harrisburg, and trains were operating on a given schedule. Traffic destined to points west of the Brazos were ferried across the river. It was not only the first railroad in Texas, but also the first west of the Mississippi. The locomotives and other equipment were shipped from the East to Galveston by sea, then by barge to Harrisburg. Necessarily the coaches and other equipment were quite small as compared to present day facilities. Some of the coaches had once been used as horsecars, four wheels to each coach, and operated on small iron rails, the coaches being connected with pin and link couplers and controlled by hand-brakes. Even with the great advance in transportation methods it represented when compared with the horse and ox transport current in those days, it requires no stretch of the imagination to picture the discomforts of travel upon that little railroad in the days of Texas' infancy. By the fall of 1859, the road had reached Eagle Lake, and the following year to Alleyton, eighty miles from Harrisburg, on the east banks of the Colorado River. Construction was discontinued at this point for some eight years. Through purchase of the Columbus Tap Railway in 1866, the line was extended to the east bank of the Colorado River, opposite Columbus, this latter being negotiated by ferry. In July of 1867, the road from Columbus to Harrisburg changed hands, remaining with its new owners until January of 1870, when it was sold to Colonel Thomas W. Pierce and his associates. Under the authority of the Twelfth Legislature of Texas, the corporate name was changed to "The Galveston, Harrisburg and San Antonio Railway Company," and its real development, and upbuilding began under the effective guidance of Colonel Pierce. He at once began the work of extending the line from Columbus to San Antonio.

The railroad history of our great empire state cannot be

138

written without frequent use of the name of Thomas W. Pierce, noted pioneer builder of early days.

While not a resident of Texas, no one has added more to the early building of Houston, Galveston and particularly the western part of the state than Colonel Pierce. He took an early interest in everything pertaining to the good of the citizens of Texas.

Born in Dover, New Hampshire, on August sixteenth, 1818, Colonel Pierce, at the age of nineteen, was appointed on the staff of the Governor of New Hampshire. Moving later to Boston, he established there in 1848 the mercantile house of Pierce and Bacon, which became in due course one of the most extensive concerns in that city. Their trade, enormous for those times, extended far into Texas, where they were large buyers of cotton, sugar, hides and wool.

The increase in their southern trade was such in 1852 they established, in conjunction with the late General E. B. Nichols, a close friend of Colonel Pierce, a branch house in Galveston, of which General Nichols was manager. The latter was also the partner of William Marsh Rice at that time and materially assisted in building up the great Rice fortune of later years. They operated under the firm name of E. J. Hart and Company, organized in 1838. Subsequently Mr. Hart moved to New Orleans and became the leading wholesale druggist of the South.

While General Nichols acted as the agent of and was closely associated with Mr. Pierce in all of his southern enterprises, he continued his connection with William Marsh Rice until the War Between the States started. A line of fifteen packet ships was organized by the firm and employed in bringing in lake ice from Boston with regular schedules. Various lines of other commodities were also brought in by these ships, and returned cargoes were made up of such Texas products as cotton, bones, hides, moss, etc., for distribution in the North and to Europe.

In addition to General Nichols, Colonel Pierce had another close personal friend and business associate in Colonel Henry B. Andrews. Major Converse was another right-hand man in Colonel Pierce's railroad activities but truly, it was a strange combination for those times; a true-blue New England Yankee, teaming up with Boys in Grey, but the mutual admiration was great and lasting between them. General Nichols honored Colonel Pierce by naming his son, Thomas Pierce Nichols, and Major Converse, not to be outdone in gallantry, likewise named his eldest son, Thomas Pierce Converse.

At this time, the G. H. and S. A. Railway maintained their general offices in Galveston, under the management of Colonel Andrews. The terminus was then at Harrisburg. Subsequently it was extended to San Antonio, and the general office moved there.

Major Converse resided in Houston, looking after the affairs of the road here when its terminus was at Harrisburg. Colonel Pierce, however, was a tireless worker, and, ably seconded in his efforts by Converse and Andrews and Nichols, the road was pushed rapidly toward San Antonio and into the Golden West.

Even now, in my mind's eye, I can see Colonel Pierce as he walked the streets of Houston, a proud military bearing and General Burnside whiskers. In general appearance he impressed me as rather closely resembling Commodore Vanderbilt who, incidently, was also associated with Pierce and at one time interested in the line of steamers plying between Galveston and the North. Few men have possessed the higher characteristics that were found in Colonel Pierce, nor his deep sense of religious obligation. At the close of the war and during the reconstruction period that was equally devastating, he found that, like many others, he had lost large sums of money. He took his losses philosophically, remarking on one occasion to a friend and sympathizer: "It matters little; thank God, money is not everything in the world."

My first introduction to the G. H. and S. A., was in 1869. My schoolmate, Harry Andrews, had invited me to visit him at Harrisburg, then the terminus of the road and one of the liveliest places in the South. This was particularly true a few years later when the Morgan Line steamers ran to Clinton. At times six hundred to seven hundred were employed at the docks and among the shipping, all of whom lived at Harrisburg, and the amount of commerce passing through there had developed the town to where, at one time, it was larger than either Galveston or Houston.

There are a few living who were invited by Colonel Andrews to participate in the celebration marking the completion of the line to San Antonio. Some two or three hundred merchants and friends were asssembled in Galveston, and a like number from Houston invited, and great acclaim and welcome was accorded them when their special train rolled into the Alamo City. A magnificent entertainment was provided for them by the citizenship of San Antonio. It was not, of course, my good fortune to have made the trip, as I was only old enough to go to the depot and bid my father and friends goodbye.

Colonel Pierce's activities, however, did not stop with the mere completion of the road to San Antonio. He turned his attention to West Texas, and while a resident of Boston and a citizen of Massachusetts, to his efforts, interest and enterprise, more perhaps than to any other man's, is due the development of the resources of western part of the state. He constructed not only one of the best equipped railroads in the state, but was largely effective in developing the coal deposits of Texas and other varied resources of the Rio Grande and outlying sections.

In way of colonization and settlement, he dispatched Colonel Kingsbury to England, where the latter arranged for thousands of Englishmen and Scotchmen to come over from the British Isle and engage principally in the sheep and cattle business in West Texas.

Colonel Pierce pursued his colonization scheme by organizing colonist-agencies, through the medium of which he induced thousands of settlers from the New England and Northern states to take up their homes on his railroad lands. He sold to these settlers on the most liberal terms, encouraging them to engage actively in cultivation of the land. He opened not only old centers of trade, but created new ones. His knowledge of the state, its varied climatic conditions and ability to produce at given points the given crops, was extensive. As a young man he had visited and traveled over nearly every portion of the state and was, consequently, familiar with local requirements.

His record as a whole is remarkable for its simplicity, its usefulness and its grandeur. He was known personally to every business man on the line of his railroad, to every foreman and to the rank and file of working men. It was generally conceded that Texas was more indebted to him for its commercial advancement than to any other one man.

At the offices of the G. H. & S. A. in Houston, my friend Harry Andrews was station agent, baggage master and what not. But in 1883 when I came to Houston to make it my home the G. H. and S. A. shops had been moved here; and the local offices of the road, established on the North Side in a two-story edifice. C. W. Sedgwick was the local agent.

He had a chief clerk (Tom Scott) and two bill clerks, one collector and an office boy. Two train dispatchers completed the staff. They constituted the entire clerical staff and management of the Southern Pacific road of those days.

Compare that with the three thousand and two hundred paid clerks, the managerial staff, the mechanics and laborers of today, and you note the evolution of the Southern Pacific Railroad. Many say that the oil industry has made Houston; others that cotton and the ship channel have made the city, but, to my way of thinking, the Southern Pacific was and yet remains the backbone of Houston and the coastal region.

KATY RAILROAD IN TEXAS

Missouri, Kansas and Texas—Very Popular with Texans

Upon completion of the new M. K. & T. railroad terminal in Houston the following letter by the author was complimented very highly by the President of the M. K. & T.

"I want to offer congratulations to the 'Katy' upon building such magnificent terminals, which will do credit to any city.

"The 'Katy' has always been very popular with the Texans, as it was the first to give us a northern outlet from the State, having secured permission from the 'Indian Territory.' There was no state of Oklahoma at that time.

"It also furnished us such traffic men as Messrs. W. B. Groseclose, A. C. Allen, J. L. West and the late R. B. Baer.

"It was largely instrumental in building up Fort Worth, Denison and other good cities in Texas, and many in Oklahoma and Kansas.

"To show you how popular it was, I attended in the early days, at the opera house, a revival, I think led by Sam Jones. After the speaker was finishing his text, illustrating the 'Broad and Narrow Paths,' he asked the congregation, 'Which road will you take?' 'My brother,' a voice in the peanut gallery shouted, 'give me the M. K. & T., via Denison.'

"My brother and I, in June 1874, went to St. Louis on one of the first through trains. Fort Worth was then a tent city, just emerged from an army post. Dallas was just completing the first brick store, the Schneider and Davis building. Galveston and Houston had their three and four story buildings, long before the 'Sixties.' Stations that only boasted one or two stores have become large cities.

"Indians, in their native garbs everywhere, greeted the train. Many of the 'bucks' displayed the bright blankets given them by Uncle Sam.

"I remember a supper we had at Vinita. Imagine, I can taste it yet—wild turkey, venison, quail, berries, wild honey, etc., the table fairly breaking down from the products of the prairie.

"I am glad to see the 'Katy' is still pinning its faith on Houston and helping to make it the metropolis of the South."

"Jesse A. Ziegler."

EARLY DAY STEAMBOAT TRIP FROM HOUSTON TO GALVESTON

Fully ninety per cent of the cotton produced in the early years of Texas passed through Houston and Galveston by boat. No one of the present or, even, of the immediately passed generation can conceive of the bustle and hurry during those early days of the "Seventies," at the Houston steam-

143

boat landing situated then at the foot of Main Street. This was particularly true an hour or so before the scheduled departure of the boats; in those days, palatial passenger boats also carried quantities of freight.

Their departure for Galvéston was usually set at four o'clock in the afternoon. Nearly always prior to their departure of the boats; in those days, palatial passenger boats drays, teams and other vehicles became deadlocked. Frequently the air would become blue with the oaths and cries of the hardy teamsters and the outraged occupants of busses or family carriages.

In my memory I can still hear the warning of the steamboat's shrill whistle and the command of the first mate calling lustily, "All aboard for Galveston and intermediate points!" and then the pell-mell rush to complete last moment arrangements. To an eye-witness of the scene, it appeared that every merchant waited until the last moment to get his goods to shipside. Stubborn mules and equally stubborn drivers necessitated that the dock policemen use their clubs on the animals and even at times upon the drivers themselves. Meanwhile the mate on deck yelled instructions or criticisms at the roustabouts in language scarcely appropriate for milady's drawing room. It was language that, if not elegant, most assuredly was altogether expressive, in fact, for exactitude of expression, it was neatly rhetorical.

When the last truck load of freight was on board, and the gangplank carried on deck, the inevitable "last man" would appear, rushing to the boatside with frantic appeal to be taken aboard. Usually it would be some influential Brazos bottom planter or individual of like prominence and popularity; and, amid the swearing of the captain and first mate, the gangplank would again be lowered, the late arrival taken aboard, and the wash of the great side-wheel paddles could be heard as the boat backed out to head down stream. Ruffled dispositions were soon stilled by the band striking up "Dixie," "Swanee River" or other popular songs of the day. With the farewell waving of many handkerchiefs and many shouted "adieus" to friends on the dock, those on board settled down for a glorious trip down the magnolia lined banks of Buffalo Bayou. The boat presented a picturesque effect with the passengers bedecked in their gala attire, and the roustabouts and deck-hands seated on cotton bales, with buckets of water at hand to put out any fires that might arise from passing sparks emerging from the smoke-stack. Usually

144

At San Jacinto Battle Ground
Through the Moss—A Ship Leaving Houston

these hands carried their banjos and guitars, and when the band was silent would regale themselves with the contemporary songs of the South. A check-up of the passenger list would usually disclose at least a few known Brazos bottom planters destined for New Orleans, eastern ports or Europe. Merchants from all over Texas journeyed regularly to Galveston, New Orleans and New York via this mode of travel, as it must be remembered that at this time the Texas and New Orleans Railroad had not been completed, nor did the Missouri, Kansas and Texas secure right-of-way through Indian Territory, now Oklahoma, and thence into St. Louis, until 1872. The only outlet of prominence, therefore, to the sea was via Buffalo Bayou or the Galveston, Houston and Henderson Railroad.

For their day and time, however, the steamboat facilities available as above were of a splendid nature. That pioneer steamboat operator, Captain J. H. Sterrett, went in person to Cincinnati to supervise the completion of four very pretentious steamboats. Their arrangement, construction and equipment, and the furnishings installed were said to be the equal of any of the larger passenger steamers then plying on the Mississippi River or the Ohio; indeed, they seemed to me at the time to be altogether palatial for river travel. These boats, as I recall, were named for pioneer steamboat men and merchants or members of their families; among them were the "T. M. Bagby," the "Diana," the "Charles Fowler," the "Lizzie," and the "Era No. Three."

As a rule, the respective captains of the boats had their coterie of friends in the interior who would book passage for weeks ahead in order to make the trip with their favorite. Many of the sugar-barons and cotton planters insisted upon this privilege of selection. Too, the stewards of the various boats were renowned chefs and had an equal following of friends in the interior who would book passage with the particular steward in order that they might, en route, tickle their palates with the epicurean delights provided by these famous chefs. In lesser degree, perhaps, the chief clerks or pursers of the respective boats had their following; and withal the gathering on board the boats was similar to a reunion of old friends of former trips.

There are perhaps a few yet living who remember the only house on Buffalo Bayou between Houston and Harrisburg. It was maintained by an enterprising farmer and his wife at a boat landing on Constitution Bend, and called

145

"Buttermilk Station." When the Captain found that he had amply time, he would land for a few minutes, permitting the passengers to refresh themselves with potions of cool buttermilk.

The big stop en route, however, was Harrisburg. Here occasionally some two or three hours were consumed in exchanging passengers and loading and unloading freight. Frequently, Houstonians would take passage to Harrisburg in order to accompany or visit with friends making the entire trip, and, disembarking at Harrisburg, make the return trip to Houston on boats going upstream.

The next landing en route to Galveston was made at Norsworthy's, located at the mouth of Carpenter's Bayou. This was followed by a stop at Dr. J. S. Massie's plantation, at the junction of Green's Bayou. Their plantation home was one of the most pretentious of early day plantation homes, but was destroyed in the hurricane in either 1875 or 1886. The estate was undoubtedly the largest slave plantation on Buffalo Bayou.

As the steamboats approached these landings, the shrill blast of their whistles could be heard for miles away; the band, of course, would strike up its melody. Ladies with their picturesque riding habits of the day, long velvet skirts and large hats with trailing plumes, came galloping up with their escorts to the wharf, to exchange greetings with those on board, or perhaps to take passage to Galveston and other ports.

Passing the historic San Jacinto Battle Grounds, formal salute was offered. A real stop was then made at Lynchburg, then a thriving little town, as all the freight going into East Texas from Galveston and Houston was transshipped there. Ox-teams were employed to carry the cargoes of cotton, wool, hides and household commodities via trail.

Weighing anchor, the boat would proceed down the channel, passing the historic home of Dr. Ashbel Smith Evergreen at Baytown, thence through Clopper's Bar (now Morgan's Point), and negotiate the wonderful trip across the bay to Galveston.

It will be remembered that these were the days of pine-log fuel. The engineer was, perhaps, love-lorn and had a pressing engagement to arrive in Galveston on time, and orders would be given to the firemen to stoke the furnace heavily. Showers of sparks would soar heavenward, leaving a brilliantly lighted trail in the prevailing southern breeze

146

somewhat akin to a playful comet. The night trips across the bay constituted, in good weather, one of the most exhilerating recreations imaginable. Passengers often remained on deck long after all the lights were ordered out, to enjoy the breeze and the starry nights; and frequently, there were races between the boats of competing lines, thus adding to the hilarity and excitement of the passage. The description of Venice by night, or a trip on the Riviera in the Mediterranean could scarce surpass the enjoyment of these night passages to Galveston.

By early morning Galveston came into view. A light breakfast was served and landing was effected with band playing and the added melody of the songs of the deckhands and roustabouts. Even at the early hour of seven or eight, the usual landing time, the docks were crowded with friends waiting to welcome the incoming guests.

Here the same procedure was carried out as told before and the boats would continue on their trips to the other ports of the world.

THE GREAT MEDICINE LAKE

Nature's Sanatarium—Old Sour Lake

In the early days, before the coming of oil, Sour Lake was known far and wide for its medicinal qualities. The Karankawas and their arch enemies, the Tonkawas, both fierce Indian tribes, came regularly to Sour Lake, as did the Caddoes, generally considered the First Texans. One of the Caddo tribes, the Tejas, gave the Lone Star State its name. These Indians came regularly to have their battle scars healed.

Many years ago, I was told that Vinegar Hill and the dense woods surrounding, where now Jeff Davis Hospital stands, was the favorite camping grounds of the Indians going to and from Sour Lake. It was called 'Nature's Sanatarium' later and was indeed a curiosity. The lake was as round as a well, an acre or two in extent and its waters were 'sour.'

The bottom of the lake was for the most part hard asphaltum, making a splendid floor for bathers. The lake was constantly boiling and bubbling, caused by currents of

147

gas escaping from the earth. This was readily proven by taking a can opened at one end and punctured at the other, plunging the can half way into the bubbling water and applying a lighted match to the puncture. When ownership of the lake rested in Sam Ashe and Dr. Tom Boyles, a large rusty stove pipe was sunk into the mud over the bubbling gas. I have seen a flame ten feet high shoot up out of the water. It burned like a gas jet and unless blown out by the wind, continued to burn as long as the pipe remained over the bubbling waters.

Practically nothing lived in these waters, except a small bug. It was almost instant death for fish or snakes to enter the lake. Even mosquitoes dared not fly over the waters as, breathing the issuing gases, they would fall dead. Often the lake was covered with a film of mosquitoes and other insects who had come to partake of the healing water and met only death.

But the gas had no effect upon man. There was a legend that the water would 'grow hair on a bald head.' I have often seen men bathing in the lake plaster their heads with the mud and let it dry in the sun, but like most hair restorers guaranteed to 'Grow hair on a billiard ball,' it did not work. If the mud baths did not live up to legend, they did have some healing powers and apparently gave new strength and vigor. It was a delightful sensation to plunge into the buoyant water and feel the pressure of the gas causing the water to bubble. It was beautiful to see ducks floating upon the water which was not too placid in spots.

The lake was surrounded by about twenty-five or more wells or springs nearly all in a state of ebullition; though but a few feet apart, these wells differed as to the taste and properties of their waters. Here you would find a group of wells that contained water sour as a crab-apple and right next to these another group whose waters were sweet. A few feet farther on, you might find wells of yellow sulphur water, and next, wells of pure white alum water. One well in particular I remember was highly charged with citric acid, and a few feet farther on was a well of pure magnesia. By mixing the waters from these latter wells, one almost had a perfect lemonade. Floating on some of the alkaline wells one could see a petroleum substance that gave the waters a strong taste of tar. The visitors or patients would drink from the wells perscribed for them.

Men and women would sit around the wells as they do

now at Manitou and Eureka Springs, drink the waters all day and carry a fresh jug to their rooms at night. These waters produced a ravenous appetite.

There were also springs of iron, magnesia and many other mineral properties which were not defined, but all in all, I believe there were some twenty-one or twenty-two wells fully analyzed, and I have no doubt that others were discoverd later. Go where you might, around the lake, you would find many jets of gas and water issuing out of the ground. I remember seeing a mangy coon wallowing in the seepage from a well, and at another place, an old donkey who would come regularly and stick his nose over the well to inhale the gas. All the animals seemed to sense the curative properties of the wells.

It was only necessary to dig a hole at such places to secure a flow of mineral water. How easily lighted these premises were at night with the gas pouring out of the ground and millions of fire-flies appearing to light the ground. Added to this was the constant sound of the many bull frogs. During the day, hundreds of chameleons would dart among the trees, changing color as they rested on leaf or wood, a perfect camouflage. To him who was affected by the beauties of nature, this was indeed a place of never ceasing wonder.

How all these waters came together at this place and for what purposes no one knows, but a noted geologist once said, "Undoubtedly they were placed there by the Living God, for the purpose of healing the nations," and I believe it true. A common sense answer might be that for many millions of years, decayed vegetable matter gathered in this hollow spot and concentrated there which caused all these gases. The trend today is toward the scientific explanation and God is given little credit for such wonders. For myself, the more I see of nature, the more I see of God. It looks to me that it surrounds us daily and only those who are blind fail to see it. Who can stand on Pike's Peak, for instance, and not be moved by the solemn stillness, or view the coloring of the Grand Canyon. Even in a modern steamer today, hundreds of miles out from land, it is merely a shell being guided by that unseen power all races of man recognize in one form or another.

Back to Sour Lake, I know of many wonderful tales told of the healing qualities of this body of water. The pioneer hardware man of Galveston, the late J. M. Brown, had during the War Between the States, a fine and valuable Negro cook who became blind. Dr. Marant Smith, the owner of the lake at that time, induced Mr. Brown to send the Negro over, which he did. After several months, he received no reports but did receive several offers to buy the slave. They drove over to Sour Lake to investigate and found that the Negro cook had regained her eyesight. She was taken back to Galveston. Mr. Brown told me this story shortly before his death.

In making my first trip to the resort, I went over with a gentleman who had contracted eczema. His face was like raw beef steak and he was not allowed to eat at the general tables, as some of the guests had protested against it. However, in a week's time, his skin was clear and not in the least discolored. I have often seen men and women suffering from granulated eyelids bathe their faces in the healing water and at the end of a week, leave the resort entirely free of the ailment. I have also known of some remarkable cures of rheumatism. One woman who had not walked a step for fourteen years visited Sour Lake and after religiously using the water for a few weeks, was able to walk very well.

The late Judge T. W. Foard organized a company and had the waters, mud, sand and minerals analyzed and spent a great deal of money trying to develop the project. He sold many by-products of the lake for years, after advertising it extensively. He discovered a white sand that was used for cleaning silverware and sold thousands of pounds of this material.

The surrounding country is mostly prairie but there are wide belts of timber, particularly on Pine Island Bayou and Little Pine Island and the lake is in the middle of grand oak trees.

The prairies were often filled with geese, brants and ducks and the woods were filled with wild turkey and game. One of the most enjoyable squirrel hunts I ever had was in this section, with a little dog who treed them for me. No one ever visited there unless he brought his gun. We had bear meat, venison and wild turkey at every meal. Pine Island and Little Pine Island Bayou were always full of game and fish. They are about two miles distant, at either hand and very big catches of bass and perch were often caught. In fact, I am sure it then would rival the Don Martin Lake fishing in Old Mexico. Many fishing parties were arranged and a fish fry always followed. The silver perch and black bass ran from a quarter of a pound to three pounds in weight and catching them was fine sport.

In the "Eighties," those who came to Sour Lake expecting marble palaces and fine hotels were disappointed. There was a commodious hotel, and "bachelors' row," which was a long string of cabins near the hotel. It was there that the biggest fish tales were told. The comforts were all the visitors could ask for as the food was always excellent and came entirely from the forests, streams and prairies.

We must not forget the noted character, "Dr. Mud," an old native Negro whose laboratory was a can of mud and with a crooked walking stick, he hobbled around prescribing for the patients. He looked and acted wise but his applications of the waters and the mud were often ineffective.

Ladies, not unlike those of today who frequent the beauty salons, applied mud to clear their complexions. In fact, mud was applied for every ache and pain.

The sports were varied. If one wanted to kill an alligator or scare up a moccasin or rattlesnake, he could be accommodated. The largest garter snake and coach whip I ever saw stopped our stage coach one morning.

The original tract was one thousand acres and was owned by Dr. Smith, who sold it in 1882 to P. J. Willis of Galveston who built a new hotel and improved the resort. The properties passed on to Captain Sam Ashe and Dr. Tom Boyles in the "Nineties." They purchased it at a Sheriff's Sale at Kountze, the county seat of Hardin County. It then became the property of the Texas Travelers Protective Association and was sold by them to the late Colonel Newton of 'The Gables.'

At the turn of the century, the Texas Company secured it and this glorious old place was turned into an oil field. Millions of dollars in black gold have been produced where the curative waters and mud had been, and no longer is it the favorite watering place of the bankers, sugar barons and cotton kings who used to gather there every summer. The social activities of this famous old resort were known all over Texas and Western Louisiana. I am told it was one of the first bases of the Texas Company's capitalization, which was originally five million dollars. I was offered a one-third interest in the thousand acre tract for nine thousand dollars, when the company first started, and there I missed a chance of a lifetime.

151

The old lake had almost been forgotten but I trust that when the oil company produces its last gallon of oil, it will restore the old place to its former greatness.

BATTLE OF RICHMOND

Famed Feud of the "Jaybirds" and "Woodpeckers"
of Fort Bend County

Sixty years ago the coastal counties of Texas were in the throes of Carpetbagger Rule. It was, in fact, the rule of all Texas and of the vanquished South. The white populace of the South, the planters, merchants and citizens generally who had fought for the Lost Cause were disfranchised. Small child that I was, I remember distinctly that my father, himself a land-owner who had shouldered his musket in behalf of the South, was not allowed to cast his ballot at election time. Yet ignorant ex-slaves who could neither read nor write, nor owned a foot of ground, were accorded the superior rights of citizenship.

In Galveston, where I was born, Wright Cuney, a Negro, was made Collector of Customs. Negroes were elected aldermen in the city and made the local laws, execution of which was chiefly through a governing body known as the Freeman's Bureau. Legislatures of the various states had their quota of Negro representatives and senators, as did also even the national Congress of the United States.

Houston was little better off than Galveston. The same element governed here, involving the city in an enormous debt that, later, the white citizenry then in power endeavored to repudiate. Wiser counsel prevailed, however, and eventually a compromise was made on the outstanding indebtedness and the bonds retired.

Fort Bend County was governed by a Negro, Henry Ferguson, and the voting strength was about ten colored to one white. The population of the county, in fact, was about two colored to one white. Conditions had become unbearable when, in 1886, a meeting was called by the prominent planters and citizens of Richmond, the county seat.

The purpose of this meeting, ostensibly, was to form a Young Men's Democratic Club, the objective being to more properly regulate the affairs of the community. Some two hundred of the southern Democrats attended. News of the meeting and the plans formulated there, came immediately to the Republicans, promoters of carpetbag rule. They proceeded to gird for the coming battle of ballots and called a similar meeting. They were able, however, to gather only about fifty white citizens. These added to the Negro vote heretofore controlled, constituted formidable opposition to the southern Democrats. The latter, being politically expedient, campaigned vigorously among the Negroes. Many of the ex-slaves remained loyal to their former masters and voted with them. The Republicans planned to control the Negro vote in the coming election as they had in the past.

J. M. Shamblin, part owner of the Fields Plantation (now included in the Sugarland Plantation), was one of the influential leaders of the community. He was a first lieutenant in the Democratic "Jaybirds" organization, a justice of the peace, and owner of one of the large gins. Accordingly, he succeeded in influencing many of the Negroes on his side.

I was seated at my desk one Monday morning when Mr. Shamblin walked in and inquired whether anyone had been in from the "bottom." I replied that Hudson Caldwell, a Negro, had brought me a bale of cotton from down there. "Let me see it," Shamblin requested. 1 pointed to the bale near him. He turned to it, brushing the cane straw off the bale, and pointing to a dim mark exclaimed, "See! this is 'P. R.' The bale belonged to Pink Rab, and was stolen from my gin Saturday night."

"If you can identify the bale as stolen, take it along," I retorted. "I can't hold it." Shamblin replied, "No. Give me a check for what you originally paid for it; you are entitled to your margin of profit on the re-sale."

This I did and requested that on his return to Richmond he have Caldwell arrested. He agreed, but his return was delayed. Meanwhile, the Negro disappeared and was never found. Two other Negroes, however, were found who were involved in the theft; one of them turned state's evidence. En route to the trial, as he passed by Caldwell's home, the wife of Caldwell gave him a cup of coffee. In it she had placed a liberal dose of strychnine. Drinking it, the Negro fell stricken, but managed to crawl over to Mr. Shamblin, then justice of the peace, and gave him his dying declaration of the poisoning and the cotton theft. This evidence Shamblin brought to the court in Richmond.

The above incident further engendered the bitterness be-

153

tween the opposing factions in Fort Bend County, and it was only shortly later that, one Sunday afternoon, Shamblin, seated in his living room with his young daughter on his knee, while reading to her from the Psalms, was shot dead through the window from ambush. Within an hour, between one hundred and two hundred "Jaybirds" were scouring the country with rifles and bloodhounds in search of the murderer. The hounds finally led them to the home of William Caldwell, son of Hudson Caldwell, and the latter was immediately jailed. But as each of the "Jaybirds" returned home that night, they found pinned upon their doors after dark, "Take warning—make no more attempt to get Negro votes."

The warning was disregarded. A stiff campaign for votes was carried on among the Negroes, and the trial of William Caldwell for murder of Shamblin was prosecuted in the courts of Richmond. Notwithstanding that Caldwell was defended by an ex-district judge and one time candidate for governor, he was found guilty of the crime and subsequently hanged in the Harris County jail.

Failure to heed the warning, however, was responsible for yet another attempted murder. Henry Frost, who had succeeded Shamblin as first lieutenant and leader of the "Jaybirds" was shot down from ambush at the gate of his home. The shot did not prove fatal, as some two months later, while fishing one morning at daylight off the pier at Galveston, I heard someone exclaim, "Hi, Ziegler. What are you doing here?" I turned and saw it was Henry Frost. Very much surprised, I stammered, "Why, I thought YOU were dead!" Jokingly, he replied, "No, I have been in Sealy Hospital but I am going back to Richmond to finish matters."

Two more Negroes were arrested in connection with the assault on Frost's life, and affairs in the community were at such a crisis that the Democrats, or "Jaybirds," called a meeting of all the whites in the county, regardless of their political leaning. At the mass meeting, both factions sat down together to work out the community problems. Among other provisions they ordained that all Negroes who were regarded as a disturbing element be ordered from the town, both parties agreeing thereto. In addition, and much to the surprise of the "Jaybirds," the Republicans, or "Woodpeckers" decided not to nominate a political ticket in the coming election, in order to further safeguard the peace of the county.

In brief, they would make Fort Bend County safe for democracy. Their attitude left the "Jaybirds" speechless.

Unhappily, however, for the continued peace of the community, almost before the ink was dry on the agreement executed by the mass meeting, a certain new element among the Republicans got together and decided the political spoils of the county were too fat a prize to be so easily discarded. They put a complete Republican ticket in the field and campaigned vigorously for votes, calling themselves Independent or Conservative Democrats. The sobriquet of "Woodpecker," however, remained with them. As election time drew near, the personal feeling on both sides grew to fever heat. In many instances, those aligned on opposite sides were associated in business. Boyhood friends, neighbors, passed each other on the street without greeting; wives of the opposing factionists refused to recognize each other at social gatherings. Numerous fist-fights and altercations occurred. Then, after the smoke of election had cleared away, it was found that the "Woodpeckers" had again won.

L. E. Gibson had been the "Jaybird" candidate for County Assessor, in opposition to Kyle Terry, originally one of the famed sons of Fort Bend, but now a member of the "Woodpeckers."

Returning from my plantation, I had boarded the train at Stafford's Point, seating myself with William Thatcher. I had scarcely become seated when the conductor handed Thatcher a telegram stating that Kyle Terry had killed Gibson. Thatcher, a brother-in-law of Terry, bade me goodbye, stating that he must return to Richmond. I continued on to Houston, where I learned that the two Fort Bend County men met in Wharton; words ensued, followed by firing and Gibson lay dead.

Retribution was not long in overtaking the "Woodpeckers." A week later, as Kyle Terry was walking up the court house steps between his attorneys, John Lovejoy and Major Marc McLemore, Volney Gibson appeared on the scene. Gibson drew and fired; Terry fell in his tracks and died there on the steps.

Gibson went home under bond. Richmond, its two factions armed to the teeth, was a smoldering keg of powder. It needed only the final touch of the match to set the magazine aflame. Whether this was deliberately brought about through trickery by a feigned altercation of the streets, or the incident in which Albert George was arrested was in truth a serious-minded altercation, will probably never be known.

155

Opinions varied at the time. Suffice it to say that Albert George apparently did engage seriously in an affray on the streets, was arrested by the "Woodpecker" sheriff, J. T. Garvey, and was en route to jail with the latter when Volney Gibson stepped into the street with a Winchester in his hand. Instantly the entire square sprang into action. On the front of the court house steps were three "Woodpeckers," Deputy Sheriff Tom Smith, H. S. Mason and J. W. Parker, the former county judge. As the two former went to meet Sheriff Garvey and his prisoner, Judge Parker recognized the latter as a "Jaybird," and noting Gibson in the street armed, sensed serious trouble. Just then Gibson raised and fired, and the Battle of Richmond, the War between the "Jaybirds" and the "Woodpeckers" was on. The day was August eighteenth, 1889.

The starting time of the battle was just at sunset. No sooner had Gibson fired, than the streets of the square became filled with armed "Jaybirds." J. W. Blakely, a former sheriff and one of the large planters of the community, was the first man killed. Sheriff Garvey was shot dead as he tried to cross the street with his prisoner. Deputy Sheriff Mason, going to Garvey's rescue, and Private Jones of the Texas Rangers, were wounded. The two Rangers had been sent to Richmond by the Governor to perserve peace, and were on the court house lawn when the firing started. They advised Deputy Sheriff Mason to retire under cover to the court house, but the latter refused to leave until Garvey's body was rescued and the wounded Mason brought to safety. Upon bringing the latter in, it was found that he had a bullet in his thigh, while Judge Parker carried a wound in his groin.

The battle, fast and furious, and with much shooting while it lasted, was brief. Richmond remained that night as armed camp, both factions resting upon their arms and prepared for further action on instant notice. The situation continued tense. Full extent of the casualties was made known when morning came; "Jaybirds," one dead, three wounded; "Woodpeckers," two dead, one wounded; non-combatants, one dead, a Negro girl accidentally shot by a stray bullet, and one wounded, the Ranger who had inadvertently exposed himself. Oddly enough, the "jaybirds" most seriously wounded was Frost, the Democratic leader and organizer of the "Jaybirds." His previous wounds from the attempt to ambush him at his gate, scarcely healed, he had engaged in the thick of the fray and received four bullet wounds in

156

the body. A few days later, they proved fatal, thus removing a colorful figure from the life of Fort Bend.

Volney Gibson stopped a rifle bullet that went through his jaw and flattened out under the skin at the back of his neck, just where the collar-button would be. He remained in the fight and the next morning, after an excellent breakfast, proceeded leisurely to the doctor to have the bullet removed.

Andrus, another "Jaybird," was brought down with a bullet through the leg; yet, fallen, he remained on the square and fired until the fight was over.

With morning came martial law and the arrival of the Brenham Light Guard and a detachment of the Houston Light Guard, acting under orders from Governor Sul Ross. Later, Governor Ross visited Richmond himself and after surveying the situation, suggested to the citizenry that they place Sergeant N. A. Aten of the Rangers in office as Sheriff of the county, believing that an impartial representative of the people would promote peace in the community. This was done after some weeks' delay, the "Woodpecker" commissioners court making the move with reluctance. It served to exert a quieting effect upon the populace. Subsequently, the "Woodpeckers" holding county offices began resigning and gradually removed themselves from Fort Bend.

Meanwhile, with the removal of the "Woodpeckers" in progress, the southern Democrats called a further mass meeting of all the white with the avowed purpose of "combining and uniting the white people of the community for the advancement and prosperity of Fort Bend County." There emerged from the meeting, in October of 1889, the "Jaybird Democratic Association" the constitution of which recited, among other items, that:

"We, therefore, declare that any white man now residing in this county, who shall undertake to lead against this association any political faction or voting population opposed to the principles and objects of this association, shall be considered and treated as a social and political outcast."

There remains today on the court house lawn at Richmond a weather-beaten monument to the three fallen "Jaybirds," Shamblin, Frost and Gibson. And it is said here, Republican votes in Fort Bend County are about as scarce as the proverbial hen's teeth!

This account of the battle was related to me many years later by Volney Gibson, with notes added later from an article from the pen of C. L. Douglas. In contemplating the whole, however, I have wondered whether my buying a bale of low grade cotton from Hudson Caldwell, a purely innocent act of purchase on my part, was the initial factor of a series of incidents that reached their unhappy climax in the final "Battle of Richmond."

PHENOMENAL WEATHER OF YESTERYEARS

Oldest Inhabitants Not Yet Old Enough to Forecast Weather of Texas

The good natured raillery of the press about the cold or warm weather in Texas brings to mind the thought that there are even yet a few of us now living who, by the ripeness of our years, are qualified by discourse on the phenomenal weather of East Texas and vicinity in generations past.

The expression has become trite that "only a newcomer or an imbecile would predict weather in Texas." Nevertheless, I find that those yet living whom even I could properly class as "old timers" are really "cagey" when it comes to forecasting Texas weather.

For example, only recently, I had the pleasure of hobnobbing with Will Lillie, a native-born, now eighty-eight, and the venerable John T. Browne, ninety-two, compared with both of whom my own eighty-one years seems to me quite youthful. They were born and lived in the log-cabin period when there were "homes without doors and without floors" as we were wont to hear. When I approached them upon the subject of Texas weather, each in turn took refuge behind the suggestion that they were "too young and too recently a comer to Texas to predict the weather."

There are, however, many of us now living who will recall the terrific cold spell of 1886, when the bayous, creeks and even Galveston Bay were frozen over.

Houston had at that time a number of Yankee cotton men connected with E. L. Dennis, W. V. R. Watson, Joseph Metcalf and other local brokers. They came into the Cotton Exchange on the morning of the great freeze with their ice-skates hung over their shoulders, prepared to take part in the carnival of fun already under way over the city. Proceeding to the Fifth Ward, near the Southern Pacific Shops, they found a great crowd of old and young gathered at the John Trenton Brick Yard ponds. These had been created by excavations from which the mud was used to make the mud-bricks of those days. The ponds were frozen solid and the crowd remained skating all day, permitting business to take care of itself. Some of the skaters pursued their way up White Oak Bayou for a mile or two, enjoying the thick ice provided by that stream. It was one of the most severe freezes Houston had ever witnessed. Beauchamp Springs, of course, was frozen solid and provided another favorite spot for skating.

While phenomenal weather often has occurred in Texas during the interim, the first record we appear to have of such was in 1818, when Jean LaFitte reported Galveston Bay covered with ice and the loss of several of his men frozen to death.

Again, Mrs. Jane Long, "Mother of Texas," gives a very graphic account of the drastic winter of 1820-21, when she was holding the little mud fort at Bolivar Point. A thick sheet of solid ice covered Galveston Bay. She observed one day a great black bear weighing several hundred pounds, crossing the ice toward the Point. Apparently he had been over to Galveston Island and was heading back to the mouth of the Trinity, from whence, probably, he had come. One shot from her faithful old muzzle-loader and the bear hastened away. The only food that Mrs. Long, her young daughter and the slave-girl Kian had during that siege of cold weather consisted of frozen fish, the latter chopped out of the ice, placed in tubs of salt and thawed out as needed. This was supplemented by occasional wild ducks also caught fast in the ice.

My personal experience in instances of the kind dates back to 1863, when Galveston Bay again froze over. We awakened one morning in Galveston and found twenty-two inches of snow in our alley; the depth doubtless occasioned by wind action at that particular point, although it overlaid the entire island to a considerable depth. In our case, it served somewhat peculiarly. For some time we had been suffering the loss of our chickens by thievery. The night of the snow my father, then stationed at the fort on West End, obtained leave and came home with his gun loaded with bird-shot. The miscreant appeared and while engaged with the chickens, was intercepted by my father, who let fly with his gun. The intruder fled, but left behind him a trail of

159

blood that we followed the next morning in the snow for several blocks, but finally lost in the road.

Governor Frank Lubbock in his memoirs stated that he was commissioned to inspect the fort on West Galveston and Velasco during the above mentioned cold spell. Riding horseback through the weather, it was necessary that he be lifted from the back of his horse when he reached the end of Galveston Island. The cold had so numbed his entire body that he was unable to move.

I was a mere school boy at the time of this spell and recall the schoolmaster gave the larger boys a recess in which to gather firewood. Most of that time was actually spent in snow-balling and similar frolic, but we did finally return, each with a load of wood upon his shoulders.

Others will recall vividly the great snow on Saint Valentine's Day in 1895, when the South was white-blanketed from El Paso to Florida. Drifts of snow from four to six feet deep formed in the streets of Houston. I had, on that occasion, to employ two Negroes to excavate a tunnel some eight or nine feet through the snow at the gates of the old Allen Warehouse (where the Merchants and Manufacturers Building now stands) in order to pass a consignment of cotton required for shipment.

When that snow fell, a general holiday was declared in Houston. No one thought of work; bankers, merchants, clerks and all joined in the sport. At the corners of the Houston National and First National Banks, the fleecy snow was four to five feet deep. I witnessed that morning a battle royal on Main Street between the old Confederate Veteran, Major A. L. Steele, Theodore Lubbock, Captain Ben Weems and others, as they wrestled and rolled in the snow and pelted each other with volleys of snow-balls.

For some reason, the main targets for snow-balls were the policemen; everyone seemed to take a shy at them. Probably the only occasion on which they felt an opportunity provided to get back at them under entirely good natured circumstances.

The entire city was quick to respond to the fallen snow. Within a few hours a dozen or more carriages appeared on the downtown streets, their wheels removed and runners substituted. Rosy-cheeked belles were accompanied by their beaux, sleigh-bells tinkled and the streets rang with merriment.

In the homes along the three principal streets, the feminine

A Graceful Battleship Enters Houston

members of the family cleared the porches and piled up armsful of snow-balls. If snow were lacking in a given yard, mothers, grandmothers and daughters scraped the drift from the doors and windows to supply the white ammunition and woe to the unsuspecting passerby. Truly, that day in Houston, "Eternal vigilance was the price of safety."

I recall, in the course of that day, an amusing incident downtown. Two visitors from "down East," frequently accustomed to the sight of heavy snows in their home environs, came walking down Main Street. At one of the intersections their tall hats and immaculate dress made them a conspicuous target. They raised their umbrellas to ward off the increasing barage. The umbrellas were ripped to shreds and their owners outraged with the severe pelting, appealed to a nearby policeman, charging that such demonstrations were mere rowdyisms. Surprised at the attitude of the Easterners, the burly Irish policeman roared back, "What ho! You should complain, you're being attacked by the best citizens of Houston."

Great snow-men were made all over the city; here and there more complicated snow-huts, houses and forts were constructed. The snow lasted two days. When it began to melt on the third day, the Western Union messengers and other youngsters, reluctant to see the fun fail, composed their "snow-balls" of snow, ice, mud and gravel. The result was a rather wicked weapon; a number of fights occurred on the streets and finally the police were called upon to officially usher out the snow.

It was estimated that the foregoing siege of phenomenal weather brought an average snow-fall of twenty-two inches between El Paso and Florida.

Then, once again, in 1899, the weather-gods selected Saint Valentine's Day on which to vent their fury. Nothing like it had ever occurred in Texas as a whole. Thermometers in the state varied one hundred degrees in twenty-four hours, an item of which Ripley in his Believe it or Not might well take note. On the morning of February thirteenth, the thermometer at Brownsville stood at eighty-eight. The next morning, at Texline, a temperature of twelve below was recorded.

The official record at Houston was six above on February fourteenth. The report came that Galveston Bay was again frozen over and a number of venturous Houstonians wanted to see the sight. All trains in and out of Houston had been suspended, with exception of the Katy from Dallas and that train was reported four hours late. About eleven o'clock in the morning we left the Cotton Exchange and proceeded over the iron bridge at San Jacinto. Advancing, we faced a bitterly cold norther. So intense was the cold and so furious was the wind that we were forced to stop every ten or fifteen steps to catch our breath. Finally, we arrived at the brewery, where the outside thermometer showed six above zero, and huddled around the boiler until time to leave for Galveston.

En route, we found every bayou, creek, water-tank and pond frozen solid. West Galveston Bay was a solid sheet of ice. At Galveston, as well as in Houston, all street car traffic was abandoned. We walked through snow and ice until we came to the beach, where Murdock's bathhouse stood. Farther down the coast the Brazos had poured its yellow fresh water into the Gulf and it had frozen. As the high waves rolled in and broke, their crest and foam would instantly freeze and pile up on the beach. The gulf reminded me of a giant bowl of eggnog, the frozen foam having the appearance of the custard.

For lack of other conveyance, we "hoofed" it from the beach to the wharf-front. There we found the entire mosquito fleet frozen in at their slips. From the grain elevators hung icicles six and seven feet long. At some of the slips lay sailing ships; their masts, sails and sides, where the water had washed, were solid sheets of ice. In the bay were several sloop schooners, with full sail set, frozen solid in the sheet of ice that covered the bay. It reminded one of those early pictures of ships caught in the Arctic ice pack. Yet, the ships and their rigging covered with ice, presented a beautiful fascinating picture, flashing back the lights of the mid-afternoon sun.

The only thing of a torrid nature that we found in Galveston that day were the hot "Tom and Jerry" and "Hot Scotch." For nearly two days, the bars of Galveston enjoyed the only real business that was carried on in the city.

Our party decided to remain over night in Galveston, because of the excessive cold to be encountered on the night journey home. On our return trip next day, we observed somewhat of the damage done by the terrific freeze. Thousands of cattle were found piled up on the prairie and at the edges of the woods. Young trees, shrubbery and fruit orchards were killed outright.

It was interesting to note, in passing, that on the days of

the intense cold waves, few Negroes were to be seen anywhere. When they did appear, one saw them with quilts or blankets thrown over their heads and shoulders, their faces covered until only the whites of their eyes shown forth. Frequently they wore several suits under these blankets, their legs wrapped in jute baggins and their feet in burlap sack cloth. Forsooth, they were truly sons of the tropics. Arrayed in such attire, they reminded me strongly of great grizzly bears or Esquimaux.

The spell above mentioned was caused, I am told, by the highest barometer reading ever known, thirty-one point six. There was no wind, but a complete dead calm, the only circumstances, I believe, under which salt water may freeze.

Later on in 1911-12, we had another spell of weather most unusual in nature. There was a mixture of flurries of snow and an intense hail. Some of these hailstones weighed in excess of a pound and while the thermometer never touched the low levels of 1895 and 1899, the damage over Houston and vicinity from the heavy hail was immense. Hundreds of trees broke under their load of ice and sleet; roofs and window panes suffered heavily, as did unprotected livestock. Greenhouses and street cars were riddled as with machine guns. It was estimated that between six and seven carloads of window pane glasses were shipped into Houston to repair the damage done by this storm.

I lay no claim to technical data as relates to Texas weather, but I have been told in late years by scientific men from that field that, what with world changes in climate and temperatures that have apparently occurred in the past several decades, these extreme, low temperatures in Houston and coastal regions, involving the freezing over of Galveston Bay, are not highly probable in the future; that, in fact, they may never occur again. Some advance the theory that the Gulf stream is gradually moving its course closer and closer to the Texas coast and that its proximity will eventually ward off the intense cold waves from the North. In some respects this appears to be evidenced by the weather report of January eighth and nineth just passed. With an extreme low of thirty below in the northwest and two below at Amarillo, we failed to register a freezing temperature at Houston. I have been caught many times in Dallas when sleet and snow fell heavily there; and returning to Houston, found myself over night in a balmy, tropical climate.

Recently, our local press, following forecasts of the Gov-

ernment Weather Bureau, came out with streaming headlines predicting twenty-four below and more. Nothing like
these predictions materialized.

Perhaps our climate is changing, or perhaps a kind
providence looks after those "children of God" who, in
present circumstances would find themselves unable to cope
with the bitter cold that has come to us in generations past.

Quite often we hear reference made to "when the stars
fell," or "when Galveston Bay froze over"; I should far rather
recall such instances from memory, then to again experience
them. I trust that our scientific men are correct in their
assumption that better days are upon us, as concerns phenomenal weather and that eventually Houstonians shall live in
an Utopian climate.

TRINITY RIVER

Steamboats Once Chugged up the Trinity River

Time, it seems, is about to complete another cycle and
history will again repeat itself, however, on a much higher
plane. This time it is the development of the Trinity River
which will reopen and re-establish another great inland waterway in Texas.

Like a great many projects of its kind, the development
of the Trinity is merely preserving another waterway and
power supply which we almost destroyed in our mad rush to
build a great and better State.

Rapid development of the railroads, later followed by the
motor truck, created the opinion that transportation by water
was no longer profitable. This resulted in destruction of
the watersheds by the ax and plow, and the once broad and
mighty Trinity River gradually dried away into comparatively a small stream.

Transportation on the Trinity River is not a fantastic
dream as some would term it today, but instead it is a very
practical engineering venture which will reopen what was
once one of the finest waterways in Texas.

As far back as January twenty-nineth, 1843, a wealthy
Englishman, Mr. Houston (pronounced Howeston), cruising
with his wife in the West Indies on their auxiliary yacht,
Dolphin, heard of the Texas coast. They were taxidermists

164

and collectors of all kinds of curios, shells and flowers and members of the Audubon Society. Mrs. Houston was also a writer, and after their second trip to Texas had a book printed about the trip in London, in 1844.

They made two trips to Texas and on the second one landed at Galveston, where they stayed for months fishing, hunting and cruising. They made a trip far up the Trinity River. On returning, they reported a steamboat, the "Ellen Franklin," had just returned to Galveston in safety after making a successful voyage up the Trinity River four or five hundred miles. This is the first time such a trip had succeeded, and at that time it formed almost an era in the canal history of Texas. The bulk of the merchandise was carried by steamboats. Captain Frankland, owner of the steamboat, assured the Houstons while trying to interest them in the project, that navigation on the Trinity River was practicable, even within sixty or seventy miles of the Red River.

A large tract of land had been granted to an English and American corporation that had induced a number of settlers to locate, and an English Company had been founded, joined by a number of business men at Galveston, to ply up and down the Trinity River. Light draft iron steamboats with flat bottom rafts attached were used.

The successful trips, results of Captain Frankland's expedition, had proved there did not exist any great impediments to navigation of the Trinity River, as the river had no shallow spots and not many snags or hindrances. It also was observed that the navigable capacities of the Trinity River would prove of immense and incomparable benefit to Galveston from a commercial point of view.

At that early date, many Galvestonians were anticipating numerous invaluable water privileges. It was anticipated that a canal connecting the Trinity River with the Red River would not be an expensive undertaking, the distance being only sixty miles and the country was level. They felt the vast quantity of cotton and other products grown in the fertile lands of the Red River would be transported direct by means of the canal and the Trinity River to Galveston, instead of being put on Red River steamers and started on a long and circuitous route to New Orleans. Furthermore, they predicted that should this mode of transportation be established, it would benefit the entire State.

During a visit to Austin, Judge M. W. Burch of the State Highway Department assured the writer that he had seen near Dallas the ribs of two steamboats that had been carried up the river, but probably, because of low water for some time, stayed there. One was the "Duke of Wellington." Captain George A. Wright, who was mayor of Palestine for a number of years, said boats had gone as far as Dallas. He rafted and steamboated for years on the Trinity River.

The destination was usually Parker's Bluff, named for the uncle of Cynthia Ann Parker, who was released from her captivity by Governor Ross from the Comanche Indians.

In the "Sixties," the writer's father's office was just across Strand Street in Galveston, from the wharf of Dargan and Tobin, wholesale grocers, and steamboat landing. I have witnessed fifty to one hundred sternwheelers and sidewheelers loaded with merchandise, steam up the bay for the river, and still recalls the old megaphone crying, "All aboard the Trinity for Liberty, Wallisville and Magnolia." One in particular, the "White River," was commanded by Captain Joe Stafford, brother of the late Colonel W. M. Stafford, with my old schoolmate, Fort Smith, son of the old San Jacinto veteran and Indian fighter, Colonel Fort Smith of the Republic, as clerk. He entertained me aboard the sternwheeler and I bid him Godspeed up the river after we feasted.

I also remember the "Silver Cloud" and "Era No. 3." The landing point for cotton was at Magnolia, but at times boats would venture far up the river and often get tied up for months on account of low water. Three boats that were tied for months on account of low water, on a spring freshet came to Galveston, tied up on Twenty-Nineth Street and unloaded cotton in May.

At some future date the Trinity River project may be a reality. In memory, I can still hear the "chuck--chuck" of the engines and the swash of the paddles of the old sternwheelers as they plowed up the mud crossing Galveston Bay for the mouth of the Trinity River.

FIRST WHITE CHILD BORN IN HOUSTON

The death of Mrs. Julia J. Loeffler at San Antonio marked the passing of one of Houston's true pioneers, who was very closely allied with the activities in the early days of the city. It is generally understood that she was the first white girl born in Houston, about one hundred years ago.

166

She was survived by a brother, Henry F. Fisher, of the law firm of Fisher & Sears in Los Angeles; a sister, Mrs. Byron McKeen of Houston; one son, Hubert A. Loeffler, who is general freight and passenger agent of the Southern Pacific; three daughters, Mrs. Adolph Wilke, Miss Tillie and Miss Antoinette, all of San Antonio.

The old Henry F. Fisher, Sr., home, where she was born, occupied the entire block where the Woods Hotel and Stude's bakery and other buildings in Houston now stand. In the center of this block was this large home. Here is where she loved to roam as a girl, in one of Houston's beautiful flower gardens, which today is in the heart of the city.

Henry Fisher, Sr., secured very valuable concessions from the state of Texas to help colonize and was intrumental in bringing about twenty to thiry thousand German, Austrian and Swiss colonists to the state. For his reward, he was granted several million acres of Texas land, obtaining six hundred and forty acres for every family and three hundred and twenty acres for every male adult, which was similar to the colonization grants given Stephen F. Austin.

Major Gustav A. Loeffler, her husband, a Confederate soldier was appointed agent of the Nobility Verein, a company of forty titled Germans from the Rhein, formed to help colonize Texas and headed by Prince Zolm, founding New Braunfels, San Marcos and later Fredericksburg. He was a noted scholar and outstanding citizen of Houston. He was later made assistant land commissioner and colonization agent, and was beloved by everyone.

Possibly one of the oldest associates of Mrs. Loeffler was Mrs. Theodore Lubbock. Theodore Lubbock, who passed away a number of years ago, had the distinction of being the first white boy christened in Christ Church, making them among the oldest natives of Houston.

To many of us she was known as Mother Loeffler. Having lived a long and useful life, she now rests among her many friends in Glenwood Cemetery, Houston.

THE LAST OF THE WINDJAMMERS

The Passing of the Sailing Vessels

History reveals that in the very early days transportation in and out of Texas was, almost exclusively, by sailing vessel. When Stephen F. Austin, in the late twenties, landed his first colonists at Brazos-Velasco, in passing down Galveston Island there was no sign of life, and the only landmarks were the famous LaFitte's Grove, the three great trees.

The enterprising merchant and founder of Harrisburg, John R. Harris, carried to New Orleans by schooner, the first one hundred bales of cotton produced in Texas; a crop that was raised by Jared E. Groce, near Hempstead, and with whom Harris had contracted in 1826 to convey the cotton to a marketable port. This cotton was brought to Houston by ox-teams through what were then the wilds of Texas.

In the "Sixties" and "Seventies" and even as late as the "Eighties," a number of large, four-masted schooners were brought in at intervals by the late Charles Bender, from Calcasieu, Louisiana, and Pearl River, Florida. These were loaded chiefly with lumber for building railroad equipment, bridges, depots and ties. The T. and N. O. Railroad was not completed until the "Seventies," and even then suffered many interruptions of service.

These ships of Charles Bender usually unloaded their cargoes on the bayou front between Main and San Jacinto streets in Houston, where the steamboat landings were then located. Quite often, also large consignments of building material and brick were transported in like manner.

When the Federal fleet was about to capture Galveston in 1862, the Confederate government had in the harbor at Galveston a boat loaded with ammunition. It was sailed quickly up the bayou to Houston, towed to the Milam Street bridge, adjacent to Henke's Ice House, and there tied up. Heavily laden and more or less leaky, the ship gradually settled in the mud and was abandoned to its fate. There are many yet living who can remember that after a strong norther affecting the tides, boys and men would dig down in the hull of the old boat and bring forth muskets, sabers, torpedoes and bombs. In fact, after remaining embedded for forty or fifty years, these bombs when carried ashore and tampered with, were the cause of a number of serious accidents among the "treasure hunters" who, apparently, were possessed of more energy than brains.

During the War Between the States, a number of Houstonians, including Cornelius Ennis, T. W. House, Henry Sherfius and others, combined to engage in blockade running. Fast sloops, schooners and other types of "greyhound sailing vessels" were obtained, loaded with cotton that commanded an exceedingly high price abroad at that time, or supplemented in part with tallow, hides, wool, wax, etc., and the race to break through the Federal blockade and get away was on. In some instances stem vessels with auxiliary sails were used. Those vessels getting through would land their cargoes in Vera Cruz, Havana and other outlying ports, and bring back, in return, those items of merchandise so badly needed in the South.

It constituted, of course, a hazardous undertaking as quite frequently the outgoing vessels were captured; or, making the outward trip safely, were captured upon their incoming trip with return cargo. However, the successful landing of either an incoming or outgoing cargo, sold at prices then existent, would offset the destruction of several ships, the profit on a cargo being enormous.

A number of schooner-loads of "Boston ice" were brought up the bayou by the late Harry Prince, founder of the American Brewing Association. He was joined in the former enterprise by Captain DeLesdernier, paternal grandfather of the present DeLesdernier children of Houston. This ice consisted of huge blocks of lake ice and the ships were unloaded by block and tackle. When the hatches were opened and the ice in course of withdrawal, the ship would become enveloped in great clouds of vapor arising from the hold as the icy cold blasts came in contact with Texas' salubrious climate.

Uriah Lott, another shipper via "windjammer," brought up cargoes of railroad iron for use on the San Antonio and Aransas Pass road, then under construction, and other commodities followed in regular sailings.

The first real ocean-going boat of the steamer class to negotiate the ship channel, and the forerunner of the present gigantic volume of traffic now passing down Buffalo Bayou, made its maiden voyage up the channel in 1915. A solid cargo of fertilizer was loaded at the Armour Fertilizer docks at Long Reach, the transaction being handled by Fred H. Sage, agent of the Texas Transport and Terminal Company. The ship employed was a Danish brig. It was likewise her last trip. Near Land's End, on the coast of Ireland, she struck a German mine and was lost. Later, another Danish ship of the same company was loaded at the same docks, taking on a cargo of cottonseed meal for Danish ports. It was a small brig, fifteen hundred to two thousand tons capacity and, unhappily, met a fate similar to that of its predecessor sister-ship in the English Channel.

Returning to the earlier days, the Mallory Line, operated first by Commodore Vanderbilt, came regularly to Galveston in the early "Fifties," carrying both passenger and freight in the clipper type of ship. This was augmented by Colonel Tom Pierce, founder of the Southern Pacific, operating under the firm name of Pierce, Bacon and Company of Boston, who ran a line of fourteen clipper ships, both freight and passenger, from Galveston to Boston. He appointed an agent in Galveston, General E. B. Nichols, who was at that time partner of William M. Rice and E. J. Hart. These vessels carried the usual cargoes of cotton, wool, moss, etc., and did a tremendous volume of business.

A trip down the ship channel today will reveal at the mouths of the bayous one or two of the old four-masters. But the majority of them yet in existence can be found at the mouths of rivers, fast settling down to Davy Jones' Locker. At the mouth of Old River was the late Captain John Atkinson's water burial ground of the Houston Direct Navigation Company, where many of the old type sailing vessels spend their final days. Nearly all of the old clipper sailing vessels have disappeared from the seas. A few in occasional service are to be found around Portland, Oregon and Portland, Maine, and Boston. Doubtless too, the Orient has yet a number in semi-active service. Their romantic days have passed; they have been superseded by the tramp steamship and the jitney line boats.

There was something about these fullrigged, four-masted clipper ships that was romantic. They resembled seagulls with flapping wings. On the bowsprit usually was displayed Apollo, a mermaid or other sprites handsomely done in hand-carved wood and covered in gold, beautiful to behold. They carried, too, the usual brass howitzer of those day, as the seas were yet infested with pirates, and these guns were invariably fired in salute when entering or leaving port. They were presented with gifts by these interior friends, and day. This mail was of a different type; thousands of large linen envelopes, sealed with great blotches of red sealing wax and containing the account-sales of our Texas cotton and other commodities, a form as then executed unknown to our present generation. English, German and Belgium mail was routed via Queenstown or Southampton and Liverpool.

In some instances these great ships remained in port for

thirty to fifty days, awaiting a full cargo or favorable winds; long enough, as was facetiously said, for the captains to become naturalized citizens. Many of the captains became great favorites with the merchants and planters of the interior. They were presented with gifts by these interior friends, and in turn brought many handsome gifts from across the seas to the wives and children of Texas homes.

It required in those days some forty to fifty days sailing from the Gulf ports to England and European ports. If contrary trade winds or other handicaps were encountered, this was increased to ninety days or more. In brief, the trip across required three months; the return trip another three months. Account sales of merchandise so shipped were long in coming in, and instances occurred where merchants, unaware of the disposition of their shipments, were bankrupt before they knew it. Often fortunes were made back on subsequent shipments before the outcome of previous shipments were known.

Many can remember Mr. Morris Kopperl, who brought many cargoes of coffee from Brazil. Often you would see quaint small crafts from Spain and Portugal. Italy would send small ships to our harbor to remind us that Columbus had discovered the new world. But the real fun began when the Chinese or Japanese vessels hove in sight with the crews rarely averaging over five feet four inches in height. It would take twenty of them to each hatch to uncover them, and when they moved the sails and riggings it reminded one of Gulliver's Travels and the Lilliputians.

BOLIVAR POINT

Bolivar Light has stood as a lone sentinel and benefactor to the seafarers for the past fifty-eight years. In view of the fact that the ship channel will be improved from time to time it is necessary to keep this light burning. The Intracoastal Canal lays directly in its path, which will be a benefactor to Bolivar Point, as well as all points it traverses.

Bolivar Point was never much of a settlement, but is quite a historical spot and boasted of habitations when there were little more than huts and hulls of vessels on the island.

General Long, in 1819 with his army, landed there and made it his headquarters. It is a matter of history that he had great aspiration of establishing an empire in South Texas and Mexico.

The day General Long arrived at Bolivar Peninsula to establish a settlement with his young wife, they could see considerable activity across the channel at the pirate settlement called Campeche, situated about where the quarantine station is now located, or a little farther south. General Long and his wife also paid their respects to Jean LaFitte, as he was leaving the island for good, then rowed back to Bolivar Point, after being royally entertained by LaFitte.

General Long proceeded to Mexico in 1821 and his noble and courageous wife resided in Bolivar for some time afterward, then returned to her native land.

Colonel Jones (Levi Jones), a pioneer merchant in Galveston, about 1870, bought a lone tract at Bolivar and laid out the city of Ishmael, and maps that were highly lithographed, showing the great opportunities, were freely broadcast. Nothing but the lighthouse and the lighthouse keeper's residence stood at the point for many years, until L. P. Featherstone and Fox Winnie built the Gulf and Interstate Railroad. When the Santa Fe purchased this road, putting in its terminals, it was really put on the map.

Later the lighthouse was dismantled and discarded, and the state placed a marker on the site of the historical Long Fort at Bolivar Point.*

*A granite marker has been placed in front of the Old Bolivar Lighthouse, at Bolivar Point, which is no longer being used, by the Texas Centennial Commission, bearing the following inscription:

Previous to the storms of 1886 and 1900, there was a great deal of subsoil on the peninsula and there was quite a bit of farming done. Bolivar watermelons became famous, and the truck was brought in by quite a "mosquito fleet." The peninsula is very narrow.

A few miles up from the point was Roll Over, a little settlement named by a wag, who stated if one would lay on his back and roll over south, he would land in the Gulf, and if taking a roll north, he would find himself in the bay.

Bolivar Point may come to its own, and the proper usages of the bayfront will be found. It will largely be developed by shipping interests. Maybe the dreams of the old realtor will come true!

HOUSTON AND GALVESTON BUILT BY CO-CITIZENS

A glimpse into the careers of the early pioneers of the Texas coastal regions reminds me of what a joint city directory, or joint history, of the Galveston-Houston of those days would reflect. It is remarkable how closely interwoven were the prominent and leading personnel of the two cities. Correspondingly, the business and social life of the two cities were entwined.

In the early "Forties" there were many prominent Houstonians who were from and had aided in firmly establishing Galveston as one of the leading cities of the South—and their names became inseparable from the combined history of the two cities.

Many of the pioneers of Houston named their sons after old Galveston friends and associates in business. This was offset in turn by many of the Galveston youngsters bearing the names of prominent Houstonians.

"POINT BOLIVAR"
"Headquarters for Long's Expedition which attempted to free Texas from Spanish Rule in 1819.

"Named in honor of Simon Bolivar (1783-1830) leader in the Spanish-American War for independence.

"Here Mrs. Long and a small group remained until news of her husband's death came in 1822.

"A lighthouse was erected here by the Republic of Texas.

"Erected by the State of Texas 1936."

173

Take, for example, the career of B. A. Shepherd. He was first a leading citizen of Galveston, largely instrumental in advancing its early commercial status. Subsequently, he moved to Houston and became the first individual in Texas to engage exclusively in the banking business. He named his son Frank for Frank Ball of Galveston.

A. P. Root of Galveston came to Houston and married the daughter of Mr. Shepherd. Later he moved to Houston and succeeded Mr. Shepherd as president of the First National Bank.

Likewise, S. F. Carter, made his active start in Galveston, then came to Houston and amassed a fortune in the lumber and banking business. In turn, Guy M. Bryan, formerly of the old Galveston National Bank, came to Houston, married Mr. Carter's daughter and succeeded Mr. Carter as president of the Lumberman's National—now the Second National Bank.

History also shows the Gail Borden, famed inventor of the condensed milk that today continues his name, after surveying the city of Houston, moved with his brother to Galveston and surveyed that city; later, became the first collector of the port there. And in 1880, Gail Johnson, nephew of Gail Borden, came to Houston and established the Houston Post.

Samuel May Williams, a nephew of S. M. Williams, his secretary and co-worker, first started activities in Galveston, then came to Houston and engaged as manager of the Milby and Dow business.

Other co-citizens of the two towns who named their children for friends resident in the other were: Colonel Harvey Sellers, first in Houston, married the niece of James T. D. Wilson, moved to Galveston and established the first cotton exchange in Texas. Mr. Wilson named his son for the late Harvey Sellers. Judge Fairfax Gray, brother of Peter Gray, named his son Ebenezer Nichols Gray in honor of General Nichols of Galveston and Houston; and General Nichols, in turn, associated as partner with the late William Marsh Rice, named one of his sons for Mr. Rice, another one for his friend Tom Pierce, co-builder with Nichols, of the G. H. and S. A. railroad, and another son, Gray, for Judge Peter Gray of Houston. A. C. Crawford, partner of B. A. Shepherd before the latter moved from Galveston to Houston, named his son Shepherd Crawford.

Alexander H. Sessums started his mercantile career in Houston when the War Between the States was closed. Later he sold his business to W. D. Cleveland, Sr., and moved to Galveston. Mr. Cleveland named his son, A. S. Cleveland, Sessums as tribute to his former friend and associate. Dr. E. H. Massie of Houston, whose great plantation was located on Carpenter's Bayou, moved to Galveston and became the partner of Mr. Sessums.

J. H. Burnett amassed a fortune in Galveston as a cotton factor, sold his interests there, came to Houston and added to his funds by investing in Houston real estate and down town buildings. Among others, the Brazos Hotel and Terminal Hotel were constructed by him. His daughter, Ellen Burnett, married J. O. Ross of Houston, and the two of them later erected the Rossonian apartments, then the showplace of its kind in Houston. A son of the couple, J. B. Ross, was named Burnett.

J. R. Cheek, originating his activities in Galveston, came to Houston and developed both Manchester and Magnolia Park additions, leaving, at his passing here, a comfortable fortune.

Captain J. C. Timmins, father of George H. Timmins of the First National Bank in Houston, started in Galveston, came to Houston and engaged in the cotton business as compress manager.

General E. B. Nichols began his active commercial career in Galveston, moved to Houston, and engaged with William Marsh Rice and E. J. Hart. Subsequently, he moved back to Galveston, and Mr. Rice retained an interest with him in the latter's business there.

A son of General Nichols, Frank Nichols, went to England and was adopted by Lord Stewart. He returned to Houston and married Ella Hutchins in one of the greatest international marriages ever performed in Houston; it was an unhappy union and the young bride did not return to England with her husband. Upon the passing of the senior Lord Stewart, the English law ruled that the adopted son, Frank Nichols, married here as Lord Stewart the younger, could inherit neither the title nor the estate.

He returned to Houston as Frank Nichols, bringing with him the famous black diamond that had belonged to Mary, Queen of Scots, herself a Stuart, and which had passed down through the family to the senior Lord Stewart and through him to Frank Nichols. I have seen the stone on many occasions at various fairs and exhibits during those earlier days.

P. J. Willis and R. S. Willis, brothers from Montgomery County, first engaged extensively in Houston and moved to Galveston, where the firm did an international business.

Cornelius Ennis, starting in Houston, made a fortune and when the Civil War closed moved to Galveston, where he engaged in the cotton exporting business. Later he returned to Houston with his son-in-law, Frank Cargill, who had married Miss Cornelia Ennis, and assisted in building the Houston and Texas Central Railway. Ennis Cargill is named for him.

Noteworthy as reflecting the co-operative enterprise of the residents of the two cities, is the undertaking in which were joined John and George Sealy and J. H. Hutchings with Judge Peter Gray, B. A. Shepherd and Colonel Ashbel Smith in founding the Bayland Orphan's home at Bayview, midway between the two cities. It was managed for years by Colonel Gillette, father of Mrs. Rockwell Hoskins of Houston. Finally when the bayou steamboat service was withdrawn, the home was moved to Houston, occupying a site near what is now Bellaire. It is now to be moved to commodious quarters on Clear Lake and its constructive work continued under yet more favorable auspices.

Again, Galveston and Houston joined in many other co-civic enterprises; during the Civil War period the two cooperated in the formation and maintenance of "Howards" associations, forerunner of the present Red Cross in America, and which former functioned, in fact, during the yellow fever and cholera epidemics prior to the War Between the States. The same spirit of cooperation was shown in advancing the lyceums of the coastal regions, the Masonic lodges, Odd Fellows and similar organizations. Houstonians assisted materially in financing the early wharves in Galveston, and Galvestonians reciprocated by lending equal assistance in the building of railroads extending out of Houston.

Reverting to Civil War days, General G. B. Magruder, when in charge of Texas and Louisiana, had on his staff about an equal division of Houstonians and Galvestonians; and it was due chiefly to their knowledge that the effective strategy of the Battle of Galveston on January 1, 1863, was worked out and Galveston recaptured from the Federals.

In conclusion, I must add a coincidence recently occurring that impressed me: At the time William A. Kirkland was made a vice-president of the First National Bank, I ap-

proached him and requested that he shake hands with me. "Willingly," he replied, "but what is the occasion?"

I explained that in grasping his hand I had shaken hands with the fourth generation of his family personally known to me. "Interesting indeed!" he exclaimed, "but wait until you see the fifth generation, my young daughter."

Sometime later I saw the charming daughter and was remarking to Captain Jim Baker that I had now known five generations of the Shepherd family. With his characteristic cordiality, he retorted, "Mr. Ziegler, that is an interesting record, but I shall go you one better—I have known six generations of the Shepherd family; when I was in school at Sewanee, I knew the elderly father of Mr. B. A. Shepherd!"

Captain Baker's experience, it occurs to me, must be almost without parallel, considering that Texas is only one hundred years old.

During the days of the Volunteer firemen, a number of times Houston has been forced to call upon the Galveston firemen for help when raging flames seemed beyond control, and always the appeal was answered in the briefest time possible with existing conditions. Not only were men, machines and hose afforded by the Galveston Volunteers, but great risk was encountered in extra fast railroad service in making flying runs on such occasions. Fifty miles in fifty-five minutes is the record run on a fire appeal, and this was accomplished by the Galveston, Houston and Henderson road in 1878, when the Main Street block between Congress and Preston avenues burned. It must be remembered that in those days a wooden tressel spanned the bay and often twenty minutes was taken to cross the bay. When the Great Galveston conflagration occurred in 1886, and forty residential blocks were wiped out, Houston sent down more than half its fire apparatus. Both organizations were always on the qui vive to answer the S. O. S. calls, this showing how closely both cities were entwined.

It is interesting to contemplate what the status of Houston and Galveston will be when we celebrate our next centennial. Doubtless long before then they will have become known as the "twin cities of Texas," for surely, at the rate the population of coastal Texas is increasing, the gaps now remaining uninhabited between them will have been filled with homes and business places along the entire route, even as Los Angeles has become one with its outlying

sister-cities. It is meet, therefore, that the two cities hence-
forth, in the next few decades, may become the "Great
Metropolis of the South!"

HISTORICAL PAPERS FOUND (DR. PEETE)

R. W. Schroeder, thirty-three years ago, found valuable
documents in a house after the great Galveston storm in
1900. Among the papers found is the appointment of George
Peete as assistant surgeon-general, signed by Andrew Jackson
in 1832, and other papers dating back as far as 1832. Also
A. Peete's diploma, from the Virginia Military Institute.*
    The family is extinct, the last surviving member having
passed away now, Mrs. Will Ziegler, the sister-in-law of the
writer, and granddaughter of Doctor Peete.
    Dr. George Peete was a large planter in Virginia, the plan-
tation is now Virginia Beach, and owning hundreds of slaves,
when the document was signed by Andrew Jackson. When the
War Between the States came, he resigned his commission and
enlisted in General Lee's army, later becoming surgeon-general
of the Confederate army. When peace was declared, he turned
loose his slaves, sold his plantations for a song. Today that
property is worth millions and the great Southern resort is in
the center of it, Virginia Beach.
    Like many other discouraged Southerners, he came to
Texas to start anew, settled in Galveston and became a very
prominent surgeon. After a short time he was made state
quarantine officer and stationed at "Fort Point" where the
state built him a new quarantine station.
    On August twentieth, 1875, he was at his post during
the storm that destroyed Indianola. The authorities sent
a tug to get him to come to the city, but he lashed chains
over the house and refused to leave until this was finished.
Alas, he waited too long. Finally, he left the station with
his favorite grandson, Fred Blount, in a large yawl, manned
by seven seamen. The waves mounted almost mountain
high and next morning, after the storm, he and his grandson and seven seamen were found dead at the drawbridge
near Virginia Point.

*The original papers of Dr. Peete's are in the hands of Mrs. E. E. Bost,
in Fort Worth, Texas.

He was an outstanding man, resembling General Lee very much. When in uniform, he was often taken for General Lee. A life-size painting by a celebrated artist was lost in the storm referred to herein. While I never saw General Lee, who was called an Apollo, I have often seen paintings of him and they were almost like Doctor Peete.

The A. Peete referred to of the Virginia Military Institute was his only son, Angus Peete, who served with distinction with General Wood in the Philippine war. When the war was over, shattered in health, he visited me, and died fifteen years ago in Chicago. The only daughter of Doctor Peete was the wife of Dr. Fred W. Blount, who was the second state health officer in Texas, appointed by Governor Sayers, and many remember him and how he fought the merchants of the state and protected the people in the last epidemic of yellow fever, called the Guitares fever. At a general meeting held here, he refused the request of the merchants of Texas to lift the quarantine. I heard him say that as long as the danger lasted, he would do nothing. "One life lost in the City of Houston was worth more to him than all the commerce in the state." He died about twenty years ago.

When Mrs. Annie Blount Ziegler died a few years ago, the widow of the writer's brother, Captain William A. Ziegler of the famous Washington Guards, the family became extinct, but it is wonderful that after one hundred and two years all this could be unearthed.

Another man that resembled General Lee was his friend, George W. Pendleton, an outstanding officer, his chief aide and member of the staff and was finally elected to Congress on the Democratic ticket, a remarkable achievement at that time, from Cincinnati as it is generally Republican.

EARLY PAPER MONEY

First Bankers in Texas—Ball, Hutchings & Co.

When the regular government of the Republic of Texas began operations, it inherited a debt of more than a million dollars, in the form of paper money. The struggle had left the republic desolate. There were no banks and no money.

179

Lands could not be sold. To avoid the absolute dissolution of the government, it became necessary to resort to some expedient that might furnish temporary relief. This could only be effected by creating something that could cover some degree of credit abroad.

Three kinds of notes were issued, viz: Ten per cent interest notes called "Star Money"; notes bearing no interest, called "red backs," after 1839; and, in 1842, the exchange bills. The "red backs" ceased to circulate after 1839 and merely became objects of speculation. In 1842 the government refused to receive them for taxes. They were not worth ten cents on the dollar. Business of all kinds became dormant and a state of chaos existed. It was a trading proposition entirely like that of the John Jacob Astor fur days.

In 1842 Congress repealed the act authorizing "red backs" and authorized the issuance of not more than two hundred thousand dollars in exchange bills in denominations of five dollars to one hundred dollars, there being no small denomination of currency of any kind available.

The firm of R. and D. G. Mills of Galveston, bankers and commission merchants owning and operating large plantations on the Brazos with headquarters in Galveston, and Mills, McDowell and Company of New York and McDowell, Mills and Company of New Orleans, were powers in the land. Owning large interests in the Holly Springs Bank of Mississippi, the firm in 1845 sent over and obtained two hundred thousand dollars worth of bank notes, mostly in small denominations. They endorsed them and the notes were circulated and accepted everywhere like gold, which relieved the situation. This was what was called "Mills money." My father, Jacob Ziegler, was employed by them as farm products supervisor and later broker, until the death of Robert Mills in the "Seventies" for a period of twenty-six years.

For circulating this money the firm was fined twenty thousand dollars by the government, as there was found on the statute books of 1842 a law prohibiting any company from circulating currency in bills of any kind. This fine was remitted later when the Supreme Court held the law did not apply to the firm such as R. and D. G. Mills, which had loaned millions to the Republic and helped finance the mercantile business of the state.

When Samuel May Williams was secretary to the immortal Stephen F. Austin in 1831-35, he was appointed by Austin as secretary to the local government because he was fluent in the use of Spanish and French and he also wrote a fine Spencerian hand. He was a tireless worker and later moved to Galveston, where he built the Williams wharf. He owned the first steamboat and operated many vessels up the Trinity River and Brazos River, and became the leading merchant, doing more than any other man to build that city.

During his visit to Mexico, as secretary to Austin, he obtained from the Mexican government a grant for the "Banco de Commerciary Agricultura," which was recognized by the Republic of Texas in 1836. The firm acted as bankers for the people of Texas for years.

Ball-Hutchings, in 1847, opened their bank in Galveston. At the death of Sam M. Williams in 1858, the good will of this bank, chartered by Williams in 1835, was taken over by the firm of Ball, Hutchings and Company, making them automatically the first bankers of Texas even before the days of the Republic, more than a hundred years ago. The firm was then composed of George M. Ball, J. H. Hutchings and John Sealy. In the "Sixties," George Sealy entered the firm. He was the father of George Sealy, now president of the Wharf Company and chairman of the board of Sealy-Hutchings Bank, Galveston.

This firm did more to finance the State of Texas than any other bank. It built more enterprises and helped to establish more mercantile and wholesale firms than any other concern at that time.

The Ball, Hutchings and Company largely built the Gulf, Colorado and Santa Fe Railroad. John Sealy was made president and when this road was completed to one thousand miles, it was the greatest deal that had been accomplished, totalling 22 millions, in Texas, as it was financed entirely by Galvestonians. Houston, however, came next, in achieving the building of the Houston and Texas Central Railroad to Denison, which was built by Houston capital alone.

When one thousand miles of the Gulf, Colorado and Santa Fe Railway was completed, George Sealy was authorized by the board to sell the road to the Atchison, Topeka and Santa Fe for seven million dollars. When the Atchison went into the hands of the receiver and the stock went to nothing, those who held some of their stock were assessed five dollars per share to pay for the receivership.

181

Ball, Hutchings and Company, while not active cotton planters, or sugar barons, nevertheless became interested in farmers, to whom they advanced more than any other as bankers, and commission merchants. Their steamboats, sternwheelers, which they partly owned, would come from the Brazos, Trinity, Colorado and Neches rivers.

I remember distinctly seeing these steamboats when they left the flats at Galveston loaded with all kinds of merchandise, implements and farm products. Upon sailing the captain or the first mate, with a megaphone, would call, "All aboard for Trinity, Wallisville, Liberty and other landings." I would remain on the wharf and wave goodbye to my father, who carried saddle bags filled with gold and silver to pay for cotton. There were no interior banks in Texas at that time and Indians and renegades were plentiful.

Later, during the course of their early day existence, the firm of Ball, Hutchings and Company, and its successor, Hutchings, Sealy and Company were large owners of the Mallory Line, financing what were perhaps the finest and greatest ships of that line; in addition to which they were extensively interested in the Wharf Company. George Sealy came later, but over a long period of years assisted in guiding the destiny of the firm. Is was often said that a visit to the offices of their firm was like walking into the House of Rothschild, Baring Brothers, or Brown, Shipley and Company, of London. Particularly was this true when they were receiving the cotton kings or sugar barons from the great coastal or bottom plantations of the state.

Mrs. Nellie League, only child of George Ball, lives now in New York. Numerous descendants of the two early partners, Hutchings and Sealy, were unknown by me as I left Galveston prior to their arrival. ⟨The present George Sealy, chairman of Hutchings-Sealy Co., president of Cotton Concentration Co., and president of the Wharf Company, carries on the industries founded by his forefathers.⟩

⟨The present establishment, the Hutchings-Sealy National Bank, remains as a monument to the first generation of bankers of Texas, and to carry forward the traditions of the Centennial Bankers of the State. It is a reminder of the days of colonization, when banking in Texas was carried on largely as a "trading" proposition; and the money of the Republic consisted largely of the famous "Red Back" bills. ⟩

FIRST BASEBALL GAME IN TEXAS

Yankee Soldiers Introduced Baseball in Texas

In 1865, the first match game of baseball was played in Texas, just north of the Ursuline Convent in a large open prairie. It must be remembered that Galveston's first city map showed ten-acre outlots, as well as city blocks. As the transports arrived, the soldiers were quartered on the vacant outlots where there were no houses; many regiments were located in the east end, many in the west end, but the big parade grounds were north of the Convent as it was much more central.

In the center of this open space stood a large flagpole and on top waved Old Glory for years. It was raised for years at sun-up, with the boom of a cannon, and lowered at sundown. Just east of it was the British consulate, established in the days of the Republic of Texas. The British flag also was raised on a large flagpole and lowered each day during the Civil War to warn the blockade fleet that there the "British lion" roared and the bombarding guns gave it wide berth. The consul, Mr. Lynn, like a patriarch, wearing a long beard, raised and lowered the flag, personally, each day.

On this parade ground was mapped out the first diamond, and the crack teams of the different regiments assembled there to give battle.

When the command "play ball" was given, all the ragamuffins and boys on the Island were on hand to size up the players. They were the critics and after the game the cry went out from them, "O pshaw! They have stolen our old game of 'town ball' and substituted a few additional features." The boys never forgave the Yankees for making the steal.

Town ball, the predecessor of baseball, was played very much like the new game, with three bases in the diamond and a pitcher and catcher. The bat, however, was flat, like a cricket bat and the ball was made of rubber entirely. If the batter struck the ball a square lick, it would bounce and skim over the rich green Bermuda grass field for a block or more. Every player would run for the ball and if it was passed between the runner and the base, he was out; but if one was fortunate enough to "sock" or "stick" the runner, he was good and out. Cricket was played by the English

183

cotton buyers, but it never took like baseball and soon died for lack of interest.

It was little dreamed that this new game of baseball would eventually become the great American game of today, enjoyed by hundreds of millions of people, and that it would spread to all corners of the world. It was brought to Texas by the Yankee soldiers.

The crack team in Galveston was the Robert E. Lees. The Houston team was the Bayou City Club and some of the players were: Joseph P. Meyers, Sir Henry M. Curtin, Charles Bullock, Tom Whitmarsh, Sam H. Haines and Judge Henry F. Fisher; the latter three are the only survivors.

The cry still goes out, "Slide you, bum, slide!" or "You can't hit an open barn door!" but the old cry of "Oh, you Sandcrabs, see us bury you!" or in turn, "Oh, you Mud-cats wait till we get you in Galveston!" is no longer heard, or the similar nicknames and pet names given one another in the two cities.

Speaking of clothes, it was not a matter of what the fans wore, but how they wore them. They were almost as naked as the "Feeji Islanders." The writer's Sunday outfit consisted of a Confederate jacket of the gray and trousers cut from Yankee breeches, with patches galore and of many colors, to remind one of Jacob's coat of old. He also possessed a pair of goat skin gloves, made by a kind soldier, perhaps the only boy on the Island to own a pair.

EARLY DAYS OF THE GALVESTON NEWS

〈During the Civil War, the Galveston News was printed in Houston, and in 1866, it was moved to Galveston. The old News building stood on the east side of the lot now occupied by the Kress Store, covering a space of about forty by fifty square feet.〉 It is now located on Mechanic and Twenty-First avenues, in Galveston.

〈The writer, who began his career in Galveston, had his first introduction to the Galveston News, with his father, in 1866, through the late Willard Richardson, who published the paper during the Civil War period and later was succeeded by Colonel A. H. Belo.〉 He also renewed an acquaint-

ance of forty years ago with Mr. G. B. Dealey, president of
The Dallas News.

It was an early morning visit, just as the paper was coming off the press and Willard Richardson was taking off the
first paper. At that time the motive power of the press was
an old blind white horse, plodding away on an old treadmill.
At a later dated visit, the blind horse had been replaced by
a big Hoe and Goss press.

Colonel R. D. Bowen was one of the earliest employees
of the News, having sold papers on the streets long before
Mr. G. B. Dealey became associated with the paper.

⟨The Galveston News was the parent organization of the
Dallas Morning News, prior to the Civil War⟩

TREMONT HOTEL

Early History and the Closing of Hotel by Washington Guards

The old Tremont in Galveston was opened as the finest
hotel in the southwest and has a very interesting background,
especially in connection with the Washington Guards and
their military achievements.

The hotel was said to have been first built in 1839. General Sam Houston made the old Tremont Hotel his headquarters at various times and made his famous anti-seccession
speech from its balcony. Later Frank Lubbock made a speech
from the same balcony, advocating the burning of Galveston
rather than to see the Federals take the city. But in 1865,
while the Confederate soldiers, part of Cook's regiment were
quartered there, the Tremont was destroyed by fire.

It was rebuilt, in 1874, as the largest structure south of
St. Louis or west of New Orleans, by Burnett and Kilpatrick.
At the opening of the new Tremont Hotel, in 1876, the
Washington Guards in ranks were called upon to appear in
full dress uniform to aid in the dedication, under the com-
mand of Captain J. W. Edmondson.

In the "Eighties," the Washington Guards was the crack
military company of the State and South, in drill and discipline, under drillmasters, Captain Albert G. McMahan and
Captain William A. Ziegler. They were the first military
organization after the Civil War to wear the blue uniforms
and receive a charter. The two outstanding military achieve-

185

ments were its efforts in quelling a mob when the city was under martial law in 1877, and during the Taylor-Sutton feud in Indianola, when the guards found only three men peacefully smoking corncob pipes on the wharves, when they expected a mob of three thousand.

Other military organizations were the Island City Rifles and the Galveston Artillery Company.

The first session of the Texas Agricultural and Mechanical College was held in the Tremont Hotel in 1876 and sixteen of these boys were put into the Washington Guards, because of their military training.

In 1936, seven members of the Washington Guards, who served as special guards of honor in 1876, when the Tremont Hotel was opened, wrote its final chapter in a gathering at the cafe.

Signing of the roster of the Tremont Hotel for the last time were the following: R. D. Bowen, Paris, 1878; Captain George A. Hill,* Houston, 1870; Fred D. Lemcke,* Houston, 1870; Jesse A. Ziegler, Galveston, 1874; Charles W. Ziegler, Galveston, 1872; O. R. Hoecker,* Galveston, 1876; Dr. John T. Moore, Houston, 1896; J. Ed Crain, Houston, 1896; Sam J. Williams, Galveston, 1893; F. Andler,* Galveston, 1870; Fred Erhard,* Galveston. Only five remain today.

The oldest living Captain of the Guards at this meeting was Captain George Hill, father of George A. Hill, Jr. He lived in Galveston from 1869 to 1885 and was engaged in the cotton brokerage business in two firms, Quinn and Hill, and Orvis, Hill and Company.

Those unable to attend were the following: The present commander of Washington Guards, George N. Yard,* Clarence Herschberger,* W. C. Ogilny, Worthy Boyd,* and Colonel William Stafford Manor,* the oldest surviving members of the guards at that time.

Dr. William Gammon, owner of the hotel, extended a welcome to the guests and also read a telegram from Major John R. Ricker of the United States reserve corps, whose father was a member of Washington Guards.

A tribute was paid by those present to the comrades who had died. A special tribute was paid John Wyatt, Negro drummer of the guards for many years.

Interesting recollections and individual reminiscences were told and repeated events of early history in which the

* Deceased.

186

Tremont Hotel and the Washington Guards were closely allied, were related. And so it was that three hours were spent and the lobby of the Tremont Hotel echoed, for the last time, the happy laughter of these old men. When the doors were closed that night they were never opened again and the old hotel was shortly afterward demolished.

COLONEL JONATHAN WATERS' PLANTATION

Near Houston, in Fort Bend County, is located the historical Waters plantation, which reflects the history of Fort Bend County, Houston and the combination of Southern and Western influences which has contributed to its development.

Colonel Jonathan D. Waters, who was born in Newberry County, South Carolina, in 1808, established this famous plantation, and became one of the largest and richest planters in the South before the War Between the States.

He owned hundreds of slaves and thousands of acres of the most fertile land in Texas, and vast herds of his cattle roamed the prairies. At that time he was president of the Brazos and Houston Tap railroad, and prominently identified with and interested in several corporations and financial institutions in both Houston and Galveston.

He donated one hundred thousand dollars to the Confederate government to aid the Lost Cause, and made many other contributions which aided the states.

The plantation is now owned by the Scanlan sisters, who obtained it from T. W. House. It was first settled in 1840 by Colonel Waters and is situated on the Brazos River and Oyster Creek in the southeastern portion of Fort Bend County, near Arcola Junction.

On the first of March, Colonel Waters planted a crop of corn on the banks of the Brazos and raised it to maturity without a fence. At that time there were no big herds of cattle in the Brazos bottoms. He came too late to be one of the Austin colonists and therefore he had to purchase land. He first bought one thousand acres from Frances Bingham, and later two thousand acres from Mr. Coples. He added to this extensive plantation two hundred acres purchased from John Shipman.

The second crop of Colonel Waters was cotton, and that year he made one hundred and eighty bales. The third crop was a failure. The caterpillars destroyed almost every plant, and only forty bales were gathered. He then purchased the Fitzgerald League property, increasing the acreage in cotton until five hundred bales were gathered at a single crop. After this, Colonel Waters began raising sugar cane, and erected a fine sugar mill and a brick yard.

Mr. Waters beautified the plantation, planting bois d'arc wind-brakes, in which were clustered the wild white Cherokee rose, making a perfect hedge and wind-brake which protected his cattle from the northers.

He became one of the most popular and beloved planters in the state. He moved to Galveston, and purchased the home of Thomas M. League, father of J. C. League, for whom League City is named.

This mansion was erected in 1855 or 1856, a Colonial building of red brick brought from Maine, three stories high, with large fluted Corinthian columns. Colonel Waters furnished it as a family hotel, and called it the "Waters' House." It was also called the "Planters' Home," as sugar and cotton planters from all over the Gulf coast stopped there. It became a fashionable resort, where gay parties were held.

I remember in the gay "Seventies," I attended a semi-masquerade ball, a cotillion often called "German Dejoiners." I represented a Russian cavalier. Captain Louis Hershberger, in order to see me fitted out properly, lent me the cutlass he had captured on the "Harriet Lane" when he boarded her at the Battle of Galveston. I had to discard this early, to finish the dancing, which consisted of the minuet and lancer promenades. The ladies were dressed in Colonial style flowered silk dresses, hoop skirts, powdered wigs and black beauty spots on their checks. The men appeared in the ballroom only in full dress suits of black broadcloth. On very formal occasions they wore double-breasted frock coats.

The style and elegance of the Germans of those days cannot be described fully. Even the sugar baron and the missus, when the "Dixie Reel" was announced, joined in, stayed through the dance "Dan Tucker," and were loath to leave the floor when the strains of "Home Sweet Home" were played.

After this they would leave in a Rocky Mountain coach, driven by four white Kentucky thoroughbreds, drive down Tremont Street, the only paved street in Texas, made of

188

white clam shells, cemented together and glistened like snow after a rain.

The late Colonel W. L. Moody, senior, purchased this beautiful place, which he converted into a private home. William Jennings Bryan, Governor Hogg and many other notables were his guests there.

Where nobility often trod, the schoolboy now holds sway, as it is owned by the Catholic church, and bears the name of a true American, Father Kirwin.

In 1866, Waters' health failed and he came to Houston. The late Dr. D. T. Stewart and Dr. Burroughs advised that a trip across the water was necessary to save his life. He was placed under the care of eminent physicians in Paris, where he lived for two years, and finally died.

His immense plantation holdings, including thirteen hundred and eighty slaves, were left to his widow. His Houston residence was on Fannin Street. His affairs being in bad shape, his widow was compelled to borrow fifty thousand dollars from the Royal Bank of Canada, through the branch house in Havana. When she was unable to meet the notes, she came to Mr. House, who paid her eighty thousand dollars in gold and assumed all indebtedness.

J. H. B. House managed the plantation until 1900; when his health failed, the son-in-law of T. W. House, W. L. Howze, took charge. The plantation was incorporated in 1905 with a capital stock of seven hundred and fifty dollars, with T. W. House as president, J. H. B. House, vice-president, and W. L. Howze, secretary and general manager.

The sugar house was completely wrecked by the storm in 1900, and Mr. House purchased new machinery throughout. Until that time the sugar house was turning out about three million pounds of sugar a year, and with the new machinery it produced about eight million pounds a year. One hundred and fifty convicts were leased from the state and about two hundred and fifty free laborers were employed. A standard gauge railroad was built on the place in 1902, and cane was hauled from the field to the mill.

One and five-ton cars were used in transporting the cane. The road was three miles long and the cars were pulled by a small locomotive. The cane was switched alongside the cane carrier, and with drop doors lowered, the cane would roll out on the carrier and then be conveyed to the mill. Before the railroad was installed the cane was handled by old-fashioned dump wagons and dumped on the yard and then carried to the cane carrier by hand.

There is no question that this land was rich, for Captain William Christian, sales manager, often exhibited stalks of cane fourteen feet long, stalks of corn ten to twelve feet long and ears of corn one and half feet long.

Colonel Waters, while he never had any children, was married three times. He rests in the old plantation cemetery besides his three wives. The monuments are still well-preserved.

The planters all sleep their sleep, their dreams are dead and only the glamorous recollections are left for us.

While I have submitted a few of my recollections of the foregoing men, I am indebted to J. J. Fenn, Walter Howze, and Sewell History for their notations.

OLD WHIP

The Famous War Horse of General Santa Anna

About 1821-22 a man named Allen Vince came to Texas from Missouri as a member of Stephen F. Austin's colony and settled at the mouth of a small stream that empties into Buffalo Bayou, about twenty miles below the city of Houston and three miles east of Harrisburg.

Here he had a grant of land located, erected a house and established a stock ranch. For the benefit of commerce passing from one side of the stream to the other, he constructed a narrow, rough, strong cedar bridge and Vince's bridge became famous in Texas history in connection with the Battle of San Jacinto. This bayou was called Vince's Bayou.

When General Sam Houston learned, the day before the battle, that Santa Anna was at New Washington, his army almost to a man implored him to fight the "Napoleon of the West." Houston consented. He ordered Deaf Smith to burn the bridge, destroying all chances for a retreat by the Mexican army. At the same time he planned the strategy which proved so successful at San Jacinto.

Mr. Vince also operated a farm on the east side of the Brazos River adjoining the plantation of John A. Fenn in the southern part of Fort Bend County and raised a fine crop of cotton and corn besides cattle and stock for his ranch on Buffalo Bayou. He also had some good horses.

Among them was a large coal-black stallion whom he called "Old Whip" from the fact it was supposed that he whipped everything else on the ranch in the way of horses.

In April, 1836, when Santa Anna arrived at the Bayou road with his army, all residents of that area had fled before him. He gathered for his own use all of Vince's horses that could conveniently be caught. These included "Old Whip" which Santa Anna appropriated for use as his own war horse. He transferred his three hundred dollar gold mounted saddle from the back of one of his inferior mounts to that of the black stallion and rode away to New Washington, on the bayshore.

Santa Anna crossed all his men and baggage on the little bridge except a twelve pound cannon and caisson of ammunition, which he was afraid would break it down and which he sent around the head of the bayou in charge of a company commanded by General Castrellion. General Houston came along soon with his army and crossed the same bridge, and after him came General Cos with five hundred more Mexican troops.

Colonel Delgado, who was on the staff of General Santa Anna, said in his notes after the campaign that after arriving at New Washington and burning a warehouse there and taking possession of other property, the president sent him out with a detachment to bring in some cattle and slaughter them for the use of the army. Cattle were so plentiful that the soldiers soon rounded up one hundred head and drove them to camp.

Now, these cattle were raised in Fort Bend County, belonging to Dr. Johnson Hunter and had been driven from his ranch on Oyster Creek ahead of the Mexican army in an effort to save them; but he was finally compelled to abandon them on the San Jacinto prairie as Santa Anna approached. There were about six hundred head, and that accounts for cattle being so numerous at that time in that section.

On the day before the battle Santa Anna had the famous black stallion near him and, when he saw the conflict going against him, put on his silver spurs, mounted in his gold trimmed saddle and fled, to the consternation of the brave Castrellion and General Almonte, who were endeavoring to rally the panic stricken Mexican troops. He dashed across the prairie toward Vince's bridge, leaving Captain Henry

191

Karnes and his pursuing troopers far behind. The bridge, however, had been burned by Deaf Smith when the fleeing Santa Anna arrived. He attempted to cross the little bayou, but "Old Whip" stuck fast in the mire and he was compelled to abandon the horse and the fine saddle and hide himself in the thicket. Almonte states that before he fled he dashed up and down the line like a crazy man, crying "The enemy is coming! The enemy is coming!" which had a tendancy to demoralize the troops. Santa Anna had made no effort to form his lines and face the enemy; had lost all idea of fighting, and sought only to save himself.

Captain Fenn, who had been captured by one of Almonte's men in Fort Bend County, stated that he did not wonder that Santa Anna was running over pack mules, baggage and infantry, as he knew "Old Whip" well and that he was once the most powerful horse in the county.

Karnes and his men came upon the scene later, Almonte stated, and found the horse covered with mud and slime. Santa Anna also was a woeful sight.

But to return to Allen Vince for a little more of his biography. When the bridge was destroyed the name of Vince was forever linked with the history of Texas. Allen Vince was the first white settler on Buffalo Bayou in the region east and southeast of Houston.

With his brothers John, Richard and William and his sister Susan he engaged in the cattle raising industry and as the land filled with settlers dealt in land and slaves.

The author of "The Raven" states that on the night of April twentieth, 1836, Sam Houston's army feasted on the Vince brothers' cattle, which at that season and in that climate on the open range, must have been in fit condition for the table or the camp-fire. It is not on record that any of Vinces fought at San Jacinto.

Emigrating from Tennessee where he was born, April, 1785, Allen Vince moved to Alabama. When his first wife died he came to Texas, sometime before 1821, and from the time of his arrival until his death in May, 1849, he was a colorful and active figure in the life of the fast developing frontier country. His name appears frequently in the various court house records of more than one county.

He is shown to have been the foreman of the first grand jury impanelled in Harrisburg County in December, 1836.

Austin's county roll for 1826 shows Allen Vince a widower

192

Beach Front, Galveston

with one dependent. The dependent, his son William, who came with him to Texas, was old enough to serve in the army of the Republic, was granted a tract of land and died unmarried in 1838. Allen Vince had another son, John.

I am told that some of the land patented to Allen Vince is in the heart of the Conroe oil field where millions is involved.

"Old Whip" was restored to his owner who kept him for many years until he died at an advanced age. He was a magnificent traveler and moved as on springs. In fact nearly all Fort Bend County saddle horses were well bred and splendidly gaited. To ride on one was like sitting on a rocking chair, a gait like a fast walk and a lope. I have often seen George Herman ride into Houston in a single day from his Fort Bend County plantation.

Many old planters who came in from the Brazos or Colorado preferred this method of traveling, particularly in wet weather when the prairies became boggy.

The large wild sunflowers, blood weeds, and coffee bean weeds grew so thick buggies could not penetrate them.

Fort Bend County furnished many race horses. The Fulshers, Huggins, Harrises, etc., provided many horses that won first prize at the state fair. Dr. George Ferris of Richmond imported an Arabian stallion and I was the fortunate owner of one of the colts. I called him "Little Reb" but should have named him "Gone With the Wind" as he would never stay hitched, and cost me a small fortune in bridles, which he would break and then run away. But, I would always find him waiting at the barn door for his feed. He was the fastest quarter mile horse on Galveston Isle. I cured him of running away by getting a stout Manilla rope. There are many fine horses now and in the early days but "Old Whip" and General Houston's white steed will go down for generations in the eyes of Texans.

I am indebted to Joe J. Fenn, the surviving son of Captain Fenn, Sorrell's History and R. B. Huntly's notes for this story.

A LEGEND OF GOOSE CREEK
The Cannon Filled With Spanish Gold

Among the earliest settlers of Goose Creek was the "Sage of Evergreens," later honored as the Ambassador to the Court

193

of St. James and St. Cloud. During the War Between the States, he as Colonel led an army and acquitted himself nobly at Vicksburg. Fancy a Connecticut Yankee leading a Rebel regiment! He was the grand old man of his day, Colonel Ashbell Smith. His cousin, Rockwell Hoskins, a graduate of Yale and Harvard, came to live with him, and was later called "The Father of the Goose Creek Oil Field."

When the old Bayland Orphan Home was founded, an Episcopal minister, Henry J. Gillett, was made manager, but when the War occurred he was made chaplain of a regiment, with the rank of Colonel.

It was here that Miss Willie Gillett lived. She later married Rockwell Hoskins. Mrs. Hoskins is still living and often speaks of the many strange things that have happened in that vicinity. One is that a noted recluse lived at the mouth of the creek, hunting game in the winter, fishing in the summer, and farming between times.

Often he would absent himself for a week or more, then reappear with pockets filled with gold and silver, mostly Spanish coins. It was generally believed that he was one of the followers of Jean LaFitte, and was aware of where some of the latter's treasure was hidden.

It has often been said that one of the favorite haunts of Jean LaFitte was Goose Creek and the Cedar Bayou country.

Anyone who has sailed up from the mouth of Cedar Bayou, with its moss-covered oaks, cypresses and other trees, knows what a fine retreat it must have been for the buccaneers. Goose Creek was then a much prettier stream than it is today, and was an important settlement, with its brick yards, wood yards, and other active industries. In the early days, as the story goes, there lived a well-known individual, Uncle Chris Casey, who was a typical Goose Creek native and I remember many persons who bought wood, bricks and cotton from him regularly.

Way back in the "Sixties" a villainous-looking foreigner often appeared in Houston. He had but one eye and a scar from a saber wound or a knife cut across his cheek. His looks were sufficient to prove him a pirate, but in addition to that, he always brought with him a bag of gold and silver coins of ancient date, Mexican and Spanish money. While he was watched carefully, no one ever discovered where it came from, and no one ever doubted his being one of LaFitte's men. Everyone in Houston had implicit faith in this.

While the existence of LaFitte's treasure was merely a

matter of supposition, there were found some strange marks on the trees at Clear Creek just out from Seabrook, and much digging was resorted to, but nothing was ever found. However, it was supposed that LaFitte with his fleet of forty or fifty sloops, schooners, and brigs often came up the cut-off from the Bay into the Creek.

The only good thing LaFitte ever did for us was when he could not persuade Jim Campbell, his first lieutenant, to follow him farther and release him.

Campbell settled on a farm at Campbell's Bayou (named for him), just fifteen miles south of Seabrook where it empties into the Bay at Half Moon Lighthouse. He became the first horticulturist in Texas, specializing in raising plums, peaches, figs, etc., and long before the fruit was ripe, Galvestonians would sail over and contract for his produce. His son Warren (named for Colonel Warren D. C. Hall, a friend of LaFitte's) died recently at the age of ninety-one. He was known to me, and I sailed with him a hundred times on a yacht, "Rosa and Lillie," which was owned by Colonel William Harvey Sellers, first president of the earliest Cotton Exchange in Texas, and uncle of our Hubert Wilson and Mrs. Eugene Dargan. As sailing master, he took us all on the bay on fishing trips, where he commanded "Hard alee," "Come about" and "Cast anchor!" We were sure to catch plenty of fish on shell reefs and sandy bottoms. I know the Campbells were familiar with every reef and every stream tributary to the bay, and I am sure they often visited near here on Trinity Bay, San Jacinto Bay, Goose Creek and Cedar Bayou. They were fine men and their descendants are prominent today.

In my boyhood days many men were pointed out to me as "LaFitte's Gang," among them "Crazy Ben," who wore earrings and looked like a typical pirate. He was a fisherman. Once when he was seated in a skiff on the channel, a large porpoise appeared. He had a harpoon attached to a chain in the bow of the boat, and with this he speared the porpoise, which carried him up East Bay at the rate of thirty miles an hour, and finally the pilot boats had to rescue him.

My grandparents, who came in 1845, found many of these pirates on the Island of Galveston, and described them as a "rum-soaked, motley crew."

As a boy, my ambition was to find LaFitte's treasure, and often visited LaFitte's Grove, the "Three Trees," on the west part of Galveston Island, and scratched around the sand hills, but found nothing. My parents' home was situated in line with these trees, and I have often seen men carrying sacks, lanterns, shovels and picks going out to LaFitte's Grove at night fall. The face of the earth has been dug up, but I have heard of only a few Spanish doubloons having been found. In fact, the entire Gulf Coast and inlets have been excavated from Port Lavaca to Barataria Bay, LaFitte's first rendezvous, and the search still goes on.

Mollen E. Moore, my boyhood friend and sponsor to our old "Washington Guard," described LaFitte's treasure thusly: When LaFitte burned his town of a thousand inhabitants on East Beach at Galveston, and standing on his flagship, "The Pride," ready to sail from Texas shores forever, he was heard to mutter, "I have buried my treasure at the Three Trees." A short time after, two of his followers returned; going to "Tres Palacious," they began digging. Suddenly they heard their picks clash against copper and they pulled out a large copper covered chest. Opening it, they found, instead of money, the remains of LaFitte's beautiful Creole wife, who had died a few days before he left for Yucatan, where he died in 1826.

The tale of the Spanish cannon sealed and filled with gold has been told for a hundred years. It is surmised that, during the period of which I am speaking, this cannon was on a sailboat, belonging to General Santa Anna which was sunk in Goose Creek to prevent its capture during the Texas Revolution.

Uncle Chris Casey often referred to the cannon filled with gold, and said that it would soon be unearthed and his dreams would come true. He was very positive and enthusiastic about the existence of these treasures, and being well versed in Texas history, could tell all about the days of Santa Anna and the many hunts for the treasures. He estimated that the cannon contained fifty thousand dollars in gold.

The only treasure ever reported found in this vicinity was a bunch of large knives found on the shores of Evergreen Bay. Whether they had been used by the pirates or by Mexican filibusters, or by the early sugar makers, could not be determined. Another time an old wagon wheel was found.

Mrs. Ivy Illfrey, a life-long resident of the Cedar Bayou community could relate interesting stories. Her grandfather, one of the early settlers of Cedar Bayou, often was host to

196

Santa Anna when he visited Texas before the Revolution. Her grandmother used to tell stories of the times when Santa Anna drank coffee at their home and visited for weeks at a time, when rodeos drew throngs of people from as far as Mexico. Later, the Mexicans and desperadoes became a constant menace to the country and the settlers had to bury their wealth and there were no banks at the time.

It was also believed that LaFitte and his gang used to come down in this section and bury their gold too. On one occasion, some marks which were found on trees, led to renewed digging there.

It is a well-known fact that in the "Thirties" a company of Mexican soldiers were carrying sixty thousand dollars of government money on the Santa Fe Trail, between San Jacinto and the Brazos River, when they were attacked by a large band of Indians. The Mexicans took refuge on a "sweet gum island" (a clump of bushes on the prairie) and buried the money in a hole before putting up a fight with the Indians. The latter being a strong force, the result was that all of the Mexicans were killed, except one man who escaped, so badly wounded that he died soon afterwards. Houston people have often searched for that "island," but its location has never been found. At one time, cowboys discovered a lot of arrow heads sticking out of a sweet gum tree on Cypress Creek in the northern part of the country, and they dug up the face of the earth near there, but found nothing.

On another occasion, a German farmer, while hunting for cattle, found a Mexican dollar not far from Cypress, where the railroad crosses the creek; again there was much digging with no success.

Like most of the stories of buried treasures, the legend of the "cannon filled with gold" and the fabulous fortune of the buccaneers, lives without foundation.

It is likely that LaFitte died without a cent as it was a custom for men of his character to squander their money. If this swashbuckling buccaneer had a fortune it is reasonable to assume that what was left of it is lost beneath the waves of the Gulf, or buried somewhere along the coast of Yucatan.

The "cannon filled with gold" will always remain an intriguing story, and as long as gold is foremost in man's mind it is probable that many will continue their search for the cannon, but whether it will ever be found or not is another story.

197

DEDICATION OF THE
SAM HOUSTON BAY-SHORE HOME

Another marker honoring "those who have gone before" was unveiled on the "Ravenmoor" estate of Milby Dow, August the eighth, 1937.

The fourteen hundred pound marble slab marks the Cedar Point homesite of General Sam Houston.

The simple ceremony was attended by a crowd of about three hundred people from Houston and surrounding towns, including Attorney General McCraw, Colonel Andrew Jackson Houston, the only living son of General Houston, and ninety-seven-year-old Jeff Hamilton, former slave and body servant of the General.

Called on without warning, the former slave stole the show from the more learned orators, as he addressed the crowd under the oak trees of Ravenmoor.

"I adore the name of Sam Houston," he said. "It has been seventy-four years since I was on this soil. It's a pleasure to be back on the 'old stomping ground.'

"I want to say to you, let peace and harmony prevail among all nations. That's my religion."

Major John C. Townes, president of the San Jacinto Centennial, welcomed the crowd to Ravenmoor.

Attorney General William McCraw, delivering the dedication speech, said:

"We should have a thrill of pride in gathering on this sacred soil to honor Sam Houston. No man has ever charmed the human heart as he did. We should feel more than privileged at having a part in this ceremony, attended by Sam Houston's only living son, Andrew Jackson, and his body servant, the good and faithful Jeff Hamilton."

Colonel Houston asked that Judge Sam Houston Payne unveil the monument.

Mr. H. Dick Golding, executive secretary of the San Jacinto Centennial Association, was chairman of the arrangements committee.

Other prominent guests at the ceremony were: Mayor R. H. Fonville, of Houston, and former Mayor John T. Browne, Houston's oldest living Mayor. There were also present officials from La Porte and Chambers counties.

The only lineal descendants of Sam Houston in attendance were Mr. Franklin Williams, grandson of Sam Houston, and Mrs. Madge Hearne.

PART THREE

HISTORICAL SKETCHES

GERMAN NOBILITY COLONIZE TEXAS

When the League of Nobility (the Adelsverein) was formed to colonize Texas in 1842 at Mayence, Rhennish Prussia, they sent their emissaries, Count Boos von Waldeck and Count Victor von Leiningen, to assist in caring for the German colonists. These men arrived in Galveston in 1842. Both carred letters from the most prominent people in Europe to Stephen F. Austin and Sam Houston. On their arrival they made Louis Klainer their fiscal agent. He was a member of the large banking and merchandising firm, Kaufmann and Klainer, which later in its day became the gigantic firm of Kaufmann and Runge of Galveston.

Count Boos von Waldeck and Count von Leiningen came to Houston and made arrangements with Henry Fisher, an outstanding man of his day, who was brother-in-law to H. Bonzano, director of the United States mint in New Orleans. He made a contract with Fisher, of the Fisher Muller Colonization Company, guaranteeing each settler with a family six hundred and forty acres of land, and each single male three hundred and twenty acres. Von Leiningen proceeded to Austin and demanded that the land be exempt from taxation for a period of four years. President Houston refused to grant this, of course, which forced Von Leiningen to return to Germany a little later.

The League of Nobility, which in 1844 was comprised of twenty German barons, princes and counts, entered into an agreement with the Fisher Muller Company. Large sums of money were spent all over Europe to settle six thousand families. Many immigrants arrived—some, however, proceeded to Missouri, Kansas and other states, resulting from the advertisements. Galveston and Indianola were designated as the main ports for the colonists to disembark. Indianola was first called "Indian Point," but later named "Powder Horn" and "Carlshaven," in honor of Prince Charles of Germany. Between the years 1842 and 1878 about sixty thousand immigrants were induced to settle here.

It was my pleasure to have seen probably fifteen to twenty thousand disembark from the immigrant ships. Needless to say, the day of disembarkation was like a big circus day. Many business houses closed up to see the fun and to transact business with the immigrants. All the pioneers and early settlers in Texas who desired cooks, house servants, and farm hands, made application to the authorities, who tried

201

to obtain them. When my mother needed a house servant, I assisted her in selecting one. I remember my mother employed a Mrs. Klatt for a cook. On the following Saturday she was stricken with yellow fever and died on Sunday; Monday her husband was stricken and died; and the following day the two sons took sick and died; thus wiping out the whole family in four days as none was acclimated.

After the needed help was selected, the bulk of the immigrants was billed and ticketed like merchandise, and herded together like sheep. Each had a large tag pinned on, giving destination and route by railroad or steamship. Ringling Brothers or John Robinson circus did not attract more attention. Often a line of one thousand men, women and children would march from the wharf to the Galveston, Houston and Henderson railroad station, the only road between Galveston and Houston at that time. They marched in the middle of the street to the depot one and a half miles away, and were kept in line by the state immigration officer or the company officials.

Often a Russian, or a German from Hamburg, could be seen wearing a fur coat in July or August, or a Swiss peasant could be seen in native attire with knee breeches and Alpine hat decorated with feathers. These were the days when the females here wore anklets and showed nothing more than their insteps. To behold the peasant women of Germany and Switzerland with dresses up to their knees, made everybody "rubberneck."

Often you could see a paddy with a short pipe stuck in the side of his mouth, wearing knee breeches, and a knapsack strapped on his back. But the real fun was to see a big fat immigrant with a round black hat, long tailed coat reaching to his knees, with his hands behind his back, smoking a four-foot porcelain pipe. Behind him followed a frail wife, weighing about ninety pounds, loaded down with bundles of bedding and clothes. Trailing her were the children with pans, dishes and cooking utensils strapped to them. The man before the emancipation of woman.

When the Southhampton or Liverpool ships arrived, you could often see the Scotchman with his bag-pipes strung on his back. When the procession stopped, he would unstrap the contraption and play his strange music, to which the Negroes sometimes tried to dance, but which they soon gave up in disgust. Many of this class of immigrants of the early days are now the bankers, lawyers and merchants of today, and many have attended both houses of the legislature in Austin.

The first Germans to arrive were F. Ernst and Charles Fordtran, who arrived in 1821. Their stories have often been told.

The next to arrive were the Klebergs and Von Roeders, in 1831, who were shipwrecked and cast ashore on west Galveston Island, where nothing was visible except three trees, or LaFitte's grove, as it is now called. Rudolph Kleberg, and other male members of the group succeeded in chartering a schooner and proceeded to Austin's headquarters at San Felipe.

It will pay any reader interested in a more detailed account of these settlers to read Professor Moritz Tillings' "The German Element in Texas" and Von Roemer's "Texas," recently translated from the German by Oswald Mueller of Houston, also Fletcher's book on "Prince Zolms." The Kleberg females and one of the male members remained in Galveston to fight the Indians, snakes and alligators, and to kill deer, which were plentiful.

After Kleberg's return, he succeeded in chartering another schooner, which took them to Harrisburg. There they rented a house from John R. Harris, the family remaining there until residence at Industry was completed. Mrs. Rosa Kleberg was a gifted writer, and her letters to the Germans at home brought many families to Texas.

Mrs. Kleberg related an amusing incident, which happened while they were living at Harrisburg. One morning, while baking bread a shadow was cast on the door. Looking up she perceived three large Comanche Indians in full war paint. Quickly she ran into the next room to get her gun, and when she returned she saw them fleeing, calling to her "swap, swap." Looking at her kitchen table, she discovered three large turkeys but her bread had disappeared.

It was my pleasure to have known a number of the older Klebergs. Many reside all over the state and in Galveston. Robert Kleberg must be remembered as having married the daughter of Captain King, of the great King's ranch, which he managed until he passed away a number of years ago. One or two sons reside at Kingsville, managing the ranch; another is the national congressman at Washington, D. C.

I was a member of the Fisher and Loeffler households for years, which gave me an intimate knowledge of the early days. Mr. Fisher's residence occupied the entire block. It was a large two-story house, and stood in the center of the block now occupied by the Woods Hotel, Shudde and Stude stores. No streets had been cut then and it was a hill covered by a vegetable garden and a beautiful old-fashioned flower garden. It was a pleasure to see his four daughters, who became the late Mrs. Gustave Loeffler, Mrs. Byron McKeen, Mrs. H. Pannell and Mrs. James Chew, roaming around the flower gardens. Their only brother still lives in Los Angeles, Henry F. Fisher, who must be remembered as senior partner of the law firm of Fisher and Sears.

I was told fifty years ago the Mr. Fisher took three million acres of patented land grants, all on sheepskin, signed by the president and other officers. In order to raise funds, he borrowed seventy-five thousand dollars on the three million acres granted him for colonization purposes, but a depression occurred shortly afterwards and he lost his fortune and many hard years of labor.

These were the old John Jacob Astor days—a "swapping proposition only." The red backs at one time could not be sold for anything. There was no currency anywhere. The Nobility League paid big money for their land, and some of it was only worth five and ten cents per acre—the surveying and costs of locating the land were more than the land was worth.

But to return to Count Waldeck. He purchased four thousand, four hundred and twenty-eight acres of land near Round Top from Robert Mills of Brazoria, and named it "Nassau." The land had some nice timber on it and was cultivated by slave labor. He made frequent trips to Houston, where the German population then was about fifty per cent of the total inhabitants, who had their singing societies, literary clubs, etc. Many prominent families had arrived, among them the Berings, Cabanas, Kosses and Harde. On one of his visits he met Morgan L. Smith, the owner of the finest equipped sugar plantation in Brazoria County. It was a beautiful place.

Its well-kept turn-rows and the park around its fine brick residence was ever a pleasant view. You could see several thousands acres of waving cane and corn as far as the eye could see. Mr. Smith had decorated the park around the residence with twenty-five thousand dollars worth of statuary. It was a sight for the gods. The sugar house was of brick, an immense structure, and resembled some castle more than a building of sugar making. It had a double set of sugar kettles. In conjunction with the sugar house was a refinery

204

for making white cut loaf sugar. Sugar was also made in cubes.

This was the finest sugar refinery in Texas. The barns or cribs, of which there were several, were of bricks, as were also the cabins of the slaves. There was a nice brick church erected on the plantation, where services were held for the slaves, the whites also attending. The services were conducted by white ministers. (Was anything like this pictured by "Uncle Tom's Cabin," or other abolitionists?) In the ravine was an immense cement reservoir that held water for the sugar house and for the refinery for making of sugar.

When Count Waldeck saw it, he was reminded of the many feudal castles on the Rhein, and, while he was the guest of Mr. Smith, was so taken with the plantation that he purchased it, six thousand acres, naming it "The Waldeck Plantation." He owned and operated it for years through the firm of Spofford and Company, his bankers in New York, whose Texas representative was the banking firm of T. H. McMahan and Company of Galveston. I remember well Mr. William I. Evarts, the father of the late Percy Evarts, who passed away recently as a city official—his brother is Curtis Evarts, the produce dealer, who still resides here. Mr. Evarts managed it for years, until it was sold, but his family reside here.

To give one an idea of the magnitude of business done in those days, there were several large merchants in the towns of Columbia and Brazoria; John Adriance in Columbia, and Patrick McGreel of Brazoria, and R. and D. G. Mills of Brazoria, often took in five thousand dollars in cash in one day, besides the credit sales, and business was mostly done on credit in those days. Mr. Robert Mills was the granduncle of our Mr. Hutchins, principal owner of Clarke and Courts. Just before Mr. Mills passed away, he pointed to a pile of his books, saying to me, they represented untold millions. When the "Lost Cause" was ended, he freed eight hundred slaves and owned eight plantations, now going back to the jungle which Stephen F. Austin had found.

Count Waldeck returned a little later than his friend Count von Leiningen. They were succeeded by Count Prince Solms-Braunfels who founded the city of New Braunfels but only remained here a short time.

But Baron von Meusebach, who finally managed the affairs of the Nobility Verein, lived and died in Sisterdale, where I had the pleasure of seeing him fifty-five years ago.

WAVE OF THE GULF

My forebearers were destined to follow the early colonists to New Braunfels, but when they arrived in Galveston ready to embark for Indianola they were met by friends from Hanover who said, "Dear people, do not go any farther." Eight hundred of the emigrants had died of yellow fever, small pox, cholera and malaria.

Zachary Taylor had arrived, and the war between Texas and Mexico was practically declared. General Taylor paid more for horses than individuals could pay, which caused a dearth of teams. No transportation was available and those that proceeded to New Braunfels suffered for want of food, medicine and water. Thousands perished. It was often said that the road from Indianola to New Braunfels was a continuous graveyard and many of the colonists' bones were bleaching in the sun.

While in the "Sixties" and "Seventies," I saw many of the colonists day after day; I often visited the German consul, Julius Frederich, and viewed the magnificent paintings of the town of Fredericksburg, the junction of the Pedernales and near the Colorado, one of the prettiest spots in the country, but I did not see Fredericksburg until 1880 when many of the original colonists still lived. Mr. J. W. Jockush, grandfather to our Mr. Julius W. Jockush, Jr., grain man, was Prussian consul at that time.

Many of the readers of this story have seen San Marcos and New Braunfels, with its beautiful Landa park. They, like Stephen F. Austin's coloinsts, picked rich land but endured many hardships to give us our present civilization, to whom we owe a debt of gratitude that can never be paid.

THE LANDING OF THE ORIGINAL SWEDES IN TEXAS

In looking back over the past century of development in Texas, one European country looms as a factor in Texas history—Sweden. Sixty years ago, in the days of sailing vessels, many full rigged ships and barks arrived from the Land of the Midnight Sun, coming regularly to the Gulf and bringing light cargoes and immigrants from Sweden, Norway and Denmark.

At that time, Texas was not so closely connected with Sweden as it is today because these ships have been replaced by steamers which come regularly to take out cargoes of oil, cotton and fertilizer. Nor even do we see the tramp steamers of twelve to fifteen tons, manned by a dozen seamen, as they have been supplanted by the big carriers, manned by a crew of hundreds. It is no longer profitable to maintain small steamers for long voyages.

I have had the pleasure of knowing many native sons of Sweden. Among them were A. Wettermark, banker associated with B. A. Shepherd in the early days, and also the genial pioneer, Gustav August Fosgard, who arrived in this country one hundred and ten years ago. We were friends and neighbors and had many business transactions together. Just before he passed away, he gave out the reminiscences of his earliest days in Texas and to preserve the facts, I took the notes to which I refer now.

On the morning of November 22, 1848, a party of Swedish immigrants landed at the foot of Main Street in the City of Houston. The steamboat was the "Reliance." They had left Sweden in the early part of the year, sailed to Boston, then to New York to find transportation to Texas. They boarded the schooner, "Stephen F. Austin" for Galveston, and from there boarded the Reliance to their destination.

This was the only way to reach the interior of Texas as Indians and Mexican bandits were ever present obstacles. There were no telegraph or telephone systems then and only a few miles of railroad in the United States. Covered wagons, ox-carts and stage coaches, and some "prairie schooners" were the methods then used for transportation.

The party consisted of two families, Anders Palm, his wife, two daughters and the "mother of S. M. Swenson." They had been on a return visit to Sweden. In their party were three maid servants, six men servants and a young boy, and none of them could speak English. The Palms had a brother, Sir Swante Palm, living in LaGrange at the time. S. M. Swenson, the nephew, resided on a plantation in Fort Bend County. The boy was a son of a well-to-do farmer in Foreisum, Sweden, who represented the district of "John Koping" in the Swedish "richsdag," the parliament.

The boy came over to prospect and view the land and then to return to his native country. He was so taken with the richness of the new country that he remained until the spring of 1866.

To inform him when the long expected party had arrived, S. M. Swenson had left word and had made arrangements with B. A. Shepherd of Houston to send a rider to Richmond with the dispatch. It took several days before the arrival of the vehicles which were to convey them to Richmond. Meanwhile, the party was well quartered in the Washington Hotel at the foot of Main Street in Houston. It was a strange sight to see these Swedish citizens in their native dress and the town turned out. As Artemus Ward said, "They saw the show for nothing and it did not cost them a cent."

They had brought with them a two-horse wagon with harness, which also attracted much attention, as well as their large brass bound chests containing clothing and some farm implements.

Mr. Fosgard had brought with him a small rifle, equipped with percussion caps and flint lock, also, two pepper box guns, which he later carried to California when the gold rush was on.

The party proceeded to the Swenson plantation at Richmond and was soon engaged in planting cotton and corn and clearing the timber and underbrush. They were the first white people to pick cotton on the Brazos. He was well satisfied with his experience as a cotton planter. The party later scattered seeking a healthier climate, some going to Industry in Austin County, some to LaGrange in Fayette County and later to Irion and Williamson counties.

Sweden is a great agricultural country and the growing season is very short and the land requires large quantities of ammonia, with which our cottonseed meal is charged, to quicken the growth. We supply to all Scandinavian countries this commodity. They also mix our cottonseed meal with rye flour, which is now fed to millions of people in that country. Cottonseed meal is also fed to sheep and cattle.

S. M. Swenson's mother returned to Sweden where she continued to live until she passed away at the age of ninety-nine. Mr. Swenson then came to Houston and founded a co-partnership with S. Lionel Hohenthal. Mr. Fosgard found employment in Houston with Mr. Shepherd, who established the first private bank in Texas. Swenson set up his life long friendship with Mr. Wettermark.

Later, Mr. Swenson moved to Austin and became one of its influential citizens. He was instrumental in bringing hundreds of Swedish families to Texas, many of whose descendants are now living in Travis and Williamson counties, particularly in the vicinity of Round Rock, Hutto and Taylor.

Scandinavians are a grand race of men. Nearly all Swedes are tall and powerful men. As a matter of strength they stand out as longshoremen and particularly as cotton screwmen, as no weakling can handle a cotton jack. I have seen them run away with a cotton truck loaded with five hundred bales for two blocks, like pushing a baby carriage.

The writer, in 1876, was a co-worker in a cotton office with John G. Palm, who wanted to give me a good time, when he learned I was going to the Philadelphia Centennial exposition, and gave me a letter of introduction to the grand old Swede, S. M. Swenson. Then for the first time I saw this great pioneer of Texas and his son, Eric P. Swenson, then a young man. Both had moved from Austin to engage in the banking business. They prospered in the East, and made an investment later in Texas which was destined to be one of their greatest.

About thirty-five years ago, my friend, Guy M. Bryan, Jr., a nephew of Stephen F. Austin, called at my office stating, "Ziegler, my family is tired of ranching and planting cotton and corn. We are going to sell all our Brazoria County lands, aggregating thousands of acres, to the Swensons."

The price Mr. Bryan named was forty-five dollars an acre, if I remember correctly. The Swensons had the land analyzed. They discovered large sulphur deposits which they soon developed.

That land which Mr. Bryan disposed of for forty-five dollars an acre, has since given up millions of dollars worth of sulphur for market. Ships loaded from Freeport, Houston and Galveston carry this product to all parts of the world, today, and ninety per cent of the world's requirements come from this state.

Fosgard, who gave me the privilege of pasturing my Jersey

cows and my Kentucky thoroughbred horses on his property, was induced by then Mayor Rice to part with his seven-acre farm south of Houston and on this spot, in the heart of the metropolis, stands one of the largest school buildings in Texas, the San Jacinto Senior High School.

I recently visited in Austin, the old Sir Swante Palm home, which was pointed out to me. It is a show place, like the French embassy was.

I recalled what S. M. Swenson had done for Austin, as did my old friend, the late John G. Palm, who for so many years was connected with the Bremond bank as cashier, and I recalled the splendid influence in the building up of Texas that the native sons and daughters of the land of perpetual snow have contributed. They are a definite part of the historical background of Central Texas.

THE LAST OF THE FILIBUSTERS
THE REVOLUTION OF 1812

(Taken from the notes of Colonel Warren D. C. Hall and Lewis W. Newton)

Life in Texas under Spanish rule was no bed of roses. Until Mexico won her independence, Texas was practically a part of the kingdom of Spain. Before the coming of the Austins, the country was overrun with filibusters, soldiers of fortune, freebooters, adventurers of all kinds. Some were very prominent, all more or less daring. They were invading Texas with small armies claiming that they had received commissions, etc., and were trying to free Mexico from the Spanish yoke. But as it turned out, each of them had the hope of forming an empire of his own.

Philip Nolan was the first to arrive, an adventurous American and the most active filibuster. His mission was mysterious and not understood when in 1800 he traveled from Natchez, Mississippi, to San Antonio. He claimed to have a passport and a contract from the Governor at New Orleans for the purchase or capture of wild horses in Texas, for a Spanish regiment in Louisiana. He seemed to have delivered thirteen hundred and eight horses on his contract made in 1797.

210

But in 1799 a new Governor of Louisiana became suspicious of Nolan's purpose and asserted that he had obtained his previous passport under false pretenses.   He charged that Nolan was the agent of the crafty General James Wilkerson of the Unted States Army and that his purpose was to make maps of the country and to incite the Indians to revolt against Spain.   He ordered Nolan's arrest if he should again enter Spanish territory.

Nolan's last expedition into Texas left Natchez in October, 1800.   When the little band of twenty-one reached the Ouachita River in Louisiana, a force of some fifty Spanish troops tried unsuccessfully to stop them.   Three of their number having deserted, the other eighteen pushed on to the Brazos River, pitched camp and captured some three hundred wild horses.   Afterwards they ranged in pursuit of horses as far north as the south fork of the Red River.   Upon their return to camp somewhere near the present site of Waco, they were attacked on March twenty-first, 1801, by a force of one hundred men sent against them from the Spanish fort at Nacogdoches.

With but twelve Americans and Louisiana creoles and one Mexican taking part in the defense, fighting Nolan and his men carried on an unequal fight for about three hours hours.   Nolan was killed, three of his companions were wounded and finally the little band surrendered.

The prisoners were held to await the decision of the Spanish Government.   After a long delay there came, at last in 1807, the King's decree that one out of five of those engaged in the fighting must be selected by lot to be hanged. Since through death and escape only nine captives remained, the Mexican authorities mercifully decreed that only one should be executed.   The prisoners threw dice on a drum head and the choice fell upon Ephriam Blackburn, a Quaker. At the last moment, he was baptised in the Catholic Church. He was hanged at Chihuahua on November eleventh, 1807. The other prisoners were scattered among the various Mexican penal settlements.   Only one of them, Peter Ellis Bean, reappeared in history.

Mordecai Richards, one of the men who had deserted at the beginning of Nolan's second expedition, later testified before a Spanish court martial concerning Nolan's purpose saying that Nolan planned to build a fort among the Caddo Indians, to explore the country and search for mines, to catch wild horses and then to return to Kentucky where he was to be authorized to conquer Texas.

Because Thomas Jefferson, then the Vice-President of the United States, had some correspondence with Nolan concerning the habits of wild horses in Texas, some historians have considered Nolan's expedition as a preliminary preparation for the acquisition of Texas by the United States. It seems unlikely that Nolan's invasions had any political significance. No further invasions occurred until 1806.

At that time, the uncertain schemes of Aaron Burr so aroused the Spanish as to cause them to gather forces near the Sabine and even to occupy Adacs. General James Wilkerson, commanding the American troops on the southwestern frontier of the United States, ordered the Spanish back across the Sabine and this order was obeyed, since just then Wilkerson was eager to concentrate his troops at New Orleans where he could pose as the savior of his country against the conspiracy of Burr, in which he himself was an accomplice. Wilkerson induced the Spanish General Herrera to sign an agreement with him which declared that the country between the "Arroyo Hondo" and the Sabine River should remain temporarily a neutral ground, over which neither Americans nor Spanish should exercise political jurisdiction.

Though the military agreement of 1806 was never formally ratified as a treaty between the two nations, it was generally observed until 1819 and the neutral ground became a place where the worst characters congregated to prey upon the American and Spanish settlements.

Historians have never been able to determine with certainty what designs, if any, Aaron Burr had upon Texas. It is possible that he hoped to detach it from Spain and use it in some way for his personal advantage.

For a time after the Burr disturbance, the southwestern frontier was comparatively free from excitement. But during 1810 and 1811, the rumbling of internal changes in Mexico furnished inviting opportunities to restless frontiersmen, who were quick to scent the chance for adventure and possible advantage in the revolutionary situation.

For centuries Mexico had been suffering under an accumulation of abuses practiced in succession by some sixty Spanish viceroys. At length, in 1810, there emerged from the Indian village of Dolores, in the state of Guanajuato, a country curate named Hidalgo, to proclaim a revolt against Spanish tyranny. Successful at first, Father Hidalgo was final-

212

ly defeated in battle on January eleventh, was captured and later shot at Chihuahua. A bitter war of extermination was waged against his followers.

The Magee-Gutierrez Expedition, of which we know a little more today than the others, followed the Hidalgo Revolt. It was in June the Hidalgo Revolution so unhappily ended that Bernardo Gutierrez, one of Hidalgo's adherents, was so fortunate as to be in the United States when his chief was defeated. Gutierrez stopped on his way back at the little frontier town of Nacogdoches and it was here that he met a United States lieutenant, Magee, who was planning the conquest of Texas. Both agreed that an armed expedition was necessary and organized a "Republican Army of the North," composed of one hundred and fifty-eight white men, as well as Mexicans and Indians. Gutierrez entered Texas in June, 1812, and Magee remained to gather supplies and recruits.

Gutierrez' force captured Nacogdoches and drove the Spaniards from East Texas. It was agreed that Gutierrez should be general, while Magee was colonel and commander-in-chief. When they crossed the Trinity River, the army had grown to over eight hundred men.

By October, they had captured Goliad. In the meanwhile, General Herrera, General Arredondo and Governor Salcedo had gathered a force of Mexican troops and advancing on Goliad, laid siege to the town for about four months, until March, 1813, when they retired to San Antonio.

Meanwhile Major Kemper of the Republican Army had been given command and under his leadership the army moved to San Antonio, which surrendered to them soon. Governor Salcedo and his officers, though paroled, were put in the protection of a Captain Delgado, who took the fourteen prisoners out of town and killed them.

In a later trial it was proved that this massacre had been ordered by Gutierrez, who was deposed. After this the Republican Army disintegrated, several Americans resigning from it in disgust; the remainder of the army was almost annihilated by a Mexican army led by General Arredondo, only ninety-three Americans making their way back to Natchitoches.

Dismal as their failure seemed to be, this was the most successful of the invading expeditions in that for a time it had made Texas practically free of Spanish rule. But after the routing of the Republican Army, all republicans and foreigners were killed or driven out of the country.

The next expedition which was made into Texas, with the hope of recovering it from Spanish dominion, was under the leadership of Dr. James Long, a Natchez merchant, in 1819. He led a band of seventy-five men who resented the United States' renouncing any claim to Texas in the Florida Treaty of 1819.

Long's band crossed the Mississippi River and marched toward Natchitoches, being joined all along the way by adventurers. The expedition now numbered over three hundred men, who took Nacogdoches with ease.

Long now declared Texas an independent republic and organized a provisional government which was to be administered by an elected council. Soon the council announced a program for disposing of the public land, and so attracted immigrants to Texas. One of the councilmen, Horatio Bigelow, established a printing office and newspaper of which he was the editor. He thus became the first newspaper editor in Texas. A fort was built on the Brazos near old Washington and trading posts were erected on the Trinity and the Brazos rivers.

Dr. Long now learned that the pirate LaFitte was occupying Galveston Island and visited him, hoping to make an alliance with him, but LaFitte declined. When Long returned to Nacogdoches, he found his men had been killed or scattered by a Spanish army. He escaped to Louisiana but later returned to join a remnant of his men who built a small fort at Bolivar Point on the north coast of Galveston Bay.

The Mexican revolutionists now affording Long another excuse to enter Texas, he and his army again entered the interior and captured Goliad in October, 1821. They were soon overpowered and forced to surrender. They were taken to Mexico, where Long was assassinated by a Mexican soldier in 1822. The rest of the Americans were released at the request of the United States Government.

As a result of this disastrous attempt and the revolt of Mexico against Spain, Texas was almost depopulated. Only a vestige of civilization remained in San Antonio and around the ruins of Nacogdoches.

The weak Spanish hold upon Texas and the unsettled conditions resulting from the Mexican revolution proved a great inducement to smugglers and pirates in the Gulf of Mexico.

The first of these adventurers who made his headquarters

214

on Galveston Island was Luis Aury. In 1816, he took possession of the island with a commission from the government of Morelos, the leader who carried on the Mexican revolt after the death of Hidalgo. Aury used the long, sandy island as base from which to carry on "privateering" against Spain. He plundered not only Spanish vessels, but those of other nations and permitted his men to smuggle Negro slaves into the United States, in defiance of the law of 1808 which forbade their importation.

Galveston was an ideal location for Aury's enterprise. There was space sufficient for watchtowers, forts and buildings, as well as range for a few cattle. The protected bay lying behind the island, with its narrow entrance from the sea and its long inlets reaching far into the interior, gave security to lawless vessels.

Fortunately, in 1816 a Spanish adventurer, Javier Mina, arrived at Galveston with two hundred men and a magnificent scheme for carrying a revolutionary expedition into the interior of Mexico. Aury joined him, and Galveston was abandoned. When after a defeat in Mexico, he returned, he found the island in the possession of Jean LaFitte.

Jean LaFitte's first base had been in Barataria Bay. It is said that Jean and his brother Pierre were able to dispose of the loot from many a marauding enterprise by posing as simple merchants and blacksmiths of New Orleans. His vessels had been the scourge of the Gulf until his rendezvous was broken up by United States naval ship in September, 1814.

This was during the War of 1812 and LaFitte pretended to have an offer from the British commander at Pensacola proposing to give him a high office in the British army and thirty thousand dollars if he would put himself and his men in the British service. He chose instead to join General Andrew Jackson at New Orleans, where he rendered valuable assistance and the government accordingly dropped prosecutions against him for past offences.

What Jean LaFitte did during the next two years is not known, but in 1817 we find him beginning his adventurous career which lasted for four years on Galveston Island.

LaFitte kept up a pretense of an organized government with heads of departments, as Aury had done, and professed allegiance to the Mexican Government which had not yet been established. He claimed to attack none but Spanish vessels.

His colony of Campeche on Galveston Island grew and prospered until by the close of 1817 the Island had become the resort of nearly a thousand desperate characters. Forts were built and LaFitte moved among his men with the air of a prince.

But some of his men grew too greedy and seized the cargoes of vessels flying the flag of the United States. When this was known at Washington, a naval vessel was sent in 1821 to break up the Campeche establishment. LaFitte surrendered without resistance and sailed once more away into obscurity.

Jean LaFitte had not been a filibuster, although all of them from Long and Magee on had tried to interest him in their schemes. He laughed at them and refused to join them, pointing out their small numbers and the disastrous battle of Medina.

Perhaps one reason he did not join them was that he had his hands full, trying to keep out of the hands of Uncle Sam's watch dogs, who were close at his heels.

The only good things that can be laid to LaFitte's account was his furnishing General Jackson with twelve thousand dollars and helping him in the Battle at Chalmette.

Many make an idol of him but to me he was nothing but a pirate, slave dealer and smuggler.

The very soldiers of fortune whose aim was to secure this land for the settlement of Americans by military force, the Austins, had the ability to accomplish by peaceful means.

"THE MOTHER OF TEXAS" MRS. JANE LONG

From time immemorial, the faithful keeping of a tryst between a man and a maid has been the theme most immortalized by the great poets, singers, writers and composers of the age.

Pondering this, I often have wondered whether it is the mere love element involved that so fascinates the onlooking world, or, possibly, the spirit of utter loyalty to a trust, that so excites the springs of admiration within us. After all, is it not that undying spirit of mutual loyalty exemplified by these historic instances, rather than the affectionate relationship, that impels our delighted attention? Or is it, perhaps, that a really great love cannot exist without due regard for an equally great sense of loyalty?

Brave and capable woman that she was, I do not believe the career of Jane Wilkinson Long, young and beautiful belle of Natchez, would have proved so fascinating in the annals of pioneer Texas, had she not possessed as he did, so unusual a spirit of utter devotion and sheer loyalty to her adventurous young husband, General James Long. Neither do I believe that, without these ardent personal characteristics with which to buoy her own spirit, she could have endured the long suffering, hardships and travail that were her lot, and yet lived to the successful accomplishment that was hers. Faith and adoration are, indeed, wonderfully stimulating qualities.

Perhaps, in some respects at least, the period in which Jane Wilkinon grew up and lived was an age better fitted for great romance than the present, notwithstanding the example quite recently before us of the relinquishment of a great throne for an equally great love.

How Jane Wilkinson Long, practically alone the greater portion of the time, once held a Texas fort for approximately two years, constitutes one of the most thrilling chapters in the early annals of Texas. First, let us take a peak into the origin and early background of this remarkable young lady.

Born in 1798, at Natchez, Mississippi, Jane Wilkinson was the daughter of General William Wilkinson, not related to the Dr. James Wilkinson Long whose name the daughter later bore. Reared and educated there, her beauty and personal charm had drawn eligible suitors from afar, before she had arrived at the age of sixteen. She was yet attending the old Academy at Natchez when, seated one day on the porch

217

of their home, her little Negro slave-girl attendant came prancing by, and exclaimed mischievously, "Miss Jane, the very handsomest man in most of the whole world has come to town!"

"But what is that to me?" asked the beautiful young school girl, as her radiant countenance peeped from beneath the folds of her green silk poke-bonnet.

"Miss Jane, you sure must see him. He's the only man I ever saw what just matches you entirely!"

It was "Kian" who spoke, the little Negro slave girl who later became so entwined in the story of Jane Wilkinson's life, and who unwittingly brought about the romance that placed Jane Wilkinson Long in so unique a niche in the history of Texas.

The man in question was Dr. James Long, who owned a plantation near Natchez, and although comparatively youthful, had recently resigned his commission as surgeon in the United States Army. He had seen service with "Old Hickory" at the Battle of New Orleans, and from his close association with Andrew Jackson had absorbed many of the latter's characteristics.

Jane Wilkinson did meet Dr. Long at her home in Natchez. He was tall, handsome and twenty-two years of age, with a heroic air about him. She was seventeen years of age, a charming slender schoolgirl of romantic type. It was a proverbial case of love at first sight on the part of both. A whirlwind courtship followed. After a week, they were married and he carried the winsome young prize off to his plantation home. Beautiful old colonial home with its magnificent grove of trees and broad lawns with old fashioned gardens bordering its pathways, the setting scarcely could have been more ideal for love and romance to have reached their heights of ecstacy.

And so it was thus surrounded, with Natchez itself at that time a hot-bed of intrigue and daring adventure, there came to Dr. Long the miraculous thought of invading Texas with a following of his own, wresting it from Spain and Mexico, carving a new empire in the west and with himself at its head make Jane Wilkinson Long his queen in truth. He proceeded with his plans accordingly.

Meanwhile, in 1816, their first daughter, Ann Long, was born. It was when Ann approached her third birthday, and Jane Long was again nearing motherhood, that the now General Long, supported by less than one hundred adventurous young Americans marched away to conquer Texas.

It was on June the twenty-eighth, 1819, two weeks after the birth of her second child, that Jane Long, because of her great devotion to him and feeling it altogether impossible to live apart form her husband, concluded to follow him. What followed that decision on her part impresses me as almost, if not entirely, without parallel.

In her convalescent condition, accompanied only by her two small children and Kian, the latter even yet a young girl, Jane Long proceeded to the boat landing at Natchez, to embark for Alexandria, Louisiana. That was to be her first pause on a perilous journey through the savage wilds of Texas, en route to Nacogdoches. It was at the Natchez landing that she was discovered by one of her former ardent suitors, James Rowan, one of Natchez' wealthiest merchants. Still devoted to her, and altogether shocked at the temerity of her plans, he refused to permit her to make the initial trip alone, and stepped aboard the boat attired as he was.

The ensuing trip to Alexandria by boat proved most severe, heavy downpour of rain coupled with intense cold; the boat became grounded on a bar and provisions and fuel ran short. No physician was present and normal medical supplies exceedingly scant. Finally, Rowan paid a youth to proceed by land and obtain horses. Carriages were out of the question for use over woodland trails. After considerable delay, the boy returned with only two horses. Undaunted, Jane Long and Kian mounted one of these, and James Rowan, with the two babies, the other, all of which, aside, impels me to suggest that "greater love hath no defeated suitor," notwithstanding any unusual skill as a horseman he may have possessed. Truly, heroes must have been born and not made.

Twenty days later, sick and exhausted, the little caravan finally arrived at Alexandria, where Jane Long took to bed at the home of her sister, Mrs. Calvert. Some time after that, the boat arrived with Mrs. Long's baggage. It brought also the distressing news that the young man who had secured the horses for their trip to Alexandria, had died from exposure incurred in that undertaking.

James Rowan, after providing Mrs. Calvert with ample funds for Mrs. Long, and a letter of credit on his house at Natchez, negotiable by her at points along the proposed route, reluctantly took return passage to Natchez.

Four weeks had now elapsed. Jane Long yet remained

219

confined to her room, apparently growing worse, her condition undoubtedly aggravated by the continued separation from her husband. Finally, her physicians, believing her mental attitude was preventing her physical recovery, consented to a resumption of her trip, admonishing her that it should be undertaken only by easy stages, with great care from exposure.

At this time, Randall Jones and a number of other adventurous young men had gathered at Alexandria and were preparing to join Dr. Long's expedition. Jane Long, with the funds provided by Rowan, purchased a closed carriage, arranged to leave the infant daughter with her sister, and accompanied by Ann and Kian, departed with Jones and his followers.

History records that the travelers averaged about seven miles per day, impeded by terrific rains, roads deep with mud, and swollen streams. Arriving at Nachitoches, Louisiana, they paused a few days from the rigors of the journey, and struck out again. The Attoyac and Sabine rivers were hazarded at flood-tide without casualty. Nacogdoches appeared in sight, and it was a matter of only minutes before the long suffering and love-hungry Jane Long was in the arms of her beloved husband.

Happiness was scarcely achieved before it was again brought to a close. General Long must leave at once for Galveston Island, there to seek the support of that glamorous pirate chieftain, Jean LaFitte, in his forthcoming effort to wrest Texas from the Spanish-Mexican yoke. General Long knew that LaFitte was particularly antagonistic toward the Spanish; that after the former's pardon by President Madison for services rendered General Jackson at New Orleans, LaFitte had fortified Galveston Island as a stronghold from which to prey upon Spanish vessels in the Gulf and Carribean waters, and counted greatly upon obtaining his co-operation in the Texas movement.

Leaving Major Cook in command of his men at Nacogdoches, General Long bade his wife farewell and journeyed to LaFitte's headquarters. There he laid his plan before the bucanneer and was deeply disappointed to receive not only the latter's refusal of support, but to learn also that LaFitte firmly advised General Long to drop any further thought of his creation of a new empire.

Meanwhile, affairs had not gone well with General Long's little army at Nacogdoches. Major Cook indulged in protracted intoxication, in the midst of which, came news that a Mexican army of some seven hundred men were approaching the town, intending to attack and put its defenders to the sword. Pandemonium ensued among the disorganized followers and they fled. Jane Long, intending to warn her husband, took her carriage, Kian and Ann, and struck out toward Galveston. En route, she met General Long, greatly downhearted because of his failure to enlist LaFitte in his cause.

He left them with a family by the name of Brown, rushed to Nacogdoches, which he found entirely deserted, although no enemy had appeared. Returning immediately to his wife, he was dismayed to find that all of them, becoming alarmed, had fled to Louisiana. Overtaking them, he accompanied the travelers to Natchitoches. It was here that he and his wife learned that the child left with her sister in Alexandria, and whom he had never seen, had meanwhile passed away. Bidding her farewell again, General Long hurried Texasward to reorganize his men, while Jane Long, Kian and Ann returned to their home in Natchez.

Regaining Texas and collecting what remained of his scattered men, they were badly defeated in battle with a Mexican contingent. Barely escaping with his life, General Long made his way to New Orleans and organized a new expedition.

Jane Long, Ann and Kian joined General Long at New Orleans, and after a brief stay, they sailed for Bolivar Point, near Galveston, intending a further effort to enlist LaFitte's support. Arriving at Bolivar, they erected a tiny fort of mud, sticks and stones, mounted a small brass cannon, and living quarters were established in army tents.

With his wife, General Long made one more trip to Galveston Island. They found LaFitte preparing to leave. He had received his ultimatum from the United States. Swashbuckling cavalier that he was, however, LaFitte could not resist the temptation of delaying his departure until he had entertained the General and his lady. While steadfastly refusing to join in the enterprise of General Long, as a farewell compliment he served them a right royal feast accompanied with the choicest of wines; and upon their departure accorded them a salute from the guns of his flagship. Partially across the bay, the Longs looked back and observed that LaFitte had fired his little town of Campeche and was blowing up the fort. Presently they saw his fleet get under way and head into the open waters of the Gulf. It was the last that Galveston Island and the Texas coastal regions ever knew of LaFitte. What actually became of him and his band has been lost in obscurity. History relates many and various tales concerning his end; none of them apparently authenticated.

To appreciate the situation of General Long, his wife and their comrades, one must go back to Bolivar Point of one hundred and twenty years ago. Now a prominent shipping point, it was then a barren peninsula. Originally it had been fortified to some extent, in 1818, I believe, by General James Wilkinson, a filibuster associated with Philip Nolan, Aaron Burr and others who also contemplated a new empire in the west. The location of Bolivar made it subject to prey by the powerful and extremely cruel Karankaway Indians, a cannibal tribe of giant statue peculiar to the coastal regions of Texas. LaFitte's pirates, and not without just cause, had so mistreated these Indians that they lost no opportunity to wreak vengeance upon the whites. Once, within sight of General Long and his wife, the Karankawas had captured a French ship with all on board and taken them to Galveston Island. Before the Long party could intervene, the Indians had reached the island with their prisoners, killed them, and were proceeding to cook and eat them. Greatly outnumbered, Long and his companions returned to Bolivar.

General Long had now increased his force to some two hundred men. Learning that the Mexican Colonel Perez was en route to Nacogdoches with a detachment numbering about six hundred men, he made his plans to intercept and attack them.

At Fort Bolivar, he detailed four of his soldiers to protect his wife, Ann, and Kian and their dog named "Galveston." Doctors Edgar and Allen, with their wives, accompanied Long's "army."

Giving his wife a farewell embrace, he admonished her, "Stay here until I return, or until you receive from me a message directing you where to join me. Hold the fort at all hazards!"

That was the last the devoted Jane Long ever saw of her beloved General.

A long and weary period of months passed without word from General Long. This historic winter of 1820-21 came on with its terrific cold. Utterly discouraged, the garrison

222

of four men concluded to abandon the fort and acquainted Jane Long with their decision, insisting that she accompany them. This she absolutely refused to do. "Go, if you wish, but I remain here! My husband left me here with the parting injunction that I remain until he returned or sent for me. I shall be faithful to that trust. If I should not survive the ordeal, at least my grave will tell him of my loyalty to his charge!"

No appeal could change her will. The four men marched away and left her there with Kian and Ann. And Jane Long was shortly to become a mother for the third time.

Their only shelter was an army tent beyond the walls of the mud fort. One morning, Kian discovered moccasin tracks left by a prowling Indian and reported it to her mistress. Jane Long rose to the occasion by hoisting upon the fort a red battle flag made from one of her flannel underskirts. She loaded and primed the little brass cannon, protecting it from the elements by an oiled canvas; and likewise loaded the several available muskets. She and Kian and little Ann took turn about keeping watch for the expected onslaught of the Indians. One morning shortly after, the war canoes of the Karankawas were noted headed for the fort. Ordering Kian and Ann to the shelter of the fort, she took position by the cannon. There she stood, lighted towrope in hand for the usual gunner's match, and when the fleet of canoes had approached within range, she touched the fire to the powder. Undoubtedly luck was with her as to accuracy of aim for the solid shot fell among the foremost canoes. Furiously she sponged the heated barrel of the cannon, reloaded and primed it, preparing for a second shot, but it was unnecessary. The accuracy of her fire, coupled with the detonating sound of the cannon, had served the purpose. The war canoes immediately fled toward Galveston Island whence they had come. Several days later, the Indians made a further attempt to attack the fort, received the same reception and went back to their haven and never returned.

Winter fell upon them with a fury never seen by colonists in those parts. Galveston Bay froze over, an incident that occurred, so far as I have heard, on only one other occasion, the winter on 1886. Jane Long watched bear and other wild animals cross over to Galveston Island from the mainland. Her food supply was enhanced by a supply of ducks that froze feet-first in the ice and had to be chopped out. Fish were had by chopping holes in the ice, using hook and line, and salting and freezing the resultant catch. Of such was their scanty larder. Snow burdened the little tent almost to the point of collapse. And while the roof sank low, Jane Long, resting upon her rustic cot, brought into the world on December the twenty-first, 1821, her third child, Mary James Long, with only Kian and little Ann to attend her. What courage and fortitude she must have possessed. Little Mary James, always a frail child, lived only a period of four years.

It was in 1822 that the little family noted one day the approach of two men. They hastily prepared to receive them as enemies. One may well imagine Jane Long's delight as she presently recognized the two as Captain Randall Jones, an early traveling companion to Texas, and his brother, James.

"My husband?" she exclaimed.

One can glimpse somewhat of the poignant suffering that must have been Jane Long's as she learned from Captain Jones that her husband had been assassinated upon the streets of Mexico City, while yet a prisoner on parole. History records that the shot was fired by one of his own men. The Long Expedition had come upon evil days. Outnumbered and cut off, they were made prisoners and the entire band taken to Mexico City.

Captain Jones and his brother took Jane Long and her family to San Antonio. Determined woman that she was, she made the trip on burros to Mexico City with Kian and her two babies, visited the spot where her husband was killed, and later knelt in prayer at his grave. While there, Ben Milam came upon her and related how, the night before his death, the General had come to him with a premonition of his end. Long had requested that Milam be "a brother to my wife, and a father to my children," a promise that the latter made and faithfully kept until his death in 1835, in the fighting around San Antonio.

Jane Long and her children and Kian remained in Texas. Locating at Brazoria, she kept boarders, while Kian did the duties. It was while here that Jane Long learned her husband had mortgaged Kian to a creditor. He foreclosed. She worked tirelessly to redeem Kian from bondage. Finally, a former suitor and schoolmate, General Peck of Natchez, bought Kian and returned her to Jane Long.

In later years, Jane Long moved to Richmond, Texas, where the Republic had awarded her a grant of land, and

Scenes of the Houston Ship Channel

maintained another boarding house. It was my privilege, on several occasions, to meet and come to know her there. Even without the romantic and historic interest attached to her, there was something about Jane Long in point of personal charm and attributes that gave her an unusual and striking personality. Truly, her friends were legion, and her admirers many. There was no end to suitors, but to one and all she declared, "I loved but one man . . . I could give my heart to no other!"

Ann Harriet Long grew to womanhood and married Judge J. S. Sullivan of Galveston.

And as to Kian, the faithful young slave-girl: it was "Kian III," granddaughter of the original Kian, long since gathered to her reward, who, on December thirtieth, 1880, when Jane Long passed peacefully away, tenderly waited upon and prepared her for that last, long sleep.

FRONTIER FORTS OF PIONEER TEXAS

The first so-called fort in this vicinity was built by General Long in 1821 at Bolivar Point on Galveston Bay, a crude affair of mud and sticks, but effective for its purpose. A few small forts were built here and there in East Texas, chiefly by the missionaries for protection against the Indians, and at one or two points by the Mexican authorities as military outposts. Of the latter, Nacogdoches was perhaps the most important. The "old stone fort" at that point, formerly located on the city square, has been removed to the residential section of the city and is now maintained as a museum. The Mexican Government had also established a fort at Anahuac, maintained at various intervals until the defeat of Santa Anna at San Jacinto.

Fort Saint Louis, the first fort of its kind to be built in the confines of the State, was built by the French explorer, La Salle, about 1684. He had first landed on the coast of Matagorda Bay (seeking the mouth of the Mississippi River) and erected a temporary habitation. This was soon deserted for a more favorable location some five miles inland near the banks of Garcita Creek. Here Fort St. Louis was built, flourished for a while and came to its tragic end.

The first fort to be built by the Republic of Texas was

constructed on the east end of Galveston Island in 1836, and named Fort San Jacinto in commemoration of that battle. It was used as a base from which to fight the buccaneers of the Gulf and the Mexican army detachments that from time to time after the Battle of San Jacinto, threatened invasion of the infant republic.

It should also be remembered that the swashbuckling pirate, Jean LaFitte, built a fort at Campeche on Galveston Island and held forth there with his pirate band numbering approximately one thousand from about 1817 to 1821. This fort was destroyed and the site abandoned by LaFitte under orders from the United States Government.

Again in 1858, Bolivar Peninsula became the site of a fort. Fort Travis, named after the defender of the Alamo, was constructed on the site of General Long's previous mud fort.

Fort Crockett on West Beach of Galveston Island was first built in 1836, named after the illustrious David Crockett of Alamo fame, and the first Texas fort of note in this vicinity of which we have any record. It was manned by twenty-eight officers and five hundred and fifty-one men. It fell to obscurity but was rebuilt by the United States Government in 1897 and remains active at present.

In 1861, the Confederates built four additional forts in Galveston for protection of the harbor; also a mud fort and breastworks on the Galveston side of the causeway and a further fort and breastworks at Virginia Point. History tells us that General Magruder assembled six thousand men at the latter point previous to his attack and capture of Galveston from the Yankees on New Year's Day in 1861. His troops extended as far up as Harrisburg and Houston and a portion also were stationed at Velasco.

The historic chain of Texas frontier forts, however, was built in 1846-48, or both before and after the United States and Mexican war. They were forty-two in number, although some of them were mere military outposts and not actual fortifications. The chain extended from Brownsville along the territory contiguous to the Rio Grande, up to El Paso and the Panhandle of Texas and terminated in the then Indian Territory, now Oklahoma.

The principal sources of supply for these forts were Houston, Harrisburg and Galveston, their supplies being hauled over-land by ox-teams.

The purpose of this chain of forts was to protect the

226

pioneer settlers of Texas from the Mexicans, sporadic raids of Mexican army detachments, depredations of Mexican bandits, white renegades and the marauding Indians, restless souls that the latter were.

The forts were connected with a government telegraph line running from Brownsville to Fort Sill. The latter was maintained only through constant patrol of mounted soldiers between the forts. A pony express, armed and carrying mail and passengers also plied along the route. The forts were constructed with rock and mortar where these items were available; otherwise, great logs and adobe were used in building them

Among the more prominent in the chain was Fort Bliss, named for General W. S. Bliss, adjutant to General Zachary Taylor. Built originally in 1848, it was rebuilt and enlarged in 1890, and today is one of the outstanding army posts of America. Located at El Paso, it commands that great gateway to the interior of Mexico.

Old Fort Ringgold at Rio Grande City, established in 1850, was named for Major Ringgold of the United States artillery, slain in the Battle of Palo Alto in 1846. Fort Ringgold witnessed many sharp engagements in its day and is yet in good condition.

Fort Brown, just outside of Brownsville, was established in 1840 as Fort Taylor. Later the name was changed to Fort Brown in honor of Major Brown, killed in action in 1847. During the Mexican War and the War Between the States, it did noble duty. Subsequently it was garrisoned by a Negro regiment that mutinied a number of years ago, raiding the city of Brownsville and developing a sensational army scandal at the time.

Fort McIntosh at Laredo, was built originally by the Franciscan Fathers in 1757, and constitutes one of the most ancient historical spots of Texas. It received its present name in 1850 from Colonel J. S. McIntosh, hero of the Mexican War, who died from wounds received in the battle of Resaca de la Palma at Molina Del Rey.

Fort McKavitt, another quaintly interesting point historically, was named in memory of Captain McKavitt, Eighth United States Infantry, killed in September, 1846, in the battle of Monterrey.

Fort Belknap, located on the south fork of the Brazos River in Young County, was constructed in 1851. Robert E. Lee, then a young lieutenant assisting General Albert Sidney

Johnston, built the fort in conjunction with his associates, the later General John B. Hood and General McClellan. They later served as Fort Croghan in Burnet County. General Lee was also stationed at Fort Mason. The old bed and table that he used was on exhibit for years in Fredericksburg, at that time the most accessible town to the fort. I have seen the two pieces there on frequent visits at the Nimitz Hotel.

Camp Radenski, an outpost of Fort Belknap, honored the name of Lieutenant Radenski, a native of Poland, an engineer and most gallant officer of the United States army in the war with Mexico. Another outpost of Fort Belknap was Camp Van Camp, built in 1858 and named for Captain Van Camp, killed by the Indians in the fight at Wichita Village in the same year.

Fort Elliot, built in 1876, was the farthest in the Panhandle of Texas. Its chief purpose was to protect the white settlers from the Indians, who fought for long years to prevent the white invaders from wresting from them their great buffalo hunting grounds. The whites slew these buffaloes by the thousands. It was a terrific waste of food and propagating stock, as they left the plains covered with carcasses of flesh, taking only the hides as a rule. The Comanche Indians were particularly ferocious in their defense of the plains, being ably seconded by the Apache and other tribes, as they depended upon the meat of the buffalo for sustenance.

Fort Rice, established fifty-three miles east of El Paso, after the close of the war, was renamed Fort Hancock for General W. S. Hancock of the United States Army. Its ruins may yet be seen and inspected by the passing motorists. In the adjacent El Paso territory, Fort Bliss also was the nerve-center for a number of outlying camps whose chief purpose was to patrol the border. The most prominent was Camp Elizario, twenty-two miles below El Paso and originally built as a Spanish mission in 1780.

Camp Harney, named for Colonel William Harney, was built at a point then called "Hellville" on the banks of the Rio Grande.

Fort Quitman, a Rio Grande River post near El Paso, was built in 1858, the name honoring General Quitman of the Mexican War.

Fort Sam Houston, in San Antonio, is, of course, the largest establishment remaining of those early day chain of forts, having, since its origin, greatly expanded. The original

228

splendor of the fort, when I first saw it sixty years ago, yet remains. It was then an old quadrangle, but rather beautifully built. Now, in the broad confines of its park, may be noted the gorgeous peacock, spotted deer, friendly squirrels and other animals adding their attractiveness to the grounds. These are maintained by the government in the state equal to those at West Point. I am told that the cannons, placed in the great walls of the quadrangle in 1857, can yet be fired. It ranks second to none of the army posts in the United States. Adjacent to it in point of territory, are Camp Bullis, Camp Stanley, Brooks Field, Kelly Field and Randolph Field, combining to make the location worthy of its sobriquet, "West Point of Texas." In the early days, among those who served at Fort Sam Houston and came later to be known among the famed were U. S. Grant, Jefferson Davis, Nelson A. Miles, Robert E. Lee and others.

Not far distant, in Kerr County, may be found the ruins of Camp Verde, founded in 1856, by the colorful frontiersman, Captain I. N. Palmer, of the United States Cavalry.

On account of the terrain throughout the western plains, upon the recommendation of Jefferson Davis, then Secretary of War, a number of herds of camels were imported for service in these parts. They were brought in from Asia and Africa and landed at Galveston and Indianola. Another herd was held at Harrisburg by Governor Lubbock for the purpose of carrying freight between Harrisburg and Houston. The main caravan, however, was transferred to the mid-southwest, and there served as carrier between the United States army posts included in the chain mentioned, and the Pacific coast. For some reason, these camels did not prove as practical in operation as did the good, old "army mule" and in due time they were abandoned. A number of them appear to have been turned loose to roam the plains, with the hope that eventually they might propagate their kind. Either climatic conditions were unfavorable to that end, or they were preyed upon to point of extinction, as in a few years no more was seen of them.

Fort Davis, named for Jefferson Davis, maintained a protective patrol over a great stretch of country, and boasted throughout its active life a substantial garrison. It was but recently abandoned as an army post, but visitors will find it yet in an excellent state of preservation.

Fort Concho, in the environs of what is now San Angelo, is in ruins. It was first called Camp Hatch. General Robert

E. Lee also saw service there. Nearby was Camp Johnson built in 1852 and named for the Confederate General Joseph E. Johnson.

In Uvalde County, near the home of John Nance Garner, are to be found the remains of the two forts established in 1849 on the Leon River. One, Camp Inge, was named for the gallant Lieutenant Inge, killed while charging the enemy at Resaca de la Palma; and the other, Camp Sabine, founded in 1856 by J. B. Pickett, another soldier of distinction. These were near the present city of Edinburg.

In the early days of Texas these frontier forts answered a great need. They not only stopped the depredations by Indian tribes, but prevented Mexican raids and effectively made Rio Grande River the boundary between Mexico and Texas. The need of them grew less and less as the country became settled and with the relations happily existing between the Mexican government and our own, we may assume that it will be only a comparatively short while before the last of them have fallen before the tranquil and understanding attitude of the nationals of both nations, even as has been the case on the Canadian boundary for over one hundred years.

On a recent visit with S. G. Reed of the Southern Pacific lines, it was my privilege to have shown to me the personal memoirs of Colonel Tom Pierce, great builder of the Southern Pacific system. His detailed descriptions of the old forts, and how, in later years, their military and other supplies were transported over the new railroads, were delightful to read. Colonel Pierce and his associate, Major T. Converse, aided by the merchants of Houston and Galveston, maintained a continuous stream of supplies to the settlers and commissariats at these forts, chief for the army itself, but frequently to supplement the stocks of the small trading posts in that section of the country.

Where the railroad did not touch the army posts direct, the supplies were sent in large caravans under escort of soldiers, as was true in the earlier shipments made direct from these cities before advent of the railroad. With the gradual pushing of the Southern Pacific west, the need of the caravans passed, and they, too, became extinct.

Reference to these caravan-trains recalls that even in the days before Texas was a republic, such firms as R. and D. G. Mills, John Adriance and Patrick McGreel employed caravans to transport commodities to Matamoros for trans-shipment to

New Orleans, Cuba and European ports. Later, during the Civil War the same route was used by such merchants as E. J. Hart, E. B. Nichols, Wm. Marsh Rice, Cornelius Ennis, T. W. House, Willis and Bros. and Ball, Hutchings and Company. Their caravans traveled, as far as Albuquerque, New Mexico and the Rio Grande border.

The Indian is no more; the bandits, renegades and bush-whackers have gone their way. Cordiality and understanding between Mexico and the United States is increasing rapidly. The opening of the magnificent new highway to Mexico City from the Texas border will do much to cement the fast growing relationship between the two countries. These old frontier forts have served their purpose. It is well that we have their remains to look upon and contemplate what the pioneer settlers of Texas endured in order that we might inherit, after them, the present great and peaceful domain that is ours.

BATTLE OF GALVESTON

Only a few are now living who can recall the arrival in Houston a few days before Christmas of 1862 of General G. Bankhead Magruder, who with his staff had been transferred here to take over the command of the Confederate armies in Texas and Louisiana.

He arrived here presaged by an excellent record of successful military accomplishments, his early laurels having been won at the first battle of the Confederacy at Big Bethel Church. It was here that the Baptists had maintained their national camp meeting grounds for over a century, just eight miles out of Yorktown, Virginia, where Cornwallis, less than a hundred years previously, had capitulated, marched his valiant English army out between the two lines of American and French soldiers and surrendered them, while the English bands played "The World's Turned Upside Down."

For Magruder's valor and signal victory at Big Bethel, he had been complimented with the Southern command above noted. He was not, however, altogether unknown in Texas, for he had previously won his spurs under General Zachary Taylor in the Mexican War of 1846-47, and was assigned from time to time to the various United States army posts in Texas. Of a creative mind, he was a clever strategist, a man with ideas, and a great deal of luck in carrying them out. Not that he was lacking in valor, but that many of his successful engagements, including the battle of Galveston, were fought under peculiarly unfavorable circumstances. In the latter instance, his forces were practically defeated and in panic-stricken retreat, when the lucky arrival of the Houston "cotton-clads," already four hours late, turned the tide of battle and gave them a signal victory.

It was characteristic of General Magruder to inspire not only the loyalty of his troops but likewise the hearty co-operation of the citizens of the community where he was quartered for the time. Upon his arrival in Houston, and shortly prior to his advance upon Galveston, he assembled both the citizens and his entire command and addressed them in a body. He did not at the time outline publicly his intent to attack Galveston specifically. He did, however, exhort to the Southerners to "fight to the last ditch, and that the line of seaboard defenses from the Sabine to Brownsville must be held at all hazards." He reviewed in detail the activities and atrocities of "Silver Spoon" General Butler; how that federal commander and his forces had sacked and destroyed the state of Louisiana, and predicted the same for Galveston and Houston if the Yankee forces ever invaded Texas. He went on to say: "General Banks has landed in New Orleans with twenty thousand men. Undoubtedly he has his eyes on Texas and its coastal inlets. He must not be permitted to set foot on Texas soil. Texans, need I tell you what reception to give him; to wait not for orders, but to

232

attack the enemy at once, and to wage that attack with all the fury of the legions of ancient Rome."

It is not inappropriate to digress for the moment just here to relate that Silver Spoon Butler did not acquire his sobriquet from any fact of luxurious birth. Quite to the contrary, one might possibly surmise that General Butler's earlier years had not accustomed him to those little niceties of silver table—that Emily Post of today would regard merely as normal essentials of the better American homes. Be that as it may, history does record that the general did have a penchant for collecting silver spoons, knives, and forks and that in the looting and sacking that usually followed his occupation of a given territory, care was taken by his subordinates to see that all such articles collected went directly to the general's headquarters. I mention it only as characteristic of the jibes hurled during that period. We were at war; looting was a phase of the war, and silver bullion, regardless of its source, must have commanded a fair value at the time. Undoubtedly, General Butler (like the rest of us) had many virtues, any one of which would have overshadowed his passion for silver spoons.

Establishing his staff headquarters in Houston at the home of William R. Baker on Rusk Avenue, General Magruder called into conference G. C. Forshey, prominent engineer of that day, and with General E. B. Nichols, Captain E. P. Turner, Major DeBray and several scouts, they proceeded to Galveston in disguise and under cover of darkness on Christmas Day of 1862. There they made a careful survey of the possibilities of the situation.

Major B. DeBray had under his command a force of some six thousand men scattered from Virginia Point to Houston, and the larger portion of which was to be employed in the attack upon Galveston. To co-operate with the attack by land, General Magruder secured from the Sabine Captain Leon Smith, father of our late Leon Smith, Houston clothing manufacturer and an outstanding naval strategist of the period. To Captain Smith was assigned the task of collecting and preparing a "navy" at Houston to engage the Yankee gunboats anchored off Galveston, supporting the federal land forces occupying the city, and maintaining the federal blockade. The attack upon Galveston was to be made simultaneously by land and sea. To further confuse the situation at sea, General Magruder obtained from Governor Lubbock the necessary authority to destroy the lighthouse at Bolivar and immediately adjacent points; and, if found necessary in the course of attack, to burn Galveston. This latter step, however, much to the rejoicing of Galvestonians, proved unnecessary.

The Yankee fleet of six warships was anchored in the channel at Galveston. The federal Massachusetts Regiment was encamped chiefly on Kuhn's wharf at the foot of Eighteenth Street. During the day they occupied the Hendley Building, constructed in the "Fifties" at Twentieth and Strand. Perhaps the largest substantial building in Galveston at the time, it also had a cupola at the top that afforded an excellent observation post for the Yankees. It is still used by the Pilots Association.

At night, however, the federal force, leaving merely a corporal's guard at the Hendley Building would retire to the wharf, under protection of their gunboats and to avoid any surprise attack, would remove the plank walk over the long trestle connecting with the island.

The Yankees made no attempt to occupy the city of Galveston by force, but showed a disposition to co-operate with the city's management, reserving to themselves the direct management of the port and shipping activities. President Jefferson Davis, in his memoirs years later, afforded considerable praise to the ill-fated commander, Colonel Renshaw, for his magnanimous attitude toward the citizenry of Galveston.

At the time of the Confederate attack, General Magruder had on his staff Judge E. P. Gray, General Nichols, Fred A. Rice, a brother of William Marsh Rice, and others already named. Captain Leon Smith, commander of Houston's "navy," had converted into "cotton-clads," the steamers Bayou City, Neptune, John L. Carr, and Lucy Guinn. Their cabins had been removed and the boilers and engines placed on the lower decks. This change in the boats had been made under the supervision of Captain Louis Hershberger and the eminent engineer, M. M. Murray, while the boats were docked just below Houston on Buffalo Bayou. Ramparts were constructed on the boats by bales of cotton closely laid, with embrasures through which the cannons protruded. Actual artillery was scant enough, but such guns as they had were supplemented with wooden cannon to simulate the real thing, and under the light of the moon left with the casual observer the impression of a fully equipped warship. Under command of Captain Smith, this fleet proceeded to Galveston to join in with the land attack.

Under cover of darkness the Confederate fleet took up its position in Bolivar Roads and lay there quietly, awaiting the agreed signal from the land forces; a single cannon shot destined to open the engagement. They were then to move out into the channel, engage the Yankee fleet and shell the Massachusetts regiment on the wharf. Aboard the Confederate fleet were a body of marines and troop of dismounted cavalry intended as a landing party to attack the Federal troops from the rear. These were under command of Colonel Tom Green, with Major T. M. Bagby commanding some three hundred sharpshooters, and Lieut. Lee Harby in charge of infantry.

Colonel A. M. Hobby, uncle of our present townsman, Ex-Gov. William P. Hobby, had effectively destroyed all of the surrounding lighthouses.

Late in the evening of New Year's Eve, 1862, General Magruder and his staff boarded the G. H. and H. train for Virginia Point, where the main body of his troops lay in waiting. At Sunset Station, now Genoa, he dispatched a courier to Morgan's Point with final orders to Commander Leon Smith as above suggested. Arriving at Virginia Point about dark, some three hundred of the Confederate troops began quietly moving across the long trestle bridge toward Galveston, on which planks had been laid to afford crossing for man and beast. All went smoothly until the army mules drawing the artillery arrived at the bridge. The mules balked at the plank walk and refused to proceed. After several futile attempts to urge them onward, the men detached the mules, muffled the wheels of the wagons and pulled the latter across the bay by sheer manpower.

How well I remember that it was just about midnight when the mother of George M. Courts, late of the firm of Clarke and Courts, came over to our house to warn my mother of the coming battle, and to take the children out to the sand-dunes on west end of Galveston Island, where the children and other non-combatants were then concentrating. We children had retired for the night, but my mother hastily awakened us, and while we were dressing and getting quilts and other needed items together, she baked several loaves of bread already made up and ready for the oven. Locking the home, we made our way in the dark toward the dunes, meeting en route many other families going that way. Some of them told us that General Magruder's troops had already entered the city and were forming near Market Square, preparatory to attacking the federal position.

The combined attack on the Confederates was scheduled to begin about midnight. Apparently, there was some misunderstanding. Magruder waited for sight of the fleet. The fleet waited for the firing of the signal gun as agreed upon; and when the hour passed and there was no signal, they became alarmed and the ships scurried back towards Morgan's Point. Meanwhile, Magruder, becoming disgusted with the apparent lack of co-operation on the part of his "navy" resolved to engage in battle on his own. History records that, haranguing his men with a brief and fiery address, he personally fired the first cannon, and the fight was on. This occurred about four o'clock in the morning of New Year's day.

The Yankees, caught totally by surprise, fought with a dash and nerve unlooked for. The result was, supported as they were by the Federal fleet which immediately came into action and caught the range of the Confederate advance, the Southern troops were thrown abruptly back upon their reserves. So great was the confusion in Confederate ranks that it appeared for a time that Magruder's army would suffer a crushing defeat and be forced to surrender before they could get off the island.

At this moment, Magruder's luck again saved the day. The "Houston Navy" hearing the cannonading about faced and returned hurriedly to the fight. Their attack from the rear caught the Yanks totally unprepared. A fierce engagement took place between the opposing fleets, in which the marines, dismounted cavalry and sharpshooters on board the Confederate fleet did terrific execution upon the personnel of the Yankee Fleet. The cannons on board were equally effective against the Federal warships. Some of the latter were blown up, while upon others the slaughter was so heavy, and immediate escape so out of the question, that the white flag was run up.

Meanwhile, the battle on land had been waged with equal fierceness. With the appearance of Captain Leon Smith's squadron, the Confederate troops had taken new heart, reformed their ranks and resumed their frontal attack vigorously. The Northern troops, greatly outnumbered and with their supporting fleet destroyed, capitulated after their artillery had been silenced by the fire of the Southern batteries.

The engagement, while of only a few hours duration, had been both vigorous and extensive. The line of fire had belched along a front of nearly two miles, extending from both sides of the wharf far up the beach, with the center of the fighting in the downtown sector. Here, for many years afterwards, were to be noted fronts of buildings battle-scarred from cannon and rifle ball. The Ursuline Sisters had refused to leave their convent, notwithstanding that during the battle it came in for a considerable shelling, and several of the nuns received minor wounds. Most of the artillery fire was within a range limit of approximately three hundred yards; consequently, it was extremely effective. In fact, in the harbor a battle royal had ensued between the artillery of the opposing fleets. The Neptune, receiving a solid shot, her captain, William A. Bowen, father of Colonel Reuben D. Bowen, drove her full speed toward the shallows and beached her in the flats.

The Westfield was blown up and sank abruptly with many of those on board. The Yankee flagship, the Harriet Lane (so named for a niece of President Buchanan) was subjected to a furious attack from the Confederate Bayou City when the latter poured a broadside into the Harriet Lane and, moving up, grappled her and a boarding party engaged in hand-to-hand encounter.

A raking fire killed more than half of the Harriet Lane's men, including her commander, Captain Wainright, and her second in command, Lieutenant Edward Lea, fell mortally wounded. It was just at this point in the battle that a singular and unhappy incident of the war occurred, for relation of which I digress for the moment.

The distinguished father of Lieutenant Lea, a Houston cotton buyer, was a colonel in the attacking Confederate army. Lieutenant Lea himself was a graduate of West Point as the war began. Under the Northern environment and his immediate surroundings it appeared to him altogether natural that he should follow the flag under which he had been trained. Unhappily, almost his first assignment was with the marines aboard the Harriet Lane, while Colonel Lea, his father, had been withdrawn from operations in a distant part of the South and added to the staff of General Magruder. Until shortly after the attack on Galveston had begun neither father nor son knew that they were engaged in the directly opposing commands. When Lieutenant Lea fell wounded on the deck of the Harriet Lane he valiantly refused to surrender

237

either his sword or the ship unless he be permitted to offer his saber to his father. Southern chivalry responded to his request. His father was located immediately and brought on board where a touching scene ensued as the dying lieutenant surrendered his sword to the colonel and died in the latter's arms. His last words were, "My father is here."

Another pathetic incident occurred in the course of the battle on land, when Lieutenant Sherman (son of Colonel Sidney Sherman, who so brilliantly distinguished himself at San Jacinto), was killed by a ball from the Harriet Lane while firing his battery, the famous Twin Sisters. Wounded unto death, as his comrades leaned over him, he whispered: "Tell my father that I died at my guns, and my mother that my last thoughts are of her." His mother had retired to her home across the bay, on Cedar Bayou, to await the outcome of the engagement. I recall having been told years ago of a singular premonition that came to the elderly Mrs. Sherman as she sat waiting in her home, listening to the cannonading across the bay. In the form of a vision, it had to do with passing of her valiant young son, and came to her, I am told, almost at the moment his tragic end occurred.

It was daylight when the federal forces surrendered to General W. R. Scurry, grandfather of our Tom Scurry. The remaining Yankee fleet had surrendered under a flag of truce. Due to excitement prevailing at the time, little attention was paid to them and several of the ships later escaped under the white flag, an ignoble act, considering the circumstances. The Harriet Lane, however, remained the capital prize of the "Houston Navy."

Subsequent to the battle, General Magruder, in his report, referred in especially praiseworthy terms of the services rendered by Colonels Cook, DeBray, Fontaine, Captains Mac-Mahan, Henry Lubbock and E. P. Turner (who later married the daughter of William R. Baker of Houston in one of the most elaborate weddings the city had then seen), E. B. Burke, Judge Peter W. Gray, Von Harten, General T. B. Howard, Major E. W. Cave, Major Bagby, W. M. Potter, G. C. Forshey and others.

A few days after the battle a tragic incident of the war occurred that always has left a vivid impression upon my memory. The Confederate boats patrolling the harbor captured an incoming yawl bearing a character known as Nicaragua Schmidt, a former Confederate soldier who had deserted to the other side. He had entered the port believing it yet in Northern hands, to accept the office of provost marshal of Galveston that had been promised him. He was seized, tried and sentenced to be shot.

All the troops on the island were drawn up in a hollow square, he was blindfolded, placed before his coffin, and a corporal's guard fired their volley. Nicaragua Schmidt toppled forward into the coffin, death instantly. I witnessed the execution in company with Willie Von Harten, whose father was the Confederate officer of the day. When Major Von Harten sighted the two of us, just as the fatal volley was fired, he lost all dignity, dashed over to where we were standing and, drawing his saber, soundly spanked Willie for attending the affair against his strict orders to the contrary. Without urging, I left the scene hurriedly.

How well I remember when my father returned to our home, two blocks from the Ursuline convent, which was turned into a base hospital, and welcomed us back from the dunes where I would estimate that seven thousand women, children and old men took shelter during the battle. A stream of wounded and dying of both sides passed our house, where I had my first view of war. My brother and I helped our mother in aiding the good sisters to administer to the wants of both friend and foe. The day after the battle father took leave of absence from his company and took my brother and I to the wharf where we boarded the battered old battleship, peacefully tied up to the wharf. The Bayou City, the Neptune, Island City and the Lucy Guinn were anchored in the channel.

Many of the officers and soldiers of the Federal army, many of them Masons, asked the victors to give their fellow brothers a Masonic funeral, which at first was not granted, but the opposition was quickly overcome and that grand old man Judge Phillip C. Tucker, grand master of Masons, performed the rites which was a double ceremony for the Confederates and the Federals killed. Judge Tucker took the second chapter of Proverbs, eleventh verse: "To speak a word in due time is like apples of gold in beds of silver." This settled the question.

The funeral cortege was a joint one, all Federal prisoners were paroled and they joined the Confederates, marching through the deep sand for two or three miles to the cemetery. I stood for hours as the procession passed near our home. The scene is still in my mind.

The battle won, the Federal fleet hoisted the white flag

239

and slipped out in the excitement to sea, the flagship West-field, Commodore Renshaw in command, ran ashore on Pelican Island in the harbor. He with a band of men had set a fuse to blow her up. They rowed away to await the blast, but it miscarried and there was no explosion. He then took a small crew and again boarded the Westfield to lay another fuse when there was an explosion, all being killed. For many years afterwards the boilers projected and I fished around the hull many times, but after the storm of 1886 she settled down to "Davy Jones' Locker."

Nearly all historians maintain the cotton clads returned and entered the battle in the nick of time and should have the credit for winning the battle.

The blockading fleet under Commodore H. H. Bell returned to its station at Galveston a week after the battle, in 1863. The Yankees, out of humor about their defeat, were disposed to get even with the Texans in any way possible.

So on the afternoon of January the tenth, their vessels moved up closer to the island. Their flagship the "Brooklyn," opposite Fort Point, and the gunboat "Sciota," without a moment's notice to warn the women and children, opened simultaneous fire. The "Uncas" joined in and thirty-six shots were fired into the city. I remember this well, as our home was in direct line with the fire of the "Uncas," so we fled to the sand hills on the first shot.

Colonel Cook hurried the E. B. Nichols guns to the south battery, which was where the Murdoch's bath house now stands, and fired four shots with telling effect, which compelled the enemy to retreat. Many buildings had been struck, though without serious damage and no lives were lost.

The next night, the eleventh, the Yankees were by way of amusement dropping an occasional shell into the helpless city. Suddenly the "Alabama" commanded by Admiral Raphael Semms, came into sight, while cruising our coast on the lookout for transports of the Banks expedition in Texas. Not knowing of our recapture of Galveston, he came suddenly upon four federal war vessels near the island. Realizing that Galveston was again in the hands of the Confederates, the "Alabama" began to move off. It was closely followed by one of the blockading vessels.

Admiral Semms, in his "Memoirs Afloat," describes the battle thus: "At length when I had drawn the stranger out about twenty miles from his fleet I furled my sails, beat to

240

quarters and prepared my ship for action. We wheeled to meet him.

"The two ships now approached each other very rapidly. As we came within speaking distance we simultaneously stopped our engines. The ships were about one hundred yards apart. The enemy was the first to hail. 'What ship is that?' cried he.

" 'This is her Britannic Majesty's steamer "Petrel," ' we replied. We now hailed in turn and demanded to know who he was. We heard enough. They were therefore our enemy.

"Presently the stranger hailed again and said, 'If you please, I will send a boat on board you.' We replied, 'Certainly, we shall be pleased to receive your boat.' "

While the Yankees were lowering their boat Admiral Semms ordered Lieutenant Kell to tell the enemy who he was, and Kell did so with, "This is the Confederate States steamer Alabama," and turning to the crew gave the order, "Fire!" Away went the broadside.

At the sound of the shots, Commodore Bell got under way with the federal ship "Brooklyn" and two other steamers and came out to the rescue.

When the action commenced the two ships had swerved in such a way that they were now heading in the same direction; each ship delivered her broadside and the action becoming a running fight.

This, however, was not very long, for in just thirteen minutes after the firing of the first shot, the enemy hoisted a light and fired off a gun as a signal that they had been beaten.

Semms says, "We steamed up to the beaten steamer which proved to be the 'Hatteras' a larger ship than the 'Alabama.' The Yankees reported two killed and five wounded, the Confederates only one man wounded."

Admiral Semms commanded every man be conveyed from the sinking ship to the "Alabama."

Commodore Bell, off Galveston Island, issued on January twenty-first, 1863, a proclamation that the city was "likely to be attacked at any time by the force under his command," and giving warning to withdraw within twenty-four hours after five o'clock that day.

On the twenty-ninth the "Brooklyn," with the gunboats "Onasco Katahdin," "Sciota" and "Alaska," opened fire on Fort Scurry (at the east end of Market Street) and fifty-four shots were fired, but no one was killed.

In a few days Colonel Cook visited the "Brooklyn" under a flag of truce and informed the commodore that the hospitals containing Federal and Confederate wounded were in range of the federal guns. The Prussian, German and English consuls protested. The commodore made no reply, but the bombardment ceased.

About January twentieth, 1863, Sabine Pass and Sabine Lake became endangered and General Magruder, still in command, had the two new steamboats, the "Josiah Bell" and the "Uncle Ben," which he had secured at Calcasieu, fitted out and duly protected by bales of cotton. Each was equipped with a suitable gun and a body of sharpshooters. The "Josiah Bell" had a rifle piece from the Tredegor Works at Richmond, Virginia, which had been hauled from Alexandria, Louisiana.

The "Uncle Ben" had two twelve-pounders on her forecastle. Captain Johnson was in command, the guns being under Captain Kieth and the sharpshooters from Spaight's battalion.

The "Josiah Bell" was under command of Captain Charles Fowler and her armament directed by Captain Odium of the Davis Guards, Dick Dowling being at the gun; sharpshooters were from Pyron's cavalry regiment.

General Magruder ordered Colonel J. S. Spaight to remain at Beaumont and sent a major of his staff to organize the expedition and direct the attack. The steamboat "Sunflower" furnished some additional supplies and the boats raised steam and crossed Sabine Lake on January twentieth, 1863.

At this time the blockade fleet was composed of two vessels, the "Morning Light," being commanded by Captain Dillingham and had a rifle piece on the poop and a battery of eleven guns. The other vessel, the "Velocity," carried two twelve pound Napoleon guns. These, the next morning, hastily retreated outside of the bar and to seaward, hoping the Confederate boats would swamp in the sea. But they were followed out about thirty miles and then prepared for battle, the "Josiah Bell," the fastest was first to fight and the "Uncle Ben" followed soon. After a few shots from the guns on the steamboats, which did remarkable execution, and soon the only man on deck of the Morning Light was the captain. "The flag went down" and the other vessel also surrendered to the Texans. Both vessels were later taken to the pass.

The "Velocity" was towed over the bar and the "Morning Light" might also have been taken in, but she was finally

242

burned to keep her from falling into the hands of the Federals.

Colonel Spaight and his battalion were ordered to Louisiana and Lieutenant Colonel Griffin was placed in command at the pass. Colonel Griffin with his command left for Bonham, and the only forces left at the pass were the artillery company of Captains Odium and Kieth, the former being the ranking officer.

No blockaders had been seen at the pass, until on September the eighth, a fleet of twenty-eight sails made its sudden appearance. Captain Odium placed his company of forty-two on the Uncle Ben with Kieth's company to meet the enemy on the lake. Captain Odium directed Dowling not to fire a gun until the enemy had reached a certain point where the channel is crooked, making navigation difficult.

At about nine o'clock in the morning four gunboats opened fire on the fort, which remained silent, as the boats had not reached the point Odium had designated. When the Clifton, the foremost of the enemy ships, had reached the point designated she struck an oyster reef and was held fast. A shot from the fort penetrated the steam drum of the Sachem, the next boat. Both were helpless and soon taken possession of by Captain Odium of the "Uncle Ben." The other vessels, with twelve thousand men, returned to New Orleans. (These were the ships who left under white flag after the battle of Galveston.)

The object of the Federals in making this formidable expedition to the coast of Texas has never been fully explained. It may have been to land and penetrate the interior of Texas in concert with General Banks, or to take possession of some eight thousand bales of cotton stored at Neblets Bluff. Whatever may have been the object this was the last attempt to occupy Texas.

In his report of January twenty-fourth, General Magruder says: "I have the honor to report that Sabine Pass has been cleared of the enemy. Two gunboats which I fitted up on the Sabine have captured the enemy's blockade squadron. They pursued the enemy thirty miles out to sea, during which a running fight was kept up. Finally they surrendered and were returned to Sabine Pass.

"The destruction and expulsion of the enemy's land and naval forces at Galveston, and the permanent occupation of the island and the east coast of Texas has been effected."

THE BATTLE OF SAN JACINTO

The Texas Army, under command of General Sam Houston, had retreated from Groce's Crossing of the Brazos, near Hempstead, following what is now the course of the H. and T. C. Railroad, toward Harrisburg, the principal village at that time. The City of Houston as such did not then exist, although there was a small settlement on the banks of the bayou and a boat landing about where the W. D. Cleveland Building now stands.

The Mexicans, under the commands of General Santa Anna, the President of Mexico, General Cos, supporting Santa Anna and General Filisola, were invading Texas and laying waste the country as they advanced. Houston's army was small, poorly equipped and composed largely of volunteer recruits. Discipline, under the circumstances, was necessarily lax. The results, they came and went, sometimes individually, sometimes in bodies, according to the demands upon them from their home, farm or other affairs, and sometimes, largely according to their mood at the moment.

General Houston, it seems, with his army in that status, was in no particular mood to risk an engagement with the superior forces under Santa Anna. He realized that one disastrous defeat by the Mexican army would spell the end of Texas liberty, a liberty, in fact, yet to be accomplished. Therefore, he deferred a decisive contact with the enemy until circumstances were more propitious, hoping meanwhile not only to catch the Mexican forces while they were divided, but also upon a field of battle more suited to the needs of an army so small and of the particular type that he commanded.

His continued postponement of definite contact with the enemy, by consistently retreating, had brought upon him the severe criticism of his compatriots; many of his recruits were leaving the colors and returning to their homes, making the oft-repeated comment that they had come to fight, not to retreat. There was even strong talk of replacing Houston as commander in chief of the army.

Such was the status of affairs when the Texas army was encamped near Groce's Crossing above mentioned. It was here that word came to General Houston that Santa Anna, was marching toward Harrisburg with a force estimated at from one thousand five hundred to two thousand men, and that Generals Filisola and Cos, with their respective Mexican commands, were operating in other parts of Texas, their plan being to converge with Santa Anna's command in the coastal region after the three Mexican armies had devastated Texas and crushed the rebellion.

It was General Houston's purpose, by leading Santa Anna away from his two supporting Mexican commands, to stake all on a decisive battle and crush him before help could arrive. Yielding, therefore, to the importunities of his men when the news of Santa Anna's approach reached them, the Texas Army immediately broke camp at Groce's Crossing and on April eighteenth, 1836, started southward. After a forced march of one day and a half, in which they covered fifty-five miles, the army arrived opposite Harrisburg. The crossing was made next morning at what is now Manchester on the Ship Channel, near the present site of the Texas Chemical Company.

That evening a dispatch-bearer from the enemy was captured, from whom it was learned that Santa Anna, with a choice division of Mexican troops, had preceded the Texas Army, burned Harrisburg and marched toward Lynch' Ferry, now Lynchburg, on the San Jacinto River.

Leaving behind their baggage, the sick, and a sufficient rearguard, Houston's army, in a forced march, continued eagerly after the enemy. Only one stop was made, a halt for only a brief period in the prairie, without refreshment, and the march continued through the night of the nineteenth. Pushing forward at daybreak, the Texas scouts encountered those of the enemy and learned that Santa Anna was at New Washington (now Morgan's Point), from whence they intended to proceed, by way of Lynch's Ferry to Anahuac.

The Texan Army, planning to prevent the crossing of the Mexicans, moved forward and took up their encampment in a grove of timber adjacent to Lynch's Ferry. This was on the morning of April, twentieth.

The greater portion of the Texans were doubtless asleep or resting from the fatigue of their forced march of the previous two days and a half; the commissary soldiers were busy slaughtering beeves herded from nearby; Houston and his aides consulting meanwhile over the contemplated plans of attack, when suddenly the camp was thrown into intense excitement and activity by the surprise approach of Santa Anna and his army, who advanced in battle formation against the

Texan position. It developed that the Mexican army had been encamped at Clopper's Point, only eight miles below.

The first contact of the opposing armies occurred about noon of the twentieth, when the Mexican army, marching in good order, took position on an eminence fronting and within easy cannon-range of the Texans. Here they posted their only artillery, a double-fortified brass twelve pounder (General Rusk states it a nine pounder) and deployed their infantry and cavalry on their right, protected by a skirting of timber.

The Mexicans opened fire on the Texans, their cannon in front, infantry on the left and the cavalry changing position in the course of the firing. Their infantry charged the left wing of the Texans. This was promptly repelled by the Texans artillery, consisting of the famed "Twin Sisters," two small brass cannons presented by the ladies of Cincinnati.

Presently the firing ceased, the Mexicans retreating and re-forming in two small groves of timber. Here they remained, opening fire now and then in a desultory manner until shortly before sunset, when a move was made to withdraw their forces. Their cavalry and artillery were moved to other locations. Colonel Sidney Sherman, in a reconnoitering movement with some sixty or eighty mounted men, advanced towards the Mexicans' position and charged their cavalry, numbering in excess of one hundred, who came out to meet him. A sharp encounter followed. Sherman lost two men wounded, but none killed and inflicted substantial losses upon the Mexican cavalry. Their infantry moved forward in support of the cavalry, whereupon Sherman's command retired, the Texas Infantry moving forward to cover their retreat, and the whole was made in good order.

About nine o'clock in the morning of the twenty-first of April, Santa Anna was reinforced by the arrival of General Cos with a force of five hundred men, who had, without sleep the night before, made a forced march to join forces with Santa Anna before the impending battle. Santa Anna accordingly, permitted them to stack arms and go to sleep. Both armies remained poised, awaiting the final clash.

General Houston, determined that the coming engagement should be decisive and that the vanquished, whoever they might be, should have no escape. Accordingly, he ordered Vince's bridge, communicating with the Brazos and about eight miles distant, to be destroyed. This was regarded at the time as the only means of egress from the field now oc-

246

cupied by the opposing armies. Erastus (Deaf) Smith and his scouts were charged with the destruction of the bridge and about four o'clock in the afternoon rode in to report that the bridge had been destroyed. This information was received with loud acclaim by the Texans, and amidst a scene of wild enthusiasm, Houston gave orders preparatory to an immediate attack upon the enemy. The Texan army now numbered seven hundred and eighty-three men.

With the addition of General Cos' command, Santa Anna now had some fifteen hundred men, fully equipped. At three o'clock in the afternoon of the twenty-first, the great portion of the Mexican army were at rest, having thrown up a breast-work some five feet high, with an opening in the middle where their cannon was stationed. It appears that General Santa Anna and a majority of his staff were asleep at the moment.

Meanwhile, General Houston had ordered the Texan army to parade their commands and take up the respective positions assigned them, all of which was really accomplished without observation on part of the enemy, because of the shelter of the woods in which the Texans were encamped. General Houston had wrought well in selecting the site of the battle. As the zero hour, about four-forty o'clock the same day, approached, the parading Texans were formed for attack. General Burleson's First Regiment was assigned the center. The Second Regiment, Colonel Sherman in com-mand, occupied the left wing. The artillery commanded by Colonel Hockley, Inspector General, was stationed on the right of the First Regiment, being sustained by four companies of infantry under Colonel Henry Millard of their right. The cavalry, numbering sixty-one mounted men un-der Colonel M. B. Lamar, afterward President of the Repub-lic, was placed on the far right, and thus completed the Texas line. The cavalry was first dispatched to the enemy's left; this being done to distract their notice and cover a movement of the main body of Texans as they emerged from the timber and moved forward over the open prairie toward the Mexican breastworks and artillery. The Texan artillery now moved up to within two hundred feet of the Mexican cannon. Commanding an open view, they immediately opened a brisk fire of grape and cannister.

The reaction on the Mexican side to the above described movements, can perhaps best be gathered from the excerpt from the report of the Battle of San Jacinto by the Mexican Colonel Delgado.

"No important incident took place until four thirty o'clock in the afternoon. At this fatal moment the bugler upon our right signalled the advance of the enemy upon that wing. His Excellency (Santa Anna) and his staff were asleep; the greater number of his men were also sleeping. Of the rest, some were eating; others were scattered in the woods in search of boughs to make shelter. Our line was composed of musket stacks, our cavalry riding bareback to and from water. I stepped upon some ammunition boxes, the better to observe the enemy, and saw that their formation was a mere line and in one rank, greatly extended. In their center waved the Texas flag. (This was the famous battle-flag presented to Colonel Sherman's Company by the ladies of Newport, Kentucky, bearing a figure symbolizing the Goddess of Liberty, and the motto, 'Liberty or Death!' and was the only flag used by the Texans at San Jacinto. It now rests in the Capitol at Austin). On both wings they had two light cannons, well manned, their cavalry was opposite our front, overlapping our left. In this array they advanced resolutely upon our camp, yelling furiously and with a brisk fire of grape, musket and rifle. The utmost confusion prevailed on our side. Generals shouted on first one hand and then another. Colonel Almonte was giving futile orders; some cried out to commence firing; others to lie down to avoid grape shot. Among the latter was His Excellency, Santa Anna. Already, I saw our men flying in small groups, terrified and endeavoring to shelter themselves behind large oak trees; all efforts were in vain; the evil was beyond remedy; we were a bewildered and panic stricken herd. Meeting no resistance, they dashed lightning-like upon our camp, and their unpleasant noises and clamor were heard in close proximity. Then I saw His Excellency running about in the utmost excitement, wringing his hands and unable to give an order. General Castrillon was stretched on the ground with a wound in the leg; Colonel Treviño was killed, and Colonel Aguirre severely injured; the enemy had now reached the ordnance train . . . everything being lost, I went . . ."

And little wonder!

As reported from the Texas side, Colonel Sherman commenced the attack from the Texan left, but the entire Texan line at the center and right advanced in double-quick time upon the Mexican breastworks, shouting the war-cry, "Remember the Alamo! Remember Goliad!" They received the scattering fire of the enemy and rushed to within point-blank shot before releasing their fire. The conflict in the breast-works lasted but eighteen minutes, the troops encountering hand-to-hand. The Texans, not having bayonets, the rifle-men used their muskets after the fashion of war-clubs, many of them being broken off at the breach. The route was complete, as Colonel Delgado has stated, although the pur-suit, the Texas cavalry leading, continued until twilight.

A Texan guard was left in charge of the Mexican en-campment, while the remainder of the army returned, bring-ing in their killed and wounded. As miraculous as it ap-pears, the Texans lost only two killed and twenty-three wounded, some half dozen fatally. Contrast that with the Mexican loss of six hundred and thirty-eight killed, two hundred and eight wounded, and seven hundred and thirty-eight prisoners.

The amount of plunder taken from the Mexicans was immense. It included several hundred horses and mules, six hundred muskets, three hundred sabers, two hundred pistols and nearly twelve thousand dollars, in specie. Among the staff loss by the Mexican Army there were: Killed, one general, four colonels, two lieutenant colonels, five captains and twelve lieutenants; wounded, five colonels, three lieuten-ant colonels, two second lieutenant colonels, seven captains and one cadet; prisoners, President Santa Anna, General Cos, four colonels, aides to Santa Anna, and the Colonel of the Guerrero Battalion. General Cos was not captured until April twenty-fourth.

I retain even yet, in memory, a vivid picture of the Battle of San Jacinto, obtained through the medium of a visit to the battle ground on April twenty-first, 1884, in company with some twenty of the original veterans of San Jacinto, and Mrs. Andrew Briscoe, daughter of John R. Harris, founder of Har-risburg, and herself one of the early historians of Texas.

I recall, subsequently, the visit of Alonzo Steele, last sur-viving veteran of San Jacinto, to Houston, and how reverent-ly he was entertained at Bryan Hall seventy-one years after the battle. A splendid portrait of him now hangs in the State Capitol at Austin. His remaining son, Alonzo Steele yet active in his nineties, is now one of Houston's venerated citizens.

In conclusion, I recall the words of Colonel Rusk: "The sun was sinking in the horizon as the battle commenced; but at the close of the conflict, the Sun of Liberty and Independence rose in Texas, never, it is to be hoped, to be obscured by the clouds of despotism!"

MARY JANE BRISCOE

Savior of San Jacinto Battle Ground

As in every battle there is a leader, so in every movement to perpetuate the memory of the historical spot and its heroes there is one figure that stands paramount. Mrs. Clara Driscoll Sevier has been called the "Savior of the Alamo" and the name of the late Mrs. Mary Jane Briscoe should be placed on the honor roll as the "savior and perserver of San Jacinto."

Had it not been for the untiring efforts of Mrs. Briscoe, the cornerstone to be laid at the battle ground on San Jacinto day might not carry the same significance. This and succeeding generations could do nothing finer than to pause and reflect the contribution Mrs. Briscoe made toward preserving the history and beauty of San Jacinto—the Shrine of all Texans.

For sixty-seven years Mrs. Briscoe labored for the upkeep of the battle ground, when this spot was almost isolated. The coming of automobiles and good roads has made it just a short distance from Houston. Until the storms of 1875 and 1886, through the efforts of this fine lady the "Sam Houston Oak" had been preserved.

Mrs. Briscoe's maiden name was Mary Jane Harris. She was the daughter of John R. Harris, founder of Harrisburg, and came to Harrisburg in the fall of 1836.

I had the pleasure of meeting her in 1884 as we walked up from the boat landing at San Jacinto toward the site of the beautiful memorial building now under construction. We were in company with about twenty-five of the old veterans, several being from Houston, and Mrs. Briscoe offered to show me just where the battle was fought. We passed the old country burial grounds where the natives had been buried for over forty years. She led us across the Lynchburg road and pointed to a swamp and timber section. It has been fifty-three years but I have never forgotten the graphic description Mrs. Briscoe gave on that occasion.

Year after year, Mrs. Briscoe's interest in the battle ground grew—in beautifying it, in preserving names, documents and relics for others to enjoy. She was called the "Belle of Buffalo Bayou" and later became the vice-president of the Daughters of the Republic of Texas and held many offices later.

On August, eighteenth, 1837, she married Andrew Briscoe, the marriage being performed by Rev. Isaac Patterson. Meanwhile the new seat of government had been established at Houston, the county seat. Mr. Briscoe was appointed Chief Justice of the county of Harris, which necessitated their residence in Houston. Mrs. Briscoe's life was closely connected with that of her husband and she always was proud of her husband's connection with the war of Texas Independence and had a sincere affection for those who had shared with him the dangers of the revolution.

Andrew Briscoe's name first became associated with the Republic at Anahuac, through an event of historical importance, and one in the chain of causes which soon led to the revolution. This event is vaguely referred to by most of the historians as the "Affair at Anahuac," but no names are mentioned in connection therewith.

Briefly, the facts are that shortly after Mr. Briscoe had moved a stock of goods to Anahuac, the town was invested by a garrison of forty men under the Mexican Captain Tenoria, who, after pretense of collecting dues on imports, seized the goods brought there by Mr. Briscoe and forbade him to make any disposition of them until permits were secured.

Protesting against the obvious injustice of the demands, Mr. Briscoe resisted the order and was thrown in jail. This immediately gave rise to a conflict between the local Briscoe following and the Mexican garrison. Reports of the situation were transmitted rapidly to San Felipe. There the news spread quickly, and resulted in a rescue party being formed by William B. Travis and Patrick Jack. This party headed for the Gulf, commandeered the ship Ohio, placed loaded cannon aboard it and sailed to attack Anahuac. They won the fight, liberated Andrew Briscoe and disbanded the Mexican garrison.

The fires of the revolution were now under way. Briscoe having been robbed of his property and having no business, turned his attention toward freeing the colonies from the tyranny of Mexico. The break into open rebellion soon became with the conflicts at Goliad and Gonzales. The battle of "Concepcion" followed. Mr. Briscoe took part in this battle. He was present and took part in the storming of San Jacinto.

Mr. Briscoe was elected to represent Harrisburg at the convention, thus becoming one of the signers of the declaration of Texas Independence and joined in the battle of San Jacinto in command of a company of regulars.

Mr. Briscoe died at New Orleans on October fourth, 1849. He was survived by his wife, Mrs. Briscoe; two daughters, Jessie, who became the wife of Captain M. G. Howe, and Adele, who married Major M. Looscan, and two sons, Parmenas Briscoe and Andrew Birdsall Briscoe.

Mrs. Looscan passed away a few years ago as one of Houston's oldest settlers and a valued and beloved historian. Mrs. Briscoe until her death was one of Texas' most outstanding women. As a member of the Daughters of the Republic and United Daughters of the Confederacy she filled many high offices. She was instrumental in getting the first appropriation through the legislature to buy the present San Jacinto Park. With the aid of a few veterans, she placed the present red granite monuments where the different armies were camped and the location of Sam Houston's famous oak, which she guarded so many years.

I do not believe a single reunion passed without her having been an active delegate at the meeting and participant in the celebration. She cherished the grounds and the shrine with her daughter, Mrs. Looscan, who took up the work where her mother left off in the different historical societies.

Her son, Parmenas Briscoe, remembered as the local agent of the Texas Transport and Terminal railroad between Houston and Clinton fifty years ago, with Mrs. Columba Harris Hume and Miss Annie Hume, nieces, the latter yet with us, all worked faithfully in carrying out the work originally started by Mrs. Briscoe. Credit also should be accorded for a material share in this work to Mrs. C. M. Milby of Harrisburg and to Mrs. J. J. (May Fenn) McKeever, who labored industriously with the legislature and other bodies to secure funds to purchase for San Jacinto battle grounds the red granite markers. My recollecton is that Mrs. McKeever spent some eleven hundred dollars of her own money in publicizing the movement at the time. Another Houstonian quite active in the movement was Mrs. H. F. Ring.

It is doubtful that any family has worked more faithfully and left more genuine contributions than has the Briscoe family and its branches. It would be fitting and proper to carry a recital of their part in the preservation of San Jacinto battle grounds in some bronze placque or other memorial within the walls of the beautiful structure now under construction. Mrs. Briscoe gave of her efforts for seventy years, passing away on March ninth, 1903.

HISTORIC STAFFORD'S POINT

The Naming of Houston

Every young man cherishes the desire to enter a profession, business or vocation. Fifty years ago, the height of my ambition was to become a Brazos bottom planter. Having been brought up and "fed" on cotton, I desired to remain in this business, as my father had come to Texas, in 1851, and engaged in the business that was destined to become one of the largest industries in the South.

I thought my troubles were ended when I purchased the historical "Varney Plantation," founded by Dr. Zeke Varney, in the days of the Texas Revolution. It is situated three quarters of a mile south of the little town of Stafford's Point. Part of the land is situated in the Oyster Creek bottom and one half lies in the prairie, running through which is a creek called "Stafford's Run." Here is where William Stafford brought his slaves in the early thirties from Virginia and farmed a half century ago. It was well farmed and beautiful peach, quince, mulberry and fig trees abounded on it.

Sometime ago my daughter, Jessie, came down from Austin and we took an automobile drive out Houston's Main Street. We kept driving until we were almost to Stafford's Point and I was telling her about the old plantation there. We inquired of some of the natives and took a winding country lane that left the Old Spanish Trail far behind. Stopping beside a huge oak tree, we decided to ask the man approaching us for further directions. It was a pleasant surprise to come face to face, after an absence of thirty years, with my old friend, Reese Packer. After greetings and a brief reminiscence I asked my old friend to show my daughter where General Filisola had his camp, the day of the Battle of San Jacinto and also where he received his orders delivered by Deaf Smith from Santa Anna "to skee-dadle," as General Houston described it.

Had the Mexican general disobeyed orders and followed Santa Anna to Harrisburg, quite a different story might have been told today and the flag of the Lone Star State might have carried a different design. Mr. Packer went with us to the edge of the timber and pointed to a vast prairie originally extending to the head of Buffalo Bayou, where the Mexican general maneuvered his army. It was here, also, according to Mrs. Adele Looscan and Mrs. Dulie C. Harris, in their memoirs, that at dusk just a few days prior to the battle, when the planters had finished their corn and were planting cotton, they heard a deafing sound like thunder. They could see a cloud of dust which might have resembled a dust bowl storm of today, only to discover that it was a large herd of buffalo coming from the Brazos River above Fort Bend. As they passed the home of Dr. Pleasant W. Rose he tried to get in a shot at them but his horse became frightened and he had to hurry away. As the night was very dark, they could not tell when the last buffalo passed. They were terribly worried because it was supposed that Indians were following the herd. They traveled eastward toward Houston, entering what is now the beautiful residential section of "River Oaks." The ground over which this herd passed looked like it had been plowed. This was the last time a buffalo herd in large numbers was seen in this vicinity but for some years a few ranged on Mustang and Chocolate bayous, south of Alvin. Mr. Hill, a cotton man from Grimes County, however, had several buffalo roving with his cattle as late as the early "Forties."

I asked Mr. Packer to show us where the old men, women and children of the colonists gathered from Brazoria, Matagorda, Fort Bend and Colorado counties and camped when they were fleeing from the Mexicans. He pointed to Stafford's Run where the group had camped and, like Filisola's army, obtained water for man and beast. Dr. Varner had built a large well which everyone in that vicinity had come to know as "supplying good drinking water."

History tells us that many planters deserted the army to meet their families there, escorting them to the Sabine where they would be safe on United States soil, intending to rejoin the army later. Many say that these people were dismayed because they thought the Hero of San Jacinto was fleeing to the Redlands and did not intend to fight or make a stand. Colonel Warren D. C. Hall, acting Secretary of War, issued an order for them to come as near Galveston as possible, if they were undecided or in doubt and they would be supplied with transportation to the island to make a last stand, but the horrifying "runaway scrape" had gained momentum. The rivers were overflowing, creeks and bayous were out of their banks, and the prairie looked like a sea of mud. Heroic wives of the pioneers were seen driving ox carts with wobbling wheels made out of round slabs of oak trees and with shift axles run through them, similar to those we see in the interior of Mexico. Scant provisions were placed on the carts and old men and children were huddled together in these conveyances. The slaves were loyal to their charges, protecting the women, children and enfeebled and putting their shoulders to the wheels to help pull the wagons out of the mud. In March, the news came that the Alamo had fallen and the Texas army was retreating. President Burnet was en route to Harrisburg. When the refugees arrived and crossed Vince's Bridge they found thirty slaves from Stafford's plantation and fully five hundred people at the ferry. The women were on horseback; roads and prairies were a bog; homes and plantations deserted and everything left behind. The Trinity River was ten miles wide.

General Ben Fort Smith appeared with a group of Negroes but they were not like the old slaves; they were more like "wild native Africans" and did not understand a word of English, and were of little assistance.

Once when I needed some Negroes to pick cotton and recondition it, I located eight or ten in Western Louisiana, who had been brought in through the Barataria country from Africa. They did not understand a word of English but by gestures I showed them how to assort the cotton and they adapted themselves remarkably. Some of these men, this was fifty years ago, had cuts on their cheeks, ears notched and other marks of identification. Some actually had rings in their noses, lips and ears; others were like pigmies and others were very large and strong. These were a decided contrast to the Negro of today.

The refugees, upon crossing the Trinity River, were informed that the Mexicans had crossed the Colorado at Liberty. It was five miles to Liberty. A few days later, a man came on horseback bringing them the news that the Texas army had crossed the Brazos and that President Burnet had arrived in Galveston with his cabinet, with the exception of General Rusk who was aiding General Houston. After remaining in Liberty for a week, the refugees heard a distant sound like thunder, which they understood came from the cannons of the Texas and Mexican armies. The reports of the cannons were so distinct that they thought the fighting was at Trinity River.

They met a group of some sixty young men who had crossed the Sabine from the United States, to give aid to General Houston, but they all were met by a man on horseback waving his hat, yelling, "Turn back. The Texans have whipped the Mexican army and the Texans are pursuing them to the Brazos River. No danger! No danger! Turn back!"

They could not quite understand the glorious news but when the courier showed them a dispatch from General Houston, giving an account of the battle and saying that it was safe for all refugees to return to their homes, they turned their faces to the setting sun, arrived at the battle grounds where they witnessed a gruesome sight but were happy in their reunions with their husbands, sons and brothers. They tarried a few days to give aid to the wounded and to bury the dead. Hurrying back to Stafford's Point, they found the gin house had been destroyed by the Mexicans and there was no encouragement to plant cotton, as the nearest gin was twenty miles away. The school house was also burned, and despair and destruction was everywhere. They began to make preparations to return to Harrisburg County, although at that time Stafford's Point was in Harrisburg County and the extreme western end of Harrisburg County extended north to New Kentucky, on the edge of Montgomery County, where the state erected a marker recently. Cedar Bayou marked the eastern limits, although Galveston was counted in as Harrisburg County.

Dr. Pleasant W. Rose, the father of Mrs. Dulie Harris, arranged to have the family residence renovated and remained there, where it is now a part of Harris County, Houston, and an active business center. Mrs. Harris writes of the hardships the Mexicans endured after the war and states that they helped to rebuild some of the ruins.

Dr. Rose lost no time in conferring with the Allen brothers who immediately after the battle began to plan and build the new town at the upper end of navigation. Dr. Rose told the people that the Allens would inaugurate a steamboat line, the boats were being negotiated for him, and have a direct line between Houston and Galveston. He told them of other plans which they would promptly carry out.

256

While the Allens shortly after were entertaining General Houston, Mrs. J. K. Allen asked her husband what name he would give the new town and he exclaimed, "After our distinguished guest, General Houston." Then and there the new town, destined to become one of the great cities of the country, received its name.

SAN JACINTO MONUMENT
HISTORICAL RELICS OF DR. D. LABADIE
PLACED IN THE MONUMENT

Among the rare relics placed in the San Jacinto monument cornerstone were three photographs sent to me by Phillip C. Tucker, Jr. of Bradentown, Florida.

Mr. Tucker, a native of Galveston, is the eldest grandson of Judge Phillip C. Tucker, the man who founded the first Masonic lodge in Galveston, and one of the first in Texas, and built the first brick house in Galveston.

He has the distinction also of being the eldest grandson of Dr. Nicholas D. Labadie, who was born in Windsor, Canada, December fifth, 1802, and emigrated to Texas in 1830. Dr. Labadie was appointed surgeon to the Mexican garrison at Anahuac, Texas, 1831. He joined the Texas army in July, 1836, at Beason's Ferry and was appointed assistant surgeon, second regiment, artillery. The doctor was in skirmish under Captain Karnes at Colorado River and that of April twentieth, in Captain William M. Logan's Company, Second Texas Volunteers under Captain Mosley Baker and General Sherman. He fought in the battle of April twenty-first, 1836, and gave first aid as surgeon to wounded on the field on the first night. He was appointed by General Houston on the morning of the twenty-second in charge of Mexican wounded prisoners. He prepared a list of the prisoners and served as first interpreter between General A. Lopez De Santa Anna and General Houston, when the leader as prisoner was brought to camp.

Dr. Labadie then was placed in charge of the hospital at Zavalla's Point. He was surgeon of draft board for the Confederation in 1862 and 1863. His original photograph was enclosed which was used by W. H. Hudie in making the famous painting "After the Battle" with General Houston lying on a Mexican blanket under the oak tree, which painting now hangs in the senate chamber at the Capitol in Austin.

An original photograph was sent from the painting after it was first made, with a request that this also should be deposited in the cornerstone which was dedicated April twenty-first at the battle grounds. Also a photograph of the first San Jacinto monument was included. It was erected through the efforts of Judge J. S. Sullivan of Richmond, Texas, the husband of Ann Harriet Long, daughter of the "Mother of Texas," Mary Jane Long, and General Long in a preceding chapter. Part of the money was raised by subscriptions of the original San Jacinto veterans, citizens of Galveston and Houston, and the state made up the deficit. It was first unveiled in Galveston August twenty-sixth, 1881, at the beach pavillion, and was washed away in the 1886 storm. Later it was placed at the community burial ground at San Jacinto Park.

It was called "The Bingham-San Jacinto Monument." It was a plain, square spire, with pediment cap, moulded base and chamfered sub-base. It was made of best Rutland, Vermont, varigated marble, fifteen and one-half feet high. The die was of white marble, upon the west front of which was cut, in bold relief, the Lone Star of Texas, resting upon a nimbus and surrounded by a beautiful wreath, in still bolder relief, of oak and laurel leaves. Below is the name: "B. R. BINGHAM" on the base: "SAN JACINTO."

Near the top of the shaft was a polished band, upon which was cut two stars on each front and one above the band on the west front. These represented the "Immortal Nine," who fell in the battle. On south front: "TWO DAYS BEFORE THE BATTLE."

"This morning we are in preparation to meet Santa Anna. It is the only chance of saving Texas. From time to time I have looked for reinforcements in vain. We will only have about seven hundred men to march with, besides the camp guard. We go to conquer. It is wisdom growing out of necessity to meet the enemy now. Every consideration enforces it. No previous occasion would justify it. The troops are in fine spirits, and now is the time for action. We shall use our best efforts to fight the enemy to such advantage as will insure victory, though the odds are greatly against us. I leave the results in the hands of the wise God, and rely upon his providence. My country will do justice to those who serve her. The rights for which we fight will be secured and Texas free."

"SAM HOUSTON"

And below this, on the plinth: "REMEMBER GOLIAD!"

On the north front of the die was the following: "ONE DAY AFTER THE BATTLE."

"At Camp on the Battlefield . . . This glorious achievement was attributed not to superior force, but to the valor of our soldiers and the sanctity of our cause. Our army consisted of seven hundred and fifty effective men. The sun was sinking in the horizon as the battle commenced, but at the close of the conflict the sun of liberty and independence rose in Texas, never, it is to be hoped, to be obscured by the clouds of despotism. We have read of deeds of chivalry and perused with ardor the annals of war; we have contemplated with highest emotions of sublimity and the loud warring thunder, the desolating tornado and the withering simoon of the desert, but none of these, nor all, inspired us with emotions like those felt on this occasion. There was a general cry which prevaded the ranks. 'Remember the Alamo! Remember Goliad!' These words electrified us. Onward was the cry. The unerring aim and the irresistible energy of the Texan army could not be withstood. It was free men fighting against the minions of tyranny, and the result proves the inequality of such a contest. T. J. Rusk."

And below, on the plinth: "WILL YOU COME TO THE BOWER." (The air to which the Texans marched to the fight.)

On the east front, upon the cap: "DEAD UPON THE FIELD OF HONOR."

Upon the die below as follows: "This monument is placed at the grave of Benjamin Rice Bingham, who fell at the battle of San Jacinto April twenty-first, 1836. Eight others fell with him, whose remains rest near his. Their names are as follows: "Lemuel Stockton Blakley, Mathias Cooper, Thomas P. Fowler, J. C. Hale, George A. Lamb, Dr. William Motley, A. R. Stevens, and Olwyn J. Trask."

Below on the plinth: "REMEMBER THE ALAMO."

"This stone is placed here to mark the spot where these heroes sleep, and to perpetuate a knowledge of their names and deeds to coming generations, by the voluntary contributions of private citizens of Texas, 1881.

"N. B.—The casket seen resting against the foot of the

259

monument contains the renowned flag, which floated over the victorious Texans forty-six years ago, now too much decayed to be unfolded."

Mr. Tucker requested the three photographs be placed in the cornerstone of the monument when it was unveiled at San Jacinto, April, twenty-first, 1937. Mr. L. W. Kemp as chairman, received them and considered them very historical subjects. He gladly complied with the sender's request.

Dr. Labadie became one of Galveston's prominent physician citizens and helped build the town, planted the first tree on the Catholic cathedral grounds. General Sam Houston complimented him very highly in his heroic work among the Mexicans after the battle when many left the field on account of the sanitary conditions.

Dr. Labadie contracted typhoid fever which nearly cost him his life. It left him with his hearing almost gone. He was well known to the writer and was the family physician at the home of his parents. His only son, Joe, passed away many years ago in Galveston. And the heroic doctor who became nationally known as an authority on yellow fever, ended his eventful career in Galveston, March thirteenth, 1867.

Judge Sullivan, a leading attorney of Richmond and later of Galveston was also known to the writer. This monument stands today west by the San Jacinto monument.

THE ORIGIN AND NEW FACTS ON THE "TWIN SISTERS"

Francis Smith, a Texan, went to Cincinnati in 1835, and eloquently appealed for funds to buy two six-pounders for Houston's army. Many Ohioans sympathized with the Texan cause, but were restrained from openly assisting the Texans because of a firm policy of neutrality then existing on the part of the United States.

Quietly, Dr. Daniel Drake and many other prominent citizens of Cincinnati banded together and arranged for funds with which to purchase the needed cannon. In order to avoid harmful publicity, the field pieces were referred to consistently as "hollow ware"; and additional funds were collected to cover the cost of an ample supply of ammunition for the guns. The ammunition, however, both in discussion and when mentioned in their resolutions adopted at the two public meetings, was always specified as "accessories and equipment for said hollow-ware."

Francis Smith arranged for prompt transportation of the guns to Texas, via the Mississippi River to New Orleans, thence by water to a Texas port, possibly Galveston or Anahuac, and hurried to Houston's army where they were publicly presented. History records that they arrived here only in the nick of time and played a most important role in turning the tide of Texas independence.

I quote, in this connection, General Houston's own report to the skirmish attack between the two armies the evening "The cannons were under command of Colonel George W. Hockley, in the center of our battle line, the First regiment and Colonel Henry Millard with four companies of infantry sustaining the artillery on the right. The enemy, advancing in column with intent of charging our line, were repulsed by a discharge of grape and cannister from our artillery consisting of two six-pounders. They thereupon fell back and fortified."

General Houston doubtless had reference in the foregoing to the skirmish attack between the two armies the evening before San Jacinto.

Reverting for the moment to the transportation of these guns from Cincinnati, and their arrival in Texas, I want to present a letter received from C. S. Mitchell of Lolita, Texas, which contains some of the most interesting sidelights on the history of the uncover. I quote it practically in its entirety: "Referring to an article by you, 'The Twin Sisters' in a pamphlet sent out by Anderson, Clayton and Company, which I have in front of me at this writing, I believe I can clear up some points relative to the famous guns.

"In the early part of 1836 the citizens of Cincinnati had cast at a local foundry, two iron six-pounder cannons and shipped to Texas as 'hollow-ware.' On each gun was a brass plaque bearing the inscription, 'Presented to the Republic of Texas by the Citizens of Cincinnati.'

"On the same boat, leaving Cincinnati at the time was a Dr. Charles Wesley Rice, a practicing physician from that city, accompanied by his wife and twin daughters, Elizabeth and Eleanor Rice, some eight or ten years of age. They all arrived in Texas together, and when the guns were presented, these little twin girls were drafted as sponsors and presented the cannons to Texas in the name of the Citizens of Cincinnati.

"They, the guns, were immediately dubbed the 'Twin Sisters.' This was the origin of the name applied to the cannons. One of the little girls, Elizabeth, afterward married Hugh Stapp, son of Elijah Stapp, one of the signers of the Texas Declaration of Independence, and was my maternal grandmother, so I am fairly familiar with the incident, having heard it related quite often.

"Now, Elizabeth was one of those sharp-eyed children who saw everything and forgot nothing, a trait, in fact, that she retained all through life. She died in 1909 in her eighties. So, while she was young at the time, she both saw and 'savvied' all about the battery of guns and often described them as 'long iron cannons with brass plates or placques in which was inscribed the legend mentioned.' To her childish eyes no doubt they appeared larger and longer than they were.

"So much for the origin of the guns. Now, as to their fate: In 1907 I tried to get track of the two famous guns, but without success. Continuing, however, in 1909 a squib of mine in the Houston Post brought two replies: first Judge William P. Hamblen of Houston, a Confederate veteran, wrote that he knew the guns and that up to 1861, when the Civil War began, they were in and around Houston, often being used in parades and celebrations. Also he stated specifically that the two guns sent to Texas by the State of Louisiana (about 1861) were not the 'Twin Sisters' as was erroneously supposed to be the case. He maintained that the 'Twin Sisters' never left Texas, and his personal description of the guns tallies in every respect with the description accorded by my grandmother, Elizabeth Rice Stapp.

"Second: A Dr. Graves, physician living at Lometa, Texas, a Confederate veteran now deceased, wrote me as follows: 'I am well acquainted with these two guns,' and here described them in detail as both Mrs. Stapp and Judge Hamblen described.

"He went on to say: 'In the summer of 1865, seeing them with a number of other cannons piled on the platform of the depot at Harrisburg for shipment north, a number of my former comrades-in-arms (they had just been discharged from active service by General Magruder) and I decided that they should never leave Texas. That night we quietly re-

262

moved them, carrying them off half a mile or so, and buried them among some weeds and bushes.'

"Now, half a mile toward the northeast of the depot would have been rather public and liable to discovery, while the same distance to the southwest would have taken them out into a level country. The probabilities are that they buried the guns on the far side of a heavy growth of senna weeds (coffee bean bushes) which would offer an excellent screen during the burial operation. It is my firm conviction the guns are still there.

"As to the two 'brass cannons,' I am not prepared to say where they came from; just two guns popularly supposed to be the 'Twin Sisters.' General Chambers' guns, often referred to (and six in number) did not arrive in Texas until after the battle of San Jacinto. Furthermore, I am inclined to believe, from all facts I have been able to gather and sift down, that the plates on the guns returned to Texas by Louisiana and bearing the inscription mentioned, were put there by the Louisiana authorities when refurbishing the guns, undoubtedly in entire good faith, but erroneously.

"One thing appears definitely evident: The original 'Twin Sisters' were never out of Texas. During the past February and March (1936) I tried to get up enough enthusiasm among the residents of Harrisburg to conduct a systematic search for these guns, so that they might again be presented to the citizens of Texas on April twenty-first, by Mary Katherine Mitchell of Lockhart, a grandniece of mine and great-great-granddaughter of little Elizabeth Rice, one of the original 'Twin Sisters.' "

Thus concludes the letter of C. S. Mitchell. Now, as substantiating the belief of Mr. Mitchell that the guns were never transported from Texas, but remain buried near Harrisburg, there comes the following extract from memoirs of Dr. H. N. Graves of Lometa, now deceased: "General Magruder had granted discharges to some seventy-two of us who had entrained at Galveston for our respective destinations in the interior of the state. Arriving in Harrisburg, when we alighted from the train we saw a number of cannons of various sizes dumped by the side of the railroad track. Looking over the pile, I was surprised to note that the famous 'Twin Sisters' were among them, and felt they, at least, should be protected from vandalism or confiscation by the Federal troops, then preparing to take possession of Texas. Therefore, to my messmates, Sol Thomas, Ira Pruitt, Jack

Taylor and John Barnett of Gonzales, I suggested that we bury the 'Twin Sisters,' to which one of them responded, 'That's right. We'll bury them so deep no dammed Yankee will ever find them.'

"My negro servant, Dan, who had accompanied me throughout the war, was instructed to assist in the undertaking, and really did most of the digging. I recall distinctly that John Barnett, even then with an attack of the measles, spent most of the time leaning against a tree and watching the rest of us work. Before burying the cannons, we took the woodwork apart and burned it. The carriages themselves we threw into the bayou, after which we rolled the cannon some four hundred yards into the woods. It developed that the earth at the spot selected was much more compact than we had anticipated, as a result of which we dug only about two and a half or three feet. There we buried the little 'Twins' in a single shallow grave, marking a number of the nearby trees. The earth was tamped down as firmly as could be done with our feet, and dried leaves and brush were heaped over the spot. Before leaving we took a solemn oath that none of us would ever reveal the secret of their hiding place until all possibility of their capture and confiscation by enemy hands was removed.

"Dan swore the oath with the rest of us. It was about 1905, forty years later, that John Barnett and I returned to Harrisburg in an effort to locate the spot. The owner of the land was absent at the time, and the terrain and environment had undergone marked changes during the interim. Corresponding with the owner, subsequent to our return home, he wrote me that he would be glad to have us 'dig up the whole creation for the "Twin Sisters" whenever you like.' "

Apparently the last visit made to Harrisburg by Dr. Graves was in 1920, when he was driven there by a young man who attended the courtesy car of the Houston Chronicle. It was the G. H. & H. depot at Harrisburg where Dr. Graves and his comrades alighted that afternoon in 1865; and if I understand his memoirs correctly, he left all documents and other data relating to the burial of the cannons to a daughter at the time of his passing, with the injuncton, "If the time ever comes when you can use these to interest patriotic Texans in recovering the 'Twin Sisters' we buried, remember it is my cherished wish that they be recovered."

One thing certain, if these buried "twins" could be unearthed and inspected, it would be a matter of comparative ease, to determine whether they are the original "Twin Sisters" presented by the citizens of Cincinnati.

So many stories, with varied descriptions as to the type of cannon, have come out of the past regarding the "Twin Sisters" and their final disposition, it is altogether difficult to determine, with any degree of satisfaction, just what to believe concerning them. Six sets of "Twin Sisters" have been named altogether. It had been always my understanding that the "Twin Sisters" from Cincinnati were cast of brass or bronze. Most certainly this was true of the two little cannons I saw many times in Galveston at the Artillery hall. This was about the year 1874.

Mr. John Sloan, manager for the Cheek-Neal Coffee Company, tells me he recalls seeing the guns there as late as 1906. Afterwards, I was told that the guns had found their way to a junk yard, being sent North and melted on account of the scarcity of brass. If these be the original "Twin Sisters" then were Dr. Graves and his comrades in error in their belief that they had buried the original guns, or had someone meanwhile dug them up and restored them to public exhibit?

Yet another story has it that two guns were buried in the mud about Virginia Flats to avoid capture by the Yankees; while another story had it that they were being transported on a vessel returning from New Orleans to Texas, or vice versa, and that in the course of voyage the vessel encountered a gale, was blown inland at Virginia Point, grounded and the guns lost overboard. This is authentic and proven many times.

All of this, however, may be either a variation of the story of the burial by Dr. Graves, or may present facts having reference to other cannon of similar size and believed by those in charge to be the original "Twin Sisters." Personally, for many years I have inclined toward the theory that disposed of the cannons as junk and shipment of them North to be melted down. However, there is a strong probability that Dr. Graves may have buried the real "Twin Sisters."

Either that, or perhaps he buried the alleged "Twin Sisters" that were returned to Texas by the state of Louisiana and forwarded to Galveston in the early part of 1861. Certainly the real "Twin Sisters," remained in Houston for many years after the battle of San Jacinto and were used in various parades and celebrations; also that they were transported to Galveston, to be used in similar celebrations there, and General Sherman's son died beside them in the battle of Galveston.

They might easily have been left there on one of those occasions and remained in the vicinity until the close of the Civil War, when Dr. Graves and his comrades discovered them discarded in Harrisburg.

As it stands, I can name three sets of "Twin Sisters": the original ones, made of bronze or brass, which Mr. Mitchell brought from Cincinnati; the iron pair now resting on the lawn at the entrance to the capitol of Texas, presented by General Chambers (and certain historians record that General Chambers really presented six such cannons to the Republic of Texas); and the pair of "Twin Sisters" uncovered during the past year at Mission La Bahia, Texas, and at first popularly supposed to be the original "Twin Sisters."

Some of these days, I hope to visit once again the adopted home of my paternal grandfather, Cincinnati, where he settled. If so, and they still exist, I shall find pleasure in delving into the musty records of the old foundries of Cincinnati in an effort to determine of just what metal the original "Twin Sisters" were made—brass, bronze or iron.

CANNONS WOMEN OF HAVANA GAVE TEXAS, LOST IN STORM

It is a little known fact that the women of Havana, Cuba, presented the scrappy Republic of Texas with two brass cannons intended to help win Texas independence from Mexico in 1836.

The only evidence of this gift is found in a Texas publication of 1879 that quotes a letter found in the official archives of the state capitol at Austin. The capitol and the archives have since been destroyed by fire.

The letter was written December third, 1836, by William G. Cook, acting secretary of war, to Thomas Toby and Son of New Orleans, fiscal agents for the Republic at that point. It announced that the secretary had been instructed by the House of Representatives to take measures to procure the custody of two cannons presented to the republic by Havana women.

These cannons were brought from Havana to New Or-

266

leans by Toby and Son's war-schooner, Tom Toby. The Tom Toby was blown ashore and wrecked near Virginia Point during a storm in October of 1837. Many years elapsed before the wreckage was searched and the cannons recovered. They were purchased by an Artillery Company at Galveston. Like the original "twin sisters" donated to the Texas revolutionary cause, by the citizens of Cincinnati, the Havana cannons have disappeared and no one knows what became of them.

PASSING OF SANTA ANNA

There are many among us who are firm believers in cause and effect—"as you sow, so shall you reap." Reverend William Butler, an outstanding minister of the gospel, who visited General Santa Anna a year before his death relates:

"Santa Anna was living in an obscure street, neglected and forgotten by all parties.

"On entering the apartment, we find the old man sitting on a sofa—behind which hung a picture of his wife, her serene highness "Dolores Tosta De Santa Anna." Arrayed as a queen, the magificence of the painting contrasted sadly with the poverty-stricken aspect of the room and furniture.

"To him, however, this could make but little difference as we soon saw that he was totally blind, as well as feeble and broken in spirit and with a tendancy to mental weakness.

"He was buried in the cemetery at Guadalupe, just outside of the capital, without honors or recognition by the government, and his remains still rest there. As I gazed upon his tomb, I could not keep from thinking of the horrible events in the history of Texas with which his name was associated."

It has long been a question whether General Houston acted nicely, in being so magnanimous, for Santa Anna caused a great deal of trouble for his country, as well as ours, during the remaining years of his life, and it is too well known that he endeavored to kill every Texan before and after his defeat.

It was left, however, to Miss Roberta John, now Mrs. Leslie Hogan, the granddaughter of his worst enemy, Sam

Houston, who visited his grave shortly after he passed away
to do a magnanimous act, returning good for evil by placing a wreath on his headstone in 1916.

WHEN TEXAS WAS YOUNG

After the battle of San Jacinto, Santa Anna negotiated
the Velasco treaty in 1836. At that time Texas claimed the
territory between the Rio Grande and the forty-second parallel north, and for ten years asserted this claim. However,
Mexico refused to acknowledge this, claiming that Texas was
not an independent Republic, and placed the boundary at
the Nueces River.

Two months after Texas was admitted to the Union,
about April, 1846, war with Mexico was declared. Again
the fighting Texans threw themselves into the fight with the
same determination and courage that won the independence
of the Republic.

Treaties, negotiated at the close of the Mexican War,
gave to the United States all the territory between the Pacific
and East Texas border. However, that part of New Mexico,
over one half claimed by Texas at that time, objected to becoming a part of the state of Texas. In 1850, the United States
paid Texas ten million dollars to establish the present boundary and finally after the Mexican War Mexico released all
her territory to the Pacific to us.

The present State of Texas, larger than any other state,
once claimed title to land comprising parts of five other states
whose boundaries have since been defined as we know them
today. These States were, New Mexico, Oklahoma, Kansas,
Colorado and Wyoming.

PART FOUR

BIOGRAPHICAL SKETCHES

WARREN D. C. HALL

Pioneer Cotton Planter and Soldier, Friend of LaFitte

Commissioned to practice law in Natchitoches, Louisiana, Warren D. C. Hall the same year became a Captain in the Magee Expedition, after the Battle of Resselo and the murder of the Spanish prisoners by Delgado. Hall, with a number of other Americans, returned to the United States and escaped the disastrous Battle of Medina. This was in 1815.

In 1817, he accompanied the expedition of Soto La Marino, but fortunately returned to the Texas coast with General Aury who occupied Galveston in 1816-17 with a small army under the Mexican rule.

In 1824, we find Hall a member of the committee of safety as a citizen of Matagorda. Aury and Mina had planned to conquer Mexico with six hundred men, but they had trouble and Hall seeing how hopeless the task was returned to Matagorda.

The Texas revolution then began and Colonel Hall was made acting secretary of war. The entire cabinet was in Galveston at the time of the Battle of San Jacinto and the sweeping effect of this battle was unknown to General Houston. Accordingly, on April twenty-sixth, 1836, Colonel Warren D. C. Hall issued from Galveston his famous order: "General Sam Houston, San Jacinto.

"If you consider it inexpedient to risk a further engagement with the enemy, and regard a retreat from the position you now occupy as inevitable,

"You are hereby directed to march the army under your command to the nearest available mainland point adjacent to Galveston Island, giving information of such move to this department and transportation will be made available to carry your command and its equipment to the island."

(Signed) Warren D. C. Hall, Acting Secretary of War.

Hall continued as acting secretary of war, but proceeded shortly afterwards to his plantation at China Grove, situated fourteen miles south of Houston. He had his farm and residence in Galveston and his name is mentioned in almost all activities of the colonists.

China Grove subsequently became the home and plantation of General Albert Sidney Johnston, who acquitted himself so nobly at San Jacinto. Johnston's residence stood on the site of the present railroad station called Bonney.

Colonel Hall often could be seen at the old Allen station on Congress Avenue, wearing his large white Sam Houston hat, lavender trousers, a long-tailed blue coat with flowing silk waist coat and a frilled and flutted white shirt, on his way to board the Columbus Tap Railroad, which he had helped build with his own money.

Colonel Hall lived at the "Three Trees," LaFitte's Grove. He would ferry to and from the plantation via Velasco at times. This was the spot where LaFitte fought the battle with the Indians.

While Colonel Hall was a friend of Jean LaFitte, he took no part in the latter's nefarious occupations of piracy, smuggling, etc.

Colonel Hall also was a close friend of Stephen F. Austin, and in the famous duel between Austin and Colonel John A. Wharton he acted as Austin's trainer. He told Austin that his only chance was to get in the first shot and make it effective otherwise he would be a dead man as he (Hall) regarded Wharton as a dead shot.

Colonel Hall was an active planter, and his plantation was one of the best in the Sugar Bowl. It consisted of rich bottom land. The residence, the sugar house and the outhouses were of brick and the grounds were beautifully terraced.

On one of Colonel Hall's regular trips to look over the plantation and to supervise the management, several Mexicans came into the dining room while he was eating breakfast and attempted to kill him. They would have done so, had it not been for his body servant, Old Tom, who came to his master's assistance. Using the big dining room chairs as clubs, he knocked them down and about until they were glad to get away before Colonel Hall got his gun. I mention this episode to illustrate the attachment between the slave and his master. After emancipation was declared (for Colonel Hall lived a number of years thereafter) Old Tom never left his master, but remained with him until Hall died. At his death Colonel Hall left Old Tom a good home of a hundred acres on Galveston Island. It was called Tom Hulbert's oyster farm, noted for his famous oyster roasts, and situated halfway between the bay and the Gulf on Hall's Bayou, where Old Tom passed his last days.

When you pick up the Harris County map, you will see the Warren D. C. Hall survey near Genoa where he located his headright. This and other surveys were granted him for

Big Five Pioneers of Houston

Left to right, seated: William J. Hutchins, Major T. M. Bagby, T. W. House. Standing: C. S. Longcope, Captain Fred W. Smith.

his excellent services to the republic. Some now are active oil fields.

Had he lived a little longer he would have seen his lands produce black gold instead of the fleecy white staple which he grew so often, and he had the foresight to pick the best.

Colonel Hall's last days were spent at the famous "Three Trees," where he still maintained a farm. His name will live for ages as one of the earliest pioneers who helped make this empire state.

THE BIG FIVE PIONEERS OF HOUSTON

*Active Managers of the Houston Direct
Navigation Company*

Possibly no other group of five men did more to the upbuilding of Houston than the five pictured in this chapter: William J. Hutchins, Major T. M. Bagby, T. W. House, C. S. Longcope, Captain Fred W. Smith.

Hearing of the new empire which was building in Texas, they all arrived about the same time to help build the New Republic. They were the first in nearly all enterprises. The building of the Houston and Texas Central Railroad, The Houston Direct Merchants Company, The Houston Eastern West Texas Railway, Cotton Presses, Cotton Mills, Oil Mills, and all other worthy enterprises. We find their names and activities in all industries. It was my pleasure and honor to have known them all, and I will try to give a brief biography and history of their activities. Some of the scenes occurred when I was only a boy.

WILLIAM J. HUTCHINS.

He was born March 13th, 1833 in Fishell, New York. He moved to Houston in 1843 and immediately embarked in the mercantile business. In 1860 he sold out to McIlhenny, Willlis and Brothers who became the largest general merchants in Texas. He was one of the original projectors and took active management in the Houston, Texas Central Railroad. The town of Hutchins, near Dallas, is named for him.

In 1861 he began the erection of the famous Hutchins House, the largest hotel in Texas at that time. In 1865 was one of the leading projectors of the City Cotton Mills, which burned down in the early days of the War Between

273

the States. The monster chimneys were blasted to make room for Camp Logan, as many remember. He helped organize the Cotton Exchange during the War. He was active in Matamoros, in receiving goods through the blockade, in bringing arms and supplies in by wagon and shipping cotton to London and Liverpool. He raised a large family, among them a son, Spencer Hutchins, who became a great social leader, often called the "Lord McAllister of Houston." Mrs. Seabrook Sydnor, a daughter, was a social leader and foremost in many clubs and civic societies. Strange, and while it often occurs, the family is extinct. His beautiful home stood on Quality Hill.

MAJOR THOMAS M. BAGBY.

A Virginian by birth, born May 1814. He located in Houston in 1837. He entered into a partnership with S. L. Allen, one of the founders of Houston, and also H. D. Taylor and others engaged in the cotton business. He was made a member of the Board of Alderman, but he never held any state offices. He was closely engaged in many enterprises with Benjamin A. Shepherd. He was a close friend of General Sam Houston, and was active in all the campaigns with him. In 1848 he married the sister of Houston's oldest citizen and mayor for a number of years (without pay), William R. Baker. They had six children: William G., Emily G., Mrs. T. C. Usher, Eloise, later Mrs. W. J. Hancock, Lucy B., wife of R. E. Tankersly and Mary B. Mrs. Usher is the only surviving child.

He was foremost in nearly all of the worthy enterprises, never refusing to sacrifice for a good thing. But as merchant and cotton buyer he was successful. He was in command of the Infantry on the "Cotton Clads" and helped capture Galveston. He owned and was interested in steamboats. Captain John Atkinson went to Cincinnati to build the "T. M. Bagby," the palace boat between Houston and Galveston. In its day it was declared nothing finer on the Mississippi River. He did not live to see his enterprises develop and prosper but passed away in 1886. It can truthfully be said that he was one of the most active in building up Houston. His heirs sold the entire block where his residence stood in 1921 to the Houston Public Library, which is a monument to his greatness.

THOMAS W. HOUSE

He, from the beginning, became Houston's foremost merchant and banker. A review of the life of this great man will show at every turn of his career that he possessed great ability. T. W. House was born in Stockest, England, on the fourth day of March, 1814. He came of reputable parentage and good English stock. It is questionable as to whether one should say T. W. House did not have the advantages of a good education. He came to America in 1835, landing in New York City where he soon found employment at the bakers trade and practiced his profession. During that year, Mr. House met a Mr. McDonald, proprietor of the St. Charles Hotel in New Orleans and was induced by him to come south and take charge of the bakery department of that famous hotel. He resided in New Orleans until the last part of 1837 when he located in Houston. This was just a short time before Houston was made the capitol of Texas. He first engaged in the bakery and confectionery business, forming a partnership with a man named Levidge. The following year he became associated with Mr. Charles Shearn with whom he was associated for ten years. The partnership between the two was well cemented when Mr. House married the daughter of Mr. Shearn. In 1853 Mr. House purchased the business of Joseph H. Stevens Company and took into partnership E. Mather. They became the largest grocers in the state. Mather retired in 1862. During the entire War Between the States there was never a suspension in business.

Mr. House engaged in the shipping of cotton to England and became a successful blockade runner with a joint account deal with that daring Captain Henry Sherfius who eluded the Federal fleets so skillfully. In 1863 when Galveston was recaptured, he bought the prize warship, the "Harriet Lane," the flag ship of the Federal blockading fleet and he fitted her out as a blockade runner, thus amassing a huge fortune. The Harriet Lane made many trips later carrying cotton. He continued in the cotton business with the late Captain William Christian as his manager, then finally became a banker exclusively. Having purchased the Arcola Sugar Mills on the Waters Plantation, he manufactured sugar for years and became a cotton planter. He was a charter member of the Houston Ship Channel Corporation, a director of the Houston and Texas Central Railroad, helped build the Houston Direct Navigation Company, the Columbus Tap Railroad, helped organize the Cotton Exchange and the Houston Water Works. He was also an active volunteer fireman and a social leader. Mr. House had two daughters and four sons. His

275

eldest son, T. W. House, Jr., became postmaster. His son, Edward M. House, his only survivor of the children, became the friend and adviser of President Woodrow Wilson and also has been called upon for advice by Franklin D. Roosevelt. Mr. House died in January 1880. The fortune he left was estimated at two and a half million, which was a huge amount at that time. The name of T. W. House will forever be linked with the early development of the city of Houston.

C. S. LONGCOPE.

He was born in Philadelphia in 1803. His family were ship owners from the early days. His elder brother established a line of vessels between the Orient and Philadelphia, but C. S. Longcope sailed on the Gulf waters and the Mississippi which finally carried him to Texas. As a shipping man, he managed the Houston Direct Navigation Company. His first activities known were at LaGrange where he married Miss Courtney McAshan in 1846. He took an active interest in the Houston and Texas Central Railroad after arriving in Houston in 1858. He engaged in the cotton factorage and commission business and later joined as his junior partner, Mr. Sam McAshan. Mr. Longcope was widely known all over Texas as a successful cotton man and merchant. In 1873 when the Cotton Exchange was organized, he was elected the first president. Like all these others he was active in all railroads, cotton compresses, steamboat matters, etc. In 1779 Sam Longcope, an older brother, published a newspaper called the American Eagle and it is still in existence in Easton, Pennsylvania. Mr. Longcope sent to New Orleans and had cast filigree iron balconies for his residence constructed in the "Fifties," the most beautiful residence in the city at that time. This house can still be seen where it stood on Quality Hill just off Franklin on Chenevert. Mr. E. (Money) Longcope, his son, is still surviving, and also his great grandson, E. M. Longcope, and other descendants live in the city which this great founder was so active in developing.

CAPTAIN FRED W. SMITH

He is a pioneer steamboat man. Known as the first vice-president and also active manager of the Houston Direct Navigation, he is one of the oldest respectable citizens of Houston. He was a native of Brookfield, Massachusetts,

276

where he was born in 1814. His father was a soldier of the Revolutionary War. He left his native state in 1836, engaged in business under the name of Taylor and Company, paying three thousand dollars for a lot now worth one hundred thousand dollars, where the Houston National Bank Building stands.

Captain Smith claims he sold the first Sam Houston hat in Houston, a headgear the style of the herder of Texas, at ten dollars in gold. Congress was in session at that time and this led to the sale of a hundred or more hats worn by the legislators. Congress was in session for four years and here thousands were sold later. Mr. Smith was appointed postmaster by President Houston and served until Texas was admitted to the Union.

On his arrival he became associated with Mr. B. A. Shepherd in different industries. He formed a stock company and was made first vice-president of the Houston Direct Navigation Company between Houston and Galveston. His boats were active carriers until the War Between the States, when they were taken by the Confederate Government and on the recapture of Galveston, January 1, 1863, they were converted into Cotton Clads. Many historians say these Cotton Clads saved the day by arriving in the nick of time when General Magruder's Infantry and Artillery were dismayed and demoralized.

At the close of the war Captain Smith was made General Freight Agent of the Houston and Texas Central Railroad, continuing as such for a number of years. In 1872 he resigned and bought the Cotton Seed Oil in Brenham, starting this pioneer industry, first of its kind in Texas. His residence occupied an entire block of ground on Caroline between Commerce and Franklin. It was a part of Quality Hill.

In 1889 he came to my office, then an old man, saying, "Ziegler, I want you to sell my block for me. I cannot any longer hear the sound of the steamboat whistles and I want to move farther out now that steamboat traffic is no more." I sold his property for twenty-two thousand and five hundred dollars which was a good price in 1889. It is now part of the I. & G. N. Depot on Franklin Street.

His daughters, Mrs. Kate Montgomery and Miss Mary Smith, still reside here.

While I named my principals the Big Five, the picture of B. A. Shepherd should appear, and they should be renamed the Big Six who did more to develop the City of Houston, and they combined should also be called, truthfully, the fathers of the Ship Channel. However, these are the names of the promoters, the men who had the vision to conceive, the willingness, perseverance and ability to carry on under tremendous difficulties and great discouragement, and are seldom mentioned. This shows how soon we are forgotten when we pass away.

GENERAL E. B. NICHOLS

Pioneer Merchant

General Nichols was born in Cooperton, New York, in 1815. His business career began in 1838 when he joined E. J. Hart and William M. Rice in the mercantile business. With them he established a wholesale business when they became the largest wholesale grocers and general merchandisers. The old store may still remain or possibly it has been remodeled, in Galveston (on the P. V. Romano site on the Strand). They did much to develop the city, building the first brick wharf, helping to incorporate the Galveston, Houston and Henderson Railroad. They were largely interested in the Galveston Wharf Company, were among the first to manufacture ice, and joined in many other local enterprises.

Mr. Hart moved to New Orleans and became the largest wholesale druggist in the South, and the firm remained in business until 1861.

General Nichols organized a regiment in defense of the confederate government, which he equipped at his own expense, and led them to San Antonio, where he received from General Twiggs the surrender of the United States equipment and the post, also the United States army.

His home and country estate were what are now the picnic grounds at Dickinson, where many generations visited and fought "woodticks and redbugs" for days afterward. There the slaves were housed and planted cotton, corn and vegetables. At one time this was called the prettiest spot in Texas.

General Nichols became a member of the Texas legislature. When General Magruder arrived in 1862, he made Nichols an officer of his staff, together with Edmond P.

278

Turner (brother-in-law of Mrs. A. A. Van Alstyne, who still resides on Broadway in Galveston), Judge Peter Gray and T. M. Bagley, the veteran steamboat owner.

At the time of the recapture of Galveston, General Magruder and General Nichols burnt mid-night oil, formulating plans for this recapture.

The Nichols home became the headquarters for General Magruder. It was a large rambling low residence, something like the Thomas Jefferson home. The same architecture is seen in Virginia today, which President Jefferson planned when a young architect. This building occupied the same space as the Sealy residence today. On the west side, the general built a schoolhouse for his seven sons: William H., who became the doorkeeper of the House at Washington, D. C.; Peter Gray, named for his fellow staff officer; Tom Pierce, named for the great builder of the Southern Pacific; George, the youngest, popular ticket agent of the railroad; Kinney, named for his friend McKinney, the first founder of Galveston; and Frank Stewart, named for Lord Stewart, who became so attached to him that he adopted him. He was "Lord Stewart" but at the death of Lord Stewart his title was taken away from him and he returned as "Frank Nichols," bringing with him the famous Stuart black diamond.

The beloved county and city official, who for so many years served the state so faithfully, Fred Nichols, also a son of General Nichols, was the last left to carry on the tradition of the name. He died in 1935 in Galveston.

I must add a few words for the noble lady who helped him, the General, to all his greatness. She was the daughter of George Stone, one of the signers of the declaration of independence, and was benevolent and charitable. She helped her neighbor, Mrs. Osterman, whose home was also a base hospital and relief headquarters when the epidemics occurred.

When the General passed away, hundreds plowed through deep sand to follow his hearse, on foot to the cemetery. The procession was a long one. The seven sons served as pallbearers. With martial steps the cortege moved to the cemetery, keeping time with the muffled drums and soft notes of the military band. Veterans of both the battle of San Jacinto and the "Lost Cause," took part in the services. A sight like this can never be seen again. It has lingered with me for sixty-two years.

WAVE OF THE GULF

The muffled drums sad rolls,
   Has been the soldiers last tatto,
No more on life's placed path shall meet
   That brave but fallen foe,
On fate's eternal camping ground
   Their silent tents are spread
And glory guards with solemn tread
   The bivouac of the dead.

ROBERT MILLS

Duke of Brazoria, Early Plantation Baron

Robert Mills, known in the early days as "The Duke of Brazoria," settled at Brazoria when Texas was a republic. Brazoria was a thriving town in those days, one of the largest in Texas. Robert and his brothers engaged in the general mercantile business in that town, under the name of R. and D. G. Mills, for some time before moving to Galveston. The brothers owned seven or eight large plantations, the largest of which was Lowwood, later owned by J. H. Hutchings of Galveston.

The brothers, reputed to be worth five million dollars, made the currency of Texas. This currency was redeemed by them as late as 1868, or just before their failure, which followed the Civil War. They advanced millions to the planters of Texas to buy machinery for making sugar and brought seed cane from South Carolina by the boatload for the planters. They brought the first tobacco from Kentucky for the colonists of the republic in Stephen F. Austin's time. It is said that in their long business career they never closed out a man for debt and had a longer career in business than any other firm in Texas.

They had plantation bells cast in Philadelphia, in each one of which fifty Mexican dollars were placed, and you could hear these bells for miles on a still day. The brothers were known far and wide for their charity. They were noble men and were examples of the best in the businessmen and citizens. David Mills died early, but I knew Robert Mills well.

Goods from Europe, as well as Texas products were sent to them on consignment and they came nearer carrying cotton from plantation to loom than any other firm. They de-

280

livered cotton to the spindles or looms of Europe and New England, running their own steamboats up the Brazos, plying through what is now the Intracoastal Canal. They carried their products from the plantations overland and by boat to Vera Cruz, Mexico. Mr. Mills lived on his ten-acre homesite in Galveston, now Kempner Park. In the center was a large plantation home with broad verandas surrounded by giant oak trees. Many can remember this site where the Garten Verein stood in later years, as the prettiest spot in Texas. His trees were his children and he knew the history of each of them. Once, when I was a lad I visited him and he delighted me with stories as to the ages of the trees and who planted them. One was planted by his friend, Colonel Stephen F. Austin, another by General Sam Houston and another by Sidney Johnston.

When General U. S. Grant arrived in Galveston from his trip around the world he also planted a tree on Mr. Mills' estate. However, the various storms in Galveston unfortunately destroyed them all.

The Mills firm brought from Mississippi two hundred thousand dollars of their Holly Springs, Mississippi, bank bills and endorsed them, and they were circulated as freely as gold. For this they were fined twenty thousand dollars, but afterward received a remittance as it was proven by decision of the supreme court that they had violated no law. Instead, they had been benefactors of the state.

Their ships flew the United States flag with the Lone Star flag below it. They carried little Howitzers which were fired as a salute on entering the harbor and departing. Remember, these were the days when pirates still infested the Gulf.

A story was told by Tom Dwyer, Sr. of Brenham, a merchant who endorsed some paper for friends who failed. The sheriff was about to attach his goods. Dwyer rode a mule to Galveston and told his friend Mills his troubles. Mills gave him the money willingly, all in gold, and Dwyer was able to pay every dollar he owed with interest and was saved from bankruptcy. Later, Dwyer became a wealthy man. When he heard Mr. Mills was in financial difficulty, Dwyer again rode a mule to Galveston and carried forty thousand dollars in gold and silver to Galveston. When he offered it to his friend, Bob Mills, it was declined gratefully as Mills, with tears in his eyes, explained, that it was only a "drop in the bucket" to what he owed.

Mr. Mills and General Houston grieved at what had befallen their beloved state of Texas and both often pleaded that the state remain in the Union. Had they both lived twenty years longer, they would have seen it rise "Phoenix-like" from the ashes and become the empire state, and the old plantations, instead of yielding cotton, cane and the like, producing millions of dollars of oil, "black gold," for the oil companies.

THE WILLIS BROTHERS

Merchant Princes of Texas

Horatio Alger, famed writer of youth-success stories, could not, in his most creative moments, have written a more fascinating story for youth than would be found in the real-life story of P. J. and Richard Willis. In the hey-day of their brilliant commercial and social activities they were known, even internationally, as among the foremost developers of Texas, both during the young republic and later on during its statehood. Even now, many, many years later, there are yet those who will recall familiarly the power of the Willis name, and the splendid heritage of accomplishment they left to the youth of Texas.

The firm of P. J. Willis and Brothers, wholesale merchants and cotton factors, operated in the coastal regions of Texas for more than half a century. It was composed of Peter J. Willis and Richard Short Willis, who in 1836, just after the Battle of San Jacinto, arrived from Virginia and settled on a farm on lower Buffalo Bayou near Houston.

Like Abraham Lincoln, they began as humble rail-splitters and farmers. Susbequently they moved to Montgomery County, where they continued their farming operations and also developed regular transportation for that territory through the medium of ox-team caravans. Finally, they accumulated enough wealth to open a general store in the town of Willis, named for them. There they continued for a number of years and prospered consistently.

Their business growing larger and larger, they moved it eventually to Houston and engaged in a larger field. They associated with them at this time S. McIlhenny, an old pioneer already engaged here, and the three operated under the name of McIlhenny, Willis and Brothers. They had the first wholesale house in Houston dealing in groceries, dry goods, boots, shoes, etc., and rapidly became a house of great prominence and influence. Sales were made as far west as New Mexico and up into Oklahoma. They also supplied the United States government forts and commissaries extending in a chain from Brownsville, north and west, to Fort Sill, Oklahoma, their commodities being delivered to these points by immense caravans of ox-trains. The firm at that time was located in the ground floor of the old Hutchins House, the famed pioneer Texas inn that stood where the Southern Pacific Building now stands.

During the period of the Civil War there was a rush, on the part of the larger merchants and wholesalers, to Matamoros, neutral port of Mexico across the river from Brownsville, where commerce could be carried on without interference from either the Yankees or Confederates. The great German merchant element which controlled the South American trade moved into Matamoros, as did great numbers of American merchants, in order to have a more convenient base from which they could supply the war demands of the interior of the United States. Trade was supplied west of the Mississippi, far up into the Mississippi Valley and even the states east of the Mississippi. Matamoros grew by leaps and bounds until it became a city of some forty thousand persons.

Imports from all countries came to its sister port of Bagdad, an island at the mouth of the Rio Grande, and as many as two hundred and fifty vessels at a time could be found in port there. It, too, grew to a population of fourteen thousand, but was entirely wiped off the map in the great West Indian hurricane of the "Seventies." Meanwhile, tremendous warehouses, some of them filling an entire block, were built at Matamoros for the purpose of storing passing commodities. Even yet the tourist may see some of these, more substantially built, that have weathered the passing years.

The Willis brothers did not join the general exodus of the larger mercantile establishments to Matamoros, but remained in Houston and increased proportionately the volume of their business against a lessened field of competition. Meanwhile, they had reorganized and now conducted the business as P. J. Willis and Brother, their associate, Mr. McIlhenny, having died during the interim. This Mr. McIlhenny, incidentally, was the father of Sam K. McIlhenny, a Houstonian of distinguished family whom some may recall as my one-time associate in the firm of Ziegler and McIlhenny.

After the close of the Civil War, there was an influx to Galveston of the greater portion of the prominent merchants of Matamoros, due to Galveston's excellent port facilities and its strategic location for serving the vast inland territory of the United States. Galveston grew rapidly in population and increased wealth, and soon became the richest city in the United States, per capita, with the possible exception of Hartford, Conn. As expressed by L. C. Luckel, an enterprising Houston realtor, at that time: "Millionaires are now so common in Galveston and Houston, that no longer does one pay them any attention—come and be one!"

As improving their position for serving the trade, Willis and Brother now moved their business to Galveston. There they continued to expand until, in their line, they were the recognized leading wholesale house of the state. Theirs was the medium that, in due course, established many other wholesale houses throughout the interior. It was in the height of their career, in 1882-83, that Texas produced the greatest cotton crop, acreage considered, the state has ever known. According to the statistician, Jepperson, the average yield for the state was 9/16 to 5/8 of a bale to the acre. In the spring of 1883 more cotton was plowed under than was produced the following year due to the lack of cotton pickers to gather the crop.

Of that tremendous crop, Willis and Brother alone, on a factorage basis, handled eighty-six thousand bales and transacted a general merchandise business exceeding eleven million, five hundred thousand dollars.

It was shortly afterwards that P. J. Willis died. Surviving him were three daughters, Mrs. George Sealy, Mrs. J. F. Goldthwaite and Mrs. W. F. Ladd, and two sons, P. J., Jr. and William H. Willis. The manner of dividing the land was in itself unique. R. S. Willis held one-half, the remaining half to be divided equally among the five heirs mentioned. The land involved amounted to some five hundred thousand acres. It was ticketed according to location and value, say, one acre of rich interior agricultural land against five acres of uncultivated East Texas soil. R. S. Willis always wore a "two-story" beaver hat, the remainder of his immaculate ensemble completing a picturesque appearance. On the day the estate was to be divided he called me into his office and asked that I participate in the division of the land. It was a simple drawing from his beaver hat in which had been placed ten tickets calling for itemized properties of

284

equal value. At his request, I passed the beaver hat around and the five heirs of P. J. Willis drew one ticket each representing his or her share of the estate. After they had drawn, the remaining five tickets represented the one-half of the estate devised to Richard S. Willis.

At the time of the above it was my privilege to be their outside cotton supervisor, including the management of their wharf press and the handling of all cotton in and out of the office, and the selling of all irregulars, as well as executing all deliveries.

When I moved to Houston some fifty-five years ago, I went into the office of R. S. Willis to bid him goodbye. Grasping my hand, he exclaimed, "Ziegler, I wish you luck in the Bayou City that I have always loved. Be seated while I relate to you some of those incidents of the happiest days of my life, when my brother and I used to ox-team into Houston from Montgomery County."

Along in the latter part of 1863, Willis held six hundred and eighty bales stored in the Allen and Pless warehouse, he told me among other things, located about where the M. and M. Building now stands.

The firm had accumulated this cotton and held it during the critical period of the war. They placed guards and deputy marshals on duty to guard it; but there came to him a good friend to advise him that the Confederate government was about to seize the cotton and conscript it for war purposes. Mr. Willis went to the firm of Ranger and Company, operating here, and stated that he wanted to sell them his cotton. Upon inquiry as to the price he wanted, replied, "If you will give me this minute on account your draft on London for one thousand pounds Sterling you may have the lot for six cents a pound." The draft was passed and the Rangers, being Germans with a London connection, as aliens, neither the Confederate nor United States governments could touch the cotton.

Employing mule-team caravans, Ranger and Company carried the cotton overland to Matamoros, the trip requiring months. From there it was shipped to Liverpool and London during the last days of the Civil War. The lot sold in England at from one dollar and fifty cents to one dollar and ninety cents per pound, creating millions of profit for Ranger and Company. Later this company tried to coup the market, miscalculated and went bankrupt.

It was characteristic of Richard Willis to be a veritable

giant in business; accustomed to making decisions quickly, he concerned himself little with the "trifling details" as he termed them. I recall one instance when I was with Mr. Willis in their cotton sampling room. A Greek buyer from the firm of Ralli Brothers entered to trade with Mr. Willis upon a very large consignment of cotton. There was some discussion as to whether the price per pound should be $14\frac{1}{4}$ or $14\frac{1}{8}$, the Greek holding out for the latter. Mr. Willis said to him, "My friend, my clerks here are too busy to make out an account sales in 'eight's' but I shall flip a silver dollar; if it comes heads you pay me $14\frac{1}{4}$, if tails you may have the cotton at $14\frac{1}{8}$." They agreed on this and in keeping with Mr. Willis' usual luck, the coin fell heads up and the trade went through for $14\frac{1}{4}$, involving twenty-five hundred bales. A far cry from then, cotton is now sold at prices varying as little as one fractional decimal point.

During the period when R. S. Willis was vice-president of the Santa Fe Railroad he called me into his office and told me I was not to take a vacation that year, explaining that he had just sold the Santa Fe five million feet of lumber, with the privilege of increasing the order five million feet more. I had been delegated to receive the lumber from Calcasieu and other mills in Louisiana, render the account sales and have the amounts credited to the various mills, that they might use the funds for further purchases of commodities from Willis and Brother. It required five months to accomplish the task, upon the completion of which I was given a bonus of five hundred dollars in lieu of my vacation.

When the first thousand miles of the Gulf, Colorado and Santa Fe, was completed, George Sealy, son-in-law of P. J. Willis, was authorized to go to New York and negotiate the sale of the road to the Atchison, Topeka and Santa Fe Railroad for nine million dollars. This he did, the transaction finally amounting to twenty million dollars. There followed, in Galveston an amazing celebration of the sale, and it was considered a great feat at the time.

Mr. Willis never lost his taste for farming, and while yet a merchant prince, he bought for his own use the historic Darrington Plantation of eighteen hundred and thirty acres, near Sandy Point. Here he installed a sugar mill at a cost of one hundred and fifty thousand dollars, and introduced for the first time in Texas the present method of sugar-refining and manufacture, and also handled the corn, sugar and cotton crops of his neighbors, with a small narrow gauge tram road running to and from his plantation. The Darrington Plantation originally had been the home of Sterling McNeil, one of Stephen F. Austin's first three hundred, and is now the state's finest farm.

At the age of eighty, still sturdy and active, Mr. Willis, with his long, white beard flowing to the winds, would mount his Kentucky thoroughbred each spring and set out for the plantation. My last sight of him, on one of these occasions, was on Main Street in Houston, en route to his farm. His palatial residence still stands on Broadway in Galveston.

Richard S. Willis, Jr. is the only son surviving of the brothers. Only three of the grandsons of his brother, Peter J. Willis, are now left. Richard Short Willis was a distinguished citizen of Texas and the Old South, a constructive dreamer who literally made his dreams come true, and who helped right nobly and well to build the region in which he dwelled.

JOHN A. WHARTON

"Father of Masonry in Texas, Keenest Blade of San Jacinto"

John A. Wharton was born in Nashville, Tennessee, in 1809, the son of John Harris Wharton, who died in 1815, and was followed two years later by his wife.

John A. Wharton and his brother, William H., were reared by an uncle, Jesse Wharton, a former United States Congressman. After receiving an academic education, John, the younger brother, studied law in New Orleans, remaining there in the practice of his profession until 1833, when he moved to Texas and joined his brother, William H., then at Columbia on the Brazos, where the latter maintained a magnificent plantation known as "Eagle Island."

From Columbia, John A. Wharton was sent as a delegate to the "consultation" at San Felipe de Austin in 1835. For a time he was a member of the General Council of the provisional government, and was sent by General Houston to New Orleans to consummate the purchase of supplies and munitions of war for the Texas Revolutionists. On his return, he joined the army and was on the staff of General Houston; as Adjutant General at San Jacinto, his bravery on that battlefield being conspicuous. The military records of the Republic disclose that Wharton served in the Texas army from December nineth, 1835, to July fifth, 1836.

Sometime prior to that, he had engaged in a duel with Stephen F. Austin, the cause of which, at this remote date, does not appear entirely clear. Austin was trained for this duel by the noted Warren D. C. Hall, later Acting Secretary of War for Texas, who admonished Austin that unless he got in the first shot, he would be a dead man, as Wharton was never known to miss. The affair was repugnant to Austin, but he did get in the first shot, wounding Wharton in the right forearm and causing not only the immediate loss of his weapon, but as a result of the wound, a stiffened right arm that remained with Wharton the rest of his life. Austin exceedingly regretted the incident and the two of them later became close friends.

John A. Wharton might well be regarded as the "Father of Masonry" in Texas, as in 1834 it was he who rode from the town of Brazoria to Louisiana and secured a charter or dispensation to organize Masonry in Texas. In a peach brake, near Brazoria, under a large oak tree on what is now known as Captain Ballowe's place, this lodge was organized on December twenty-seventh, 1834, with the following charter members: Warren D. C. Hall, Anson Jones, John A. Wharton, Asa Bringham, James A. E. Phelps, J. P. Caldwell and Alexander Russell. The young lodge had during its early existence a hectic career. In 1836, when the Mexicans captured Brazoria, one of the members of the lodge broke down the door, recovered the charter and fought with it in his saddle bags at the Battle of San Jacinto. Later on, when Masonic affairs in Texas were adjusted, Houston retained the charter and the lodge operating thereunder is now known as Holland Lodge No. 1, Houston, while the lodge at West Columbia has the archives and other documents in connection, and is known as St. John's Lodge No. 5. Brazoria itself yet retains the Charter Oak of Masonry under which the original lodge was formed. A few years since, Mrs. Jane Ballowe Holt deeded to the Grand Lodge of Texas an acre of ground surrounding this venerable oak, her father having been an active member of the fraternity.

In 1837, William H. Wharton, his brother, was among those on the ill-fated "Julius Caesar" when it was captured off Velasco by a Mexican man-of-war and all passengers taken to Matamoros and placed in prison. John Wharton, with thirty Mexican prisoners and a flag of truce, sailed for Matamoros in an effort to effect an exchange of prisoners, but he, too, was seized and placed in confinement. In due course, however, the two of them escaped. Anthony Strobel of Brazoria County relates an interesting incident anent the manner in which William H. Wharton passed unrecognized under the eyes of his guards:

"He, William H. Wharton, was visited in prison by Father Muldoon, a high dignitary of the Catholic church. On the occasion of his second visit, he remarked to Wharton, 'When I come again, I shall bring you the garb of a Catholic Priest. Array yourself as a priest, walk out, and no questions will be asked of you. But, Mr. Wharton, if you value your safety, until you reach the Texas border, fail not to remember that you are a Catholic Priest.'"

Wharton did so and reached his home in due course. Truly, Father Muldoon was a rare friend in time of need, when it is remembered that Wharton was a staunch Presbyterian. The two, however, had been friends of long standing, and Father Muldoon had often visited "Eagle Island," home of the Whartons. Both were college men and both were men of means, it being related that Father Muldoon owned some hundred leagues of land in his own name. In Fayette County, the little town of Muldoon remains as a memorial to the good father. Unhappily enough, the two of them never met after Wharton's escape from prison, as it was not long after that he came to his death while on a visit to the home of his brother-in-law, Leonard Groce, near Hempstead.

Upon his return to Texas, John A. Wharton again became active in affairs of the Republic, serving as Secretary of War under President Burnet, and a member of the House of Representatives from Brazoria, in the first Congress. Declining candidacy for a second term, he remained at home, engaging in the practice of law as a member of the firm of Wharton, Pease and Harris, the latter being E. M. Pease and J. M. Harris.

John A. Wharton died in Houston on December seventeenth, 1838, while serving as a member of the House of Representatives in the third Congress.

On the afternoon of his death, officers of the army assembled at Kesslers Arcade to pay tribute to his memory. Colonel Sidney Sherman was called to the affair, and William S. Fisher made secretary of the meeting. It was agreed that all officers of the army then in Houston would, at the time designated, form in front of Wharton's late residence and march in formal procession to place of interment. On the following day his remains lay in state in the Capitol. When both Houses had adjourned to attend the Masonic services conducted by Holland Lodge, of which Wharton was a member, Vice-president David G. Burnet, who delivered the oration, said in part:

"The keenest blade on the field of San Jacinto is broken! The brave, the generous and the talented John A. Wharton is no more! But surely it will be engraved upon the tablets of our history that Texas wept when Wharton died!"

The two Wharton brothers were greatly devoted to each other, and so moved was William H. Wharton upon the loss of his younger brother, that he changed the name of his son, Waller, named for Judge Waller of Waller County, to John A., a lad who later became a General in the Confederate Army.

John A. Wharton was interred at the old City Cemetery in Houston, now on West Dallas Avenue, where the State of Texas in 1932 erected a fitting monument. The town of Wharton was named for the two brothers, a deserving tribute, because of the residence in those parts of many of the Whartons' former friends and associates.

The will in full of John A. Wharton follows, being characteristic of both the man and the times:

"Republic of Texas,
"County of Brazoria:

"I, John A. Wharton, citizen of the Republic and County aforesaid, being desirous that my own will, and not the law, shall prevail in regard to my property and effects in case of death, do hereby make my last will and testament:

"Item: I devise and bequeath to my brother, William Harris Wharton, all my property, real and personal and mixed, constituting him my sole heir and universal legatee:

"Item: My debts being considerable, I wish them paid out of monies that may be collected from notes and accounts due me, and not to sell any of my lands, negroes, horses or bank stock:

"Item: I positively forbid my brother from dividing my property with any of my other relatives, except they move to this County within eighteen months of this date; and in that case he may exercise his own pleasure.

"Item: I consider it unnecessary to suggest to my brother to educate our guardian children, or to assist any of our

290

relatives who may move to Texas and who are honest and industrious and enterprising, or to make suitable presents to my friends.

"Written in my own hand on this twenty-third day of July, 1837.

"John A. Wharton,

"Signed in presence of: Thomas A. Thompson and H. P. Brensler."

The passing, in 1878, of the widow of William H. Wharton, terminated that immediate branch of the family in Texas. She had been preceded by her husband, her son, General Wharton of the Confederacy, his wife and his daughter, Kate Ross Wharton, and was finally placed to rest beside the granddaughter in the old family ground of Eagle Island, the manorial home of the Wharton's near Brazoria.

BENJAMIN A. SHEPHERD—FIRST BANKER OF HOUSTON

A search through the early and mid-annals of Houston would develop no individual of a more interesting, or more constructive type than is reflected in the career of Benjamin A. Shepherd, pioneer merchant and founder of the present First National Bank in Houston.

Born May fourteenth, 1814, in Fluvanna County, Virginia, seat of the old family home established by his forefathers in the early settlement of America, he passed his youth on the parental estate. He remained there, acquiring his education until the age of sixteen, when he entered the employ of a country general store as clerk, thus laying the foundation of that keen personal insight into business for which, in later years, he was noted.

At the age of nineteen, in order to broaden his sphere of experience and usefulness, and afford a greater field for his budding ambition, he left the home-field, and mounting horse, went to Nashville. (There is to be seen in the director's room of the First National Bank today, a letter written by young Mr. Shepherd to his mother in the course of his trip to Nashville.) Here, seeking employment in a new field, he made connection with an old established mercantile firm; and, by close application to the problems before him, drew the cordial regard and respect of his employers. As a token of their friendly esteem, when he left them some four years later to seek yet fresher fields, the management of the firm presented him with a very fine watch. He carried the time-piece throughout his career, fondly cherishing the memory of that early connection and its friendships.

Removing from Nashville in 1837, he proceeded to New Orleans, where he became engaged with a large wholesale commission house as chief bookkeeper and credit adviser. It was during his service with them that the country passed through one of its most distressing early panics. Credit over the nation appeared wholly destroyed, and many of the old established houses went down in the hurricane of financial disaster. The experience Mr. Shepherd gained during that trying period left a deep impression upon him. It served materially to make him by nature prudent and conservative and to qualify him as the excellent and conservative banker he became in later years. Profiting by both observation and experience, he chose the safer and surer course of building his fortune.

In 1839, Mr. Shepherd, having been attracted by the promising outlook in the new Republic of Texas, moved to Galveston. With A. C. Crawford, he engaged in the wholesale crockery importing business under the name of Crawford and Shepherd, a line of endeavor that, alas, now with present tariff regulations, is altogether impractical. Their wares arrived, packed in hundreds of crates made, in the fashion of that day, of grape-vines, staunch and secure. It is an interesting type of crate, long since discarded, and I doubt that many of the present generation have ever seen one. This business continued until Mr. Shepherd established one under his own name. The close friendship with Mr. Crawford, however, continued throughout the latter's life. Mr. Shepherd was, in fact, the god-father of Crawford's eldest son, named Shepherd Crawford as a tribute to the elder Crawford's friend. This son I knew intimately, he being one of my schoolmates at the Old Academy.

Some years later, Mr. Shepherd moved to Houston, forming a partnership with A. J. Burke, under the name of Shepherd and Burke, and conducted an extensive mercantile business until 1855. Disposing then of his mercantile business, he engaged exclusively in the business of private banker and founded what was the first house in the state devoted exclusively to banking. The friendly association of the Burke and Shepherd descendants has continued through successive generations, Henry B. Bringhurst, now Assistant Vice-president of the First National Bank, being a grandson of A. J. Burke.

Mr. Shepherd now devoted all of his time in building up his banking interests. It continued in healthy growth until the War Between the States. The status-quo between the North and South grieved him sorely; nor did he like the business outlook and the result that he felt was to be anticipated from the war. Accordingly, he notified all of his patrons to withdraw their deposits and he retired from the banking business for the duration of the war. During its course, however, he engaged actively in other enterprises that contributed to the upbuilding of Houston. Among other interests, he was president of the Houston Direct Navigation Company, a line of steamboats plying between Houston and Galveston, prior to the advent of the railroad between the two cities. He was also an influential factor in promoting the H. and T. C. Railroad, and a member of its first board of directors. Prior thereto, in fact, he had organized a company to grade and construct a plank road on the Washington stage road, now Washington Avenue, and considerable amount of this work had been accomplished when the Houston and Texas Central purchased it for a roadbed. He next turned to organization of the City Cotton Mills in connection with T. W. House, Sr., and P. J. Willis and Brothers, and W. J. Hutchins, at a cost of one hundred thousand dollars and became its first president. This mill was subsequently destroyed by fire, and resulted in a total loss to its stockholders, occurring, as it did, in the turbulent days of the Confederacy, when no insurance was available. Its chief product was of the rough-goods type, called Osnabergs, used largely for clothing the slaves, making cotton-picking sacks, or the wagon-covers and tarpaulins so sorely needed by the Southern Army. The mill stood where Cleveland compress is now located, near the present Hill Street bridge. Years ago, I went out to see workers blast away the towering brick smokestack of the cotton mill to make way for the compress. It occurs to me now as a singular coincidence that the great grandson of Mr. Shepherd, W. A. Kirkland, is the son-in-law of A. S. Cleveland, one of the owners of the compress.

During the War Between the States, Mr. Shepherd's sympathy, of course, was with the Southern cause. His eldest son, the only one of sufficient age to join the army, had enlisted with the First Texas Regiment of the famous Hood's Texas Brigade, and Mr. Shepherd himself did much to alleviate the suffering of the families of the soldiers while the latter served at the front. The cruelty of the fratricidal conflict were heavily upon him, however, and he refrained from any direct activity connected with it, declining, even, to engage his boats in blockade running. In fact, the records indicate that he initiated no new business enterprises of any nature during the period of the war.

In 1866, with the close of the war, Mr. Shepherd re-established his bank under the name of B. A. Shepherd and Company, having admitted to partnership, A. Wettermark, previously for many years his confidential clerk, and his nephew, J. A. Shepherd. In 1867, having acquired a large interest in the First National Bank of Houston, organized shortly before by T. M. Bagby, he merged with it the business of his private bank and became president of the merged institution. He continued in that capacity for the remainder of his life. Oddly enough, notwithstanding the merger, the national bank continued to be known to the public as "Shepherd's Bank," and among the older generation one still frequently hears the institution referred to by that name. Today, each draft issued by the bank bears an admirable likeness of its early founder.

The writer recalls with interest his early banking transactions with Mr. Shepherd when the bank's capital was comparatively small. Hedged about by strict banking regulations of the day, the bank was unable to loan more than ten per cent of its capital and surplus to any one borrower. There was nearly always available, however, in Mr. Shepherd's personal account at the bank, a few hundred thousand from which he might, if he felt justified, complete the needs of his larger borrowers during their seasonal requirements. Under his management the bank prospered and became a recognized factor in the upbuilding of the city's commerce. He was ably seconded by his son-in-law, A. P. Root, who first was cashier of the bank, then vice-president, and finally succeeded Mr. Shepherd as president when the latter passed away. Under Mr. Root's guidance, the bank continued to expand conservatively, and upon his death, passed to the directing management of a second son-in-law, that grand old Houstonian, Owen L. Cochran, father of the present vice-president, W. S. Cochran. Mr. Shepherd's own sons had passed away early in life and took no active part in the bank.

In 1889, prior to his death, Mr. Shepherd, in keeping with his usual thoughtful consideration for his less fortunate townsmen, founded a trust fund of twenty thousand dollars, the proceeds of which annually were to be distributed to the needy of Houston in such manner as the trustees of the fund might elect. This trust fund continues in operation today.

At the death of Mr. Shepherd the ownership of the bank's stock passed in turn to his immediate descendants, comparatively little of it being held outside of the family. The present chairman, John T. Scott, entered the bank in the early "Nineties" as a young bookkeeper, passing successively the various official ranks culminating in his present title.

In point of type, Benjamin A. Shepherd reflected the quiet, christian gentleman. He amassed a large fortune outside of his banking activities, cared little for public acclaim and never sought public office; yet he delighted in assisting to build the city wherein he lived, first Galveston, and finally Houston. He passed away on Christmas Eve, 1891, during a cold, rainy spell of weather that made the streets of the city a sea of mud. I recall distinctly that it was impossible for the funeral cortege to traverse Washington Avenue to Glenwood Cemetery; instead, it proceeded to the Houston and Texas Central Depot, from which point the casket was placed on mule-street-cars and accompanied by hundreds of friends, transported from there to Glenwood. So great was the attendance that the street car company was unable to furnish sufficient cars to carry his friends to the final resting place of the great builder of Houston.

CAPTAIN SAM S. ASHE, PIONEER SHERIFF OF HOUSTON

The Bravest Man I Have Ever Known

To one whose privilege it is to look back over that long vista of years when Houston was characterized as the "little village on the banks of Buffalo Bayou," and Harris County itself a favorite camping ground for Indians, Mexican bandits and renegade Americans, it is interesting to contemplate in passing whether, with crime, vice and the professional gangster organized as apparently as they now are, the peace officer and constabulary of today are required to have as great or greater degree of personal bravery and discretional judgment in emergency, than was possessed by many of the old time sheriffs and other officials responsible for the peace and well-being of their communities in pioneer days.

Pondering upon many incidents of that nature that came under my observation in those yesteryears, it seems to me that, with customs and conditions existing as they were at the time, that the average instance of its kind was more acutely dangerous to those involved, fraught with more far-reaching consequences to the community as a whole, than would be found in the simple capture and arrest of the law-violator of today. In perhaps a majority of those instances of note, the situation was so acute, account of local politics, friendships or family connections, that a single indiscretional act of the arresting peace-officer would have touched a match to the power-keg, the "explosion" of which would have instigated a relentless warfare between given opposing factions and reacted to the detriment of the community as a whole. Consequently, in those periods, unless the sheriff, constable, or other officer serving, were possessed of the knowledge of exactly when, and when not, to "draw" or was lacking otherwise in cool, courageous and steady procedure, as a rule, he did not remain long in office.

Outstanding among those men of early Houston who made a complete success of such office, was Captain Sam S. Ashe, who, among his other leading activities in the city, was sheriff of Harris County.

Captain Ashe was born in Bowsville, Tennessee, June the fourteenth, 1808, the son of John B. and Eliza Ashe. His

BIOGRAPHICAL SKETCHES

For four years, we had little or no tea, coffee or white flour; even sugar was rare and such clothes as we had were of homespun made in Huntsville. There was equally misery in certain sections of the North, particularly in the spinning districts, as with no cotton obtainable, tens of thousands of the mill employees were left without work and because of this became wards of public charity. Likewise, Manchester, Lancashire and Oldham, spinning centers in England, had thousands of inhabitants who were destitute. So acute did the situation become on the North Atlantic seaboard that many of the New England states threatened to secede from the Union if no relief was given.

England befriended the South to a considerable extent, both in way of direct aid and by helping to finance the war. The Honorable Judiah P. Benjamin, of President Jefferson Davis' cabinet, and George Wigg, cotton buyer of New Orleans and Galveston, were made fiscal agents of the Confederate Government in England, where they worked assiduously to further the war. France, who was dependent almost entirely upon the South for cotton, fared even worse. Napoleon endeavored to relieve the situation by intervening and joining with England. Two large warships (rams) that Napoleon intended to sail to Charleston and end the blockade, were, at the last minute, bought up by certain Englishmen who were Northern sympathizers. Subsequently, after the fall of Vicksburg, and the defeat of the Southern forces at Gettysburg, the South began to totter, and both England and France withheld their aid, then came the final crash.

During the course of the war, I lived with my parents in Galveston. Often at midnight we would be awakened by the booming of guns from the Federal fleet. In a few moments the sky would be filled with sky-rockets and Roman candles, the signal to all Yankee warships that some poor, unfortunate blockade runner had been sighted. Immediately, the fleetest of the ships would give chase the entire length of the island, thirty miles. As a rule, the blockade runner, when hard pressed, would throw overboard the deck cargo in order to lighten her load. If this proved insufficient, then the cargo between decks was thrown into the sea. Frequently, the blockade runners, built in such manner as enabled them to sail in shallower water than their pursuers, would escape to the Mexican coast. Often, they could be caught, fired upon and forced to beach their ship. Here

301

they would settle down to Davy Jones' locker, the ship breaking up and the cargo covering the waters. Such incidents presented sights amazing to my childhood eyes. There were bales of drygoods, domestics, linens, etc., and cases of canned goods floating pell-mell. All of the able-bodied men were at the forts, while the half-starved, nearly naked, old men, women and children would gather upon the beach and wade out in the Gulf up to their necks floating the salvaged articles to shore. It was the rule that "finders are keepers." To prevent mildew, the goods were first soaked in rainwater, then spread out in the sun to dry. Once after a blockade runner had been driven ashore, the entire end of the island looked like a huge Chinese laundry. The canned goods and other eatables spread out to dry, reminded one of a big auction sale.

The blockade runners were usually small side-wheel steamers, frequently assisted by auxiliary sails, and built especially for speed and intended, in case of need, to negotiate shallow waters.

In addition to T. W. House, Sr., and Captain Sherfius, the large firms of Ball, Hutchings and Company, P. J. Willis and Brothers, W. J. Hutchins, B. A. Shepherd, Cornelius Ennis and a few others, including one English firm and two small other foreign concerns, engaged in this hazardous occupation. It required immense capital, as when a ship was lost, the vessel and cargo represented potentially a tremendous fortune. On the other hand, if a successful landing was effected once the bold runner had slipped through the enemy lines, the delivered cargo also represented an immense sum, and often made up for the loss of two or more cargoes previously lost.

The blockade runner, i. e., the commander of the ship, was necessarily of bold and daring type, and an excellent navigator. Of all the commanders of that period, most certainly no man was more aptly qualified for the job than Captain Sherfius. Time and again he slipped through the Yankee fleet, traded his outgoing cargo at other ports for the supplies needed at home, and negotiated the return landing successfully. One of his tricks before venturing out with a cargo would be to mount the tallest building in Galveston, where, with a pair of powerful field-glasses, he would fix the location, just before sunset, of each of the Yankee watch-dogs. This data he would reduce to a small, but accurately drawn, map, and use the whole as a chart.

Then, as the dark of the moon came on, the blockade runner would steal out of the harbor, make a dash, and be through the enemy's lines before they were aware of his presence.

He appeared always certain of himself and his record justified such confidence. I recall that on one occasion when Captain Sherfius was preparing to venture out with his ship, he felt so sure of his return at the appointed time that he invited a number of his friends to attend his wedding on a given date. Some weeks later, he showed up on the date previously named, bringing with him a huge wedding cake baked in Vera Cruz, Mexico. I remember quite well at the wedding reception which followed, Captain Sherfius regaled those present by relating a number of his blockade running experiences.

Perhaps the most distinguished craft commanded by Captain Sherfius was the "Harriet Lane," which brings to mind a diverting thought relative to the "only navy Houston ever had," consisting of the famous "cotton-clads" used to recapture Galveston. They were barges fitted out along the bayou and at Harrisburg, by General Magruder, who came fresh from the battlefields of Virginia. Captain Sherfius was placed in charge of the "Harriet Lane" and continued his daring efforts until the close of the war.

The Harriet Lane was purchased by T. W. House from the Confederate government for fifty thousand dollars in gold. He fitted her out for a blockade runner for Captain Sherfius.

Whenever the commander of the blockade fleet at Galveston, the Harriet Lane, the Satchem, the Clifton, Westfield, wanted to break the monotony, they would order Galveston bombarded. We would flee each time for the sand hills.

The only thing left of the historic boat, Harriet Lane, is the ship's bell which rests under a canopy at Sam Houston Park, the clapper gone.

Mrs. J. E. Price in Houston is the owner of the two gold framed mirrors which hung on the beautiful cabin walls; Captain Ellsberry, her grandfather, bought them from Mr. House. Another relic remaining is the ship's lantern, now the property of Mrs. H. Ray of Houston.

William Bowen of Los Angeles has the Bible of the Neptune duly autographed as the ship's Bible. Miss Dot Andrews of Galveston, granddaughter of Captain Hershberger, is the possessor of a cutless which he captured as one of the officers to board the Harriet Lane.

After the war the Harriet Lane was made into a cotton carrier and frequently came to Galveston as late as the "Nineties" for a cargo.

SAMUEL M. McASHAN

Pioneer Banker and Merchant, Active in the Days of the Revolution

The subject of these memoirs traced his ancestors from a French Huguenot origin. The McAshans, as might be surmised from the name, coming from Scotland; the Agees, from which he is descended on his mother's side, coming from France.

He was in the early settling of this country, when each family took up its abode on this continent, securing a foothold with colonies of Virginia, where he became identified with the political, religious and social surroundings and entered with zeal upon the new life spread out before him. With such experiences as they had in their native countries, they could hardly be expected to do otherwise than align themselves with the Colonials in their struggles with the Crown, and to contend on all proper occasions for the enjoyment of their religious liberties. All of them stood by the settlers before the formal rupture, and when the war came at last, those able for field services took up arms and fought with Washington and LaFayette and some of them sealed their faith in the cause of freedom with their lives.

Those who served in the revolution were John McAshan and John Agee, grandfathers of the subject of this sketch, and great-great-grandfathers of the present S. M. McAshan of the South Texas Commercial National Bank today. After the conflict, such of the ancestors of our sketch as survived settled down as planters.

Nemiah McAshan, father of S. McAshan, was born in the year 1763. He married Elizabeth Agee in 1789. In 1844 his parents went to Texas and settled at LaGrange, where they both died. They had, like many old time families, sixteen children.

Samuel M. McAshan was born in Buckingham County,

Original Members of Houston Exchange—Floor Scene, 1891

Seated, left to right: R. H. Hooper, Capt. Geo. W. Kidd, A. Gallatti, Alex Coghill, Frank Cargill, H. W. Garrow; in rear: C. H. Lucy and J. M. Lee; standing: E. S. Richardson, Geo. W. Neville, Wm. M. Reed, Sam J. Hubbell, Jesse A. Ziegler, Wm. B. Martin, Albert Nelms, J. M. Burwell, Tom Young, Felix Houston.

Virginia, March 11, 1829. He was fifteen years old when his family moved to Texas. At eighteen he became a clerk for Ward and Longcope in LaGrange; later in business for himself. At the close of the war in 1863, he moved to Houston. In 1864, he entered the store of T. W. House, first as bookkeeper. When Mr. House organized his bank he was made cashier and later at the death of Mr. House, assisted the son of T. W. House largely in building up his cotton banking business and entered into the railroad building, compress and other matters, and largely managed the affairs of this large and vast estate.

Those who believe in heredity and evolution feel that this was a family of bankers. The son of the first cashier of T. W. House, James Everett McAshan, helped organize the Commercial National Bank, and his son S. M. McAshan is now president of the South Texas Commercial National Bank. Mr. Harris McAshan has lately been elected assistant cashier, making four generations of bankers. Mr. S. M. McAshan, Jr., an executive in the firm of Anderson, Clayton and Company, is in line as a banker also. Mr. Samuel E. McAshan, the youngest son of the first banker, still remains with us, also, his son Allen D.; the only daughter of the original banker, Mrs. H. R. Dupree and her son, M. E., are still with us.

On May 11, 1855, he married Miss Mattie R. Eanes. To them were born four children; three of them are, Samuel Ernest, Annie E., wife of R. H. Kirby, and Virginia, wife of H. R. Dupree. The family were always strict Methodists. He passed away in this city in 1904.

Mr. McAshan lived to see a great deal of the making of Texas history and was an interested spectator in all that has gone before him.

When he came to Texas, there was not a mile of railroad, nor a telegraph line, and also no town of any size. The population was confined to the settlements along the larger streams and to the few villages that existed at all. His son, who unfortunately passed away in the prime of life, helped to found what is about the largest bank in South Texas, became an honored Trustee of the great Rice Institute and other honored positions.

His grandson is now the President of this bank and lives to carry on what two generations before him started.

In Samuel McAshan's younger days, he was one of the

boys that "ran with the machine," as one of the most active members of the Houston Volunteer Fire-Department.

Had Mr. McAshan lived a little longer, he would have seen the city he helped to build become the second largest city in the South.

WILLIAM MARSH RICE

Founder of the Rice Institute

William Marsh Rice was in truth one of the very early pioneers of Texas, having established himself in Houston in the fall of 1838, when the village was in its infancy.

He was born in Springfield, Massachusetts, in 1816, of thrifty, New England stock, being one of approximately eight children. He grew up there, attending the schools of Springfield until the age of fourteen, when he discontinued his common schooling and went to work. It should not be said, however, that William Marsh Rice discontinued his education. He was, by nature, an inveterate reader, student and philosopher, and the greater portion of his evenings he devoted to such pastime.

Fresh from public schools and utterly without experience, his first job was with a small country store, drygoods, groceries, notions, etc. Upon first approach, the proprietor was dubious, but becoming favorably impressed with both his air of earnestness and his spirit of entire frankness, he told young Rice to report for duty the following morning.

When William Marsh Rice went to work the next morning, it was the initial step of a successful commercial career that led to the accumulation of millions. It constituted the first link in an interesting chain of circumstances that has made possible the celebration of the twenty-fifth anniversary of the now noted Rice Institute, September twenty-third, 1937.

His living quarters were in a little room above the store. His duties began almost before daylight and continued through lamplight. Urged on by an indomitable will to succeed, possessed of dynamic energy, and a spirit of thrift and economy comparable only to the native New Englander, he made himself valuable from the start. Seven years later, Mr. Rice became the sole owner of that store

306

through purchase, part cash and the balance in notes. Under this management, the business continued to grow and prosper.

It was about this time that echoes from the Field of San Jacinto announced the victory that led to the independence of Texas. To the South a new republic was being born. Young Mr. Rice had read and heard much of it, and the lure of opportunities to be had in this new land excited his sense of adventure, as he contemplated there the possibilities of accomplishment.

Once he arrived at a definite conclusion, it was characteristic of William Marsh Rice that immediately he placed his thought into action. Disposing locally of all such items as he would not require in his new location, he boxed his entire remaining stock of merchandise and shipped it by sea to Galveston. The owner followed by stage and boat to the new republic.

Alas, for best laid plans of mice and men! The boat by which his stock of goods had been shipped was never heard of afterwards, probably having gone down at sea with all hands on board in one of the autumnal hurricanes of that period.

At daylight one morning later on, William Marsh Rice landed at the pier at the foot of Main Street, from the sturdy little steamer, "Bayou City," then plying regularly between Galveston and Houston. He presented at the time, 1838, an impressive figure, very black hair, deep blue eyes, ruddy New England complexion, erect carriage and striking presence.

For him, it was a unique situation: in a strange land, utterly alone, without funds, friends and even acquaintances. Undaunted, he set out to make contacts, and it is said that before nightfall he had obtained a clerkship in one of the new mercantile establishments of Houston.

His personality, extremely aggressive, yet thoroughly cordial and friendly, carried him far. In due course, the business came to be known as Rice and Nichols, exporters and importers, and wholesale grocers of Houston. The firm had an excellent standing and operated from the Gulf to the Red River, and from Sabine to the Rio Grande. E. J. Hart, another prominent merchant of Houston, the founder of the firm, E. J. Hart and Company, was associated with Rice and Nichols until the War Between the States, when he withdrew to join the Confederate army at New Orleans.

Later, he became one of the largest wholesale druggists in the South.

General Nichols withdrew from the firm when Colonel Thomas Pierce, builder of the Southern Pacific, and then operating a line of ships from Boston to Galveston, appointed him to act as agent for the line at Galveston. General Nichols thereupon moved to Galveston.

Mr. Rice continued the business at Houston, occupying what is now the old E. Kiam corner at Main and Preston avenues. Later, he built a store on Main and Commerce, adjacent to the southwest entrance to the Main Street Viaduct, which structure did not, of course, exist at that time.

William Marsh Rice continued in Houston until the close of the Civil War, when he removed to New York and New Jersey, where he maintained his residence the remainder of his life. He never lost, however, his devotion to Texas as a whole, and Houston particularly, his visits to the latter being of frequent occurrence.

A man of comparatively small stature, he was, nevertheless, a giant in business, and one of the great builders of Houston's pioneer period. Assisting in the promotion of the H. & T. C. Railroad, it was largely through his wealth and commercial influence that the road was early successful. Associated with him in the venture was Paul Bremond, another pioneer builder of Houston, whose daughter Mr. Rice married. Unhappily, she died without issue, and Mr. Rice subsequently married the daughter of General Horace Baldwin, another Houstonian of prominence, which wife also passed away without issue.

Mr. Rice was known as a man of great means, with large holdings in virgin timber lands of Louisiana and Texas. He, with the cooperation with E. J. Hart, built the first brick wharf in Galveston. He was a frequent visitor in Houston later and spent many winters in these parts.

It was during one of his visits in Houston, in 1891, that having in mind the founding of a great university of learning, he called together his younger and devoted brother, Captain Fred A. Rice, long associated with him in business, and his close friends, A. S. Richardson, Secretary of the H. & T. C. Railroad, Caesar Lombardi, of William D. Cleveland and Company, Emanuel Raphael, a business associate of many years of F. A. Rice, J. E. McAshan, father of our present S. M. McAshan, and Captain James A. Baker, and outlined to them his plans for founding the Institute.

These plans contemplated after Mr. Rice's death, the use of practically his entire estate, and that the institution would bear his name. He felt that his great fortune having been made in Texas, the benefits of it should properly pass to coming generations of the youth of that land wherein it had been made.

Nine years after the incorporation of William M. Rice Institute, in 1900, Mr. Rice died in New York City. In 1907, the litigation involving his estate was settled on a will drawn in 1896. The estate, then amounting to approximately five million dollars, was turned over to the Trustees of Rice Institute, who immediately proceeded with plans for completing the project. In 1912, the Institute was thrown open to the public. Its growth from that time has been phenominal. Correspondingly, the original estate has increased greatly in value, and other special endowments have been added by Houstonians and others until it is now one of the heaviest endowed institutions of learning in America, ranking at the same time as one of the leading higher educational institutions of the world.

We should regard it not only in that respect, but in truth, a lasting monument to the personality of its founder, a man of unselfish, generous ambition in behalf of the youth of the land who were to follow after him. It stands as a striking example of what may be accomplished by one man possessed of the qualities mentioned, an infinite capacity for accomplishment, and an indomitable will to succeed!

GENERAL ALBERT SIDNEY JOHNSTON

Once Owner of the China Grove Plantation

Just thirty-two miles south of Houston, on the old Columbia Tap at the little town of Bonney, is a beautiful granite marker, one of the first to be erected in the State by the Daughters of the Republic and the Daughters of the Confederacy. It marks the site where once stood the home of that illustrious Son of Texas, General Albert Sidney Johnston.

The historical old plantation, "China Grove," was the home of this brave soldier who resided there at intervals, when not engaged in the defense of his State and Country.

When his wife died in 1835, Johnston sold his farm near St. Louis, Missouri, and moved to Louisville, Kentucky, to make his home. It was in the latter place that Johnston heard a stirring speech about Texas from the lips of the Father of Texas, in the old Second Presbyterian Church. He was so impressed by the brilliant speaker that he decided to join him and help the cause of the Texans in obtaining independence from Mexico.

Arriving in Nacogdoches, after a hurried trip, he met General Sam Houston and enlisted as a private under General T. J. Rusk. Rusk soon recognized Johnston's ability as a soldier and made him adjutant with the rank of Colonel. Shortly afterwards the unfortunate duel between Johnston and Felix Huston took place. Johnston was badly wounded and was forced to return to Kentucky where, through careful treatment and nursing, he regained his health. He returned to Texas in 1838 and became Secretary of War under M. B. Lamar.

It was this time that Johnston purchased the China Grove Plantation, in the early forties, having married the niece of his deceased wife, and with his two children by his former wife, moved his family to China Grove. The plantation lies partly in Oyster Creek bottom but a good portion of it was prairie land. Johnston found most of the land a virtual jungle, full of wild game and beasts. He soon began to beautify the place, planting rows of Bois d'Arc (mock orange) trees, which became entwined with wild Cherokee roses. The combination formed a perfect wind brake protecting his cattle. In order to get quick shade trees around his home, Johnston planted Chinaberry trees in large numbers, hence the name of the Plantation, "China Grove."

He had only a small number of slaves in comparison to some of his neighbors, but they planted corn, cotton, sugar cane and a large variety of vegetables, which were marketed in Houston and Galveston. There were orchards of plums, peaches, and figs which supplied his table. He was noted for his hospitality and his friends were legion. They came to visit with the family and to admire the plantation, especially the big fig trees. He had selected Yellow Celeste fig trees and they grew to large proportions. He was proud of his home and the latch-string was always to be found on the outside of the door.

China Grove was principally a sugar plantation. The

310

manor was a fairly good-sized plantation residence. The sugar house was of brick. Many are living today who have seen the walls after it had burned down. Johnston, a lover of flowers, always maintained a beautiful garden and well kept grounds around the place. His son, William, as he grew up, came to live there and helped his father beautify the place. William was his father's constant companion during his stays which were usually in the winter and spring. In 1849, he was made Paymaster in the United States Army, with headquarters at Austin. He became a resident of Austin but visited China Grove often. General Johnston often said that the happiest days of his life were those days spent on his Texas plantation. The subsequent owner of China Grove was Colonel Warren D. C. Hall.

After Texas was annexed to the United States in 1845, General Johnston enlisted in the services of the United States Army. He was given command of the Pacific Coast and remained in the service until Texas withdrew from the Union, when he resigned his commission and, with a number of others, came overland to Texas. He was placed in command of the Confederate Army in Tennessee, coming overland from California, and in the fatal Battle of Shilo, when victory was almost within his arms, he was struck by a Minie ball and died on the sixth day of April, 1862. His command was given to several officers but none could be found who could fill Johnston's place. This event led to the decline of the Confederacy.

This brave General's wish was that his remains be interred in Texas soil. His wish was granted and his body was shipped to Austin, full military honors paid him, and his remains were interred in the State Cemetery, which had been established by the Texas Legislature in 1854 as a patriotic shrine for Texas, "The Arlington of Texas." The Daughters of the Revolution and Daughters of the Confederacy arranged for a sum of money to enable the placing of an appropriate monument to General Johnston. The sculptress, Elisabet Ney, immortalized General Johnston by carving a life-size statue of the General in uniform, which is internationally famous.

Thus ended the life of one of Texas' noblest sons, who now rests among his comrades in conflict, whose bodies were brought from the four corners of Texas through the untiring efforts of L. W. Kemp of Houston.

The old plantation had long since declined until it is

now a ghost of its former beauty and splendor, and is gradually going back to the jungle that it was when General Johnston found it. It became the property of a Houston bank but they parted with it to an oil company who, as late owners, will produce oil, "black gold" instead of the "fleecy staple" and the Golden Yellow Sugar Cane.

China Grove Plantation, however, will remain in the hearts of all true Texans as the shrine of one of the noblest Generals the Republic and State of Texas has ever known.

SAM McNEIL

Pioneer Cotton Man

Sam McNeil, oldest cotton man in Houston, and probably in Texas, was a native of New Orleans who came to Houston in 1877 and was immediately associated with Major Albert Ruttkay, a prominent exporter, who was the nephew of General Kossuth, the noted Hungarian patriot. At the death of Major Ruttkay, McNeil founded the firm of Horton and McNeil. Mr. Horton passed away shortly afterwards but Mr. McNeil remained active in business until a few years ago.

He was the senior warden of Christ Church and had served for many years as vestryman. He was identified with a number of business concerns and social organizations.

He was a self-possessed man of mild temperament, generous almost to a fault, with his family and friends. His word was his bond, and he was always ready to extend the hand of fellowship to the many newcomers who profited by his wisdom of the cotton trade. As a judge of cotton he had no peer. He was an authority on grade and staple, and he was known throughout the State as the "noblest Roman of them all."

He was always proud of having worn the uniform of the Continental Guards of New Orleans of which he was one of the earliest members, which endeared him to the citizen soldiery of Texas, particularly the Light Guard and Washington Guards, in whom he took great interest.

He was a devoted husband, and made friends everywhere he went and kept them. Death, the "grim reaper," called him after a useful life. He was a kindly, chivalrous, religious, courteous, Southern gentleman.

312

BIOGRAPHICAL SKETCHES

MAJOR E. W. CAVE

Pioneer Promoter of the Houston Ship Channel

Much had been said and written about the ship channel and great praise has been justly given to men of the present day who have brought it to the present wonderful effectiveness and importance. However, the names of the real promoters, the men who had the vision to conceive and the willingness, perserverance and ability to carry on under tremendous difficulties and great discouragement are seldom mentioned. This shows how soon we are forgotten when we pass away.

I have had the privilege of perusing some original letters written by one of those early pioneers in the development of the Houston ship channel. These letters were written sixty years ago by Major E. W. Cave. I was then living in Galveston. He paid frequent visits there and I sat at his feet listening enraptured to his fairy tales of the bayou as I viewed them at that time. I thought he was rubbing "Aladdin's lamp" too strongly, but I enjoyed them all the more. He was a man of untiring energy and a most forceful speaker. He could present a subject as clearly and convincingly as any man I ever knew. I particularly remember his description of the banks of the bayou which he said were upheld by cypress trees, oaks and other shrubs and were carpeted with Bermuda grass which held the banks in place and prevented their washing away. He told that the bayous were usually sluggish streams, but in this one being fed by numerous springs and lakes, there was always a good flow and current.

Another one of those who in the early days worked so hard for the development of the bayou was S. L. Allen, one of the founders of the city of Houston.

I listened in those days with pleasure also to descriptions of trips on the bayou by Captain Fred W. Smith, first vice-president of the Houston Direct Navigation Company, which in those days handled most of the cotton from Houston to Galveston, where it was delivered direct to steamers in the harbor, avoiding the use of the Galveston Wharf Company, which was not very pleasing to them or to the merchants of Galveston.

Major Cave was assisted in his efforts in behalf of the

313

deepening of Buffalo Bayou by Captain George W. Kidd, pioneer secretary of the Houston Cotton Exchange. They often burned midnight oil (this was during the days when John D. Rockefeller's kerosene was the best luminant known) in getting up data and statistics, searching every nook and corner for information which they compiled and sent to Washington.

W. D. Cleveland was also a constant worker with them. Their reports were done in long hand as there were no typewriters then, but their letters were excellent examples of good penmanship.

All information was sent to Honorable Charles Stewart, congressman for a decade in Washington, and it was through his influence that the project was finally recognized by the government and appropriation for deepening the bayou was secured. He was followed by Captain J. C. Hutcheson, who did noble work for years thereafter.

The resident assistant engineer of the United States station in Galveston at the time, Captain R. B. Talfor, was a strong advocate for the project, which in those days was called myth, and by many spoken of as the "elimentary canal" outside of Houston.

H. W. Garrow, prominent member and for many years president of the Cotton Exchange, was a very active and able worker too.

I will remember the trip of the delegation from Washington who came down here for an inspection of the ship channel. They were taken down on a tug. Fortunately we had had a heavy rain and the bayou was on a rampage. We had a big dinner at Clinton arranged and supervised by Captain John Atkinson, who was superintendent of the Houston Direct Navigation Company and also the master fish chowder maker. He was always the host on these festive occasions. After this everybody was in a mood to view the bayou, soundings were made, but Major Cave did not like the way it was being done, so he grasped the lead line and giving it a whirl, he exclaimed, "Six fathoms, eight fathoms, ten fathoms by the Mark Twain." He took good care when he gathered up the slack line that the congressional committee could not see the markings on the line. They were wonderfully impressed with the depth and made a good report and the result was that he succeeded in getting the largest appropriation we had had up to that time. The real fight that Houston made was when the toll chain or log was removed at Morgan's Point and our waterway was opened free to the world. This was done largely by these pioneers. While the mention of their names now gives me sorrow, I would like to see them gain a little more prominence now and then. Colonel Tom Ball and others later took up this work and completed it and their achievement speaks for itself.

COLONEL CORNELIUS ENNIS

Dreamer of Empire—Railroad Builder—Houston's First Cotton Merchant

No truthful history of the early commercial and industrial development of Texas coastal regions—Houston, Galveston and the immediately adjacent interior—could be written without portraying at least a resume of the interesting career of Colonel Cornelius Ennis, whose descendants, after several generations have intervened, yet remain active in the civic, social and commercial affairs of the city.

Of giant stature and commanding presence, Colonel Ennis, for the period in which he lived, was also a gigantic organizer of resources and a great builder of empire. A true pioneer, he was largely instrumental in formulating those plans and procedures that, in later years as they came into fruition, were responsible for making of the young Republic of Texas, a now great commonwealth. His tireless energy, coupled with a grim determination to attain success in the face of difficulties apparently unsurmountable, enabled him to fairly wrestle from nature itself the worthwhile places and products to be used to the great advantage of those who followed after him.

It is to pioneers of the type of Cornelius Ennis that we, of the Texas of today, have to be grateful when we contemplate our enjoyment of the present comforts, pleasures and luxuries surrounding us.

They came to Houston in the days when railroads were thought to be impracticable, when telegraphs were largely a superstition—a brave and hardy set of men, traveling over Texas from end to end, on horseback and in wagons, the North star for their guide by night, and the compass by day; or, if happily preceded by some comrade previously bent their way, they followed his footsteps by means of the trail he had blazed—a simple notching of the trees as he passed on. Such roads as there were, were practically impassable during the rainy season; bridges were exceedingly few and far between, and many anxious hours were spent at the fords, knowing that such crossings were the favorite attacking points for the hostile Indians. These founders of empire made such journeys with pistols, Bowie-knives, and with loaded gun across the knees; and eternal vigilance was indeed the price of safety. Yet, no true pioneer worthy of the name has been deterred by perils that beset the way. They have braved, alike, the terrors of the barren desert, and the icy-blasts of the North; nor, have they feared to go among savage peoples, nor, in fact, to travel any foot of earth or sea, did it appear to lead, ultimately, to their land of promise or, maybe, even to high and unusual adventure.

Cornelius Ennis was born in 1813, in Essex County, New Jersey. His great-grandfather, William Ennis, had come from the North of Ireland in the latter part of the seventeenth century and settled with his wife in New Jersey. Mr. Ennis' mother was a Miss Doremus from one of the original Holland families, who had early colonized New York and New Jersey.

After receiving such education as the facilities of his home environment afforded, Mr. Ennis went to New York in 1834. Three years later he began a trip down the Ohio and Mississippi rivers, in search of a suitable location in which to apply his energies. In Mississippi he met a great many people from Texas. All of them were enthusiastic concerning the agricultural and commercial opportunities offered by the new republic, and there were recitals of stories of gallantry and courage relating to victories of the War for Independence, and other adventurous incidents. The picture that young Ennis envisioned fired his imagination, and he forthwith made his plans to enter Texas.

Returning to New York in May of 1837, he spent a month purchasing a stock of drygoods, drugs, etc., and embarked for Galveston. Arriving there, he found Galveston very sparsely settled, without a hotel and without wharves. Accordingly, he proceeded to Houston, then barely two years old.

In Houston, Mr. Ennis immediately established himself in business, purchasing a location on Main Street, and enlarging the building already there, to accommodate a general mercantile and drug business. His business flourished and increased steadily from the first. By 1840, with the coming of the first cotton to Houston as a cotton-market, Mr. Ennis had established himself as Houston's first cotton-merchant. The staple had been grown in Fort Bend County and came to Houston in search of a stable market; and Mr. Ennis, sensing the value of attracting the cotton business of the future to Houston, proceeded to create a dependable market for the product.

The cotton business of the city then, as now, was done on the North Side of the Bayou. There were no bridges, but the cotton was ferried across at the foot of Main Street. Later on, a small bridge of wood and concrete was constructed, and this later gave way to the little iron bridge at Milam and Commerce streets.

A new departure in business, and one noted with much interest at the time, as promising much for the future, was the first shipment of cotton from the port of Galveston to Boston, made by Mr. Ennis in 1841. He subsequently became one of the largest cotton buyers and shippers in the State.

Turning his attention now to the interior of Texas, Mr. Ennis promoted first the building of the "plank" road out the present Washington Avenue (then Washington Road) to Hempstead; this to facilitate commerce and travel between Houston and the territory served. He was active in the incorporation of the H. & T. C. Railroad, and the now thriving North Texas town of Ennis, once the terminus of the H. & T. C., which was named in his honor. He served admirably as General Superintendent and Comptroller of this road, and also as purchasing and fiscal agent for them, in the course of which he made several trips to New York, obtaining there the needed funds to finance the road to completion.

317

Mr. Ennis helped build the International & Great Northern Railway; and, while mayor of Houston, built the "Houston Tap" Road, to the construction of which he gave his personal attention. As mayor, he served the city during 1856-57 without remuneration. Much of his time was taken up at that period in carrying out protective measures against the Mexican bandits, renegade Americans and hostile Indians who made a practice of preying on the territory adjacent to Houston, thus impeding the growth of the city and its commerce. Enlisting the aid of the State authorities, Mr. Ennis waged so vigorous a campaign against the depredators that survivors, their former comrades dead or in the penitentiary, fled the country for fresher fields afar!

During the War Between the States, Mr. Ennis was engaged in the hazardous business of blockade running, exporting cotton to Havana, thence to Mexico and to England. In 1864 he went to Havana and met Jack Moore, a bar pilot of Galveston, whom he sent to New York to purchase, at the expense of Mr. Ennis, an iron-clad steamer for blockade-running purposes. The price paid was forty thousand dollars in gold. Mr. Moore brought the ship to Havana, loaded her with one thousand two hundred Enfield rifles, ten tons of gun-powder, three million percussion caps, clothing and other supplies for the Confederate Government. The entire shipload was delivered to the Southern forces in due course. Alas for the Lost Cause! I was told years ago by one of the descendants of Mr. Ennis, that they had found among some of his old possessions, an account-statement acknowledging receipt of these supplies, and a "warrant" commonly known as the Confederate Government's "I. O. U." payable to Mr. Ennis, for one hundred thousand dollars—for all of which he received, not one penny. Forsooth, blockade running in those days had its perils financial, as well as physical!

After the war, Mr. Ennis continued his export of cotton and opened an office in Galveston. I remember distinctly my first introduction to this great captain of industry. My father was one of his brokers, having care of the loading of all his export cotton. One morning, in 1869, I was handed a bill of lading and other documents and told to deliver them to Mr. Ennis. When I entered his office he was standing at his desk—a high desk, after the fashion of that day, there being then no flat-top or roller top desks of the type now used —and he impressed me as being a tremendous man. He was, in fact, of giant stature, standing six feet three inches or more, and weighing, approximately, two hundred and seventy-five pounds. Oddly enough, his two partners, Frank Cargill and N. Anderson, were both about five feet five inches in height, and stood there in consultation with him. Child that I was, I had just finished reading "Gulliver's Travels," and the scene left a vivid impression on my mind of the Giant Gulliver talking with the Lilliputians!

Eventually, Mr. Ennis and his associate, Mr. Cargill, returned to Houston, continuing active here until their passing, years later.

Among other interests, Mr. Ennis acquired a large interest in the Galveston-Dallas News. His eldest daughter married Colonel Alfred H. Belo, who became president of the News. The second daughter married Mr. Cargill, and the younger one followed in marriage to Caesar Lombardi, an outstanding merchant of Houston at the time, and once partner of W. D. Cleveland. Mr. Lombardi died while president of the Dallas News. Mr. Ennis' only son, a splendid future before him, died early in life.

The Ennis home, a large colonial structure, was located on Congress Avenue at Chenevert Avenue. Only a few years since it was torn down to make way for business use, I think, perhaps, a filling station. Christ Episcopal Church knew both Colonel Ennis and his lovely wife as ardent supporters and workers in its cause; and I learn that through the passing generations their descendants still attend this beautiful old chapel. To my own knowledge, Mr. Ennis accomplished a world of quiet, lovable charity, little known except to those for whom it was done. In the terrible epidemics of yellow fever and other maladies which swept the Houston of those days, both of them gave heroically of their time, labor and funds to alleviate suffering of the community.

Tall, great of stature and holding himself always erect, Colonel Ennis bore himself proudly to the end. He passed away leaving upon the community the indelible imprint of a man of great mind and great accomplishment.

ADELE BRISCOE LOOSCAN

No history is complete without the frequent use of the name of Adele Looscan, who has done more and written more Houston and Harris County history than any other. She was the granddaughter of John R. Harris, the founder of Harrisburg and you might say Houston. Harrisburg was taken into its city limits and automatically became Houston years ago, which makes Houston much older than when the Allens laid out the city.

The old Looscan home was built by that gallant Confederate soldier and leading attorney, who was considered one of the most congenial men in the city, Colonel M. J. Looscan. He was known to nearly everyone as "Mike." The house also was the home of Adele Looscan's mother, Mary Jane Briscoe, whom many call the "preserver of San Jacinto Battle Ground."

It was the writer's pleasure to have known this estimable lady whose activities are so well known. It was fifty-four years ago at the Battle Ground where she made known to me the spot where the battle was fought, and with twenty-five or more of the old San Jacinto veterans, pointed out to us where the different camps of General Houston's army were located and, also, Santa Anna's army location. Later she, with the aid of the grandfather of George A. Hill, Jr., who was a member of the San Jacinto Veterans Association, had the red granite markers placed. Much credit, also, must be given to Mrs. Charles M. Milby, Mrs. J. J. McKeever and others, whose private funds helped to secure these markers.

Mrs. Briscoe was not in the battle but heard the booming of the guns and lay awake all night wondering at the outcome. At daybreak, she, a girl of seventeen years of age, fresh from the New York Boarding School, rode out on her favorite pony to give such aid as she could perform. She saw the various locations of the armies and until she passed away, took a keen interest in the grounds.

In the old Looscan home a number of women met in 1865 and organized the Ladies Reading Club, which has been active ever since. Forming of a women's club in those days was said to be a radical step. News of the organization of the clubs was kept from the newspapers. The club had about twenty-five or thirty members, regarded as very intelligent. Mrs. Looscan was its first president and out of it grew what is now the City Federation of Women's Clubs, although the Reading Club is still in existence with an exclusive membership restricted to fifty; it is so highly regarded that it has a waiting list.

Mrs. Looscan was largely instrumental in bringing Victoria Woodhul and Tennessee Claflin, the first English

Woman Sufferagist, who were the first great Women Emancipators, which the writer remembers well.

A little gracious old lady, the mother of Mr. Jack Mason of the Mason Building, now the J. E. Josey Building, slipped the writer a five dollar bill into his coat pocket and asked him to escort her and her daughter to the meeting. No man could be found to accompany the ladies, as no grown-up man wanted to attend the "hen party," as it was called in those days. It was the first time he had heard the ladies lambast the male element, good and plenty and they called "a spade a spade." Victoria Woodhul got up and asked why all this mock modesty today in calling a "leg of the table, a limb of a table." In those days when a leg was mentioned in the presence of the fair sex, it created blushes from all sides.

In this old residence was organized the first chapter of the Daughters of the Republic of Texas, in 1901. The first president was Mrs. Anson Jones, whose husband was a president of the Republic of Texas. Mrs. Briscoe was the first vice-president. The current story of how the organization came into existence is that, Colonel Guy M. Bryan, president of the Texas Veterans Association, his niece, Miss Betty Ballenger of Galveston (who passed away recently), and Colonel Bryan's daughter, Miss Halley, had read and discussed Yoakum's "History of Texas." The conversation eventually drifted to perpetuation of names and identification of women connected with the Republic and finally definite steps were taken to form the survivors and their descendants into an organization, which since has grown into one of the States' foremost societies. Mrs. Looscan continued her activities in many other organizations and many meetings were held in the old home until she was stricken. One of the last letters she wrote before her illness, the writer is the proud possessor of, and values it highly. The letter was complimenting him on his historical writings.

No family contributed so much history of the days of the Revolution as Mrs. Dulie Harris, Mrs. Briscoe and Mrs. Adele Looscan. The "Runaway Scrape" by Mrs. Harris and Mrs. Looscan has been read by many thousands and will be read by millions in generations to come.

The writer thinks that Mrs. Briscoe and her associates, together with Colonel J. M. Hill, as chairman of the Veteran's committee and others who aided her in securing the beautiful park at San Jacinto will be recognized and their names placed in bold letters in the San Jacinto Monument which will soon be unveiled to the honor of those that gave us our Independence.

Mrs. Looscan had the first Anniversary Annual Ball of the Battle of San Jacinto held in the first hotel built by Ben Fort Smith.

Mr. Briscoe had a large part in the organization of Harris County in 1836, and became its first County Judge with the title of Chief Justice. At this time he lived in Houston and built his home for his eighteen year old bride, Mary Jane Briscoe. It was situated on the corner of Main and Prairie avenues, now the Byrd corner, and was planned on the style of Thomas Jefferson, a young architect before he became famous. Later the house passed into the hands of Dr. J. S. Roberts.

It remained intact as many can remember until the "Nineties." Mrs. Roberts, the mother of the late Mayor Ingram Roberts, the great all time Houston historian, had a beautiful old fashioned flower garden in the late "Eighties" and it was one of the show places of Houston.

Colonel Andrew Briscoe was a noted jurist in his day, also was active in securing a charter for the first railroad in Texas, constructing the road bed, which was later built to the Brazos River by General Sherman. He was also a merchant in the early days, conducting a store in Anahuac, as well as, in Houston. Noted men, no matter what their profession or occupation, carried "side lines."

During his activities in Anahuac he was charged by the Mexican government with not paying sufficient revenue taxes, in fact, he was opposed to the tax placed on the colonists. For this reason he was imprisoned. This aroused his fellow comrades and a report was sent to San Felipe, in June 1835, and at a meeting there a resolution was drawn up authorizing the immortal, William B. Travis. Gathering up about thirty men, they sailed for Anahuac. The sloop ran ashore a half mile from the landing; a shot rang out from her stern to notify the garrison the colonists had arrived. The cannon was carried ashore and as they approached, the Mexicans fled in great disorder. General Terona surrendered, agreeing not to take up arms against the Texans when Andrew Briscoe and Thomas M. Jack were duly released. This act, unquestionably, was one of the first events that brought about the Revolution.

Mr. Briscoe went to San Antonio to assist Fannin and

Bowie but only for short time. He had been elected from Harrisburg as a member of the convention to assemble, March the first, 1836. He arrived in time to sign the declaration of independence.

Mr. Briscoe died in the late summer of 1849, leaving two sons, Andrew Birdsall Briscoe and Parmenas, and two daughters, Jessie Wade Briscoe and Adele Briscoe.

The Harris, Briscoe and Looscan families have contributed more South Texas history than any other family, in fact, there is very little more of the early history to be found at our libraries than theirs.

COLONEL WILLIAM T. ELDRIDGE

The Late Sugar King. Sugarland Plantation

Banker, sugar manufacturer, railroad magnate and agriculturist, that he was, no man of the present century has, single-handed, done more to develop the resources of South Texas than the late Colonel William T. Eldridge.

It was in 1896 that the writer first met Colonel Eldridge. He was then the farm-products sales-manager for Vineyard, Walker and Company, private banking firm and agriculturists of Eagle Lake. We were destined to meet many times thereafter and, over a period of years, to transact a very considerable volume of business and to develop a friendship which holds many warm recollections.

Subsequently the writer as a member of the committee of the Houston Cotton Exchange serving in conjunction with Colonel Eldridge in the entertainment provided for Carter H. Harrison a special fund of the Cotton Exchange; the Commercial Club was then in its infancy; Carter was owner of Harper's Weekly and also of "Puck," the great humorist magazine, and likewise, a son of Benjamin Harrison, former president of the United States.

Colonel Eldridge was anxious that Mr. Harrison have an ample opportunity to view the agricultural and manufacturing resources of South Texas and provided splendidly to that end. Among the excursions made with Mr. Harrison was one to the Sugarland Industries, where Colonel Eldridge pointed out to him, among other items, the unusual productiveness of the soil, sugar cane towering, as it seemed, to the skies—fourteen to twenty feet high, corn ten to fourteen feet and cotton five to seven feet high.

At the little dinner given to Mr. Harrison he was asked to offer a few kindly comments on the resources of Texas; and, in his characteristic humor, he arose and proceeded: "Gentlemen, you ask of me next to an impossibility in point of compass and range. The resources of South Texas are entirely too great to satifactorily encompass in one after-dinner speech; for, when I look around me what do I see? On the one hand, vast acres of land, the soil of which is richer than the head-waters of the Nile; the trees upon it grow "whiskers" (moss) more flowing than the beards of the patriarchs and prophets of old; so productive is it that, we stick a hair-pin into it and up sprouts a telegraph or telephone wire. Again, if we stoop down and pick up a handful of South Texas soil, giving it a sound squeeze, out flows petroleum!"—and so on. Kepple, the editor of "Puck," the greatest humorist of that time, followed Mr. Harrison, poking considerable fun at Colonel Eldridge because of the latter's portliness, which Kepple claimed could have been produced by foods that had been grown only on the fertile soils of South Texas. His son succeeded him in size and also weighed nearly three hundred pounds.

Some five years ago, it was the writer's pleasure to again visit Colonel Eldridge at Sugarland. Meanwhile his portliness had increased—so had the Sugarland industries. Upon exchange of greetings, the writer remarked to Colonel Eldridge, in passing, "I just dropped in to see you—it is getting bigger and bigger." Surveying himself, and thinking possibly back to the humorous comment of Kepple, Colonel Eldridge replied: "Ziegler, you don't mean that," pointing to his son, who weighed over three hundred pounds. "Why, I only weigh three hundred pounds now!" Laughingly, the writer rejoined, "No, Colonel, albeit you seem to be holding your own most splendidly in a personal way, I was really thinking of Sugarland and the tremendous expansion in its industry and operation." It had grown into one of the most completely equipped enterprises of its kind, a bank, sugar mills, mattress factory, general store, other manufacturing plants, and an extensive agricultural undertaking.

Colonel Eldridge was not only a large man physically; he was a giant organizer and a master agriculturist. In addition to his thousands of acres of sugar cane, he was a large producer of cotton, corn, cabbage, tomatoes, potatoes and other vegetables for the market. Correspondingly, he was a great lover of flowers, and for a number of years made a virtual "perfume shop" of Sugarland by raising tube-roses on an extensive scale for re-seeding purposes alone. These were shipped to all parts of the country. Branching out, he produced successfully for several years a self-bleaching celery for which there was excellent demand. His efforts along experimental lines with other marketable products served materially to enhance the program of farm diversification then being undertaken in South Texas.

For years, the fires of the sugar mills at Sugarland were never allowed to go out, but were banked during the periods of short runs. It was a fascinating sight to watch the Lilliputian cars running in and out of the mill loaded with the "makings," and to hear their continual rumblings, akin to a miniature railway train, for such, in fact, they were.

When, subsequently, tariff conditions made it unprofitable to grow sugar cane, Colonel Eldridge imported thousands of carloads of raw sugar from Cuba, Porto Rico, Honolulu, the Philippines and various Latin-American countries. It was in 1927 that the last sugar was ground at the mill. Today, so far as the writer knows, there is no sugar cane grown commercially anywhere in Texas, but much is grown and manufactured into sugar in Louisiana. The Fort Bend-Brazoria area, once a vast sugar plantation, is now planted in other crops. Increased cost of wages, insect infestation and tariffs have sounded the death knell of this once great industry. Today all sugar refined by the Imperial comes from the outside sources above mentioned.

Colonel Eldridge became owner of the Sugarland properties in 1908; shortly after his death he was succeeded by President I. H. Kempner, of the Kempner Estate in Galveston, and from this time forward there was a gradual improvement in all phases. The refinery's output was increased successively, due largely to improved machinery, its present capacity being in excess of one million, five hundred thousand pounds a day. Convict labor, used in previous years, was done away with and vast improvements made in the living conditions, with the result that for many years now Sugarland had been a model industrial community, supporting one of the finest school systems in the State, a well equipped hospital, churches, parks, etc.; it is the "back door" of Houston, twenty-five miles out on the number three highway.

The evolution from early "baronial" days of the great

estate is complete. The old plantation houses of the Kyles, Ellises, Cunninghams, Adams and others have long since passed away. The social life on the original Sugarland plantation must have been great. There are still living in Fort Bend County a few of the older residents whose children remember "going to the Terry Plantation"—as it was originally named, for the great and good times had there. At the turn of the century there was living an ex-slave who had lived on the original plantation, granted to S. M. Williams, Secretary to Stephen F. Austin. This old darky, in conversation, vividly recalled the operation of the early sugar mill in pre-Civil War days; that the mill had two rollers, was operated by "mule-power," and that the open kettle process, similar to that in vogue in Louisiana, was used. The molasses was drained off in troughs to one thousand pound hogsheads for shipment.

Upon parting from Colonel Eldridge that day at the close of the writer's visit, they were standing on the depot platform, looking over the vast estate. He turned to the writer and exclaimed: "Ziegler, you are looking over forty thousand acres in the highest state of cultivation, a veritable farm-basket of South Texas." And so it was—improved by a master-builder. It was then encompassed by his own circularly-built railroad to further expedite the handling of the necessary equipment and the commodities produced. The various divisions of the plantation were splendidly maintained; in driving through it, one could discern no more weeds than might appear upon the average well kept city lot.

Colonel Eldridge continued the management of the Sugarland properties until his passing in 1932, thus living to see the fruition of his early dream of a modernly equipped plantation-industry. The H. Kempner Estate is now one of the principal owners. Mr. I. H. Kempner is president. It continues under the able management of Gus Ulrich, formerly executive assistant to Colonel Eldridge, over a long period of years. Mr. I. H. Kempner, Jr. serves as assistant manager of the industries. Walter F. Woodul is one of the trustees.

Sugarland constitutes one of the outstanding show-spots of the State in point of modernized plantation life and operation.

BIOGRAPHICAL SKETCHES

ROBERT JUSTIN KLEBERG

With the exception of the Father of Texas, Stephen F. Austin, and the Hero of San Jacinto, Sam Houston, possibly no other man and his descendants have made more continuous history in Texas than has Robert J. Kleberg.

Kleberg was born in September, 1803, in Westphalia, Germany, in the former kingdom of Prussia. His parents were Lucius Kleberg and Veronica Kleberg, "a lady of culture, sweet of temper and good sense."

Robert J. entered the University of Goettingen (birthplace of the writer's forebears), in the kingdom of Hanover and in less than three years received his degree as Doctor of Law. After his graduation, he decided to emigrate to the United States. His reasons were, in his own language, "I wish to live under a Republican form of government with unbounded personality, religious and political liberty; free from the tyrannies, the many disadvantages and evils of the old country." (Prussia smarted at that time under a military despotism.) Kleberg added, "I expect to find in Texas, above all other countries, the blessed land of my most fervent hopes."

To show that many of the early colonists shared Kleberg's dream about Texas, I quote from a letter before me, written in June, 1827, by my grand uncle to my grandfather from Reinish Bavaria (then part of France) : "Dear Brother: We are so tired of all the religious frenzy and the Napoleonic wars here that as soon as we can sell out, we will follow you to the United States." My paternal grandfather had arrived in the United States from Germany and settled in Ohio in 1826, when my father was but three years old. My maternal grandfather and family landed in Galveston from Hanover in 1845. My grand uncle fought with General Zachary Taylor a year later in the last war with Mexico. They and many others were induced to come to Texas from letters received from the Klebergs and others.

Kleberg's order to accomplish his desires had been heightened by a letter received from Fritz Ernst, a German friend, who had immigrated to Texas in 1821, together with Chas. Fortrand who had founded the town of Industry, in Austin County. (This was Texas' first German colonist to settle Texas.)

On September 4, 1834, Robert Justin Kleberg married

327

Rosalia Von Roeder, a member of an old family of nobility, and with his wife, three brothers, one sister and a servant girl, embarked for the United States, well provided with money, clothes, farming equipment, wagons and all necessities of life. The voyage required sixty days, ending at New York, from whence they sailed to New Orleans on the steamer, "Congress," in company with the titled Von Roeder family. These were, Lt. A. S. Von Roeder and wife, his daughters Louisa and Caroline, and his sons, Rudolph, Otto and William, and Miss Antoinette Von Doup, a niece of R. J. Kleberg.

After eight days, the immigrants were wrecked, just as Cabeza de Vaca had been three hundred years before, on a sand bank off Galveston Island. It was impossible to name the exact spot where they were cast ashore, but it was about the center of the Island. The boat was approximately sixty yards from shore. They described the Island as "a dense wilderness, inhabited by wolves and snakes of all varieties, and the waters infested with alligators. There were also a number of deer and myriads of ducks, geese and other fowl."

After constructing large tent-like huts from the mast spars and sails off the wrecked boat, with separate compartments for the women and children, Robert Kleberg and Rudolph Von Roeder set sail on a schooner for Brazoria. En route to San Felipe where the two were going by foot from Brazoria, they encountered an Indian which Von Roeder was intent upon shooting but Kleberg interceded and the Indian soon realized that they were "tribesmen of those remarkable new-comers who kept their pale faces hidden behind thickets of beards." The Indian traded the "new-comers" venison for arms and advised them that Cat Springs was only a short distance from there, where Kleberg was to locate his relatives who had preceded him there by a few years.

In the meantime the remaining party was taken from Galveston Island by Captain Scott and sheltered at his home on Scott's Bay. From here they later moved on to Harrisburg and rented a house from John R. Harris, awaiting the arrival of Robert Kleberg and Rudolph Von Roeder who had letters from prominent people in Germany and were seeking Stephen F. Austin for the purpose of obtaining a land grant.

Returning with the coveted land grant, Von Roeder and Kleberg were informed by their families that all had gone well on Galveston Island, as the weather was "mild and balmy," and that they had existed by fishing and hunting. Those who could not fish or shoot had driven the wild deer to the hunters, gathered wild berries, etc. Remembering that the entire colony was of noble birth makes us realize the extreme hardships these pioneers really endured.

The men proceeded then by ox cart to Cat Springs to build two or three log houses for their families, which they accomplished with great difficulties, and finally founded Cat Springs in Austin County.

Mrs. Rosa Kleberg recites a humorous incident which occurred one day at Harrisburg while she was baking bread. Upon noting a shadow fall across her doorway, with a startled glance she saw three fierce looking Indians standing before her. Greatly alarmed, she hastened away to her gun but upon returning found in place of her freshly baked bread three large wild turkey gobblers on the table. Running away with the bread, the Indians were calling back "Swap, swap."

Soon rumblings of the War for Independence began; the little colony moved hurriedly to their new Cat Springs homes and in a short time Rudolph Von Roeder went to San Antonio where he participated in the Battle and storming of the Alamo. Not long after the "Runaway Scrape" began, the men called a meeting of their colony to decide whether to cross the Sabine into the United States or to join the revolutionists in their quest of freedom. Almost without a dissenting vote, the decision was to aid the Colonists in gaining their Independence. Ox carts were hastily provided for the flight to Stafford's Point where many of the Colonists, with their wives, children and old men and women, about forty families in all, had gathered for their flight to the Sabine. The archives at Austin show that there were, besides Kleberg and the Von Roeders, about forty or fifty other Germans who enlisted with General Houston, many of whom were cited for bravery. Several were with Fannin at Goliad, only one survived the massacre but I have been unable to ascertain his name. Robert Kleberg, with Louis and Otto Von Roeder, enlisted with Mosely Baker's company which was a part of the Texan army at San Jacinto. Von Roeder had been an officer in the Prussian army.

It was after the Battle of San Jacinto had been won by the Texans that a courier of Sam Houston halted the fleeing families of the revolutionists with the glad tidings of the victory and started them on their return trip homeward. Their arrival revealed that their new homes had been razed by the Mexicans. They proceeded then to the huts left on Galveston Island, which they found to be infested by mosquitoes, and no drinkable water was available. Mrs. A. S. Von Roeder died here and was buried in LaFitte's Grove, the famous "Three Lone Trees." Life on the Island was still primitive. One night frantic cries of one of the women aroused the entire colony. Mrs. L. Kleberg pointed out an alligator, with jaws wide open, heading toward the children. The monster was finally dispatched with fire and sword before he had reached the children. They recited that at that time, in 1836, not a white family resided on the Island.

Leaving Galveston Island to the mosquitoes, snakes and alligators, our friends moved on to a small village called Liverpool, at the head of Chocolate Bayou, eight miles south of Alvin. From here they returned to Cat Springs to rebuild their pre-war colony, where they resided until 1847, moving to Dewitt County where Robert Justin Kleberg died in 1888. Wherever he lived, he was a builder. It was natural, therefore, after having developed Austin and adjoining counties, that he helped to develop DeWitt County and the neighboring section.

Mrs. Rosa Kleberg was a very talented woman, a writer and musician. She had the first piano at Harrisburg which was burned along with her books and paintings by Santa Anna and his men. Her letters to friends in Germany and others influenced many in coming to Texas.

The Colonists lived on friendly terms with the Indians, who supplied them with game and looked after their livestock, bringing them in from the woods when they strayed away, in return for which services the Indians received ammunition, trinkets and odd things which were brought over from the old country. The Indians were said to present a ludicrous sight when they came themselves before the white people to trade. They came adorned with ribbons, stove-pipe hats and all manner of fancy dress.

The services of Robert Justin Kleberg were rewarded by President Houston with his appointment as Associate Commissioner of the Board of Land Commissioners. President Lamar appointed him Justice of the Peace, a highly important office at that time. Being a judge and a noted jurist, he settled many of the knotty questions of the day.

Robert Kleberg's son, Rudolph J. Kleberg, married the daughter of Captain King, of the King Ranch, the largest ranch in the world (about a million and a half acres of land). The Kleberg family owned the controlling interest. Their son, Richard, represents the Nueces District in Washington as a member of Congress and recently his daughter became the wife of Forest Lee Andrews of Houston.

Many remember M. J. Kleberg, the late beloved and outstanding attorney of Galveston who moved from Austin County in the early days. His son, Walter, is the eminent physician and County Health Officer of Galveston Island.

Truly the name Kleberg is linked with every era of Texas history and with many sections of the State.

LONDONDERRY LADS, ONE OF HOUSTON'S BENEFACTORS

Henry Frederick MacGregor

The contributions made to Texas during the past century by native sons and daughters of other states is difficult to estimate. They came to Texas before government was established, they endured every hardship known to man, and they remained to see the State take its place among the brighter stars of the Nation. Among these adopted sons was Henry Frederick MacGregor of Londonderry, New Hampshire.

Born of pioneer stock, and possessed of rugged character, ready to work and endure hardships, with vision, stamina and ambition to build for the future, H. F. MacGregor came to Houston in the early "Seventies." He liked the adopted city he had chosen for his home and set to work immediately to gain a foothold. In 1883 he had been promoted until he was now an official in the Street Railway Company in Houston. It was under his management that the mule car gave way to the electric car, and it no longer became necessary that Mr. MacGregor actually use his physical strength to get a car back on the track from whence it had "detoured."

One of the secrets of the success Mr. MacGregor was to attain was that no part of the job was "beneath" him. If it meant applying veterinary care to the work stock of the street railway company, he did that without question. If it meant dealing with employees of the company, he did that well and knew them and their duties as well as their problems. Whatever the job required was always done. He had that rare combination of characteristics—versatility and courage to venture, with the proverbial Scotch thrift and frugality to act as a balance.

331

Mr. MacGregor was an early real estate enthusiast. He bought property and planned for the future. His home at Berry and Fannin was a show place when completed, and the landscaped grounds caused many a head to turn when passing by. It was on MacGregor Avenue in MacGregor's first Main Street addition that I built my first home, after the turn of the century and where my children, Jessie and Evelyn, were born. We were old friends, neighbors, fellow club members and civic workers and I like to recall the years of pleasant social and business contacts we had.

Like a plant, he had deep roots, and though he grew tall and strong, he branched out in many directions. One of the strongest roots he had was in his home. He had married Miss Elizabeth Stevens, a native Houstonian, in 1885 and he often said that his home life was his stay and his inspiration. In social welfare work, in public philanthropies, in religious and social realms, Mr. and Mrs. MacGregor had worked side by side. They were members of the Presbyterian Church and Mrs. MacGregor's chief work was as long time president of the Young Women's Christian Association. The Activities Building of that organization at Rusk and Austin streets stands as a constant remainder of the faithful service Mrs. MacGregor gave to the Y. W. C. A.

After the sale of his Street Railway interests, Mr. MacGregor became engaged in laying out and developing residence subdivisions, principally in the South End. Among these subdivisions were MacGregor South End Addition, Blodgett Addition, Glen Park, Kenilworth Grove, Southmore and Blodgett Park Subdivisions. Riverside Terrace First Section was developed principally from land holdings acquired by Mr. MacGregor for development purposes. In the early days, many people had grown to respect his judgment and wherever he bought land, there was certain to be many followers.

Most New Englanders being Republicans, following the War Between the States, Mr. MacGregor came to Texas a Republican. While many adopted sons of the East joined the majority party for a voice in local affairs, MacGregor, of the rock rib variety, chose to remain a Republican. While it was said facetiously that a Republican convention could be held in a telephone booth, MacGregor remained faithful, as always, to his party at a time when white Republicans were few. Later he became a power in State and National politics and during the administrations of President Taft and President Harding, was Republican National Committeeman from Texas. He was host to President Harding when he visited Texas.

While active in business, Mr. MacGregor found time for varied civic interests and social affiliations. He was a director of the South Texas Commercial National Bank and a director and Treasurer of the Houston Printing Company, publishers of the Houston Post. He was an active worker with the Houston Fruit and Flower Festival and its colorful No-Tsu-Oh. He was one of those active workers who overcame every obstacle and finally brought deep water and navigation to Port Houston. He was once President of the Z-Z Club, a member of the Thalian Club, the Houston Country Club and the Caledonian Society.

Those who knew Mr. MacGregor knew also his wife. No partnership ever existed that was more beautiful or more useful than theirs. Their interests were the same and their energies were expended toward public benevolences and beneficences. At the time of his death, September 3, 1923, Mr. MacGregor was serving as Chairman of the Board of the Herman Hospital Estate and devoted much of his time to the interests of the Herman Charity Hospital.

Mrs. MacGregor continued much of the good work started by her husband and carried out his wishes in the matter of donating gifts to the city he, as a lad of seventeen, had chosen for his home. Among his gifts to Houston, Mrs. MacGregor his executrix and fellow trustees, having made the choice, are MacGregor Park on Bray's Bayou in the South End section, money for the acquirement and improvement of MacGregor Parkway and Drives skirting Bray's Bayou linking Herman and MacGregor Parks. Peggy Point, named for his beloved wife, and Memorial Fountain on the Almeda Road opposite Albert Sidney Johnston High School is another gift to Houston.

The city has honored Mr. MacGregor by placing his name on scenic drives, a public school, and at one of the major units of the Houston park system.

But while he gave so generously of his wealth to his adopted city, he never forgot the place of his birth. His public benefaction at Derry, New Hempshire, is a public park upon which his funds, augmented by personal contributions by Mrs. MacGregor, built a public library building and endowed the park for maintenance and for public amusement and recreation.

WAVE OF THE GULF

The name, Henry Frederick MacGregor, brings to mind a builder and benefactor—who helped to build a city and, its progress definitely assured, turned to give to those generations to follow a chance to play, to thrill at the scenic beauty of the countryside along fascinating winding bayous, and to pause and reflect on the joy of living in this Metropolis he had discovered in 1883.

* * *

And so the end of my tales.

We do not know how far we have traveled unless we occasionally stop and look backward. The wave of the Gulf that washed ashore Cabeza de Vaca, first white man to inhabit Texas, and his little band of Spanish explorers in 1528, spread farther than the most vivid imagination could have pictured.

Pioneers, settlers, communities and industry swept the newly discovered land until an Empire was born. Texas—after serving under six flags—today appears as one of the brightest stars in the national field, and the Texas Gulf Coast section as one of the most progressive.

We cannot do or say too much for the noble men and women who went before us, many of whom gave their lives for the civilization, culture and prosperity we now enjoy.

Roll on, Wave of the Gulf.

334

INDEX

INDEX

Adacs, 212.
Adelsverein, 2, 205.
Adkins, Mrs. Thurman, 111.
Adriance, John, 1, 2, 205, 230.
Agee, Elizabeth, 304.
Agee, John, 304.
Aguirre, Col., 248.
"Alabama," SS, 240, 241.
Alabama, State of, 16, 192.
Alabama Indians, 15, 16, 17, 18, 19, 57.
Alamo, 259.
"Alaska," SS, 241.
Albert Sidney Johnston High School, 333.
Albuquerque, New Mexico, 231.
Alexandria, Louisiana, 219, 221, 242.
Allen, Dr., 222
Allen, Mr., 75.
Allen, A. C., 14, 26, 45, 46, 47, 48, 49, 142.
Allen Brothers, 8, 23, 24, 25, 29, 30, 32, 34, 45, 46, 49, 79, 80, 86, 87, 98, 106, 107, 136, 160, 257, 272.
Allen, Charlotte M., 14.
Allen, J. K., 14, 26, 45, 46, 257.
Allen, Mrs. J. K., 257.
Allen, Mrs. Rosa, 30.
Allen, Samuel L., 13, 14, 15, 16, 19, 29, 54, 87, 274, 313.
Allen & Pless Warehouse, 285.
Allen, Pool & Company, 29.
Allen's Station, 131.
Alleyton, Texas, 138.
Allin, Capt. B. C., 97.
Almonte, General, 191, 192, 248.
Alsace-Lorraine, Germany, 4.
Alsbuys, The, 1.
Alvin, Texas, 111, 330.
American Brewing Association, 169.
American Eagle, 276.
Anahuac, Texas, 225, 245, 250, 322.
Anaties, Prof. Louis, 62, 63.
Anderson, Sallie, 298.
Anderson, N. 319.
Anderson, Clayton & Company, 114, 261, 305.
Andler, F., 186.
Andrews, Miss Dot, 303.
Andrews, Forest Lee, 331.

Andrews, Henry B., 138, 140, 141.
Apache Indians, 18, 228.
"Archer, Branch T.," SS, 90.
Arcola Junction, Texas, 187.
Arcola Sugar Mills, 275.
Arkansas, State of, 22, 56, 77, 227.
Armour Fertilizer Works, 127, 169.
"Army in Gray," 7.
Arrendondo, General, 213.
Arto, Jack, 132.
Ashe, Bettie, 297.
Ashe, Judge Chas. E., 299.
Ashe, Eliza, 296.
Ashe, Gaston, 297, 299.
Ashe, John B., 296, 297, 299.
Ashe, Mary P., 297.
Ashe, Richard, 297.
Ashe, Sam S., 71, 148, 151, 296, 298, 299.
Ashe, Sam, Sr., 297.
Ashe, William, 297.
Ashe & Ziegler, 299.
Ashville, North Carolina, 297.
Astor, John Jacob, 180, 204.
Atchison, Topeka & Santa Fe Railway, 181.
Aten, Sergeant N. A., 157.
Atkinson, Capt. John, 89, 91, 170, 274.
Atlanta, Georgia, 34, 106.
Audubon Society, 165.
Aury, General Luis, 215, 271.
Austerman, Mrs., 279.
Austin, Texas, 8, 18, 22, 23, 165, 187, 203, 208, 209, 210, 266.
Austin, County of, 10, 106, 192, 208, 329, 331.
Austin, John, 1, 26, 45.
Austin, John Brown, 1.
Austin, San Felipe de, 8, 287.
Austin, Stephen F., 1, 2, 4, 8, 104, 115, 167, 168, 180, 181, 190, 201, 203, 205, 206, 209, 272, 280, 281, 287, 288, 326, 327, 328.
"Austin, Stephen F.," SS, 207.

Baer, R. B., 142.
Bagby, Eloise, 274.
Bagby, Emily G., 274.
Bagby, Lucy B., 274.
Bagby, Major Thomas M., 14, 46,

INDEX

Bremond Square, 40, 113.
Brenham Cotton Seed Oil Mill, 277.
Brenham Light Guards, 157.
Brenham, Texas, 8, 281.
Brensler, H. P., 291.
Brewster, Col. Bob, 85.
Bringham, Asa, 288.
Bringhurst, Mrs. G. H., 31, 132.
Bringhurst, Henry B., 293.
Briscoe, Andrew, 251, 322, 323.
Briscoe, Andrew Birdsall, 323.
Briscoe, (Mary Jane) Mrs. Andrews, 249, 250, 320, 321, 322, 323.
Briscoe, Jessie Wade, 252, 323.
Briscoe, Parmenas, 252, 323.
"Brooklyn," SS, 240, 241, 242.
Brooklyn, New York, 69.
Brooks Field, 229.
Brown Family, 221.
Brown, J. M., 149, 150.
Brown, J. S., 124.
Brown, Shipley & Company, 182.
Brown, Walter Norton, 49.
Browne, John T., 26, 82, 158, 198.
Brownsville, Texas, 161, 226, 227, 232, 283.
Bryan, Guy M., 174, 209, 321.
Bryan, Wm. Jennings, 189.
Buffalo Bayou, Brazos and Colorado Railway, 138.
Buffalo Bayou Ship Channel Company, 95.
Bulloch, Charles, 184.
Burch, Mrs. Jessie Ziegler, 253, 332.
Burch, Judge M. W., 165.
Burke, A. J., 293.
Burke, Major E. B., 238.
Burleson, General, 247.
Burnet, County of, 62, 228.
Burnet, President David G., 255, 290.
Burnet, Texas, 22.
Burnett, Ellen, 175.
Burnett, J. H., 175.
Burnett & Kilpatrick, 185.
Burns, Major Bob, 51.
Burr, Aaron, 212, 222.
Burrows, Dr., 189.
Bute, James, 40.
Butler, General "Silver Spoon," 232, 233.
Butler, Rev. Wm., 267.
Byers, Charles, 61.

Byers, George, 61.
Byrd's Store, 31.

Cabanas Family, 204.
Caddo Indians, 147, 211.
"Julius Caesar," SS, 288.
Cages, The, 36.
Calcasieu, Louisiana, 168, 242.
Caldwell, Hudson, 153, 154, 158.
Caldwell, J. P., 288.
Caldwell, William, 154.
Caledonian Society, 333.
California, State of, 137, 208.
Calvert, Mrs., 219.
Camp Bullis, 229.
Camp Elizario, 228.
Camp Harney, 228.
Camp Hatch, 229.
Camp Inge, 230.
Camp Johnson, 230.
Camp Logan, 274.
Camp Radenski, 228.
Camp Sabine, 230.
Camp Stanley, 229.
Camp Van Camp, 228.
Camp Verde, 229.
Campbell, Ben, 97.
Campbell, Jim, 195.
Campbell, J. I., 39.
Campbell, Warren, 195.
Campeche, Texas, 172, 216, 221.
Cargill, Ennis, 176.
Cargill, Frank, 176, 319.
Carlisle, Mrs. Natalie Taylor, 38.
Carr, Mrs. M. B., 111.
"Carr, John L.," SS, 234.
Carroll, Mr., 85.
Carter, O. M., 75, 110.
Carter, S. F., 112, 174.
Carter, W. T., 39.
Casey, Uncle Chris, 194, 196.
Cash & Luckel, 108.
Castrillon, General, 191, 248.
Castro, Henry, 4.
Castroville, Texas, 4.
Cat Springs, Texas, 328, 329, 330.
Catholic Church, 189, 211, 289.
Cave, E. W., 74, 91, 97, 238, 313, 314.
Cavitt, Major, 1.
"Cayuga," SS, 90.
Cedar Point, Texas, 198.
Chalmette, Battle of, 216.
Chambers, County of, 198.
Chambers, General, 263, 266.
Chambers, Rev. and Mrs., 19.

339

INDEX

341

342

INDEX

INDEX

INDEX

INDEX

San Marcos, Texas, 167, 206.
Sanders, John W., 106.
Sandy Point, Texas, 286.
Santa Anna, General, 136, 190, 191, 192, 196, 197, 225, 244, 245-249, 253, 267, 320.
Santa Anna, Dolores Tosta de, 267.
Santa Fe Railway, 172.
Santa Fe Trail, 197.
"Satchen," SS, 303.
Sayers, Governor Joseph D., 179.
Scanlan Family, 37, 44, 60, 187.
Schmidt, Erich, 33.
Schmidt, Nicaragua, 238.
Schmidt, Vetter, 26.
Schneider, Capt. E. B., 54, 101, 102, 129.
Schneider & Davis, 143.
Schnitzer, Miss Martha, 45.
Schrimps Field, 26.
Schroeder, R. W., 178.
Schulte, Henry, 102.
Schuhmacher Grocery Company, 55, 90, 102.
"Sciota," SS, 240, 241.
Scott, Captain, 328.
Scott, John T., 295.
Scott, Tom, 142.
Scurry, Tom, 238.
Scurry, General W. R., 238.
Seabrook, Texas, 70, 126, 195.
Sealy, George, 176, 181, 182, 279, 286.
Sealy, Mrs. George, 284.
Sealy Hospital, 154.
Sealy-Hutchings Bank, 181.
Sealy, John, 176, 181.
Second National Bank, 112, 128, 174.
Second Presbyterian Church, 52.
Sedgwick, C. W., 49, 141.
Seibert, Billie, 84.
Seibert, F. C., 85.
Sellers, Col. Harvey, 174, 195.
Semms, Admiral, 240, 241.
Sessums, Alexander H., 174, 175.
Sevier, Mrs. Clara Driscoll, 250.
Sewanee (School), Tennessee, 177.
Sewell's History, 190.
Shamblin, J. M., 153, 154, 157.
Shearn, Charles, 275.
Shearn, Chas. P., 52.
Shearn Methodist Church, 46.
Shell Building, 38.
Shepherd, B. A., 33, 40, 60, 174,

176, 177, 206, 208, 209, 277, 291, 292, 295, 302.
Shepherd, Capt. D. P., 135.
Shepherd, Frank, 174.
Shepherd, J. A., 294.
Sheppard, Benj. S., 138, 274.
Sheppard & Stafford, 77.
Shepperdson (Statistician), 104.
Sherfius, Capt. Henry, 50, 168, 275, 299, 302, 303.
Sherman, Lieutenant, 238.
Sherman, General Sidney, 138, 238, 246, 247, 248, 257, 289, 322.
Sherman, Mrs. Sidney, 238.
Shilo, Battle of, 311.
Shipmans, The, 1.
Shipman, John, 187.
Shudde Store, 204.
"Silver Cloud," SS, 166.
Simpson, Ernest A., 125, 129.
Simpson, Ernest L., 125-128.
Simpson, Mrs. Wallis Warfield, 125.
Simpson, Spence & Young, 125-128.
Sisterdale, Texas, 205.
Sloan, John, 265.
Smith, Alfred D., 123, 124.
Smith, Mrs. Alfred D., 36, 123, 124.
Smith, Col. Ashbel, 176, 194.
Smith, Col. Ben Fort, 76, 322.
Smith, Deaf, 190, 192, 247, 253.
Smith, Francis, 260, 261.
Smith, Fred. W., 35, 91, 276, 277, 313.
Smith, Fort, 166.
Smith, Col. Fort, 166.
Smith, Capt. Leon, 233-236.
Smith, Dr. Marant, 150, 151.
Smith, Miss Mary, 227.
Smith, Morgan L., 2, 204, 205.
Smith, Obediance, 76.
Smith, Tom, 156.
Smithville, Texas, 111.
Smithwick, Noah, 17.
Solms-Braunfels, Prince, 167, 203, 205.
Sorrell's History, 193.
Sour Lake Hotel, 299.
Sour Lake Springs, Texas, 20, 28, 70, 71, 147, 149, 150, 151.
South Carolina, State of, 187.
South Texas Commercial National Bank, 38, 65, 304, 305, 333.
Southern Pacific Railway, 22, 49, 54, 58, 64, 74, 94, 106, 112, 121,

351